A CERTAIN TERROR

This anthology is a project of the Program on Militarism and Nonviolence of the American Friends Service Committee (AFSC), based in Ann Arbor, Michigan. The Program seeks to explore and root out the social and cultural props of militarism. Like all AFSC programs, our work arises from the Quaker belief that all human beings have spiritual worth and that any form of violence infringes human dignity.

I THINK THAT THE INABILITY TO LOVE IS THE CENTRAL PROBLEM, BECAUSE THAT INABILITY MASKS A CERTAIN TERROR, AND THAT TERROR IS THE TERROR OF BEING TOUCHED. AND IF YOU CAN'T BE TOUCHED, YOU CAN'T BE CHANGED. AND IF YOU CAN'T BE CHANGED, YOU CAN'T BE ALIVE.

James Baldwin

"A CERTAIN TERROR"

HETEROSEXISM
MILITARISM
VIOLENCE
& CHANGE

Edited by
Richard Cleaver
& Patricia Myers

Great Lakes Region
American Friends Service Committee
Chicago ✶ *1993*

Published by
The Great Lakes Regional Office
American Friends Service Committee
59 East Van Buren, Room 1400
Chicago, Illinois 60605

A project of
The Program on Militarism and Nonviolence
Michigan/Northern Ohio Area Office
American Friends Service Committee
1414 Hill Street
Ann Arbor, Michigan 48104
Richard Cleaver, program director

Design and composition by Patricia Myers and Richard Cleaver
Text set in 9 pt. ITC Cheltenham with chapter heads in 14 pt. Avant Garde
Printed in the United States of America
by Malloy Lithographing, Inc.
5411 Jackson Road
P.O. Box 1124
Ann Arbor, Michigan 48106

Library of Congress Catalog Card Number: 92-75570
ISBN 0-9635516-0-4

In memory of

James Baldwin (1924-1987)

&

Audre Lorde (1934-1992)

SPONSORS

Bill & Mary Carry
Nancy & Norris Lee
Clay & Adria Libolt
Geraldine McNabb
The Soap Opera
David A. Wood & Brian J. Mulhern
Jan Wright
Several others who wish to remain anonymous

This project could not have been undertaken
had it not been for early support from
The Funding Exchange
in the form of a grant from
The OUT Fund

CONTENTS

Some Additional Strategies

Visions

ACKNOWLEDGMENTS

The editors have had help of many kinds from many quarters. The task of setting down acknowledgments of that help always raises the spectre of omission, the more so because it is by its nature undertaken at the end of a long process. Our gratitude to all who assisted in this truly collective endeavor is no less where unexpressed.

Deborah Theado was a member of the original editorial team, until she accepted a grant to do research in Angola, which made commuting to meetings even more difficult. During the period of her service, her contribution was invaluable, and we are very grateful for it. Because she had no control over the eventual directions the project took, she can bear no responsibility for our decisions in her absence; but she does deserve a full measure of thanks and honor. Michael Patrick O'Connor was also a member of the editorial working group. We are grateful for his participation and his subsequent advice on matters of book preparation.

Aimée Picard, in the Chicago AFSC office, spent many (often frustrating) hours tracking down copyright holders and obtaining permission to reprint the articles in this collection. Her role in the final result is therefore considerable, and we cannot speak too highly of her diligence in the search and, what is more, her boundless cheerfulness in undertaking it. Also in the Chicago office, Michael McConnell and Darlene Gramigna shared with us the fruits of their experience on similar projects; Nicole Gotthelf, Miki McNary, Francisco Piña, Lorna Stone, Ellen Youniss and doubtless others even more invisible filled in a variety of gaps large and small before they became yawning gulfs. We thank them for their generous, quiet and efficient assistance.

Credit for obtaining the grant that made it possible to begin this project goes to Paula Amman. She also undertook supplementary fundraising along the way. More than that, she provided support in a variety of other ways, not least in the recommendation of Riva Lehrer to design the cover. Often Paula's role was simply to lend an ear to editorial frustration and give appropriate reassurance that the job would one day be complete. Similarly, Penny Ryder and Jan Wright, staff in the Ann Arbor office of AFSC where much of our work was done, offered support and assistance in countless ways. Often they bore the brunt of dismay at obstacles and emergencies of all kinds, and patiently took steps to soothe and assist.

Barbara Bogosian, Kathryn Stern, Patti Rose and Erika Trass all spent hours staring at computers screens entering the text. Without them there would be nothing to read; for this necessary and unglamorous task our lasting thanks. Kathryn Stern also transcribed the tape recording of the conversation that was to become "Language, Identities, Politics."

The equally unglamorous task of proofreading was undertaken by many people at various stages, among them Anne Beebe, Andy Farmer, Rose Hochman, Frances Large, Nancy and Norris Lee, Richard Lee, Sharon Miles, Jim Toy, Susan Woerner and Jan Wright.

The project was carried out under the care of the Michigan Area Peace Education Committee of the American Friends Service Committee, which is responsible for the Program on Militarism and Nonviolence. Many members of that committee, past and present, have already been named and thanked in some special capacity. Many others deserve to be; rather than risk omission from the long list of committee members over the years, we will thank them collectively. We make an exception in naming the subcommittee which oversaw an earlier version of this project: Mary Carry, Tom Gaughan, Gerry McNabb, Paquetta Palmer and Leonard Suransky. Jeff Epton, former staff in the Ann Arbor office, was an invaluable support during his tenure as well. Two colleagues elsewhere in AFSC, Warren Witte and Kay Whitlock, saw this collection at an earlier stage in its history and offered supportive and helpful comments.

There are still other people who have offered suggestions and leads along the way, often without realizing it. They are, as the overworked phrase has it, too numerous to mention but they have contributed nevertheless. One source of information to which we turned more than once, however, should be named here: the staff of Common Language Bookstore in Ann Arbor. It is an especial relief to find people whose livelihood is in selling books showing such enthusiasm for one's own.

Richard Cleaver would like to offer particular thanks to the staff of the Labadie Collection at the University of Michigan for their gracious assistance in hunting down out-of-the-way articles from often obscure periodicals. This archive is a valuable resource for anyone doing research in lesbian/gay history and in the history of radical movements for social change. I feel fortunate to have it so near to hand. I would also like to thank Ann Larimore, of the University of Michigan, for a variety of helpful suggestions and acts in support of this project. She can little suspect how much her encouragement of this work has meant to me.

Patti Myers would especially like to thank her friends and family for their ongoing support and understanding. Heartfelt appreciation to Linda, Barbara, Diana, Sharon, Stephanie, Emily, Siâned, and Kelsey, who is dearly missed. Thanks also to Billie and Jim of the Lesbian-Gay Male Programs Office at the University of Michigan.

AIMS AND OUTLOOKS

LANGUAGE, IDENTITIES, POLITICS:
A CONVERSATION
Patricia Myers, Richard Cleaver,
and Michael Patrick O'Connor

Each essay in A Certain Terror *opens with a paragraph or two introducing the essay and is followed by a set of discussion questions and a brief listing of additional sources. The editors hope you will find this helpful in exploring the issues of heterosexism, violence, militarism, and change. We envision this volume as a study aid to activist groups. An initial working group, including Michael Patrick O'Connor and Deborah Theado along with the two editors, determined the themes to be explored and the selection and arrangement of the essays chosen. Final editing and the production of headnotes, questions, and lists of readings were done by Patti and Richard. We begin the collection with a discussion among three members of the initial working group. Welcome.*

RICHARD CLEAVER: We've gathered together to give the readers a clue as to who the people putting this collection together were, why we were putting it together, what our outlook on the whole project was, and to raise some questions that we want people to keep in mind while they're reading and discussing the material here. Let's start by introducing ourselves.

PATRICIA MYERS: I feel I'm somewhat of an outsider with the American Friends Service Committee because I've never been involved with it before, nor have I been specifically involved in peace-oriented stuff. I have worked in feminist organizations that are committed to nonviolence, but it is a slightly different tack. I primarily come out of feminist organizing in the early eighties, as a young lesbian in the Ann Arbor area, working in shelters for battered women, doing stuff around sexual assault, some direct action, organizing lots of demonstrations, petition drives, that sort of thing. At the same time I've done a lot of educational work specifically around homophobia and that's why I'm here. I've learned something about militarism, although I've always had some ideas about how it works, but mainly I have an extensive knowledge of homophobia, and a tremendous amount of experience educating people about homophobia.

I'm particularly interested in educating activists about homophobia, which is what has kept me involved in this project during the times when I've felt over my head or overwhelmed by the amount of material we had. I kept thinking there's a group of people somewhere, affiliated somehow

This article was edited by Patricia Myers, based on the transcript.

with the AFSC that doesn't have much information about homophobia, and if we can just figure out how to get them this information, then it's going to change the way that they think about lesbians and gay men. And that's going to ripple out to all of these other communities.

MICHAEL PATRICK O'CONNOR: I became involved with this project because I thought I could help sort out some of this material and I was interested in reading about what people have been saying about the whole set of issues related to militarism and social structure. I was active as an undergraduate in the anti-war movement. I came out as a gay man about 1975, when I was doing graduate work. I've been active in AIDS service organizations since 1985, in prisoner education. I began working with AFSC in that capacity.

There's an age range among us. I'm the oldest; I was born in 1950 during the Korean War.

Richard: I'm almost as old as you are. I was born in 1952, during the Korean war.

I put together the first version of this project, as part of my work as director of AFSC's Program on Militarism and Nonviolence, which is publishing this collection. I've worked in that program for ten years. It's a peace education program, but we wanted to try and work on ways to make the peace movement broader, and in particular, make it a place where lesbians and gay men felt safer. That was the original impulse for this project. I've worked as an openly gay man in the peace movement, one way or another, since I was a college student in the early 1970s, so I bring my study of militarism to this project.

What I was hoping to do in initiating this project was to bring together some of these threads, which to me feel very much like expressions of the same general world view, particularly the idea that being a gay man and being against war, being dedicated to non-violence, are very much wrapped up together. But I never really had to examine those things until other people started asking me in the peace movement, "Well, so, what difference does it make that you're gay?" Or, in the lesbian/gay movement, "Why are you giving all of your time to this straight movement, instead of your own people?"

Patti: I have been in organizations where commitments to other arenas of social change were considered distractions from the gay stuff in particular. It could be anything depending on the group. Feminist stuff: "You spent too much time focused on that, that's not really central to what it is that we're doing." Or anti-racist work, or class; those aren't supposed to be central to our work.

Richard: Which I don't in fact agree with.

Patti: Of course not. If you say, I want to change the world and I want everybody in the world to have a better chance, a happier life, or whatever, you can't go very far with that. You have to figure out what you yourself can do, or what you and your organizational buddies can do. It has to be fairly manageable and somewhat focused. But I don't think it's helpful just to do gay organizing in a vacuum without thinking about anything else. I don't think it's even possible.

Richard: To say that you can is to imply that to be a gay man or lesbian is to be one thing—one male thing and one female thing—and to deny that these other issues of gender and race and class and physical ability and the rest aren't also present in lesbian/gay communities, which, I think, for too long we have tried to pretend. Those of us who have the privilege of staying away from some of those issues, too often we've chosen not to address them.

Michael Patrick: Although one of the subjects of the book is that these things are not all comparable with being Black, even though there exists an overall category of minority. Likewise, being a lesbian is not the same as being a gay male, even though there exists the category of sexual orientation or preference. There are some discrepancies.

Patti: You have this list of categories, and they are similar, and yet somehow different. If you combine, for example in my case, white, female, working class, lesbian, feminist, it makes an interesting mix. When you change any of those particular characteristics, flip any one of them to a different side, then it looks different. Each of those categories is important, because experience affects how I think and how I'm able to move around in the world. But I think we always have to keep in mind the other combinations. Each of our particular perspectives on the world is very, very limited. The problem then is generalizing from me to the rest of the world. And I think that's connected with privilege, with taking all kinds of things for granted. Privilege means being able to think that I am perfectly "normal" and ordinary, and that what I am is the same as everybody else. And then there are other ways in which I am constantly reminded that I'm not, in fact, perfectly normal and ordinary.

Richard: And we get these reminders, the reminder that you're normal and the reminder that you're not normal, at strange times and in strange places. The different contexts we find ourselves in as we move through our daily lives sometimes reinforce a sense of normality, sometimes reinforce a sense of abnormality.

Patti: And sometimes it's both at the same moment. When I go to the laundromat, it's perfectly normal for me, as a woman, to be doing laundry for myself and everybody else that I'm affiliated with. But it's also very different for me to be doing laundry for my female partner, or to have political T-shirts that I'm washing and hanging up. There are ways in which it is both/and. It's not either/or.

Richard: Which, in the long run, calls into question the whole idea of normality. I hope it does.

Let's talk a little bit about the words that we use to describe ourselves in our sexuality, particularly since that's one of the major boundaries we've drawn for ourselves in making this collection. Different people have used different words at different times. Of course, it's not like there's this day when you flip the calendar and suddenly take on a whole new set of words—it's a process.

As people were beginning to build some bonds of affinity during World War II, they were still calling themselves "homosexuals," applying to both men and women. Then, after Stonewall, through some process that I couldn't begin to reconstruct now—it seemed almost overnight—we were learning to call ourselves gay, meaning both women and men. Very soon women began to stop us in our tracks and say, "Wait a minute, calling men and women gay perpetuates women's invisibility."

Patti: It is just like the generic "man," it doesn't always mean men and women. People occasionally intend for it to mean men and women, but then you read something about "homosexuality in America," and it only talks about men. Or you read "Gays in the U.S.," or "Gays in the Twentieth Century," and it only means men. For a while, people were careful to say, "lesbians and gay men," but people tend to say "lesbians and gays," so that "gay," once again, excludes women.

Richard: Most often if you were to say the word "gay," you would not only mean male, but you would mean white and you would mean not only middle class, but quite comfortable middle class. Part of the image of gay people that is promoted in *Time* magazine or in the mass culture of society is not only that they're male and white, but that they live in cities and that they have a lot of money to spend because they don't have any dependents.

The whole question is bound to arise again soon around the term "queer." One of the things being promoted is its inclusiveness, not only with regard to women and men, but also to people who had desires in both directions. It was perfectly clear to me as I first started using the word "gay" in the early seventies that it included people who were attracted to women and men both. It wasn't a bipolar term. We were all quite clear that it was possible to be attracted to both, even if that didn't describe our personal experience. We didn't like the term homosexual, because, first, it implied that sex was the most important thing. (We may have gone too far in the other direction: now we want to pretend that sex doesn't have anything to do with it....) Second, it implied that you could only be attracted to other men or other women.

Now people talk about "queer" as a way of dealing with the whole phenomenon of people identifying themselves as bisexual as opposed to identifying themselves as gay or lesbian on the one hand, or heterosexual, "straight," on the other hand.

Michael Patrick: But there are bisexual people who say that "bisexual" needs to be recognized explicitly as another sexual minority along with lesbians and gay men.

Patti: I also think people talk about "queer" as a sensibility that is wholly removed from bodies and people and sex and desires. I get pretty nervous about that. In the academy, when something simply becomes a scholarly tool, like feminism or gender as analytical tool, it ends up having no connection whatsoever to lived lives. When someone talks about a gay sensibility or a queer sensibility that is wholly unrelated to her particular experience of the world, in that sense, you can have queer heterosexuals. That's a step beyond what we've been talking about, but I also think that's where things seem to be going, I'm afraid.

Another concern with a name like Queer Nation is the element of nationalism, which I think brings us to consider militaristic values.

Michael Patrick: Why don't we introduce Queer Nation?

Patti: Yes, but first, before we move on from talking about language, we should probably say something about the words "homophobia" and "heterosexism." The word most folks are more familiar with is probably "homophobia"—and I think that word does have its uses, when we're talking about individual attitudes. But we chose the word "heterosexism" for our subtitle because we wanted to highlight two issues.

First, we're dealing with a social structure, a system of oppression, an "ism" as we say, that is based on an assumption that heterosexuality, whatever that is, is natural and superior.

Second, we want to remind people that this structure is a patriarchal one, and the word heterosexism, because it enfolds the word "sexism" into itself, does that.

Now, back to Queer Nation.

Michael Patrick: Yes. In 1986 or so there was a growing feeling that the institutions that had arisen in the early eighties to deal with the AIDS crisis, such as Gay Men's Health Crisis in New York, had become stultified social agencies that had no political verve anymore. People in New York City, most publicly symbolized by Larry Kramer, began to create a movement of political demonstrations focused on particular highly charged political problems involved with AIDS, including drug companies making a lot of money and the FDA holding up drug tests in ways that were bureaucratized and archaic. They called themselves ACT UP, which became a chain of organizations across the country, a chain of small groups of demonstrators to create a fuss. It was associated with a new punkish style of activism that also involved good graphics, tasteful designs, shocking colors, neon colors, late eighties colors. Out of ACT UP's freshness in frankly raising issues about money and politics and power, people who were involved with ACT UP said everything that is wrong with Gay Men's Health Crisis is wrong with all the rest of the national lesbian and gay organizations, so why don't we start thinking in terms of making demonstrations to replace them? Out of that grew an organization, again, not at all nationally centralized, called Queer Nation, with a fairly aggressive political stance, even more aggressive than ACT UP.

Patti: My experience has been that gay men had no politics until AIDS came along, whereas lesbians were organizing on behalf of battered women and assault and health care and thinking about power and decision making and strategies and so on.

Richard: I think that was true by the middle seventies, not before. There are some generational things going on here, too.

Patti: Maybe. From what I know of Queer Nation, the goal has been a kind of equal opportunity, which is a strange phrase to apply to a radical group, but the idea of nationalism is that everyone who belongs to the "nation" comes in at an equal footing. Queer Nation seems committed to consensus decision making, committed to a very aggressive political stance, in which presumably everyone can participate. There is an acknowledgment that there are specific differences, primarily in terms of sex and race.

It is not enough, however, just to assign equal footing. We have to acknowledge that we come in with all of the privilege and lack of privilege that we started out with outside. It doesn't make us any more able to speak our minds, or interrupt less often, just because now we're in a room full of other gay people who are committed to challenging some particular legal decision or some exclusionary policy or whatever.

Richard: Some things can't just be declared to be the case. That brings us yet one more time to this power of language. I think this is a very American thing, actually. One of our myths about ourselves in the U.S. is that we are a people of few words, devoted to action, but we actually have an enormous faith in words, particularly the written word, to change anything, to define reality.

Patti: I think that's all very good but I also think that it's true that some people only want to work on what affects them, in a limited sense. And if there are all these other folks shouting about their needs when they don't affect me, then, "I don't want to work with that group." Again, it's a matter of privilege: "I don't have to. I can go someplace else and start a new organization. I can center my life around being surrounded by people who are just like me." The more privilege and power you have, the more able you are to surround yourself with people who are just like you.

The other distinction we're talking about centers on a whole range of strategies that have existed since the beginning of time, as far as I know. There are folks who believe the way to do things is to assimilate, to look as much as possible like everybody else. Then you have things like "passing," and then you have questions about who is going to be out, and what does it mean to be out, and to what degree out, and that means you're talking about gender roles. "I'm going to look like a real woman, I want you to look like a real man. I don't want you to look like a pansy or a fairy. I don't want you to look like a bulldyke and wear leather." And then there are folks who think that the way we'll be most able to express ourselves as fully as we can is to push and push and push to be accepted at face value, for whoever we are. Assimilationists and... I don't know what the label is.

Richard: Nationalists. That's one way of putting it.

Patti: I think integration is a way of thinking about this difference in strategy. I don't think that there's anything special about lesbians and gay men in terms of having those kinds of struggles. Nor do I think that there is anything new about the struggles.

Richard: We could make an analogy between our situation and, for example, that of Jews. We don't really have any materials in this collection that deal with anti-Semitism, but in fact there are some strong parallels between Jew-hating and queer-hating, not least because groups like the Ku Klux Klan lump both together, along with race hatred against African-Americans and Arab-Americans and Asian-Americans and the rest. But to return to our analogy with Jews: the question of assimilation has always been a very hot topic among Jews in this society, because Jews can pass—that is, some Jews can pass, or some Jews choose to try to pass. The question of assimilation, and the questions that go with it such as intermarriage, are very conflicted in some communities.

Patti: People with disabilities, for instance. Some people with disabilities can pass, some cannot pass. Some lesbians and gay men can pass, some cannot pass.

Michael Patrick: I don't know if that's true.

Patti: I know it's true. I know that my life is very different because I look average, and that I am with a lot of women who do not look average. They clearly are not "normal" women, and they get harassed endlessly.

Michael Patrick: They *can't* look "normal," you mean?

Patti: They *don't* look "normal."

Michael Patrick: That's different.

Patti: No, I don't think so. I think it is true that some can pass and some cannot pass. There are more who can pass, and choose to do so. Butch–femme roles among lesbians, and women who pass as men, are important parts of lesbian history. Women who look like men but who are women, and look like women at the same time, who don't look enough like men to be mistaken as men—I also think that those women, those butch women are a very important part of lesbian history. They don't pass.

Richard: I think the same thing can be said about some men. I know some very effeminate men who don't think of themselves as gay, who, however, are assumed to be. They have to build their lives around what people think about them as well as what they think about themselves.

Michael Patrick: That's why I think that the group of women you're talking about is not directly related to what we're talking about when we say sexual orientation or preference. It overlaps with it....

Patti: It does matter how you identify yourself, but I also think that there is a point where it doesn't matter.... In terms of gay-bashing it doesn't always matter. It is much more important what other people think of you than how you identify yourself. You're going to get beat up because they think you're gay, and not because you are.

Or maybe you have identified as gay but for this last year you've been sleeping with someone of the other sex. I don't think that it matters so much after a point.

Richard: I think it changes its meaning in different situations.

Patti: In different contexts.

Richard: I'd like us to back up and talk about the debate about "sexual orientation" versus "sexual preference." Maybe we ought to talk about those two terms and their implications, and indeed the implications of "sexual," the other half of the phrase, too. One of the most obvious points, related our earlier discussion of passing, is: "Well, if it's just a preference, how is it different from choosing chocolate ice cream over vanilla ice cream, and why should it have any political content?" In responding to this way of dismissing the whole issue, we have to ask, is it necessary that the characteristic on which we base our identity, our class if you will, be immutable in some way? Our movement, in public—and I emphasize that since we're more forthcoming among ourselves—has talked about orientation as if it were immutable, because we make an analogy with race. For some reason we find it difficult to compare ourselves with people in other categories. Society seems to prefer to recognize the civil rights of minority groups based on unchanging characteristics.

In fact, though, you could compare sexuality with political preference. We certainly don't think that people should be discriminated against because they choose Democrat versus Republican, although if their choice is Communist... Similarly if we are talking about religion, although there are limits to toleration of religious differences, too. At different times in our history Catholics, Jews, atheists, and even now Muslims have been regarded as not quite legitimate members of society. It remains impossible to imagine anybody being elected president of the United States who doesn't claim to be religious on some ground. Nevertheless, we recognize as a principle of our political life that those choices are legitimate. It is reasonable under our political theory to give people a choice, and not penalize them for their choices.

So I don't think sexual "orientation" is quite the right term, although we have put a lot of our eggs in the basket of immutability, at least for tactical reasons. I think "preference" is a more truthful term.

Michael Patrick: The problem of sexual versus affectional and preference versus orientation is created by the society into which we are trying to fit, rather than anything we want to accomplish in terms of defining ourselves politically. When the homophile movement started and then was succeeded by the gay liberation movement, there was no compelling need for a term to label what was under discussion. We were defining ourselves as "homos," as "queers," and we were defining ourselves in relation to the rest of society. Somewhere in the course of institutionalizing the gains of the gay liberation movement, and the homophile movement, it became necessary to find a way to describe what was under discussion. To identify the opposition of homosexuality and heterosexuality. There is nothing logical about having to identify the opposition. It can exist without a label for it. So in a sense the problem is secondary, created by society.

So there's a certain amount of baloney even in thrashing it out.

Patti: Right, a whole lot of baloney.

Richard: Except that it has implications for the strategies we choose.

Patti: Right. Except, the religious Right uses "affectional preference" to get around the hoopla around sexual orientation. And if the fundamentalist Christians are really committed, which they are, to excluding lesbians and gay men, homosexuals, queers, dykes, and faggots, sodomites, inverts, Pollyannas, whatever, they're going to figure out ways of doing it.

If you talk about biology, "born-this-way gay," you can make political arguments about why this is a good position. And you can make political arguments about the dangers: treatment and cure of homosexuality, electroshock therapy, lobotomy, castration, clitoridectomy, and ovary removal, and all kinds of things in order to cure the biological problem. If you're talking about choosing to be gay, you can also talk about Homosexuals Anonymous, and criminal status, and all the kinds of ways in which people make bad choices. I think ultimately it doesn't matter.

Lesbians and gay men, it seems to me, don't have the same kinds of opportunities, freedoms, privileges, and responsibilities that people who are not lesbians and gay men have. People ought to have those opportunities, freedoms, privileges and responsibilities. Talking about how we got to be this way is not really what the discussion is about. Whether or not I can be a lesbian for fifteen years and then have a long-term, committed relationship with a man—am I still a lesbian? Or do I call myself bisexual? According to the Centers for Disease Control, lesbians are only those who haven't been involved with men since 1978. Or the question you raised earlier, does gay only mean someone who has never felt any kind of desire, even in the *middle* of the night, for someone of the other sex?

Richard: Right. In the middle of a *cold* night.

Patti: Or if they have, have they ever acted on it? Or what about all the people, well, I don't know about gay men, but I know there are lesbians who really get off on gay male porn. Now, what is that?

Michael Patrick: Pretty weird, if you ask me.

Patti: Oh no, c'mon. It's because gay men have porn, and lesbians haven't had porn for such a long time.

Richard: Or, at least not as much and not as easy to get ahold of.

Patti: Does that mean they're not lesbians?

Richard: Yet another example I heard recently is that the next March on Washington is not to be called "Lesbian, Gay and Bisexual," but

"Lesbian, Gay and Bi," because they decided they didn't want "sexual" in there. I think there's a considerable danger that sex will drop out of this discussion, if we don't give it some attention.

Michael Patrick: That, in general, is related to the track of assimilation. What does assimilation mean? Assimilation means people who fall under these various headings that we've been discussing want to live with the rest of society for various reasons, and to various degrees. There is always a small fringe group which does not want to do that at all. The current version of that identity is the Radical Faerie groups that tend to live as far apart from mainstream society as possible.

Richard: There's an element of separatism in the queer movement as well.

Michael Patrick: Women are less likely to do this because women are less naïve about politics.

Patti: Or less likely to...

Michael Patrick: ...to pretend that they can walk away from everything.

Patti: Oh, I don't know. There are lesbian land farms.... I think that there are lots of ways in which assimilation versus something else gets played out. I think about going to Cleveland and having breakfast with some friends of friends, and using the "L-word" fairly loudly over breakfast as I tend to do. "I teach a lesbian studies course, I read this lesbian novel, my sister petitioned for this lesbian group," blah, blah, blah. And these people are uncomfortable about my dramatic lesbianism, and would much prefer that I be quiet, not use the "L-word," figure out some other way of conveying what it is that I'm talking about. Well, I think that's a question of assimilation. They're more likely to fit in at a restaurant and not raise eyebrows, induce stares, have wait staff spill coffee on you. A friend of mine was just up from Alabama with an even clearer story about secrecy and assimilation. All they say is "Do you think she's one? Is he one? I think she's one." You can't even whisper "gay." I don't think it's just the big picture, not just what a group's political strategies are, but I also think it's the ways our politics inform our breakfast conversations.

Richard: There are really two dynamics working there. One is the dynamic of privilege, and one is the dynamic of safety. And those cut across each other in unexpected ways. On one hand you can point to a lot of people who assimilate to claim privilege, like all of the closeted white gay males in the Reagan Administration who ended up getting busted for giving aid to the Contras. All kinds of straight radicals came to me after that and said, "You see, it proves that gay men can't be revolutionary." Well, it doesn't prove that to me at all, any more than Clarence Thomas proves that African-American males can't be revolutionary either. It's easy to figure out why those people want to assimilate—they have a lot to lose, compared to some of us. But it's also easy to see why somebody in a small town in Alabama would have a lot to lose in a different way. The price they would have to pay would be very high. I vary my behavior according to the context, too.

Patti: You have to. Maybe it's not simply about privilege and safety, maybe it's also about credibility. I believe your credibility is diminished when you're open in certain circles. I think that's a problem; I think that coming out is a way to challenge that. In the university, only certain programs "have politics"—for example, Women's Studies, ethnic studies, economics sometimes. Everybody else is "neutral," value-free, non-ideological. This is the same kind of problem. Lesbians and gay men when they come out are suddenly somehow biased, or unable to tell the complete human story.

Richard: This whole intellectual problem of objectivity, which is to say, who is a credible witness, who can bear testimony about their lives, is one of the props of militarism. One of the reasons why people can actually contemplate building weapons that can make the world uninhabitable is because they break the world down into small boxes. That way they can keep their emotional distance. If you can't keep your emotional distance, you're not going to progress far enough to make a career, whether an academic career or a political one. The way decisions about how to use those weapons are removed from the political arena is to say, "That's a technical problem. I, Congressman X, or Senator Y, have to rely on the generals to give me the answers to that question, because I don't have all the technical information I need." Well, it's not a technical problem really; it's a political problem.

The result of this distancing is that we now [in 1992] have $4.3 billion in the budget for Star Wars, and nobody seems to be asking the question of whose missiles we're going to shoot down now. Just because we can shoot down somebody's missiles, we seem to think somebody out there must want to shoot missiles at us. Well, somebody may, but we haven't identified who it is, and maybe not having the missiles on our side would reduce the number of people who would want to shoot at us. But that's politics; we can't let it interfere with this technical problem.

Patti: Science. Oh, the objectivity of science.

Michael Patrick: Authority questions do go in the other direction. What about the great lesbians and gay men of history approach to liberation? I suppose some people, when they learn so-and-so they admire was a lesbian or gay man, get very excited and feel good about themselves.

Patti: Absolutely.

Michael Patrick: But on the other hand, I don't feel great about that.

Patti: The thing is—you can't stay there. You can't stay there with feeling great about knowing who these folks in history were who may have at some point been somehow connected to someone of the same sex. That's not enough. What does it mean? What difference does it make?

Richard: It may not be entirely without utility. As Michael Patrick said, authority questions can cut both ways. It may make a difference to some members of Congress, when they're considering whether to let lesbians and gay men stay in the military, to discover that Frederick the Great was a great general who also liked to play around with other men. They may find themselves thinking, "Well, gee, maybe playing around with other men is not mutually exclusive from being a great general." Although I almost wish it were.

Patti: That brings us back to militarism. What does that have to do with what we've been talking about and with this collection?

Richard: One basic connection is what the society is afraid of. We've already mentioned that however we frame our arguments about who we are, and decide on our strategy about how to get justice, the Right will find ways to make us outsiders. That's one of the most important marks of the militaristic society we live in. It needs enemies. It needs to identify some group as a potential danger to society, and right now, with the Communists gone, lesbians and gay men and bisexual people are up for the role. We heard that in the speeches at the Republican convention this year.

We talked about what peace activists need to know about homophobia and heterosexism. It's important to recognize that education needs to go the other direction too. What is the nature of the society we live in? How do some of these other issues we've already raised, like race and class and gender, contribute to the very militarized and security-conscious and fear-ridden society that we live in? What is the special function of homophobia among all those other fears that I believe are tolerated, if not cultivated, to keep a few people in positions of relative privilege?

Patti: In a lot of ways I think I'm certainly a member of that other audience. I don't have nearly the same orientation to militarism as you two do. I was born in 1959, and my life wasn't framed by a larger military history in the same way yours were. My family is not affiliated with the military in any way. I knew of people in the military but for them it was simply something to do when you got out of high school, if there wasn't anything else to do. As I was scrambling around trying to figure out how I was going to pay for college I checked into the military as a possibility and decided that it absolutely wasn't one. I couldn't tolerate the disciplinary structures that would be imposed. But I feel more torn now at 33 than I did ten years ago. I felt fairly clear that violence and militarism meant certain things, and it feels a lot more ambiguous now.

Richard: I think it *is* more ambiguous now. Part of the ambivalence that a lot of people, particularly lesbians and gay men, feel toward the military has to do with the fact that it has become such a central institution in this society. You can't really escape it, unless you have a certain amount of privilege. People do have to stop and think now as they figure out a way of paying for college. The military has gotten first claim on the resources of society in such a way that it is not possible for people to avoid having to figure out how to lay their own claims to the social resources they're entitled to without running up against the military. More and more, people aren't free to say, "I wouldn't touch that with a ten-foot pole."

Patti: At a very personal level for me it's about being involved with someone who was in the Army and was kicked out for being queer. She has very mixed feelings about it. So it's impossible to take a pure anti-military stance, because it meant something to her, it was a way out for her and for other people. Plus there's the right to fight stuff. The military is a major institution that clearly discriminates. We can either spend a whole lot of energy trying to convince the military not to discriminate, or we can try to transform society so that we don't have it at all.

Michael Patrick: Also there are the economic advantages to a long-term military economy. The U.S. profited in the period from the end of World War II until certainly the present recession, the Bush recession. It didn't profit in a way that we may necessarily approve of, but it has profited.

Richard: Well, I think it profited in the short term, but now the bill is coming due—in fact it started coming due as long as fifteen years ago. It was a false prosperity that ate up a lot of the very stuff that made it run for a while.

Patti: So what were some of the particular connections between militarism and homophobia that we wanted or hoped to explore with this volume of essays?

Richard: For me at least a lot of it has to do with the nature of socialization in our society. We live in a society that values the martial virtues, the frontier virtues. An American is a good marksman, self-reliant, able to survive, and so on. All of these virtues pertain to men, of course: this is a patriarchy, after all. Some of the frontier virtues actually present problems integrating into a well disciplined force. But nevertheless we cherish rugged individualism, the image of the tough guy. John Wayne is very powerful in the socialization of men in this society. I always felt that image of manhood made it impossible for me to succeed. It always put me on the outside of the fast track to being a full member of society. I was manifestly not that kind of man. I didn't even want to be that kind of man; but it was obvious that I was going to have to pay some kind of price for refusing. All this was plain to me long before I became sexually aware in any way. All the way back to my childhood, I knew both that I had to refuse violence and that to refuse violence was to dissent very seriously. For me it's always been a gut connection that then raised a whole other set of questions about what it means to be a lesbian or gay man in society.

Michael Patrick: The Stonewall riots and the beginnings of a gay liberation movement came along and raised not only those questions but others as well, the questions that were framed by feminism. What does it mean to have a sexual identity, what does is mean to have an identity at all?

Richard: What does it mean to be a man or a woman?

Michael Patrick: Those questions help us return to questions of militarism, figuring out why militarism is so deeply involved in our society. On the one hand there is the emotional connection that we can't deny. And on the other hand there is the rhetorical matter we raised earlier. You raised it, Patti, as the right to fight, and before that we talked about the Frederick the Great argument. They do tend to run together in ways that can be quite unfortunate. There are people who will make the argument that because Julius Caesar was queer, it's okay to be queer. That's logically meaningless. It has very little emotional ground, and it's rhetorically very dangerous.

Richard: It presumes that Julius Caesar is the kind of person we all want to be.

Michael Patrick: Right. And we don't.

Patti: There's nothing magical about being gay either. Being gay doesn't make you more...

Michael Patrick: ...sophisticated.

Patti: Or humanitarian, or politically savvy, or concerned about the world, or anything.

SUGGESTIONS FOR FURTHER READING

Barry D. Adam. 1987. *The rise of a gay and lesbian movement.* Boston: Twayne Publishers.

Allan Bérubé & Jeffrey Escoffier. 1991. Queer/Nation. *OUT/LOOK* 11, 3:12-23.

James Chesebro, Ed. 1981. *Gayspeak.* New York: Pilgrim Press.

Charles Fernández. 1991. Undocumented aliens in the queer nation. *OUT/LOOK* 12, 3(3):2-23.

Celia Kitzinger. Heteropatriachal language: The case against "homophobia." *Gossip: A Journal of Lesbian Feminist Ethics,* 5:15-21.

Joseph Neisen. 1990. Heterosexism or homophobia: The power of the language we use. *OUT/LOOK* 10, 3(2):36-37.

THERE IS NO HIERARCHY
OF OPPRESSIONS
Audre Lorde

We open this anthology with a short essay by Audre Lorde, one of the most well-loved and respected contributors to this anthology. Lorde once described herself as a "Black feminist lesbian warrior poet doing her work." Here she defines three important terms (heterosexism, sexism, and racism) that will continue to be examined throughout this volume. This essay speaks to the tendency, even among those deeply concerned with issues of social justice, toward ranking forms of oppression in order to prioritize the focus and strategies of particular movements, organizations, or individuals.

Lorde clearly warns of the shortcomings of taking this particular stance, as does Cherríe Moraga in one of the recommended essays for this section. In Moraga's words, "in this country, lesbianism is a poverty—as is being brown, as is being a woman, as is being just plain poor. The danger lies in ranking the oppressions. The danger lies in failing to acknowledge the specificity of the oppression. The danger lies in attempting to deal with oppression purely from a theoretical base."

I was born Black, and a woman. I am trying to become the strongest person I can become to live the life I have been given and to help effect change toward a liveable future for this earth and for my children. As a Black, lesbian, feminist, socialist, poet, mother of two including one boy and a member of an interracial couple, I usually find myself part of some group in which the majority defines me as deviant, difficult, inferior or just plain "wrong."

From my membership in all of these groups I have learned that oppression and the intolerance of difference come in all shapes and sizes and colors and sexualities; and that among those of us who share the goals of liberation and a workable future for our children, there can be no hierarchies of oppression. I have learned that sexism (a belief in the inherent superiority of one sex over all others and thereby its right to dominance) and heterosexism (a belief in the inherent superiority of one pattern of loving over all others and thereby its right to dominance) both arise from the same source as racism—a belief in the inherent superiority of one race over all others and thereby its right to dominance.

"Oh," says a voice from the Black community, "but being Black is NORMAL!" Well, I and many Black people of my age can remember grimly the days when it didn't used to be!

I simply do not believe that one aspect of myself can possibly profit from the oppression of any other part of my identity. I know that my people cannot possibly profit from the oppression of any other group which seeks the right to peaceful existence. Rather, we diminish ourselves by denying to others what we have shed blood to obtain for our children. And those children need to learn that they do not have to become like each other in order to work together for a future they will all share.

The increasing attack upon lesbians and gay men are only an introduction to the increasing attacks upon all Black people, for wherever oppression manifests itself in this country, Black people are potential victims. And it is a standard of right-wing cynicism to encourage members of oppressed groups to act against each other, and so long as we are divided because of our particular identitites we cannot join together in effective political action.

Within the lesbian community I am Black, and within the Black community I am a lesbian. Any attack against Black people is a lesbian and gay issue, because I and thousands of other Black women are part of the lesbian community. Any attack against lesbians and gays is a Black issue, because thousands of lesbians and gay men are Black. There is no hierarchy of oppressions.

It is not accidental that the Family Protection Act, which is virulently anti-woman and anti-Black, is also anti-gay. As a Black person, I know who my enemies are, and when the Ku Klux Klan goes to court in Detroit to try and force the Board of Education to remove books the Klan believes "hint at homosexuality," then I know I cannot afford the luxury of fighting one form of oppression only. I cannot afford to believe that freedom from intolerance is the right of only one particular group. And I cannot afford to choose between the fronts upon which I must battle these forces of discrimination, wherever they appear to destroy me. And when they appear to destroy me, it will not be long before they appear to destroy you.

DISCUSSION QUESTIONS

1. What are some examples of statements or behavior that insist a person rank her oppression?

2. What are some of the similarities and differences between heterosexism and other forms of oppression? From what sources do various forms of oppression arise?

3. How important is the experience of oppression when evaluating a political theory or action? On what other basis can coalitions be formed?

4. What are the implications for peace activists of Lorde's argument against constructing hierarchies of oppression? How can peaceworkers think about their priorities to make coalition-building with anti-racist, anti-patriarchal and anti-heterosexist activists more effective?

SUGGESTIONS FOR FURTHER READING

Elly Bulkin, Minnie Bruce Pratt & Barbara Smith. 1984. *Yours in struggle: Three feminist perspectives on anti-Semitism and racism.* New York: Long Haul Press.

Marilyn Frye. 1988. Oppression. *The politics of reality,* Trumansburg, NY: Crossing Press.

Audre Lorde. 1984. *Sister outsider: Essays and speeches.* Trumansburg, NY: The Crossing Press.

Cherríe Moraga. 1983. La güera. *Loving in the war years.* Boston: South End Press.

Marlon T. Riggs. 1991. What time is it?! Ruminations of a snap queen. *OUT/LOOK* 12, 3(3):112–19.

James Tinney. 1983. Interconnections. *Interracial Books for Children Bulletin,* 14(3–4):1–5.

MAKING AND UNMAKING MINORITIES: THE TENSIONS BETWEEN GAY POLITICS AND HISTORY
John D'Emilio

The question of whether lesbians and gay men are properly considered a "minority" within the framework of United States civil rights policy and practice is hotly contested. In the broader political arena, it is explicitly challenged by the right wing, which opposes the inclusion of such categories as sexual orientation and sexual preference in local or national civil rights legislation. In its most extreme form, this position has resulted in the suppression of information such as that described in Shira Maguen's article on teen suicide in this collection.

The political implications of making lesbians, gay men and (a greater controversy in some quarters) bisexual people a "minority" in the classic sense, however, have been given less attention within these communities. John D'Emilio, author of a classic study on the subject, Sexual Politics, Sexual Communities: The Making of a Homosexual Minority in the United States, *looks at some of these implications in the following paper, given at a symposium, "Sex, Politics and the Law: Lesbians and Gay Men Take the Offensive" (New York University Law School, February 22, 1986). Marilyn Frye's article, "Lesbian-Feminism and the Gay Rights Movement," later in in this collection, also raises some questions about the usual formulation. Some of the history of the political debate is touched on as well in Richard Cleaver's "Sexual Dissidents and the National Security State, 1942–1992."*

Since 1969, when the Stonewall Riots in Greenwich Village gave birth to the current phase of gay and lesbian political struggles in the United States, the gay and lesbian movement has evolved from one emphasizing gay liberation to one emphasizing gay rights. Within that shift in terminology lies a major alteration in social analysis, political strategy, and ultimate goals. In its gay liberation phase, the lesbian and gay movement employed a language of political radicalism. It saw itself as one piece of a much larger political impulse that strove for a complete reorganization of institutions, values, and the structure of power in American life. Gay liberation sought to achieve its aims by organizing masses of gay men and lesbians whose political activity would occur largely outside courts and legislatures. These activists viewed and accepted categories of homosexuality and heterosexuality as oppressive social constructs. The movement perceived human sexuality as diffuse and polymorphous in nature, and potentially destructive of rigid social hierarchies.

Our the past fifteen years, the movement has become exceedingly diverse. Today, gay and lesbian organizations include a host of constituencies—men and women, black, Hispanic, Asian and white, young and old, entrepreneurs, middle-class professionals, and unionized workers. Homosexuals have formed political clubs, churches, synagogues, health centers, and theater companies. Although no unified vision or political strategy animates these constituencies, we can say that as Stonewall has receded into the past, the movement as a whole has become less politically and socially radical. Its portrayal by the media, the statements of many movement leaders, and the program of action of individuals and organizations convey an image of the gay movement as one in quest of equal rights. That evolution, from gay liberation to gay rights, places the political and social struggles of lesbians and gay men in a familiar, well-established equal rights framework, deeply rooted in American history. This history has provided gay men and lesbians with several models of struggle employed by minorities in search of equality. Blacks, women, ethnic groups, and religious minorities seek this equality through social movements, legislative agendas, and litigation. Recommending an analogous course of action for gay men and lesbians may be tempting.

Although I would not dispute the value of either judicial or legislative protections that guarantee due process, equal protection, and equal access, I would suggest that the "traditional" minority group model raises certain problems when applied to gay men and lesbians. These difficulties emerge most clearly if one approaches the question from an historical perspective. Over the last decade, historians have done pioneering research that goes far beyond the uncovering of gay heroes. Historians have advanced toward a reconceptualization of the nature of human sexuality, and are creating theories with implications for both lawyers and social activists. My goal, therefore, is to interpret the work of gay and lesbian historians for an audience that may be unfamiliar with it.

I shall begin with my own book (1983), which is a history of the gay and lesbian movement in its formative stages—the two decades between the founding of the Mattachine Society in Los Angeles in 1950, and the Stonewall riot in 1969. The book's subtitle, "The Making of a Homosexual Minority in the United States," goes to the heart of this new conceptualization. During this period, a gay and lesbian minority emerged as a definable social group with a self-conscious sense of itself as different from the majority. This minority did not always exist; it lacks a historical presence in American society.

Central to this argument is a view of human sexuality as exceedingly malleable. Sex is more than a configuration of bodies in space; it takes its definition from the values and structures of particular cultures, and from the consciousness of individuals within a society. Sexuality consists of acts with meanings. Although the acts may have a universal existence, the meanings may vary considerably. And it is through meaning, through an understanding of behavior which culture provides, that patterns of behavior take on social significance.

This view of human sexuality as socially constructed has led many historians, on the basis of the evidence uncovered thus far, to conclude that sexual identity—in particular, a social world divided into homosexuals and heterosexuals—is a fairly recent historical invention. To phrase it baldly, the reason a gay political movement did not exist before the post-World War II era was not because gay men and lesbians were slower to recognize injustice than were blacks or women, nor because the oppression was so severe that protest was too dangerous. Rather, the explanation lies in the fact that until the modern era, a gay and lesbian "minority" did not exist. Many contemporary Americans take it for granted that sexual orientation is a fixed category that indicates an essential difference in human beings. Yet, in the mid-18th century, or even mid-19th century, American society did not label people as heterosexuals or homosexuals.

Jonathan Katz's book, *Gay/Lesbian Almanac* (1983), illustrates this conceptual distinction. Katz divides his book into two parts: "The Age of Sodomitical Sin, 1607-1740," and "The Invention of the Homosexual, 1880-1950." By examining in detail two eras separated by more than a century, Katz highlights the sharply distinctive sexual characteristics of each. In the former period, sodomy and sodomitical behavior were punished and excoriated as sin and crime. Clerics and magistrates were preoccupied with certain proscribed behaviors, with discrete sexual acts. Sodomy was but one of many sexual activities persecuted under the law. Others were adultery, fornication, rape, buggery, and public lewdness. Sodomy was not an offense unto itself, a category that demarcated one type of individual from another. Instead, it represented a capacity for sin inherent in everyone.

Katz describes a profoundly different social reality during the years 1880–1950. In medical writing, in literature, and in the testimony of men and women themselves, one finds an effort to redefine the meaning and the experience of homosexual behavior into a distinctive identity. Sex becomes the distinguishing characteristic that describes the essential nature of some men and women. No longer simply an act, homosexual behavior instead serves as a marker of identity. That identity encompasses personality, emotional state, sexual desire, and even, according to some, physical characteristics. The homosexual can exist apart from any sexual activity: if one feels that one is a homosexual, that is sufficient. Colonial Americans would have found such assertions incomprehensible. To them, a sodomite was someone who had committed the sin of sodomy.

The distinction between homosexual acts and homosexual identity represents more than playing with words. The concepts describe two profoundly different forms of homosexual expression, rooted in different social contexts. The process of creating a sexual identity involves a complex dialectic between external labeling and self-definition. In the century since the 1880s, the medical profession, courts, legislatures, government agencies, the mass media, educational institutions, and religious bodies have articulated a system that both describes and controls the social category they helped to create. In tandem with this categorization process, men and women have elaborated complex, diverse ways of living based upon their sexual desires. They have adopted distinctive styles of dress, have evolved an argot of their own, and have carved out social spaces—private friendship networks, public cruising areas, bars, bathhouses, clubs, and most recently, political organizations—that have allowed this sexual identity to take shape. Along the way, communities of mutual interest and experience have evolved. This reinforcing process of social labeling and individual self-definition has created a homosexual minority in the last half century.

Although there seems to be a fair consensus among gay and lesbian historians that a homosexual minority has come into being in the modern era, fewer of these historians agree about precisely why this phenomenon occurred. One hypothesis is that the emergence of American industrial capitalism in the late 1800s provided an opportunity for individual autonomy that was a precondition for the development of a gay identity.

Throughout the United States diverse gay and lesbian identities and communities developed. These communities emerged among female faculty of women's colleges, among the single working women and prostitutes of boardinghouse districts in large cities, among entertainers in Harlem, and along the fringes of bohemian communities in places such as New York City's Greenwich Village. As time went on, they interacted with one another and were all subject to the external forces of social control in ways that may not have homogenized them, but that did nonetheless create commonalities among them: blacks and whites crossed paths in the clubs and cabarets of Harlem; college-educated social workers and prison administrators encountered prostitutes and other working-class lesbians in the courts and in penal institutions. Distinctive subcultures were forming, but the lines between them were sometimes blurred.

Before moving on to suggest some of the implications that this historical analysis has for contemporary legal and political strategies, let me add one more word about history. What many historians are saying about sexuality departs from common folk belief in another significant way. Popular wisdom might summarize the history of sex as follows: first, there were moralistic Puritans, then repressed Victorians, followed by liberated moderns. Individuals, the story goes, have become sexually freer since the 1920s.

In contrast, historical writers have argued that this repression/freedom model misses the essential nature of the last two centuries of change in Western attitudes toward sex. Sexual activity has gradually, though not completely, been detached from a reproductive, gender-based matrix, and has been reconstituted as an entity in itself. Sexuality has been elevated in importance; it has become, for heterosexual and homosexual alike, a marker of personal identity. Our happiness and our sense of self-worth often revolve around our sexuality, and the emotional relationships that attach to it. Perhaps this elevated importance of sexuality is a sign of freedom. But it has also amplified the possibilities for public intervention in personal life and for new methods of social control.

From this perspective, it is perhaps easier to understand why public conflicts over sexuality have become so significant in the last century. From the seventeenth through the mid-nineteenth century, one searches in vain for a politics of sexuality in America. As long as social and economic conditions kept sexual expression deeply embedded in a procreative family-centered context, neither motive nor opportunity existed for social battles to rage around sexual issues. Since the Civil War, however, sex has generated political controversy of growing intensity and scope. Issues such as obscenity, birth control, prostitution, homosexuality, and abortion have proven capable of mobilizing vast numbers of Americans. In this century, sexual issues have situated themselves nearer to the center of political concerns. At times, the leading edge of sexual politics seems to represent "freedom," while at other times the forces of "repression" appear to have the upper hand. Yet, both sides are united in the magnified importance that they attach to sexuality. If we have more sexual freedom than the Victorians had, that freedom is at best double-edged.

Are there ways in which this historical interpretation can clarify political strategies and tactics, especially in relation to the law? My comments about the present will not be as neat as my historical analysis. But let me at least describe some of the tensions and problems that arise when we place history alongside contemporary politics.

Take, for instance, the possibility of moving the courts to rule that gay men and lesbians deserve judicial intervention to guarantee equal protection under the law, i.e., that we are a minority subject to discrimination. To achieve this, one would at least have to demonstrate convincingly a history of discrimination. This task is feasible if we restrict ourselves to the last generation. Unquestionably, gay men and lesbians have been subject since the 1940s to pervasive, systematic discrimination in many spheres of public life. The military moved from simply court-martialing and discharging personnel who engaged in proscribed sexual behavior to excluding a whole class of men and women, regardless of their sexual activities, on the basis of their sexual inclinations—in other words, on the basis of their sexual identities. The federal government banned the employment of gay men and lesbians, and many state governments and private employers followed suit. Urban police forces arbitrarily conducted mass arrests at gay bars; probably tens of thousands of men and women were arrested every year.

For the pre-World War II generations, however, there is little courtroom-ready evidence of discrimination. Homosexuality was a far less visible phenomenon. Society did not so clearly categorize on the basis of sexual orientation. The laws and public policies of a later time had not yet taken shape. Unlike blacks against whom discriminatory laws stretch back to the seventeenth century, the "gay minority" has captured legislative attention only recently. A minority must exist before it can be oppressed, but a socially-defined, self-conscious homosexual minority simply does not exist very far back in the nation's past. In addition, some discriminatory practices, such as the ban on civil service employment, have already been abolished. Given this historical record and the recent Supreme Court decision in *Bowers v. Hardwick*, what is the likelihood federal courts will consider gay men and lesbians in need of protection?

As another example, consider a key item of a gay rights agenda—the modification of municipal, state, and federal civil rights statutes to include sexual preference. Clearly it is desirable to prohibit discrimination in housing, employment, and other areas of life. Yet central to the oppression of lesbians and gay men, and to society's ability to shape and enforce it, are the homosexual and heterosexual categories themselves. The identity and the oppression are bound together. Is it not deeply ironic and troubling that a strategy which relies on civil rights laws is a strategy which strengthens the categories that allow a system of oppression to continue? Is it possible that other approaches—litigation based on the freedoms of speech and assembly or legislative proposals that blur gender-based distinctions—might be both more successful and be more consistent with the history we have uncovered?

Whatever the legislative goals we choose to pursue, however, I am certain of two things. First, the issue that gay men and lesbians are facing is not simply one of a minority struggling for civil rights or equality. The issue is sex and its place in society and individual lives. The call for minority rights is simply one way of framing part of this larger issue—an issue that taps into the deepest layers of human and social irrationality. Secondly, whatever our short-term goals, we need to frame arguments for them consistent with the core of historians' discovery that sex is a malleable social construct. In this way we will achieve an educative goal beyond our immediate aim.

Let me illustrate this second point with a personal experience. About three years ago, I found myself in a debate concerning gay rights. On one side were a congressman and a retired Navy admiral; a representative of a prominent national gay rights organization and I were on the other side. The congressman made statements to the effect that homosexuals are willful, perverse sinners violating biblical law. In response, my partner declared that all the best medical evidence demonstrated conclusively that there was no choice involved, and that sexual identity is determined long before puberty.

Now, there was nothing new or startling about that statement. It is an argument made frequently in courts and legislatures, and articulated by many of our most committed activists and allies. But I heard it more clearly during this debate than I ever had before. It is a sincerely held viewpoint that squares well with the gut-level feelings of most of us. It also seems to promise political benefits; surely you will not punish us for something we cannot help.

This statement, however, ignores several valid arguments. Magnus Hirschfeld and other German activists used a variant of this argument earlier in the century when they claimed that homosexuality was not a willful perversion, but a congenital condition. The argument did not deter Nazi persecution. Secondly, at a psychological level, there is something dreadfully wrong about basing a political movement on individual and collective helplessness. Do we really expect to bid for real power from a position of "I can't help it?" And thirdly, what if the argument is simply not true?

A fatal weakness attends any gay political movement which defines itself as a fixed minority in quest of equal protection based on its minority status. To do so implies acceptance of a sexual paradigm that itself shapes and stengthens the oppression we are battling. To argue that our identity, our sexuality, is in effect an accident of birth or of early conditioning is to embrace a sexual ideology that negates the choices we have made. So long as we accept these pre-set terms we have lost much of our freedom of choice. Fifteen years ago we supposed the terms of gay oppression to be that gay was bad, sick, and criminal. So the movement proclaimed that gay is good. Now it is clear that the terms of that proclamation are the acceptance of the mutually exclusive categories of homosexuality and heterosexuality.

All of us have made sexual choices throughout our lives. This phenomenon exists for heterosexuals and homosexuals alike. Because the hegemonic models of sexuality offer only two possible self-definitions, we have retrospectively interpreted our activities as the unambiguous manifestation of our one true being. Francis Matthiessen, as a young gay man in the 1920s, illustrates this process in a comment he made after reading Havelock Ellis: "How clearly," he said (Hyde 1978, 47), "I can now see every act and friendship of my boyhood interpreted from my proper sexual temperament." Many of us have likewise experienced a moment when we said, "This is who I am"—and in the process homogenized and flattened the complexity of our lives.

A century ago, certain American men and women were making radical personal choices, pursuing untrodden paths of sexual desire. The paths they marked became the outlines both of new sexual definitions, and of new oppressions. In many ways, we are still traveling those same paths. It is time to carve out new personal and political paths, to lay claim to the possibility of choice, to embark on new journeys of sexual definition. In doing so, we will challenge not merely the particular inequalities which a minority faces, but also the meaning, the structure, and the place of sexuality in our society for everyone. A multifaceted movement which takes on that task, in its own community and in society, will provide lawyers and lobbyists with a social and political context that can radically reshape our legal and legislative strategies.

DISCUSSION QUESTIONS

1. Must a personal characteristic be innate to deserve protection in our civil society? Is sexuality more like race and gender or more like religion and political belief? What strategic difference does this make?

2. What are readers' experiences with coming to terms with their own sexuality? How do we feel about the categories we identify with, or the existence of categories at all? How might this be different for lesbians, for gay men, for bisexual people, for heterosexual people?

SUGGESTIONS FOR FURTHER READING

John D'Emilio & Estelle Freedman. 1988. *Intimate matters: A history of sexuality in America.* New York: Harper & Row.

Steven Epstein. 1987. Gay politics, ethnic identity: The limits of social constructionism. *Socialist Review,* 93/94:9–54.

Lillian Faderman. 1991. *Odd girls and twilight lovers: A history of lesbian life in twentieth-century America.* New York: Columbia University Press.

Jonathan Katz. 1983. *Gay/Lesbian almanac: A new documentary.* New York: Harper & Row.

Lindsy Van Gelder. 1991. The "born that way" trap. *Ms.* (May/June).

SEXUALITIES AND IDENTITIES

Testimonies

Heterosexuality is a condition in which people have a driving emotional and sexual interest in members of the opposite sex. Because of the anatomical, physiological, social and cultural limitations involved, there are formidable obstacles to be overcome. However many heterosexuals look upon this as a challenge and approach it with ingenuity and energy. Indeed it can be said that most heterosexuals are obsessed with the gratification of their curious desires.

WHAT EXACTLY IS HETERO- SEXUALITY ?

...& WHAT CAUSES IT ?

HORMONAL IMBALANCE?

One theory advanced is that heterosexuals have an imbalance in their sex hormones:- instead of the normal mixture of the two, they have an excess of one or a dearth of the other, resulting in an inability to enjoy full and satisfying relationships with their own sex.

ECONOMIC CONDITIONING?

FEAR OF DEATH?

Our society grants financial and other incentives for exclusively (i.e. neurotic) heterosexual coupling: from tax concessions to council houses. To be gay is expensive and many people simply cannot afford it.

A terror of mortality lies beneath much heterosexual coupling. Driven to perpetuate themselves at any cost, most heterosexuals are indifferent to the prospect of the world-wide famine that will result if the present population explosion continues unchecked.

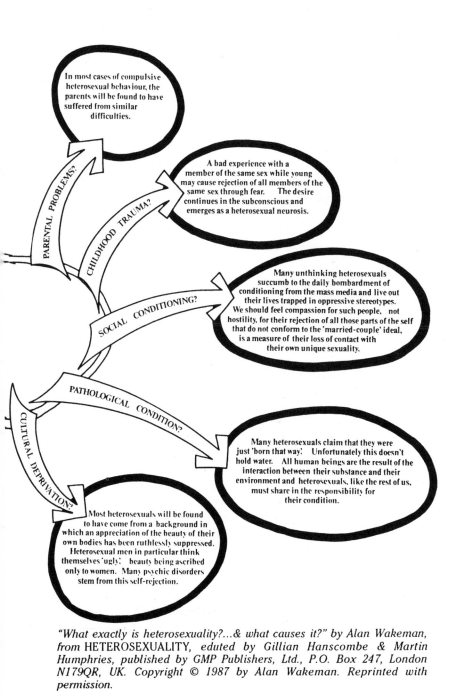

"What exactly is heterosexuality?...& what causes it?" by Alan Wakeman, from HETEROSEXUALITY, *eduted by Gillian Hanscombe & Martin Humphries, published by GMP Publishers, Ltd., P.O. Box 247, London N179QR, UK. Copyright © 1987 by Alan Wakeman. Reprinted with permission.*

FOR THE STRAIGHT FOLKS
WHO DON'T MIND GAYS BUT WISH THEY
WEREN'T SO BLATANT
Pat Parker

you know some people
got a lot of nerve.
sometimes, i don't believe
the things i see and hear.

Have you met the woman
who's shocked by 2 women kissing
& in the same breath,
tells you that she's pregnant?
BUT GAYS SHOULDN'T BE BLATANT.

Or this straight couple
sits next to you in a movie
& you can't hear the dialogue
Cause of the sound effects.
BUT GAYS SHOULDN'T BE BLATANT.

And the woman in your office
Spends your entire lunch hour
talking about her new bikini drawers
& how much her husband likes them.
BUT GAYS SHOULDN'T BE BLATANT.

"For the straight folks who don't mind gays but wish they weren't so BLATANT," by Pat Parker, from MOVEMENT IN BLACK *by Pat Parker, published by Firebrand Books, Ithaca New York 14850. Copyright © 1978 by Pat Parker. Reprinted with permission.*

Or the "hip" chick in your class,
rattling a mile a minute—
while you're trying to get stoned
in the john
about the camping trip she took
with her musician boyfriend.
BUT GAYS SHOULDN'T BE BLATANT.

You go in a public bathroom
And all over the walls
there's John loves Mary,
Janice digs Richard,
Pepe loves Delores, etc. etc.
BUT GAYS SHOULDN'T BE BLATANT.

Or you go to an amusement park
& there's a tunnel of love
& pictures of straights
painted on the front
& grinning couples
coming in and out.
BUT GAYS SHOULDN'T BE BLATANT.

Fact is, blatant heterosexuals
are all over the place.
Supermarkets, movies, on your job,
in church, in books, on television
every day and night, every place—
even in gay bars.
& they want gay men & women
to go hide in the closets—

So to you straight folks
i say—Sure, i'll go
if you go too,
but i'm polite—
so—after you.

SUPERDYKE, THE BANANA METAPHOR
AND THE TRIPLY OPPRESSED OBJECT
Sharon Lim-Hing

Sharon Lim-Hing's play raises many important issues in a format not otherwise represented in this collection. Humorously, she explores the themes of race, ethnicity, lesbian roles, style, political correctness, generational differences, and sex. Reprinted from a Canadian collection of writings by lesbians of color, Lim-Hing's contribution is the only commentary on lesbian and gay men's lives from an Asian perspective in this collection. In it, she is critical of the white gay community's racism and expectation that they will be educated by lesbians and gay men of color and inter-racial relationships, especially with white lesbians.

CHARACTERS:
DOROTHY – intellectual
FRANCIS – butch
LAN – punk
RACHEL – bisexual
SHEEMA – femme

All five characters must be played by Asian (should be of various ethnic origins, including South Asian) or half-Asian actresses. Their individual characters (i.e., intellectual, butch, etc.) can be indicated by dress.

* * *

One side of the stage represents DOROTHY's *kitchen or dining room. The other side when lit represents the street. When the curtain opens,* DOROTHY, FRANCIS, LAN, RACHEL AND SHEEMA *are sitting around a table in* DOROTHY's *apartment, having just finished dinner.* LAN *is slouched over, perhaps smoking a cigarette.* DOROTHY *is wearing glasses and reading a book.* FRANCIS *sits with her legs spread widely apart and arms folded or her hands firmly on her knees.* SHEEMA *sits in a femme-y position and checks her makeup in a compact mirror. After a few seconds' pause for the audience to observe the characters,* RACHEL *gets up.*

"Superdyke, the banana metaphor and the triply oppressed object," by Sharon Lim-Hing, from PIECE OF MY HEART, edited by Makeda Silvera, published by Sister Vision: Blackwomen and Women of Colour Press, Toronto, Ontario. Copyright © 1991 by Sharon Lim-Hing. Reprinted with permission.

RACHEL: I'm so full I just have to get up and move around.

SHEEMA: Next time we'll have to remember: Asian lesbian potluck, not Mongolian feast.

DOROTHY: Delicious mater paneer. I never realized that chianti classico could complement Korean, Indian, Chinese, Vietnamese and Japanese food—all in the same meal.

LAN: Rules are made to be broken.

SHEEMA: I think I've just done my garlic quotient for the next two weeks.

FRANCIS: Garlic and rice—keeps the hair black and silky!

LAN: Speaking of lots of black, silky hair, that was a great Asian Lesbian and Gay Association party last night. Music sucked, though.

FRANCIS: At least you can dance to it. Unlike some of your favorites.

LAN: You can dance to Lydia Lunch. You just have to have the right pair of shoes. Don't you get sick of listening to the same stupid messages all the time? *(Lan stands up)* Pump up the jam, pump it up, DJ spin that wheel...

Dorothy stands up.

DOROTHY: I rather enjoy the mindlessness of contemporary North American disco-derived music. One could do a fascinating study on the abject cynicism regarding heterosexual relationships, particularly when transposed onto the schema of a gay dance floor.

LAN: Well, it makes me want to vomit.

SHEEMA: Please don't! You might splatter my skirt. Anyways, it rots your enamel.

RACHEL: And you're forgetting the most important thing—it's so danceable.

Rachel does some quick vogueing.

FRANCIS: Hey, who was that woman Michelle was with?

RACHEL: That's the fourth white woman I've seen her with...

DOROTHY: In as many weeks.

RACHEL: She's a bonafide North Pole female monarch.

Sheema stands up.

SHEEMA: Girl, she's the queen of snow queens.

LAN: She's the snow queen and potato duchess all in one!

Francis stands up.

FRANCIS: So! I don't see why you have to be so judgmental. It's Michelle's business who she goes out with. Anyway, we all have our own little things that we go for. Michelle just happens to like sickly pale skin.

RACHEL: I wonder what your "thing" is, Francis.

Rachel looks at Francis who looks away.

LAN *(As if to herself)* Sticky rice.

SHEEMA: It would be her business if she were only going out with these women. But when she's sleeping with them, then it's our business too.

FRANCIS: To gossip about, you mean.

SHEEMA: Think of us as the friendly neighborhood crime watch committee.

DOROTHY: I do believe it was you, Francis, who asked the question, and I quote, "Hey, who was that woman Michelle was with?"

SHEEMA: Whoever she was or is, her eyeshadow was just a tad overstated, don't you think?

FRANCIS: I can't believe anyone would wear eyeshadow. To a party. For fun. I mean, it's the 90s. Get with it!

SHEEMA: *(Looking at Francis' clothes)* Exactly, Francis.

RACHEL: Not everyone has mastered the dubious skill of being a girlie-girl like you, Sheema.

DOROTHY: Yes, I imagine there are so many different aspects of societally determined female appearance to remember. But there are so many other truly intellectually engaging questions to ponder. Say, who was that cutie with the bolo tie?

LAN: You mean the bolo tie in the form of a massive labrys? Or the one with the giant pink crystal labia?

DOROTHY: I mean the cutie-pie.

RACHEL: I think they were both cute. The women, not the ties.

FRANCIS: You think anything in pants looks cute.

RACHEL: As a former lesbian, coming out as a bisexual, I resent that. You know people call bisexuals fence sitters. Well, it feels pretty good sittin' on that fence. I'd like to launch a new term: Bi-envy. *(Turns to Dorothy)* Are you saying that the pudgy one was not cute? Do I smell some fat oppression here?

DOROTHY: What I'm saying is the "pudgy" one lit a campfire in my panties. Get it? "Pudgy?!" *(Mimics Rachel)* Do I smell some fat oppressive language here?

SHEEMA: Jeez! Let me out of the P.C. squadroom. *(Checks her watch)* The Goddess of Swatch Watches be praised! It's time for me to eclipse. I have a late rendez-vous.

LAN: With who?

SHEEMA: With someone you all don't know so you can't gossip about.

FRANCIS: Sheema, will you be safe walking to the subway? There's been a lot of gay-bashing around here lately.

SHEEMA: Do I look gay? Rape is my primary worry, not gay-bashing.

LAN: Don't worry, next year Asian-bashing will be back in style.

RACHEL: Aren't you afraid if you had to run in those heels you couldn't?

SHEEMA: No, 'cause these heels make great eye-poker-outers. And between Model Mugging and kung fu classes, I'm ready. *(Goes into a fighting stance)* In fact, I'm praying they'll try. *(Makes a savage jab)* Watch out for that flying dismembered penis!

RACHEL: It's ricocheting! Everyone duck!

Everyone ducks.

SHEEMA: *(Dusting her hands together as if after a hard job)* That's another rehabilitated rapist.

DOROTHY: It's a bird, it's a plane, it's Superdyke! But how come she's not white like Superman, Batman, and Robin!

SHEEMA:	*(Indignant)* Dyke? Don't call me a dyke.
RACHEL:	*(Teasing)* Hey, there's a hair on your leg.
SHEEMA:	*(Shocked)* Where?
RACHEL:	Nope, guess it's just a run in your hose.
FRANCIS:	*(To Sheema)* So do you shave your armpits too?
SHEEMA:	Bien sûr. Even though I get razor burn. My skin turns red and if I sweat within two hours after shaving it feels like I'm rubbing salt in my wounds.
FRANCIS:	That's insane! Why do you bother!
SHEEMA:	You did say, "No pain, no gain."
FRANCIS:	Yes, but I was talking about my quads and lats, not my armpit hairs! Armpit hairs are sexy. I love summer, wearing shortsleeve shirts, flexing, taking a swig of beer. *(Pantomimes her words.)*
RACHEL:	*(Staring at Francis' armpits)* I used to have an armpit hair fetish, but I'm in recovery now. I don't shave either.

Rachel shows her armpits. She and Francis look at each other's armpits, then glance up simultaneously to meet each other's gaze. Sound of a triangle is heard. They look away quickly.

| SHEEMA: | Sorry I can't join in the bulldagger session, but I've go to go. *(Glibly)* Fifteen minutes keeps the suspense wet, thirty is fashionable, but forty-five and she won't let me in. |

Exchange of goodnights. Exit Sheema.

| FRANCIS: | I can't believe that kid. Dorothy, remember the good old days, when jeans and a checked flannel shirt were just fine for every occasion. |

DOROTHY: I don't remember what I wore. I just remember my eighth grade teacher, Mrs. Hutcheson. *(A dreamy look on her face)* She said my logarithms were perfect. She always wore long skirts, so I could only see her knees when her skirt would occasionally get hitched up on the chalk holder. I even loved her funny nervous twitch when all the kids laughed at her and she didn't know why...

LAN: How pathetic!

RACHEL: I'm a little worried about Sheema. This extreme femme-y-ness. And, I think she has a lot of unresolved banana issues.

DOROTHY: Banana issues?

RACHEL: You know, banana. Yellow on the outside and white on the inside. Can't face up to her Asian identity.

LAN: Oh, I thought that's what we called gay Asians who don't want to join the Asian American Lesbian and Gay Association.

FRANCIS: Don't we all have "unresolved banana issues?"

DOROTHY: I believe some of her behavior is due to the fact that her parents want her to finish her studies so she can go home and marry the man of their choice.

LAN: Can't she just say no? That's what I did, and my family never bothers me any more. In fact, we don't have any contact whatsoever.

FRANCIS: It's more complex than that.... There's got to be a better metaphor than banana.

LAN: How about a hard boiled egg? Brown on the outside, white on the inside, but with a heart of gold on the inside.

DOROTHY: Summer squash? That's still a bit elongated, though.

RACHEL: Lemons? Grapefruit are yellow on the outside and pink on the inside. *(Looks at Francis)* Certain sensuous melons? *(Pause)* By the way, Francis, would you like to help me organize next month's rap?

DOROTHY: What's to organize? You simply choose a topic then let everyone know about it. *(Lan kicks Dorothy)* Ouch!

FRANCIS: Sure, I'll help. Why don't I walk you home? I mean, I was going to visit my friend George and...he lives near your street, I think.

RACHEL: *(Smiles)* You've never been to my house. How do you know where I live?

FRANCIS: I...must have seen your address on the mailing list.

DOROTHY: It's almost one in the morning and you're going to visit your friend. I thought you said you had soccer practice at nine A.M. tomorrow. *(Lan kicks Dorothy again)* Ow! Why do you persist in inflicting bodily harm on others with those steel-reinforced toes?

LAN: Well, it's late. *(Yawns exaggeratedly)* You guys better be on your way.

Exchange of goodnights. Francis and Rachel go out Dorothy's imagined front door. Stage lights go out, except on Francis and Rachel, to represent street.

RACHEL: *(Stretches)* Ah, the wide open spaces of Somerville.

They walk in silence for a minute or two.

FRANCIS: So, Rachel, is it true that...bisexual women will leave a woman for a man?

RACHEL: That's a bit like asking if a lesbian will leave a woman for another woman. Depends on a lot of different things.

FRANCIS: Guess you're right.

RACHEL: Francis, is it true what they say: butch on the streets, femme in the sheets?

FRANCIS: *(Laughs)* That's something you just have to find out for yourself.

RACHEL: Hmm, sounds challenging.... Here's my house. That's my bedroom window.

Points and holds Francis by the shoulder, as if to better show her the right window.

FRANCIS: So, what would we discuss at the next Asian Lesbian and Gay Association rap?

RACHEL: Monogamy?

FRANCIS: Non-monogamy.

RACHEL: Taking the initiative in a new relationship!

FRANCIS: Unrequited love.

RACHEL: Sexual fantasies.

FRANCIS Sexual rejection.

RACHEL: Throwing caution to the winds!

FRANCIS: Shyness.

RACHEL: Kissing?

FRANCIS: Kissing.

They kiss.

FRANCIS: Think it's safe for us to kiss on the sidewalk?

RACHEL: *(Dreamily)* No. I think I'm in danger of spontaneous combustion.

FRANCIS: Rachel, I don't feel comfortable standing outside here. Why don't we go inside?

RACHEL: Okay.

Rachel makes motions of opening her front door. Before Francis goes in and closes the door, she looks at audience and winks. Exit Rachel and Francis. Lights back on at the dinner table part of the stage.

DOROTHY: Did you hear that laughing? Hey, what was all that rap organizing business about?

LAN: Dorothy, you may be writing your thesis on the incidence of sapphic activity among bovines of the Jersey breed on free-running farms, but at times you can be a bit spacey. Two dykes conniving to converge into a seething compound of slippery female organs—without seeming too obvious or too eager...neither too much the sex addict nor too much the co-dependent.

DOROTHY: You mean...oh, I get it! Hope it works out for them. You know, since Jean and I broke up a year ago, I just can't imagine having a serious relationship. Though I would consider a quickie affair with Lily Tomlin.

LAN: Have you asked her to check her schedule?

DOROTHY: How about you, Lan? Any woman on the horizon?

LAN: Oh, lots of women! But that's where they stay—far away on the horizon. Anyway, you know I'm celibate. I don't know what came first, no lovers or validating my state by a declaration of celibacy. Sometimes I don't know why I even bother to wear this button. *(Indicates pink triangle pinned to her pants crotch)* Guess I'm just a lesbian in theory. And in practice I'm chronically horny.

DOROTHY: Look on the bright side. Celibacy is as safe as you can get.

LAN: Thanks. Sometimes your utter optimism just dumbfounds me. People like you remind me why I decided to be celibate. So what're you doing tomorrow, Dorrie?

DOROTHY: Workshop on racism for the Gay and Lesbian Political Action Association.

LAN: Ugh! I can't believe you're still running around trying to educate white, gay liberals. It's not your job to educate them, it's their responsibility to educate themselves.

DOROTHY: Well, they're trying, and I want to help them. It is frustrating at times, though, the same assumptions, the same veneer of understanding. But we are part of the gay community, are we not?

LAN: I think I am, but no matter how obnoxious I may act, Asians are invisible in the "gay community," as you call it. To hell with educating whites. They'll never see you or me as a person. To them you're a triply oppressed object, or a politically correct icon. I'm just me, I don't represent all Asian lesbians. And sometimes I just want to have fun, waste time, ogle girls, like everybody else.

DOROTHY: Life isn't all fun, Lan.

LAN: Ha! Don't I know it. But you can try to squeeze in some fun between the angst and the agony.

Pause.

LAN: Been to the new women's bar?

DOROTHY: You mean Closets? No.

LAN: Music sucks. But people are friendly...enough.

DOROTHY: Well, why don't we pop in. It's only one o'clock. *(Puts her arm around Lan in a friendly way)* I'll buy you a ginger ale.

LAN: You're on.

Dorothy and Lan walk off together. Lights fade.

THE END

DISCUSSION QUESTIONS

1. How is the topic of bisexuality addressed within your local organizations? How are bisexual issues similar to and different from the particular needs of lesbians and gay men?

2. What are some of the implications of the "model minority" stereotype of Asian-Americans? How can this, and other stereotypes, interfere with organizing?

SUGGESTIONS FOR FURTHER READING

Jan Clausen. 1990. My Interesting Condition. *OUT/LOOK* 7, 2(3):10-21.

Ellen Herman. 1988. Getting to serenity: Do addiction programs sap our political vitality? *OUT/LOOK* 2, 1(2):10-21.

Loraine Hutchins & Lani Kaahumanu, Eds. 1991. *Bi any other name: Bisexual people speak out.* Boston: Alyson Publications.

Barbara Noda, Kitty Tsui, & Z. Wong. 1979. Coming out. We are here in the Asian community. A dialogue with three Asian women. *Bridge* (Spring).

Jean Swallow. 1983. *Out from under: Sober dykes and our friends.* San Francisco: Spinsters Ink.

Ara Wilson, Carol Queen, & Robin Stevens. 1992. What do bisexuals want? *OUT/LOOK* 16, 4(4):21-35.

Christine Wong. 1979. Yellow Queer. *Frontiers,* 4(1).

REPEAT AFTER ME:
WE ARE DIFFERENT. WE ARE THE SAME.
Jewelle Gomez

In this paper given at a symposium titled "Sex, Politics and the Law: Lesbians and Gay Men Take the Offensive" in 1986, Jewelle Gomez raises the question of multiple identities and oppressions, and the ways individuals find to maneuver around them. There is often a tendency in social movements, especially those based on identity, to create a monolithic image of Gay Men, or Lesbians, or African-Americans.

In real life, identities often cut across one another: class and race modify each other in complex ways, as Gomez points out. In groups experiencing racist or colonial oppression, raising questions of sexual oppression (whether gender or sexuality) can seem threatening. Other members of the group react by making those who raise these questions invisible, by denying difference. Gomez speaks of the necessity of moving beyond the need to render some members of the group invisible because they are different, and to build politics that will accommodate and celebrate differences.

It is as if people cannot feel they exist except by affirming, with a shudder, that they are different from something that they are against. (Goodman[1960] 1962, 233)

The substance of my talk is expressed in its title. As I prepared my notes I realized I was having difficulty because everything I wanted to say has been articulated in such a variety of ways in our history. Long before the Rainbow Coalition took shape during the last presidential election, it was evident that diversity is a strength we need to explore rather than deny. The groups that have poured themselves into the foundation of American society had different views of what that society can and should be. This abundance of perspectives ought to help us formulate solutions to society's problems; instead, it causes destructive frictions. That we are always struggling with stereotypes is not a new idea. Nor is the concept unfamiliar that these sometimes subtle and undramatic battles are the substance of true social change.

"Repeat after me: We are different. We are the same," by Jewelle Gomez, from a symposium, "Sex, Politics, and the Law: Lesbians and Gay Men Take the Offensive" held February 22, 1986 at New York University Law School. Copyright © 1986 by Jewelle Gomez. Reprinted with permission. Since footnotes have been abridged, readers are urged to consult the original publication for additional references: REVIEW OF LAW & SOCIAL CHANGE *XIV: 935–941 (1986).*

An additional problem with this presentation is that it is delivered to a group that is already, for the most part, converted. Those of you who came to hear what I have to say are probably already thinking about these issues. Those who most need to hear my remarks are probably not here. They are not interested in the varied experiences of lesbians and gay men. They are not concerned with the issues of race and class—how they make us different, how they make us the same. Since they are not here, I ask you to be responsible for communicating these issues to those who ought to hear them.

And it is as simple as the title. We are the same and we are different. I am familiar to some of you. I have read my poetry, given speeches, made you laugh or think. I am acceptable because I do not present an immediate challenge to most of you. By virtue of my being on this panel, I have been rendered "safe." You assume I will do the appropriate things, and all of the gut responses that white, middle-class people have to black women, to black women who grew up on welfare, to black women with dreadlocks, are stifled because I am up here. But make no mistake: we are different— as night and day.

I grew up with my great-grandmother who had to make the choice between wearing stockings in the New England winter or allowing me to go to the movie on Saturday morning—my one childhood obsession. This choice was one that many poor parents have had to make, but when you are white and poor, poverty is considered a temporary setback. If you are black and poor, it is considered to be a result of your laziness, or lack of family structure, or domineering mother, or some other inherent inferiority. In other words, you are only getting what you deserve.

This experience has made me different from most of you from the day of my birth. We should not make the common error of equating the black experience with that of immigrants, for most black people in America did not come to the United States as immigrants. That fact is at the core of the conflict between Afro-Americans and Afro-Caribbeans in this country. It has rarely been addressed in public forums on racism and our political structure. When conservatives and, lately, liberals have said "they" should pull themselves up by their bootstraps, they meant me.

In high school, my guidance counselor told my great-grandmother to switch me from the college course to the business course, because in 1963 there was not much hope of sending a poor colored girl to college. My great-grandmother had been tugging like hell at those mystical bootstraps only to receive these bizarre mixed messages from the so-called authorities who were still under the misconception that I was an immigrant, as their parents had been. They assumed that I, like those who had chosen to come here from Italy, Germany, and Ireland, was here by choice, and that I understood and accepted the rules and the sovereignty of the government that held power over me. But the immigrant's experience is not mine.

The difference in our experiences has given rise to some of the most despicable words and ideas ever given credence in the Americas: lynching, miscegenation, Ku Klux Klan, "separate but equal," "nigger." While each immigrant group has had its share of derogatory names, it has also been true that each, with the possible exception of the Jews, has been able to go on to become accepted as American. Black people have never shared that luxury. No voting rights bill was needed to allow Italian or Irish immigrants the right to vote. It was assumed that underneath it all they were human and intelligent and could be educated to have a part in this society. But we have always been the other, the "negro," the "black," but never the American—unless we were hitting a home run or playing jazz in Paris. I have been an outlaw in this country since my birth and the birth of my great-grandmother, who helped to teach me my place even as she hoped desperately that I would grow beyond its boundaries.

Although that experience has stigmatized us and short-circuited our expectations, it has also helped us to develop a magical, insular world that protects us from "them," or you, as the case may be. Black people in this country have developed a complex system of family relations that has little resemblance to the nuclear model that is imposed on Americans. The black middle class would have you believe we are the same; it is just not so. While we have developed a black middle class which emulates the white middle class obsessively, the majority of black people in this country are not in that category and never will be. The statistics on poverty and infant mortality in the black community should make that fact clear.

Despite these differences, the black family model is every bit as legitimate as the one we used to see on "Father Knows Best." It is a creative hybrid of working-class, ethnic American and African sense-memory. Our families are extended and strong. I have as much loyalty to my "aunt" who worked in the same bar with my father for twenty years, and who took numbers, as any of the Kennedys has for Rose. Our loyalty is as pervasive and enduring as any other community's concept of family loyalty. The black family taught me that we are considered outlaws and that we must support each other in order to survive. It taught me that the issues of sex and sexism are as crucial to the understanding of our "place" in this society as skin color.

"Ultimately blacks in America are prisoners of the American sexual mystique..." (Altman 1971, 194). There have been few more illuminating words for me, and they remain as true today as they were sixteen years ago. We have all heard the myth of the black stud and the negress slut. Yet few of us have really come to terms with what these images meant to our participation in this society after the Civil War. We have concentrated on establishing that blacks should vote, that we can live in the same neighborhood as whites, and that we can be educated. But what have we done to counteract the image that blacks are purely sexual beings? Gunnar Myrdal's 1944 study showed that most whites believed that the highest priority for blacks in our fight for equality was the right to have sex with and marry white people (60-61). Whites believed that economic opportunity was the last of our priorities (61).

While most of us would smile indulgently at our ancestors' reliance on the mythological figures of the stud and the slut, most of us, meaning Americans (I do think in solidarity with "Americans" at times). have not been able to replace those laughable stereotypes with anything more realistic. Calvin Hernton's analysis of one national myth—of the sanctity of white womanhood—applies inclusively: "[B]ecause this myth is acted upon *as if* it were real both by blacks and whites alike, then it *becomes* real as far as the behavior and sensitivities of those who most encounter it are concerned" (1966, 7). Blacks in this country have been reduced to our sexual functions. During the period of slavery, those sexual functions were a key to the economic survival of the plantation owner. Blacks were bred like any other livestock. We were bought and sold based on our breeding value. A plantation owner needed a woman to mate with his "black buck," so he bought a wide-hipped "bitch" to improve his stock.

After slavery, the stereotypical experience that whites had with blacks was often just as remote and mythological: the mammy, whose function was implicitly sexual, i.e., to nurse the children and fulfill all of the wifely duties except sex. This last function could be fulfilled by the whore on the street, most often black. The black man has been pictured as the feared rapist, the mindless laborer, or the powerful brute. Somewhere inside of most Americans (black and white), these stereotypes continue to fester.

Since the Civil War, most black Americans have been striving to overcome this mythology. We, that is to say my foremothers and forefathers, have been pressing our clothes just so, straightening our hair to a sheen, speaking most appropriately, averting our eyes from improper sights, and bolstering the image of the importance of the "family," so that white people would discard the stereotypes and begin to look upon us as just "regular" human beings. Given that most black people would rather not talk about sex in public (that is, in front of white people) at all, is it any wonder that the gay rights movement leaves the black community trembling with fear and anger? For a people that has spent its entire modern existence in this country trying to shift its identity away from sex to encounter within itself a sub-group which has been totally defined by its sexual preference is both a shock and a threat.

Even for the black gay (and the black community always knows who we are), being black has always been the primary identification. I am afraid it will always be so. Why? Because I have been black all of my life. I have recognized that difference since my first encounter with the rest of the world. I also knew I was gay early, but that was not an issue when I was eight years old. At eight, everything sexual is intense and peculiar. Sexuality does not become an issue until later in life, when one is asked to make sexual decisions. I would guess this observation is true for many black gays. I do not mean that the issue of being gay is less real for blacks.

I mean that by the time I learned that being gay was a reality with which I would have to reckon, I was already struggling with another reality—black skin—that was immensely more devastating in my daily life.

When I go into a store, people see a black person and only incidentally a woman. Being black invalidates even my femaleness. In an Upper West Side apartment building late at night when a white woman refuses to get on an elevator with me, it's because I am black. She sees a mugger as described on the late night news, not another woman as nervous to be out alone as she is.

In a yuppie restaurant, when the bartender insists that the waitress tell me how expensive the Courvoisier is, even though I've just spent $100 on dinner, I know he is acting out of his perception of me as a black person, not because he sees a woman or a lesbian. It is as clear as the skin on my face.

I can pass as straight, if by some bizarre turn of events I should want to. Or I can pass as a compliant woman who accepts the patriarchal hegemony. But I cannot pass as white in this society. I will forever relate to the world from that perspective, until white people expand their definition of American. When American means Afro-American as well as Italo-American, then maybe black people will be able to break down our own mythology.

We act on our myths as if they were real. Blacks and whites behave as if all of the sexual taboos that we have grown up with are God's law. But the sexual taboos that we adhere to are, in many cases, outdated. Procreation and female fidelity are concepts whose importance is based on the need for the survival of the human race. In 1986, we have world hunger, unemployment, unchecked medical extension of life, and legally binding wills; propagation of the human race is much less relevant. However, black Americans bought the sexual norms just as everyone else did, perhaps even more enthusiastically since they were so important to our acceptance.

The gay rights movement has often stressed the independence of the gay experience. It has been important to our emotional health to separate from biological families because they are often the ones who hurt us while we search for a way to have a meaningful life. But the Civil Rights movement was a family movement. For most Afro-Americans the idea of separating from family is appalling and possibly fatal. The family (not the nuclear thing "they" talk about, but our family as we construct it) is our survival mechanism, and few of us would be willing to relinquish it. It is impossible for us to imagine moving forward without our families.

While the gay movement has made a strong step in the direction of the development of non-traditional families and has pushed for a redefinition more in keeping with the actual world in which we live, most gay activists have not dealt with the importance of coming to terms with the ones who birthed us. Many black gays will obfuscate; they will hedge about their lives and their loves, but they do go home for the holidays. During the 1960s, black people laughed at the hippies, not because of their ideas about sexual liberation and pacifism, but because the hippie movement insisted it could cut itself off from the family. They would live independent of the influence and money of their benefactors. For blacks this was a cruel joke. Even now, it is not easy finding gays (or leftists, feminists, or nationalists) who will accept that some parts of our past can be a path to the future.

For many blacks today, it is the same cruel joke to hear gay people (defined by the media as white and male) saying they are independent of their past and are creating a new utopia of gayness and liberation. We know that the new world as described in the pages of the *Advocate*, the *New York Native*, and *Christopher Street* is not so different from that depicted in *New York Magazine*, or the *Village Voice*, or any other mass market publication, gay or straight. The new world is not very different from the old. White men are free to explore new constructs and to break sexual barriers, while we, the blacks, Native Americans, Latinos, and Asians are supposed to tag along like so many Tontos.

Black people cannot be invisible in this society, even if we want to be. Even if I have moved on to the middle class, the welfare patina does not wash off as easily as you might imagine. I still act out of that experience. I understand that the law means one thing for you and another for me— because I am black and because I was poor. Make no mistake about it, in spite of being on this panel here at the great New York University in the great New York City, in my heart, I am that same poor kid trying to look respectable for the welfare worker's visit. Ask Bernadette Powell what it means to be black and poor in this country (Jones 1985). She would tell you it means she can't be the victim of rape or battery. Ask her what she thinks of the difference between the sentence she is serving in jail for killing her abusive husband, and the sentence Jean Harris is serving (Harris 1986). Qualitatively, it is as different as night and day. These differences are the function of class and race in our society. "Equality before the law" means little in the face of these realities.

We needed the Civil Rights Movement to save our lives from lynching and discrimination. The sanction of law was needed to attack institutionalized racism. However, if we examine the lives of the majority of black Americans and see the poverty and segregation in which they still live, we see that the law has not done much good for them. My hope is that the gay rights movement will not make the same mistakes. Our survival depends not so much on the laws that are passed, although they are crucial, but on the attitudes we carry in our hearts and pass along to others.

If black Americans can ever let go of our feeling that we are the supreme victims (a title for which we sadly vie with Native Americans), then maybe we can begin to believe in our own worth and value in this society. If gays can ever open ourselves to the full struggle for human rights, and not wait for non-whites, the disabled, or women to be in the room before making it an issue, maybe the concept of gay liberation will have the depth of meaning we all think it should. When white gay rights activists begin to look at the struggle from the multiple perspective that black gays cannot avoid, maybe the movement will begin to address the core issues that affect *all* people in this country.

If we can all forget about capturing a piece of the already overextended pie, we might make a change in this society. Gays have not yet decided whether the status quo is worth saving or whether we should be trying to change the entire structure. We need to find a solution to that question quickly. While we here are considerably different from one another, the people who oppress us are rather much the same. They all have the same idea that they know the right way and the correct behavior, and that it is their duty to see that those of us who are not correct stay out of their schools, their neighborhoods, and their homes. And they definitely do not want me to marry their sister!

According to the law, blacks and gays have always been on the outside, so our confrontation is not just with the law but with who we are and what we believe about each other. The issue of sexuality will always be a difficult one in this puritanical culture. For the black population it will be even more so. We, blacks and gays, need to shed our fear of examining our differences. We must acknowledge that the world does not see us in the same way, and what is more important, that we do not see the world in exactly the same way. Only thus can we sustain any meaningful activism and bring about change in our society.

DISCUSSION QUESTIONS

1. What are some examples of the ways activists erase differences in the forms of oppression? What happens when we overgeneralize from our own experience? How can analogies with our own experience be helpful? How can we theorize so that comparisons between oppressions lead to discovery of patterns of oppression without oversimplifying?

2. In particular, what are some of the ways heterosexist oppression is different from other forms? What are some of the similarities with, e.g., anti-Semitism or ableism? What can we learn about oppression from such comparisons? What can we learn about strategies of resistance and change?

3. What are some of the ways readers censor themselves with respect to their differences when working in mixed groups? How is this harmful? How can we decide when it may be appropriate?

4. What does Gomez mean when she talks about "letting go of our feeling of being victims?" How is this feeling an obstacle to political action? Is there a danger that letting go will result in the history of oppression being ignored? How is letting go voluntarily different from being told by the oppressors, "That's all ancient history—this is now?"

SUGGESTIONS FOR FURTHER READING
Cheryl Clarke. 1983. Lesbianism as an act of resistance. *This bridge called my back: Writings by radical women of color.* Cherríe Moraga & Gloria Anzaldúa, Eds. New York: Kitchen Table: Women of Color Press.

Jewelle Gomez. 1991. *The Gilda stories: A novel.* Ithaca, NY: Firebrand Books.

Gloria Hull, Patricia Bell Scott & Barbara Smith, Eds. 1982. *All the women are white, all the blacks are men, but some of us are brave: Black women's studies.* New York: The Feminist Press.

Makeda Silvera, Ed. 1991. *Piece of my heart: A lesbian of colour anthology,* Toronto: Sister Vision Press.

PIETÀ
Michael Lassell

A man who is ill
visits his mother
in her nursing home.

You don't look well, she says.
Neither do you, he says.

My friends are all dying, she says.
My friends are dying, too.

I'm afraid that when I die
there will be no one left to
say prayers at my grave, she says.
It's my fear, too, he replies.

And they sit and weep,
each dropping tears onto
the hands of the other,
waiting for the after
that follows hard
the heels of time.

"Pietà," by Michael Lassell, from DECADE DANCE, *by Michael Lassell,
published by Alyson Publications, Boston, MA. Copyright © 1990 by Michael
Lassell. Reprinted with permission.*

TWO POEMS
Ron Schreiber

mother's day (5-11-86)

"he's stable," is all I can answer
"weaker yesterday," "a little stronger

this morning." it's mothers day,
and my own mother calls me.

they're going out for brunch.
I'm visiting the hospital, buying

food for John's dogs & cats, food
for my cats, watching the game

between the Sixers & the Bucks,
trying to finish reading journals

from students, wondering, as the day
goes on, whether I'll visit again

this evening—with Suzanne, John's
parents probably, who knows what

cousin or uncle is already there. I
need time alone with you,

you need that time from me, where
we're easy & simple together, hoping

that you'll get out of the hospital
to stay next time—for a few weeks or

months. "are you afraid of dying?"
I ask, and you answer, "no."

"mother's day (5-11-86)" and "9-17-86," by Ron Schreiber from JOHN, *by Ron Schreiber, published by Hanging Loose Press/Calamus Books, 217 Wyckoff Street, Brooklyn, NY 11217. $9 Paper. Copyright © 1989 by Ron Schreiber. Reprinted with permission.*

9-17-86

Saturday Jack told me
his therapist was dying.

Mauricio—married now,
with one son—died Saturday

night; I'll go to his memorial
service today. yesterday

Paul Fowler was diagnosed;
I called him in the hospital,

where he feels good. Bob
Johnson died (that's why we

have Lisa 8 hours a day
instead of 5). & John

is still living: Monday

night fried clams & butter-
scotch pudding. Barbara

—on vacation in Italy for
two weeks—thinks John will

still be alive when she gets
back. Lisa & I don't think so,

but it's all baffling.
"what do we know?" we ask

each other. while outside
it closes in, raw weather.

cold rain.

CHILDREN OF GRANDMOTHER MOON
Clyde M. Hall (M. Owlfeather)

Owlfeather is a Shoshone-Métis/Cree. This article describes some of the challenges contemporary Native Americans face in negotiating the complexities of sexuality and identity. The problem is made more complex by the multiple meanings sexualities have in cultures that partake of both traditional norms and the rest of society.

It is important that readers keep in mind this is the only piece in this collection that is written in the voice of a Native American. In such cases, readers need to resist the temptation to make a single voice speak for all Native Americans. Not only are there Native American women as well as men, not all Native Americans live on reservations, and the traditional organization of sexualities was not the same in all North American cultures.

In particular, there is a strong tendency among white readers to see Native culture through a romantic lens, as an idyllic golden age. This tendency is pervasive in U.S. culture, where it functions as a kind of veil for the brutality of the conquest of this continent. In the case of gay men, it is made stronger by the fact that some indigenous societies seem to have made more space for males to relate across gender roles and sexually to one another than our own culture does. This phenomenon is often called berdache.

Grandmother Moon comes slowly
    over the eastern hills.
Chanting a song, a song of a lost age,
    its meaning a mystery.
She comes dressed in orange calico.
Her hair wrapped in otter fur.
Her moccasins made of soft deer skin.
No one hears as she makes her journey
    to her lodge in the west.
Before her goes the owl, flying by night.
Singing, "hush, respect your grandmother
    She is old and knows many things.
    Say nothing as she passes."

Sometimes she sends owl out, to warn her people
    of someone about to die.
He chants a verse, three times
    for three nights,
    before it happens.
This makes her very sad, her people are few.
You can tell she weeps
    because you find
    Her tears
On the grass and trees when she's gone.

The reservation where I live is a harsh place, situated on a high plateau valley in the west. Most people wonder why anyone would want to live here. The temperature ranges from one hundred degrees in the summer to forty below in the winter. Life is indeed hard. It takes a certain kind of person, or people, to call this place "home." My people have lived in this place from many, many generations and consider it more than home; it is the place from where we come and to where we return. It is our mother and our special place in the world.

Many people ask me, "Why do you stay here? You have a good education, you have traveled the world and lived in many places, many different lives, so why return? There is no work here, little or no pride; there is depression, desolation, no hope. And for a person such as you, a gay Indian, what is there for you here, except perhaps criticism and humiliation?"

All of the above is true. But still I am here and surviving. I have a supportive group of friends, Indian and non-Indian, gay and straight. I hide my lifestyle and interests from no one. I participate in Indian traditional dances and religion. In a small town and in a tribal group of four thousand people nothing is hidden.

I returned to the reservation four years ago. I still remember a time when I vowed that I would never return. But despite all the situations listed above, the fact remains that I did return because there is something here that exists for an Indian person nowhere else: the sense of belonging, of family and of the land. You are not only a person, alone, but an extension of a family and a group of people, a "tribe," that has existed before the written word and history. It is a unique place and people, something that non-Indians cannot really imagine or feel. True, the culture is shattered, broken...and the people's lifestyle is in tatters and perhaps even still in culture shock to some degree. After all, my great-grandfather and great-grandmother saw the last of the buffalo killed. A lifestyle they knew and loved, with the rigors of moving camp and living in tipis, going anywhere they pleased, was destroyed.

Indian life and existence today is a paradox of the old and new. Christian beliefs are held along with native traditions. Western lifestyles are combined with traditional Indian lifestyles, and a number of people get hopelessly lost. Not respecting themselves or anyone else, some get angry, some get drunk, and some deny the Indian culture or anything Indian because they think it is useless in this present day and age.

No wonder a young man of nineteen years that I know and sleep with sometimes says to me, "I don't want to have people call me a queer or a faggot, but I want to be with you," or that I have a long-standing married lover who throws rocks at my window when the moon is full, wanting me to come out and play. He says, "I'm married, but I have always loved you and always will." Gay and bisexual Indian men and women are no different from anyone else in their fear of criticism. But I think it is more intense within a tribal structure, because our traditional way of correcting behavior is public chastisement and ridicule. And today, the view of the gay Indian man or woman has been twisted to fit the mix of Christian and Indian beliefs in contemporary tribal culture.

In the old days, during life on the plains, the people respected each other's vision. Berdaches had an integral place in the rigors and lifestyle of the tribe. The way they were viewed was not the same as the contemporary Indian gay lifestyle and consciousness that we have now— they were not fighting for a place in society and to be accepted by that society. They already had a place, a very special and sacred place. They were the people who gave sacred names, cut down the Sun Dance pole, and foretold future events. They were renowned for their bead and quillwork and hide-tanning abilities and fancy dress. (Not all berdaches dressed in women's clothes; it depended on their vision.) It was considered good luck to have a berdache on a war party or on a horse-stealing raid. If a man wanted to, and had the ability to take a second or third wife, many times a man of the berdache vision would be chosen.

But all this changed with the coming of the reservation period in Indian history and the systematic crushing of all things Indian. The berdache visionaries were one of the outstanding targets, especially those who dressed and had the mannerisms of the opposite sex. (Some of these men were married to women, but maintained the dress of their vision.) The last record of a berdache on my reservation was in the early 1900s.

You must understand that in the period of 1880 to 1910, if you were found or caught practicing Indian beliefs or dress, you could be jailed. Even if an Indian man wore his hair long, which was his pride, he could be jailed and punished. The great summer Sun Dance was suppressed. In one district of my reservation the dance was stopped by cutting down the Sun Dance pole in the midst of the ceremony. In another instance, the dance was held on a Mormon rancher's property where the government had no jurisdiction. So it was with little wonder that the vision of the berdache was forgotten or suppressed to the point that it was no longer mentioned and barely remembered. When it was mentioned, it was with shame and scorn, due to the influence of Christianity on Indian people. It is into this type of belief system and society that gay Indian men and women are born today.

On my reservation, it is traditional for the firstborn of a generation to live and be raised by the grandparents. They are called the "old peoples' children," and they are taught the knowledge, traditions, songs and lifeways of the tribe. Usually these people either become respected members of their community and tribe or turn out to be totally useless!

I was raised in this manner and lived a wonderful childhood. I was raised by my grandmother in a little one-room cabin that she and my great-uncle built in the 1920s. We had a wire strung for drying meat and hanging dish towels and clothing. In the center of the room we had a big round oak table covered with oilcloth. My grandmother's friends would come to visit and have coffee. Sometimes my great-aunts or great-uncles could come. I always knew my place, but would sometimes sit with them and drink coffee with lots of sugar and canned milk in it. I always enjoyed these visits and still feel more comfortable with Indian elders than with people my own age. I lived through their tales and my grandmother's own stories. In the winter she would tell "coyote stories." I felt very secure hearing those stories of our family and tribe and would listen very intently after the fire had burned down and everyone was bedded down for the night. The winter nights were wonderful when those stories were told, with the snow blowing around the edges of the cabin.

Our life was very simple by non-Indian standards. In the mornings when I was older I would chop wood and pump water—those would be my chores at the start of each day. After breakfast, which was either oatmeal or pancakes, my sister and I would venture forth to greet the day and many adventures.

My relationships with children my age were limited. Besides my sister and several cousins, I had very few young friends. Even at an early age I was attracted to members of my own sex. I was dreaming in my childhood. I knew that I was different in my attraction to other boys and men. I always had this dream in which a bearded man would open his arms to me and say "Come." When I was eight years old, I experienced my vision and found out how truly different I was.

It was during a hot, dry and dusty Idaho summer, when I was eleven, that I had my first real contact with another male. I had more freedom then. I had both a pony and a red bicycle. With those possessions my circle of friends widened. I met a boy who lived a few blocks down from my grandmother's cabin. He was a local white boy some years older than myself. I admired his independent and cocksure ways. He seemed to be everything that I was not: good in sports and, above all, sure of himself in every situation. He had tousled brown curly hair and was somewhat stocky. He became my hero in the eye of my budding desire.

The local boys our age frequented several well-known swimming holes on the reservation. We always picked one that was well secluded with overhanging trees and green grass on the banks. One day toward the end of summer—on the kind of day when the light is hazy and diffused and the air is barely moving and heavy to breathe—my friend and I decided to have an impromptu swim before returning home. The water was cool and clear as we dove in. I came up from under the water first. He came up right behind me and reached around and into my shorts (we always swam in our undershorts.) I noticed that he was hard, as he rubbed against my backside. As his hands reached around me...I became aroused and hard, too. It felt good and right, like something that was supposed to be. I knew then that this is what I had been waiting for and I have never looked back since.

After that summer and after many more rendezvous, my friend moved away. I was dumbstruck. I had found a companion, someone to share with and be my friend, closer than a brother or a buddy. But then he was gone. My young heart experienced for the first time the loneliness and the ache of missing someone that you love. Since that time I have found many more boys and men of all races in many different cities and countries and situations. But of course, there is no time like the first time. It is something that is burned in my memory, like those hot Idaho August days, so long ago.

It is unfortunate that among today's gay Indians the great tradition and vision of the old-time berdache has been suppressed and is nearly dead. Gay Indians today grow up knowing that they are different, act in a different way, and perceive things in a different light from other Indians. They know these things, but sometimes are afraid to act or acknowledge their gayness. If they do, they try to accept and emulate the only alternative lifestyle offered to them, that of the current gay society of bars, baths, and, until recently, numerous sex partners. It is no wonder that many succumb to alcohol or drug addiction and early death. Today I see so many of my Indian brothers and sisters with the same vision living a life that is damaging to themselves, denying or fighting against what they really are. I see and know many gay Indians on the reservation and elsewhere that think along the following lines: "It's okay for you to go to bed with me. I will talk to you in bars or when I want to fuck. But don't come around me in Indian society, at pow-wows, or other tribal functions. I don't want our people to know. Nobody knows my secret but everyone knows what you are and what you like to do."

To escape this kind of thinking and the oppressive lifestyle that gay Indians are often forced to live on the reservations, many go to the city and follow the way of the non-Indian gay society—taking up the latest trends in fashion, carrying on in the bars, or dancing the night away in discos and after-hours clubs and, of course, having sex, lots of it. I followed this way myself for many years, but in the end I became tired of it all. Deep inside I knew that, as an Indian, something else was needed—

something more than poppers, drugs, booze, fashion, restaurants, bars, gay shops, cock rings, leather, drag, and the latest dance hits—especially for a person of substance and especially for an Indian person. Most Indian people, gay or straight, have been instilled with a respect for all things, a love for the earth and all things living. The current gay lifestyle, although it is an up-front gay existence, is not an Indian way. Most gay Indians become lost in it, not only to themselves but to their cultures, tribes, and sometimes families as well.

In the past ten years, however, efforts have been made by gay Indians who live in the cities to found support groups and social organizations for urban gay Indians as well as those across the country on reservations and in other rural areas. They are to be commended. Organizations such as Gay American Indians of San Francisco and the Native Cultural Society of Vancouver, British Columbia, are at least there to provide the positive statement and support needed by so many gay Indians. They exist to say, *"We are here, we exist, we are INDIAN and we are GAY!!"* That is very important, not only to those in the cities but also to the gay Indian living on the reservation. Many live in such isolation that they cannot react to other gay Indian people in a positive way and are afraid to associate with other gay Indians because of social ostracism or criticism.

In the old days, groups of berdaches lived on the outer edge of the camp. They lived together in a tipi or a group of tipis that were usually the best made and decorated in camp. The old-time berdaches had a pride in their possessions and in themselves. They knew who they were and what place they had in Plains Indian society.

I believe this is exactly what needs to happen again with gay Indians today. There is a need to take pride in one's self and to respect other gay Indian people. There is a need for a resurgence of that old pride and knowledge of place. Traditions need to be researched and revived. If traditions have been lost, then new ones should be borrowed from other tribes to create groups or societies for gay Indians that would function in the present. An example of this is the contemporary pow-wow that takes elements from many tribal groups and combines them into an exercise in modern Indian tradition and social structure.

I am not saying that we should all go "back to the blanket" or return to the reservation. But somehow, there should be a blending of the old with the new, to develop more within ourselves and our consciousness—as a people living on the "outer edge," possessing a unique and valid vision and a place in the history and contemporary lifestyle of our country.

When you are born into this world, you reach for either a bow and quiver, which is blessed and protected by the Sun, our Grandfather, or you reach for an awl and sewing bag, which is blessed by the Moon, our Grandmother. From that time on you will follow that vision and be blessed.   —Traditional Indian belief and teaching

DISCUSSION QUESTIONS

1. How do the readers relate to the traditions of their own cultures? What are some of the strengths in those cultures? What weaknesses? How do lesbian, gay male and bisexual readers negotiate a safe space among the contradictions of culture?

2. It is sometimes suggested on the left that lesbian and gay men's issues are an exclusively "white, North American" preoccupation, and that attempts to introduce them in international or multicultural settings is a form of cultural imperialism. This article suggests that in some cases other cultures may enjoy better arrangements for dealing with sexual diversity. What other cultural experiences can readers share to support this? Is it possible that homophobic or heterosexist structures in colonized societies are the result of colonialism, rather than a true expression of indigenous values? Are there cases where the issue of cultural imperialism is used by straight North Americans to avoid dealing with their own heterosexism?

SUGGESTIONS FOR FURTHER STUDY

Paula Gunn Allen. 1986. *The sacred hoop: Recovering the feminine in American Indian traditions.* Boston: Beacon Press.

Evelyn Blackwood. 1984. Sexuality and gender in certain Native American tribes: The case of cross-gender females. *Signs,* 10(1):27-42.

Beth Brant, Ed. 1984. *A gathering of spirit: Writing and art by North American Indian women.* Montpelier, VT: Sinister Wisdom.

Beth Brant 1985. *Mohawk trail.* Ithaca, NY: Firebrand Books.

Chrystos. 1989. *Not vanishing.* Vancouver: Press Gang.

Ramón Gutiérrez. 1989. Must we deracinate Indians to find gay roots? *OUT/LOOK 4,* 1(4):61-67.

Naomi Littlebear. 1983. Earth-Lover, survivor, musician. *This bridge called my back: Writings by radical women of color.* Cherríe Moraga & Gloria Anzaldúa, Eds. New York: Kitchen Table: Women of Color Press.

Will Roscoe. 1988. The Zuñi Man-Woman. *OUT/LOOK 2,* 1(2):56-67.

SEXUALITIES AND IDENTITIES

Intersections

N. Leigh Dunlap cartoon from MORGAN CALABRESE: THE MOVIE, *by N. Leigh Dunlap, published by New Victoria Publishers, Norwich, VT, p. 10. Copyright © 1987 by N. Leigh Dunlap. Reprinted with permission.*

I AM YOUR SISTER:
BLACK WOMEN ORGANIZING
ACROSS SEXUALITIES
Audre Lorde

"I do not want you to ignore my identity." Audre Lorde was an eloquent voice for building bridges and coalitions. Here she points out the fact that even in situations where sexuality may not seem to matter, lesbians, gay men and bisexual people carry their identities with them in all their work. Often we do so clandestinely, but when we do, we pay a price. The personal resources available to movements for social change are too limited to afford such a price: we need to be able to recognize and make creative use of the strength of all our people. We will be able to do so if we remember Lorde's words: "We do not have to become each other in order to work together."

Whenever I come to Medgar Evers College I always feel a thrill of anticipation and delight because it feels like coming home, like talking to family, having a chance to speak about things that are very important to me with people who matter the most. And this is particularly true whenever I talk at the Women's Center. But, as with all families, we sometimes find it difficult to deal constructively with the genuine differences between us and to recognize that unity does not require that we be identical to each other. Black women are not one great vat of homogenized chocolate milk. We have many different faces, and we do not have to become each other in order to work together.

It is not easy for me to speak here with you as a Black Lesbian feminist, recognizing that some of the ways in which I identify myself make it difficult for you to hear me. But meeting across difference always requires mutual stretching, and until you *can* hear me as a Black Lesbian feminist, our strengths will not be truly available to each other as Black women.

Because I feel it is urgent that we not waste each other's resources, that we recognize each sister on her own terms so that we may better work together toward our mutual survival, I speak here about heterosexism and homophobia, two grave barriers to organizing among Black women. And so that we have a common language between us, I would like to define some of the terms I use: *Heterosexism*—a belief in the inherent superiority of one form of loving over all others and thereby the right to dominance; *Homophobia*—a terror surrounding feelings of love for members of the same sex and thereby a hatred of those feelings in others.

In the 1960s, when liberal white people decided that they didn't want to appear racist, they wore dashikis, and danced Black, and ate Black, and even married Black, but they did not want to feel Black or think Black, so they never even questioned the textures of their daily living (why should flesh-colored bandaids always be pink?) and then they wondered, "Why are those Black folks always taking offense so easily at the least little thing? Some of our best friends are Black..."

Well, it is not necessary for some of your best friends to be Lesbian, although some of them probably are, no doubt. But it is necessary for you to stop oppressing me through false judgement. I do not want you to ignore my identity, nor do I want you to make it an insurmountable barrier between our sharing of strengths.

When I say I am a Black feminist, I mean I recognize that my power as well as my primary oppressions come as a result of my Blackness as well as my womanness, and therefore my struggles on both these fronts are inseparable.

When I say I am a Black Lesbian, I mean I am a woman whose primary focus of loving, physical as well as emotional, is directed to women. It does not mean I hate men. Far from it. The harshest attacks I have ever heard against Black men come from those women who are intimately bound to them and cannot free themselves from a subservient and silent position. I would never presume to speak about Black men the way I have heard some of my straight sisters talk about the men they are attached to. And of course that concerns me, because it reflects a situation of noncommunication in the heterosexual Black community that is far more truly threatening than the existence of Black Lesbians.

What does this have to do with Black women organizing?

I have heard it said—usually behind my back—that Black Lesbians are not normal. But what is normal in this deranged society by which we are all trapped? I remember, and so do many of you, when being Black was considered *not normal*, when they talked about us in whispers, tried to paint us, lynch us, bleach us, ignore us, pretend we did not exist. WE called that racism.

I have heard it said that Black Lesbians are a threat to the Black family. But when 50 percent of children born to Black women are born out of wedlock, and 30 percent of all Black families are headed by women without husbands, we need to broaden and redefine what we mean by *family*.

I have heard it said that Black Lesbians will mean the death of the race. Yet Black Lesbians bear children in exactly the same way other women bear children, and a Lesbian household is simply another kind of family. Ask my son and daughter.

The terror of Black Lesbians is buried in that deep inner place where we have been taught to fear all difference—to kill it or ignore it. Be assured: loving women is not a communicable disease. You don't catch it like the common cold. Yet the one accusation that seems to render even the most vocal straight Black woman totally silent and ineffective is the suggestion that she might be a Black Lesbian.

If someone says you're Russian and you know you're not, you don't collapse into stunned silence. Even if someone calls you a bigamist, or a childbeater, and you know you're not, you don't crumple into bits. You say it's not true and keep on printing the posters. But let anyone, particularly a Black man, accuse a straight Black woman of being a Black Lesbian, and right away that sister becomes immobilized, as if that is the most horrible thing she could be, and must at all costs be proven false. That is homophobia. It is a waste of woman energy, and it puts a terrible weapon into the hands of your enemies to be used against you to silence you, to keep you docile and in line. It also serves to keep us isolated and apart.

I have heard it said that Black Lesbians are not political, that we have not been and are not involved in the struggles of Black people. But when I taught Black and Puerto Rican students writing at City College in the SEEK program in the sixties I was a Black Lesbian. I was a Black Lesbian when I helped organize and fight for the Black Studies Department of John Jay College. And because I was fifteen years younger then and less sure of myself, at one crucial moment I yielded to pressure that said I should step back for a Black man even though I knew him to be a serious error of choice, and I did, and he was. But I was a Black Lesbian then.

When my girlfriends and I went out in the car one July 4th night after fireworks with cans of white spray paint and our kids asleep in the back seat, one of us staying behind to keep the motor running and watch the kids while the other two worked our way down the suburban New Jersey street, spraying white paint over the black jockey statues, and their little red jackets, too, we were Black Lesbians.

When I drove through the Mississippi Delta to Jackson in 1968 with a group of Black students from Tougaloo, another car full of redneck kids trying to bump us off the road all the way back into town, I was a Black Lesbian.

When I weaned my daughter in 1963 to go to Washington in August to work in the coffee tents along with Lena Horne, making coffee for the marshals because that was what most Black women did in the 1963 March on Washington, I was a Black Lesbian.

When I taught a poetry workshop at Tougaloo, a small Black college in Mississippi, where white rowdies shot up the edge of the campus every night, and I felt the joy of seeing young Black poets find their voices and power through words in our mutual growth, I was a Black Lesbian. And there are strong Black poets today who date their growth and awareness from those workshops.

When Yoli and I cooked curried chicken and beans and rice and took our extra blankets and pillows up the hill to the striking students occupying buildings at City College in 1969, demanding open admissions and the right to an education, I was a Black Lesbian. When I walked through the midnight hallways of Lehman College that same year, carrying Midol and Kotex pads for the young Black radical women taking part in the action, and we tried to persuade them that their place in the revolution was not ten paces behind Black men, that spreading their legs to the guys on the tables in the cafeteria was not a revolutionary act no matter what the brothers said, I was a Black Lesbian. When I picketed for Welfare Mothers' Rights, and against the enforced sterilization of young Black girls, when I fought institutionalized racism in the New York City schools, I was a Black Lesbian.

But you did not know it because we did not identify ourselves, so now you can say that Black Lesbians and Gay men have nothing to do with the struggles of the Black Nation.

And I am not alone.

When you read the words of Langston Hughes you are reading the words of a Black Gay man. When you read the words of Alice Dunbar-Nelson and Angelina Weld Grimké, poets of the Harlem Renaissance, you are reading the words of Black Lesbians. When you listen to the life-affirming voices of Bessie Smith and Ma Rainey, you are hearing Black Lesbian women. When you see the plays and read the words of Lorraine Hansberry, you are reading the words of a woman who loved women deeply.

Today, Lesbians and Gay men are some of the most active and engaged members of Art Against Apartheid, a group which is making visible and immediate our cultural responsibilities against the tragedy of South Africa. We have organizations such as the National Coalition of Black Lesbians and Gays, Dykes Against Racism Everywhere, and Men of All Colors together, all of which are committed to and engaged in antiracist activity.

Homophobia and heterosexism mean you allow yourselves to be robbed of the sisterhood and strength of Black Lesbian women because you are afraid of being called a Lesbian yourself. Yet we share so many concerns as Black women, so much work to be done. The urgency of the destruction of our Black children and the theft of young Black minds are joint urgencies. Black children shot down or doped up on the streets of our cities are priorities for all of us. The fact of Black women's blood flowing with grim regularity in the streets and living rooms of Black communities is not a Black Lesbian rumor. It is a sad statistical truth. The fact that there is widening and dangerous lack of communication around our differences between Black women and men is not a Black Lesbian plot.

It is a reality that is starkly clarified as we see our young people becoming more and more uncaring of each other. Young Black boys believing that they can define their manhood between a sixth-grade girl's legs, growing up believing that Black women and girls are the fitting target for their justifiable furies rather than the racist structures grinding us all into dust, these are not Black Lesbian myths. These are sad realities of Black communities today and of immediate concern to us all. We cannot afford to waste each other's energies in our common battles.

What does homophobia mean? It means that high-powered Black women are told it is not safe to attend a Conference on the Status of Women in Nairobi simply because we are Lesbians. It means that in a political action, you rob yourselves of the vital insight and energies of political women such as Betty Powell and Barbara Smith and Gwendolyn Rogers and Raymina Mays and Robin Christian and Yvonne Flowers. It means another instance of the divide-and-conquer routine.

How do we organize around our differences, neither denying them nor blowing them up out of proportion?

The first step is an effort of will on your part. Try to remember to keep certain facts in mind. Black Lesbians are not apolitical. We have been a part of every freedom struggle within this country. Black Lesbians are not a threat to the Black family. Many of us have families of our own. We are not white, and we are not a disease. We are women who love women. This does not mean we are going to assault your daughters in an alley on Nostrand Avenue. It does not mean we are about to attack you if we pay you a compliment on your dress. It does not mean we only think about sex, any more than you only think about sex.

Even if you *do* believe any of these stereotypes about Black Lesbians, begin to practice acting like you don't believe them. Just as racist stereotypes are the problem of the white people who believe them, so also are homophobic stereotypes the problem of the heterosexuals who believe them. In other words, those stereotypes are yours to solve, not mine, and they are a terrible and wasteful barrier to our working together. I am not your enemy. We do not have to become each other's unique experiences and insights in order to share what we have learned through our particular battles for survival as Black women.

There was a poster in the 1960s that was very popular: HE'S NOT BLACK, HE'S MY BROTHER! It used to infuriate me because it implied that the two were mutually exclusive—*he* couldn't be both brother and Black. Well, I do not want to be tolerated, nor misnamed. I want to be recognized.

I am a Black Lesbian, and I *am* your sister.

DISCUSSION QUESTIONS

1. (For non-gay readers:) What personal experiences do you have of homophobia being used as "a terrible weapon...used against you to silence you, to keep you docile and in line"? How did you react? Could you have reacted more constructively?

2. (For lesbian, gay male and bisexual readers:) What personal experiences do you have of being cautioned against damaging the movement by your openness? How did you react? Could you have reacted more constructively?

3. (For all readers:) What are some cases of non-gay activists "protecting" lesbian, gay and bisexual movement workers from homophobia? What are the effects of such protection for social change efforts over the long haul?

4. What are some of the ways homophobia and heterosexism are expressed and understood in differing communities? What alternative strategies might be necessary, depending on the community?

SUGGESTIONS FOR FURTHER STUDY

Gloria Anzaldúa, Ed. 1990. *Making face, making soul, hacienda caras: Creative and critical perspectives by women of color.* San Francisco: Aunt Lute Foundation Books.

Jewelle Gomez & Barbara Smith. 1990. Taking the Home Out of Homophobia. *OUT/LOOK 8*, 2(4):32-37.

bell hooks. 1988. Reflections on homophobia and Black communities. *OUT/LOOK 2*, 1(2):22-25.

Barbara Smith, Ed. 1983. *Home girls: A Black feminist anthology.* New York: Kitchen Table: Women of Color Press.

William J. Weatherby. 1989. *James Baldwin: Artist on fire: a portrait.* New York: Donald Fine.

DID YOUR MOTHER DO
VOLUNTEER WORK?
Marilyn Murphy

In this "Introduction to the Class Issue," Marilyn Murphy explores more deeply the myth of the classless society and the differences in underlying attitudes that result from different class upbringings. For example, middle-class children are expected "to embody, in their very person, the standards that poor and working class people are supposed to emulate." By contrast, in working-class families, "[o]utward conformity and obedience to authority is valued, not respect or belief in the authority itself." These differences are often masked by the myth of classlessness, but disguised as they are, they do serve a function in the "good order" of society. Frequently, as Murphy points out, they serve the same function, on a smaller scale, within our own movement organizations.

Murphy, on the other hand, looks at these attitudes through the eyes of one whose work is to challenge that order. Because the readers of this anthology are likely to have this same attitude toward the social order, this article seems especially important to include.

For the past fifteen years at least, radical feminists, most of us Lesbians, have been writing, speaking and conducting workshops about class as a major influence in the development of our values, attitudes and behavior; as a system of personal and institutional oppression; as a cause of friction in our personal relationships; and as an issue which divides women and creates obstacles to our working together to liberate ourselves and our sisters from personal and institutional oppression of all kinds. Our other intra-movement issues: racism, internalized homophobia, able-bodiedism, anti-Semitism, ageism, fatophobia usually are acknowledged as issues, if only by those women suffering from their effects. Even Lesbians who insist the fat woman or the disabled Lesbian, for example, is "misunderstanding" their attitudes, remarks or behavior will acknowledge that the issues do exist. This is not usually true about class.

Before we can even begin a discussion about class differences and their effects, we first have to demonstrate that they exist. People in the

U.S. are willing to concede that the very, very rich and the very, very poor may not be like the rest of us, as long as we can keep our belief that the rest of us are pretty much the same. Most people in the U.S. are middle-class, we say, not too rich and not too poor, more or less equal. This myth of a mostly classless U.S. society is an important factor for keeping our class system in place and unthreatened by revolution or trade unions. The invisibility of class oppression, this denial of "difference," insures a cohesiveness of belief in the United States as a place where most of the people have a more or less equal opportunity to live the "good life." It intensifies the belief, congruent with a "classless society," that the only real barriers to success are laziness, ignorance, immorality, cowardice, heredity, lack of ambition or perseverance and/or the inferiority of one's sex, race, ethnicity. It teaches us that "anyone" can make it in the U.S. just by "wanting it enough," by working "hard enough." Because even members of oppressed classes and groups internalize these beliefs to a greater or lesser degree, they are more likely to think of themselves as "failures" than as members of an oppressed class—and so are their oppressors.

Also, those in the U.S. who experience oppression for other, more apparently "obvious" reasons than class, such as people of colors, Jews, Lesbians, disabled people, usually do not attribute their problems to their socio-economic class, or they believe class oppression is not important in light of their other oppression. In a certain sense, this is true. Racism, for example, limits the participation of people of colors in institutions like unions which are organizations of and for working people. Therefore, it is difficult, and does not seem particularly profitable to people of colors themselves to try to separate racism from class oppression.

In addition, the upward mobility, whether real or imagined, of some poor and working class people whose teachers or social workers chose them for "special" treatment when children, or who received scholarships, grants, loans, the GI bill and/or who worked and sacrificed for an education, who made money, who were lucky enough to become rich as athletes or entertainers, who married up—like Cinderella, convinces most people, including the upwardly mobile and those they leave behind, that class differences and the resultant oppression do not "really" exist. It also masks the reality that upwardly mobile poor and working class people bring to our new lives the values, behaviors and attitudes we learned in our childhood and youth, that we are living middle class life-styles with a poverty or working class perspective, that we are frequently out of sync with our new environment.

My purpose in writing this paper is to share some of what I have learned from my own personal experiences, from academic study, and from the women I have worked with in creating, facilitating and participating in feminist programs on class differences since 1975. This paper continues to be a "work in progress" changing as we learn more, as we refine our ideas. Much of what follows are generalizations, fitting the experiences of some Lesbians more or less than others. This is not an exercise in comparing oppressions or blaming. We are not responsible for the privileges of our birth. The class system exists for the benefit of those at the top, and is designed to keep the classes separated and antagonistic. I offer these thoughts as an exercise in understanding.

I hope this paper helps Lesbians with working class and poverty origins to identify some of the values, attitudes and behaviors we learned during childhood. With this knowledge, we can abandon those which are no longer appropriate in our lives and those which are oppressive to others. We can recognize and cherish those others which vitalize and enhance our lives, our relationships and our struggles to eliminate the oppression of all women. I want poverty and working class Lesbians to recognize when our "out of sync" feeling comes from class differences, so we can let it go as "inappropriate" when we need to, or to stand firm for what we know from our life experiences is right and true. I hope middle-class Lesbians will become more class conscious, ridding themselves of values, attitudes and behaviors that are oppressive to working and poverty class Lesbians and to the hidden, upwardly mobile poverty and working class Lesbians in their midst. I want them to be able to catch themselves when a Lesbian's style, grammar, clothes, or "deportment" inclines them to dismiss the ideas she presents. I'd like to see middle-class Lesbians remember that their feeling of confidence and "rightness" of their rules, decisions, judgments comes, at least some of the time, from their class privilege. In these ways, all of us can learn to work, love and relate to each other in more authentic, more powerful ways, as allies and sisters in the struggle for our liberation.

"KNOWING" THE RULES

Family and society teach children the values, attitudes and behaviors necessary for their survival. In the United States, these survival skills differ markedly depending upon one's class origins. In fact, class origin is the predominant factor in the development of values, attitudes and behaviors more so than religion, sex, ethnicity, education, or geographic region. Only for U.S. Jews and people of colors do religion and ethnicity modify the impact of class origins. This is so no matter how often we say or are told that we all learn "middle-class values." We are taught middle-class values, attitudes and behaviors in school, but poverty and working class children have already internalized their class values by then. Only middle-class children really learn values in school because, for them, learning and experience are congruent. The owning class, of course, is not educated in public or parochial schools. I think we can assume their education is congruent.

The owning class, those who own most of the wealth of the world, are the people who make policy. In this country, they make policy for a constitutional, capitalist, hierarchical democracy. Middle class women and men are expected to be the managers of our society, to make and enforce rules which implement the goals of the policy makers. They are expected to keep the country orderly so that business can be conducted with the least amount of interference by the workers, both the employed and the unemployed. They must set the behavioral standards most conducive to order in the society and ensure those standards are conformed to by those in their charge, the poor and working class people. Middle class people are expected to embody, in their very person, the standards that poor and working class people are supposed to emulate. To do this, middle class children are taught to respect those standards and rules. Beyond that, they are taught to respect the authority and the right of the middle class to make, to model and to enforce the rules. Therefore this respect must be internalized by the middle-class child. The middle-class child is expected, not only to conform to standards of behavior set by her class, she is also expected to conform in attitude to those standards, to believe in the intrinsic value of the standards. She is expected to experience guilt when she does not respect authority enough to conform to it. Great stress is placed on her intention when she does not conform. The question is *why* she did this or not do that. Attitudinal conformity is the goal of middle class childrearing.

The working class child learns to obey authority, learns that disobedience gets her in trouble, gets adults in trouble, gets the family in trouble. For example, the working class parent is less concerned about *why* a child stole, and more concerned about the possible consequences of the act. We are taught to hate and fear the "real poor," to be grateful that we are "not like them," that we are "better" than they are. Children whose parents want to "better" themselves or want the children to have the "chance" they "missed," are urged to behave, speak, make friends, "be like" the middle-class children they know. Upwardly mobile or not, working class parents know, and working class children learn, that rebelliousness can bring swift punishment, expulsion from school, job loss, eviction, poverty. Outward conformity and obedience to authority is valued, not respect or belief in the authority itself. In fact, contempt for the middle class is likely to accompany obedience and conformity.

Poor people, at present fifteen percent of the population according to U.S. Bureau of Census, 1990, neither respect nor obey the rules, nor teach them to their children. They learn to do whatever is necessary to keep themselves alive. They are contemptuous of working-class attempts to "better" themselves by following the rules, by hard work. They "know" that respectability is a veneer that covers middle-class corruption and hypocrisy. They "know" that their chances of making it rich by their wits and luck and crime are better than trying to make it by following the rules, by working long hours as day laborers for minimum wage or less.

With understanding and a commitment to change, our class differences about rules could create new ways of having a revolution. Feminists and Lesbians are attempting to change or overthrow or amend the rules of the patriarchy, that is the values, attitudes and behaviors that oppress us. But even in the Women's Liberation Movement, middle-class women usually "know" the rules by which to do this. They know the "right way" to do the "right activity" to accomplish what they perceive to be the "right" goals for all women.

Working- and poverty-class women of colors and white women are frequently frustrated, disgusted and angered by the use of parliamentary procedure by the more traditional feminist organizations, the National Organization for Women and the National Women's Studies Association, for example, especially when it is used to thwart our efforts to be heard. The "leadership" of NOW and NWSA are notorious for complaining that "they" (women of colors and working- and poverty-class women) are trying to destroy "our" organization by "their" unreasonable demands.

Women, mostly middle-class, who developed what we know as "feminist process" knew how systems accomplished goals through hierarchy and rules of order. They tried to change the methods so that women could accomplish our goals by empowering, egalitarian means. We rotated facilitation, spoke from the "I" position, gave every woman her chance to speak, spoke one at a time, did not interrupt, talked about our feelings. We made decisions by consensus. Sometimes working and poverty class women of colors and white women interrupted, spoke more than one at a time, expressed our feelings of excitement, enthusiasm, disagreement, anger in what was perceived as a "disorderly/disruptive/ violent" manner. Then, often, "feminist process" became rules for behavior enforced by middle-class women for their comfort and as an example for the rest of us. A process that could be a liberating means in the struggle for the liberation of all women frequently became oppression for some of us.

Because middle-class women are expected to administer the rules, to teach adjustment, conformity and compliance to others, their students, clients, patients, cases, clerical staff, salespersons, domestic workers and children, they are more severely conditioned to be "ladies" than the rest of us. Middle-class women are taught to express their "appropriate" feelings in a calm, quiet, lady-like manner. They learn authoritative intonations and body language that can bring order out of chaos created by persons whose emotions, sometimes, are out of control. They learn to smile and give the impression of reasonableness and fairness, in their personal and their private lives, no matter how they really feel.

The Women's Liberation Movement exposed the programing of all women, but especially that of middle-class women, to be lady-like, that is, to be "out of touch" with real feelings. When middle-class feminists began to get "in touch" with their real feelings, they still expressed them in a calm manner. They didn't get angry in ways poverty and working class women understood—raised voices, yelling, saying words they might be sorry about later, jumping up and leaving the room. Instead, they tried to teach us to say, as they were learning to do, "I feel angry because you did..." Then, instead of giving us a chance to respond, their "feminist process" made us wait until everyone before us in the circle had their chance to speak. Then, we were expected to express ourselves by saying "I feel..." Rigid adherence to these rules controlled and eliminated passion. This process only works when the poverty and working class women don't really care about the issue. Our attempts to modify this process to meet our needs were, and continue to be dismissed as un-feminist by those who "know."

Some middle-class feminists did try to express feelings the way they thought we did. They talked tough, yelled, made threatening gestures. We thought they were acting, were insincere, were demonstrating a different form of the intellectualizing of "I feel anger because..."

Women raised in crowds know how to talk loud, to yell when necessary. We learn to follow more than one conversation at a time, interrupt in order to get our two cents in. We communicate with our hands and faces too. Our language tends to be colorful and descriptive. We express ourselves differently than women who grow up in large homes, where children have their own rooms, where conversations can take place in various rooms, where the families are small and nuclear, where individuals are not competing for attention. These differences are interesting. They need not be oppressive in our groups or in our love and friendship relationships.

White middle-class women's unconscious assumption of "rightness," this arrogance, often silences poverty and working class white women and women of colors in Lesbian and feminist organizations, friendship circles and romantic love relationships. Some of us conform, agree, "pass," manipulate consciously, for our own financial, career benefit, for love and friendship. Others of us do this unconsciously, living out our internalized oppression, still hoping to become the ideal woman we've been imitating, always on edge, out of sync, afraid of being "found out" and "disgraced." The rest of us join organizations, make friends, become lovers across class lines, then argue, feel hopeful, hopeless, furious and despairing; or we give up the struggle again and again and again as matters of feminism and love move us.

Scare City

Financially privileged people of colors and Jews know how easily racism and anti-Semitism can sweep away privilege. This knowledge causes them to have some of the values, attitudes and behaviors common to people of colors and white people whose family of origin is working or poverty class. Their privilege simply allows them to live in a more "affluent neighborhood" in "Scare City, U.S.A." than the rest of us. Our growing up is a lesson in living with scarcity (living in Scare City). For some of us, food was scarce, or clothes, or space in the bed or at the table. Some did without beds or tables. Some had just enough of everything, except maybe underwear and shoes. Some of us had parents who were skilled workers, putting money away for the rainy day, the next depression, the factory closures, the crop failure. Most lacked regular medical and dental care, did not get music or dancing lessons or go to summer camp. Some of us were in and out of foster homes, relatives' homes, reform school or juvenile hall. A lot of us did some, much or most of the care for younger siblings, the cooking, grocery shopping, housework. If we had jobs, most of us had to give all or some of our earnings to the family. Some of our parents worked more than one job at a time, some of our mothers did ironing and child care in our home. Few of our parents did "volunteer work," unless for the church or the trade union. Our working parents usually were paid by the hour, were sometimes injured on the job, often had special work clothes or uniforms, and experienced or feared lay-offs or seasonal, intermittent or chronic unemployment. Some of us lived on welfare or "relief." Some of us stole, and so did our parents.

The fear of deprivation, the experience of "never enough," of making do, of resources carefully counted, apportioned and stretched to meet needs, of limited time and space, of doing without, develops an attitude, a feeling state of scarcity that can haunt poverty and working class children all of our lives. This internalized feeling state of scarcity makes us very different from middle-class women. The difference can be described as growing up knowing there was more cake in the kitchen if you didn't want a piece at dinner, or knowing if you didn't eat it now, it would be gone. It is the difference between "there's more where that came from," and "a bare cupboard," between an internalized belief in abundance and internalized scarcity.

Women raised in "Scare City" have our own food issues to add to the issues common to all women in our country. We try to eat everything on our plates, even if we don't like it. We worry about getting enough to eat. We bring a stash of food when we attend conferences, festivals, gatherings that include meals. We feel anxious in food lines at such events, worry that the food will give out before we get our share, take less if it looks like there won't be enough for those behind us, wish the organizers would serve "family" style. When Lesbian-feminists first made vegetarianism a feminist issue, I was angry, called it a "middle-class affectation." I know better now, but I still equate meatless meals with poverty. I've not been able to change that yet, and I suspect this attitude is underneath much of the resistance to vegetarianism in the Lesbian-feminist community.

Everything relating to money and material possessions is emotionally charged for those of us who were raised in scarcity, but who live our adult lives in a middle-class environment. In our childhood and youth, we sometimes, often, or always experienced shame and humiliation about our clothes, our house, our neighborhood, especially if we had privileged friends, and/or were the "poor kids" of our high school or college. To us, even now, having the "right" clothes is so anxiety-producing that we can't bear to shop, wear the same "good" clothes for years, affect a "style" of our own, compulsively buy clothes and/or never go anywhere unless we are sure we will be properly dressed. Not to be "properly dressed" implies that we are "too poor" to wear the "right" clothes or too ignorant or have "bad taste." These are occasions of shame, to be avoided at all costs.

Of course middle-class women sometimes dress improperly for a particular event, but their embarrassment is situational, not a resurgence of internalized oppression.

Some upwardly mobile poverty and working class women are frugal to the point of stinginess. Some of us deprive ourselves of the "luxuries," like Birkenstocks or tickets to a Lesbian event in a vain attempt to have enough money in the bank to feel "secure." Others can't save, spend what we get as we get it. We "know" if we don't spend it now, some family emergency will occur, mother's car or sister's teeth, and the money will be gone anyway. Others save and save and then splurge or give the money away. Sometimes we buy something, a car for example, and get one with a stick shift because it is cheaper, even though we want an automatic *and* even though we can afford it! Or we will buy a refrigerator without the icemaker we really want, not because it is "frivolous" or because we cannot afford it. We pull back because we feel like "spendthrifts" and that makes us feel guilty, guilty! These behaviors are mostly irrational responses to internalized oppression, to our internalized belief in scarcity. They are different from the behavior of middle-class women who are thrifty or who are simply poor money managers.

When upwardly mobile poverty and working class women need to borrow money, we resist asking middle-class friends. We know that somewhere inside middle-class women is the belief that poverty is the fault of poor people. We don't want to risk a friendship by asking. Better to ask one of our own, who may turn us down, but won't patronize us while doing it. It would be nice if middle-class women with a friend in need would offer to help her, in a sisterly way, and save her the feeling of shame her oppression taught her.

When we lend middle-class friends small amounts of money or objects that are not expensive, books for example, and they are not returned in a timely manner, we usually are ashamed to ask for their return. Asking causes us to feel petty, small, "in need." After all, our friend treats the situation as minor, else she would return what she owes, wouldn't she? We feel ashamed that we remember the debt she has forgotten.

Women from poverty and working class families have mostly poor people or people with limited means for relatives. These kinds of people often cannot afford health or auto insurance. Their savings "for a rainy day" disappeared in the last storm. These are ordinary people whose lack of material resources escalate family problems to one family crises after another. They expect, and usually receive, help from their upwardly mobile daughter, aunt, grandchild. It is insulting to us when middle-class women assume such families are "addicted" to crises, that they bring them on themselves. Middle-class people have their sorrows and tragedies too, but their privilege, money, connections, knowledge protects them, keeps their problems from becoming overwhelming crises.

On a related subject, the unexamined belief that formal education and intelligence are synonymous is oppressive to people denied that education by class and race oppression and is self-aggrandizing to those whose class privilege ensures an education they could not earn by intelligence. We all know the truth of this after a moment's reflection. Yet uneducated and poorly educated women continue to be objects of ridicule. Grammar and pronunciation mistakes by self-educated people cause laughter in women who are otherwise polite and sensitive. Women like myself, growing up in families or neighborhoods without educated English speakers, learned "correct," mostly accentless speech the hard way, by reading and imitation. Usually, we have a reading vocabulary that is much greater than our speaking one, in part because we are unsure of the pronunciation of words. Years ago, I used the word "pseudo" in the conversation with educated people, but pronounced it "swaydoe." The laughter that followed taught me to check with educated allies, though I still make mistakes and cringe at the laughter.

Money issues in inter-class Lesbian relationships can be pretty terrible, especially since the middle-class woman "knows" what is right, and her upwardly mobile companion lover cannot explain her own money behavior in rational terms. The middle-class partner "knows" that they will be able to go on the Olivia cruise, for example, if they are careful in their spending and if each saves so much a paycheck. That is how she and her family managed to take vacations regularly. Her working class partner has good intentions, but she "knows" something is bound to happen that will eat up their savings. So when she goes shopping for a Sunday brunch for friends, she buys bagels and lox, those little pastries that cost eight dollars a pound, *and* three bottles of nice, not "good" champagne. An argument about money will spoil that party. Also, she is proving she can afford to feed her friends "the best," and that she knows what is "the best" for brunch. Of course the working or poverty class woman will have a hard time taking her companion lover seriously, and taking her advice, when she says, "Don't worry. Everything is going to be fine," upon learning the IRS threatens to put a lien on their house. This is especially true when the former has evictions and homelessness in her past.

Another class difference related to scarcity that can cause problems in inter-class love and friendship relationships is "support." When a middle-class Lesbian expresses her support for a friend or lover, she usually does so by listening, by sympathy, by soothing, loving words, by remembering she is having a problem, asking her how she is feeling. This behavior can leave a troubled poverty or working class Lesbian feeling unloved, uncared for and unsupported. Where she grew up, "support" means sympathy, but also material help. If she's having trouble at work, she expects suggestions for solving the problem, discussions about changing her job, offers of financial assistance. If it's love problems, she expects advice, ideas to solve the problems, reminders about other women who have eyes for her. After all, that's what she gives when her lovers and friends confide their troubles to her. She knows that words are nice, but only action pays the rent! Her middle-class friends and lovers usually feel overwhelmed and unsupported by her businesslike response to their wish for sympathy and love.

Working and poverty class women worry about the finances of the organizations and groups of which we are members, while our middle-class sisters are nonchalantly ordering a better grade of paper for the flyers. Class issues of scarcity and abundance need to be discussed, in order to have a spending policy all the women can be comfortable with. We argue with middle-class women about the need for sliding scales and fee reductions, *without* requiring proof of need (which is humiliating to women in need,) and eliminating scholarships (which imply "merit," like the deserving or the smart poor) and work exchange (by which poor women do much of the work that all the women attending the event would have been obliged to share.) We "know" that women who need assistance are seldom the ones who "take advantage" of financial aid.

Work itself is a class issue. Working and poverty class women "know" what work is. We saw our parents or our neighbors work or come home from work. We "know" work is physically hard, often dirty, sometimes dangerous, and always exhausting. Sometimes work is interesting, but usually it is not. Work is where you go even when you feel terrible, unless you have a job that allows sick days. Work can ruin your health and kill you. Most upwardly mobile working and poverty class women feel like frauds in our middle-class jobs. The jobs are not really work to us. We feel guilty about the money we make, so much more than our parents made for standing on their feet all day and taking abuse. Women like us tend to work too hard and work when we are sick. We usually do not respect middle-class women when they complain how hard their jobs are, when they stay home from work for "mental health" days. If we could overcome our prejudice and follow the example of our middle-class sisters, we might live longer, healthier lives.

Part of the problem women like myself have with work and some middle-class women is their belief that they, and their families, "worked hard," and therefore "earned" and so "deserve" the status and money and refinements they enjoy. We grew up with people who worked hard, who worked long hours, who did without things others consider necessities, who suffered and died to provide for their families. For their efforts they received little money and no refinement or status. Is this what they "earned," what they "deserved?"

When middle-class women ignore the advantages their class privilege provides, they erase the power of class oppression in their imaginations, but leave it flourishing in the material reality of poverty and working class women's lives. We all become equal in opportunity, but inferior in achievement. This erasure by middle-class feminists is particularly painful because of our continuing common struggles against the societal erasure of sexism and racism and their effects upon the aspirations and achievements of all women. We must unlearn classism and learn to cooperate across class lines, respectfully sharing our privilege, knowledge and experience with each other, before our actions will reflect our rhetoric. Free our sisters! Free ourselves!

DISCUSSION QUESTIONS

1. Murphy points out some of the differences in style that distinguish the ways those of different class backgrounds interact. What are some issues in our organizations that may have their origins in class differences? What are some strategies we could use to address the difference and find better ways to work together?

2. Many groups, especially in the history of lesbian and gay men's organizing, have continued to be almost entirely middle class. How does this weaken our movement? What are some concrete suggestions, based on this and the other articles about class, that we could make for building a multi-class movement?

3. Even though many poor and working-class lesbians, gay men and bisexual people have not joined the middle-class gay organizations, this has not meant that they do not live openly queer lives. What are some examples of lesbian, gay male and bisexual working-class styles?

4. Some of these poor and working class styles have been outwardly adopted by middle class groups, often without acknowledgment. For instance, as David Morris points out in the article cited below, fashion is often outwardly "working class," while remaining, because it is "fashion," a middle class style. What are some other examples? What are the social, political and economic implications of this kind of appropriation?

AUTHOR'S SUGGESTIONS FOR FURTHER READING

Worlds of Pain: Life in the Working Class Family, by Lillian Rubin, and *The Hidden Injuries of Class,* by Richard Sennett and Jonathan Cobb are well worth reading. For those of use who were encouraged by our teachers to "rise above our origins," *Hidden Injuries,* although written by and about boys and men, is particularly insightful. Barbara Ehrenreich's *Fear of Falling: The Inner Life of the Middle Class* is insightful about the middle class.

ADDITIONAL SUGGESTIONS FOR FURTHER READING ON CLASS

Sara Bennet & Joan Gibbs. 1980. *Top ranking: A collection on racism and classism in the lesbian community.* Brooklyn: February 3rd Press.

Caryatis Cardea. 1990. Lesbian revolution and the 50-minute hour: A working-class look at therapy and the movement. *Lesbian philosophies and cultures.* Jeffner Allen, Ed. New York: State University of New York.

Carla Trujillo. 1992. Confessions of a Chicana PhD. *OUT/LOOK* 15, 4(3): 23–27.

Janet Zandy, Ed. 1990. *Calling home: Working class women's writings.* New Brunswick, NJ: Rutgers.

SOURCES ON JEWISH IDENTITY AND ANTI-SEMITISM

Evelyn Torton Beck, Ed. 1982. *Nice Jewish girls: A lesbian anthology.* Trumansburg, NY: The Crossing Press.

Elly Bulkin. 1984. Hard ground: Jewish identity, racism, and anti-Semitism. *Yours in struggle: Three feminist perspectives on anti-Semitism and racism.* Elly Bulkin, Minnie Bruce Pratt, & Barbara Smith, Eds. New York: Long Haul Press.

Lesléa Newman. 1988. *Letter to Harvey Milk: Short stories.* Ithaca, NY: Firebrand Books.

Adrienne Rich. 1987. *Blood, bread and poetry: Selected prose 1979-1985.* London: Virago Press.

Irene Zahava. 1990. *Speaking for ourselves: Short stories by Jewish lesbians.* Trumansburg, NY: The Crossing Press.

COMMITMENTS
Essex Hemphill

I will always be there.
When the silence is exhumed.
When the photographs are examined
I will be pictured smiling
among siblings, parents,
nieces and nephews.

In the background of the photographs
the hazy smoke of barbecue,
a checkered red-and-white tablecloth
laden with blackened chicken,
glistening ribs, paper plates,
bottles of beer, and pop.

In the photos
the smallest children
are held by their parents.
My arms are empty, or around
the shoulder of unsuspecting aunts
expecting to throw rice at me someday.

Or picture tinsel, candles,
ornamented, imitation trees,
or another table, this one
set for Thanksgiving,
a turkey steaming the lens.

"Commitments," by Essex Hemphill, from BROTHER TO BROTHER, edited by
Essex Hemphill, published by Alyson Publications, Boston MA, 1991, pp. 57-
58. Copyright © 1991 by Essex Hemphill. Reprinted with permission.

My arms are empty
in those photos, too,
so empty they would break
around a lover.

I am always there
for critical emergencies,
graduations,
the middle of the night.

I am the invisible son.
In the family photos
nothing appears out of character.
I smile as I serve my duty.

MAYBELLE'S BOY
Lamont B. Steptoe

I get from other men
what my daddy never gave
He just left me a house
full of lonesome rooms
and slipped on in his grave

Now
when muscled arms enfold me
A peace descends from above
Someone is holdin' Maybelle's boy
and whisperin' words of love

BROTHER TO BROTHER: INTRODUCTION
Essex Hemphill

This essay by the poet Essex Hemphill is an abridged version of his introduction to the anthology Brother to Brother: New Writings by Black Gay Men. *The anthology was begun by Joseph Beam as a companion piece to his groundbreaking anthology of black gay writing,* In the Life. *He was unable to finish this project before he died of AIDS-related complications. Hemphill asked Beam's estate for permission to complete his work.*

Hemphill here describes both the need for ways of making the voices of black gay men heard, and the rich if hidden history of those voices. His survey of this literature is invaluable in helping others to find the voices whose absence was so disconcerting to him. In addition, he raises difficult and important questions about how those voices have been appropriated by the white gay male and literary establishments. Like Jewelle Gomez, he also discusses the idea of "home" and its complexities for lesbians and gay men of African descent.

MASK MAKER, MASK MAKER, MAKE ME A MASK

If I had read a book like *In the Life* when I was fifteen or sixteen, there might have been one less mask for me to put aside later in life.

I approached the swirling vortex of my adolescent sexuality as a wide-eyed, scrawny teenager, intensely feeling the power of a budding sexual drive unchecked by any legitimate information at home or on the streets. I had nothing to guide me except the pointer of my early morning erection, but I was not inclined to run away from home to see where it would lead. I couldn't shame my family with behavior unbecoming to an eldest son. I had the responsibility of setting an example for my younger siblings, though I would have preferred an older brother to carry out that task, or a father to be at home.

There would have been one less mask for me to create when long ago it became apparent that what I was or what I was becoming—in spite of myself—could be ridiculed, harassed, and even murdered with impunity. The male code of the streets where I grew up made this very clear: Sissies, punks, and faggots were not "cool" with the boys. Come out at your own risk was the prevailing code for boys like myself who knew we were different, but we didn't dare challenge the prescribed norms regarding sexuality for fear of the consequences we would suffer.

I searched the card catalogue at the local library and discovered there were books about homosexuality in the "adult" section. I wasn't allowed to check out books from that section because I was only in sixth grade, but I could read them in the library, which I did, avidly, stopping in almost every day after school for several hours, and continuing this practice until I had devoured everything. What was there for me to read in 1969 was in no way affirming of the sexual identity germinating within me. The material regarding homosexuality considered it to be an illness or an affliction, and at worst, a sin against God and nature. I knew what masturbation was before I learned to masturbate. The books were very informative about the practice, but not very instructional. The books made no references to black men that I can recall, nor were there black case studies for me to examine, and in the few pictures of men identified as homosexual, not one was black.

Nothing in those books said that men could truly love one another. Nothing said that masturbation would be comforting. Nothing celebrated the genius and creativity of homosexual men or even suggested that such men could lead ordinary lives. Nothing encouraged me to love black men—I learned to do that on my own.

When I finished my month-long reading marathon, I put away the last book knowing only that I had homosexual tendencies and desires, but beyond that awareness I didn't recognize myself in any of the material I had so exhaustively read. If anything, I could have ignorantly concluded that homosexuality was peculiar to white people, and my conclusion would have been supported by the deliberate lack of evidence concerning black men and homosexual desire.

There would have been one less mask to tolerate had I not invested time trying to disinherit myself from the sweet knowledge about myself. I tried to separate my sexuality from my Negritude only to discover, in my particular instance, that they are inextricably woven together. If I was clear about no other identity, I knew, year by year, that I was becoming a "homo." A black homo. My outward denial consisted of heterosexual dating which served to lower suspicions about my soft-spoken nature. But the girls I dated will tell you I was barely interested in overcoming our mutual virginity.

Had there been the option of reading *In the Life* when I was a pubescent homosexual, I might have found time to dream of becoming a damn good carpenter, a piano player, a gardener, or a brain surgeon, but instead, a part of my life has been spent making strong, durable masks, and another part has been spent removing them, destroying them whenever possible.

Had *In the Life* been there when I was sneaking around the library looking for my reflection, I would have discovered the affirmations lacking for me in the otherwise strong black novels I was also reading. The modern Negro texts of protest and the black writings of the 1960s never acknowledge homosexuals except as negative, tragic, or comedic characters.

Surely it is one kind of pain that a man reckons with when he *feels* and he *knows* he is not welcome, wanted, or appreciated in his homeland. But the pain I believe to be most tragic and critical is not the pain of invisibility he suffers in his homeland, but the compounded pain and invisibility he endures in his own home, among family and friends. This occurs when he cannot honestly occupy the spaces of family and friendship because he has adopted—out of insecurity, defense, and fear— the mask of the invisible man.

Had there been *In the Life* when I began to have erotic dreams about boys in school, had it been there when I began to steal glances at boys in the showers, I might have spared the girls I pretended to love the difficulty of trying to understand a guy who was merely fence-sitting, waiting for the wind to blow him north or south. I might have spared myself the humiliations of pretense and denial. I might have had the courage to stand up for myself when confronted as a faggot.

I was such a good mask maker. The last one I am now removing was perhaps my most deceptive, my most prized of all. Once it is off my face, I imagine nailing it to the wall like the head of some game, tracked and killed for the sport of it. But this isn't sport. This is my life—not game. Had there been *In the Life* when I needed a father, a brother, a lover, a friend; had it been there when I needed to say no instead of yes and yes when I knew no was cowardly; had it been there to affirm my compounded identity when I was reading Ralph Ellison's *Invisible Man* or Richard Wright's *Native Son,* then perhaps a more whole picture of the black male might have formed in my consciousness. *In the Life* might have mitigated and nurtured my germinating sexual identity, or at the very least I would not have spent part of my life becoming an expert but useless mask maker.

DOES YOUR MOMMA KNOW ABOUT ME? DOES SHE KNOW JUST WHAT I AM?

Throughout the 1980s, many of us grieved the loss of friends, lovers, and relatives who were one moment strong, healthy, and able-bodied, but then in an instant became thin-framed, emaciated, hacking and wheezing, their bodies wracked with horrible pain. Sometimes brave souls would return to the family roost to disclose their sexuality and ask permission to die in familiar surroundings. Too often, families were discovering for the first time that the dear brother, the favorite uncle, the secretive son was a homosexual, a black gay man, and the unfortunate victim of the killer virus, AIDS. Some parents had always known and some had never suspected that their son was a black gay man, a sissy, a queer, a faggot. For some families this shocking discovery and grief expressed itself as shame and anger; it compelled them to disown their flesh and blood, denying dying men the love and support that friends often provided as extended family. In other instances families were very understanding and bravely stood by their brethren through their final days.

Joseph Beam, in his powerful essay "Brother to Brother: Words from the Heart," defined home as being larger, more complex and encompassing than one's living room:

> When I speak of home, I mean not only the familial constellation from which I grew, but the entire Black community: the Black press, the Black church, Black academicians, the Black literati, and the Black left. Where is my reflection? I am most often rendered invisible, perceived as a threat to the family, or I am tolerated if I am silent and inconspicuous. I cannot go home as who I am and that hurts me deeply (1986, 231).

Beam articulated one of the primary issues black gay men are faced with when our relationships with our families and communities are examined. We cannot afford to be disconnected from these institutions, yet it would seem that we are willing to create and accept dysfunctional roles in them, roles of caricature, silence, and illusion. In truth, we are often forced into these roles to survive. This critical dilemma causes some of us to engage in dishonest relationships with our kin. It can foster apathy between us and the communities of home that we need and that need our presence. The contradictions of "home" are amplified and become more complex when black gay men's relationships with the white gay community are also examined.

The post-Stonewall white gay community of the 1980s was not seriously concerned with the existence of black gay men except as sexual objects. In media and art the black male was given little representation except as a big, black dick. This aspect of the white gay sensibility is strikingly revealed in the photographs of black males by the late Robert Mapplethorpe. Though his images may be technically and esthetically well composed, his work *artistically* perpetuates racial stereotypes constructed around sexuality and desire. In many of his images, black males are only shown as parts of anatomy—genitals, chests, buttocks—close-up and close-cropped to elicit desire. Mapplethorpe's eye pays special attention to the penis at the expense of showing us the subject's face, and thus, a whole person. The penis becomes the identity of the black male which is the classic racist stereotype re-created and presented as "art" in the context of a gay vision.

Mapplethorpe's "Man in a Polyester Suit," for example, presents a black man without a head, wearing a business suit, his trousers unzipped, and his fat, long penis dangling down, a penis that is not erect. It can be assumed that many viewers who appreciate Mapplethorpe's work, and who construct sexual fantasies from it, probably wondered first how much larger the penis would become during erection, as opposed to wondering who the man in the photo is or why his head is missing. What is insulting and endangering to black men is Mapplethorpe's conscious determination that the faces, the heads, and by extension, the minds and experiences of some of his black subjects are not as important as close-up shots of their cocks.

It is virtually impossible while viewing Mapplethorpe's photos of black males to avoid confronting issues of objectification. Additionally, black gay men are not immune to the desire elicited by his photos. We, too, are drawn to the inherent eroticism. In "True Confessions: A Discourse on Images of Black Male Sexuality," Issac Julien and Kobena Mercer (1986) accurately identify this dichotomy when they observe that Mapplethorpe's images of black males reiterate "the terms of colonial fantasy" and "service the expectations of white desire." They then ask the most critical question of all (6): "What do [Mapplethorpe's images] say to our wants and desires as black gay men?"

It has not fully dawned on white gay men that racist conditioning has rendered many of them no different from their heterosexual brothers in the eyes of black gays and lesbians. Coming out of the closet to confront sexual oppression has not necessarily given white males the motivation or insight to transcend their racist conditioning. This failure (or reluctance) is costing the gay and lesbian community the opportunity to become a powerful force for creating real social changes that reach beyond issues of sexuality. It has fostered much of the distrust that permeates the relations between the black and white communities. And finally, it erodes the possibility of forming meaningful, powerful coalitions.

When black gay men approached the gay community to participate in the struggle for acceptance and to forge bonds of brotherhood, bonds so loftily proclaimed as the vision of the best gay minds of my generation, we discovered that the beautiful rhetoric was empty. The disparity between words and actions was as wide as the Atlantic Ocean and deeper than Dante's hell. There was no gay community for black men to come home to in the 1980s. The community we found was as mythical and distant from the realities of black men as was Oz from Kansas.

At the baths, certain bars, in bookstores and cruising zones, black men were welcome because these constructions of pleasure allowed the races to mutually explore sexual fantasies and, after all, the black man engaging in such a construction only needed to whip out a penis of almost any size to obtain the rapt attention withheld from him in other social and political structures of the gay community. These sites of pleasure were more tolerant of black men because they enhanced the sexual ambiance, but that same tolerance did not always continue once the sun began to rise.

Open fraternizing at a level suggesting companionship or love between the races was not tolerated in the light of day. Terms such as "dinge queen" for white men who prefer black men, and "snow queen," for black men who prefer white men, were created by a gay community that obviously could not be trusted to believe its own rhetoric concerning brotherhood, fellowship, and dignity. Only an entire community's silence is capable of reinforcing these conditions.

Some of the best minds of my generation would have us believe that AIDS has brought the gay and lesbian community closer and infused it with a more democratic mandate. That is only a partial truth that further underscores the fact that the gay community still operates from a one-eyed, one-gender, one-color perception of "community" that is most likely to recognize blond before black, but seldom the two together.

Some of the best minds of my generation believe AIDS has made the gay community a more responsible social construction, but what AIDS really manages to do is clearly point out how significant are the cultural and economic differences between us; differences so extreme that black men suffer disproportionate number of AIDS deaths in communities with very sophisticated gay health care services.

The best gay minds of my generation believe that we speak as one voice and dream one dream, but we are not monolithic. We are not even respectful of each other's differences. We are a long way from that, Dorothy. I tell you Kansas is closer.

We are communities engaged in a fragile coexistence if we are anything at all. Our most significant coalitions have been created in the realm of sex. What is most clear for black gay men is this: We have to do for ourselves *now,* and for each other *now,* what no one has ever done for us. We have to be there for one another and trust less the adhesions of kisses and semen to bind us. Our only sure guarantee of survival is that which we create from our own self-determination. White gay men may only be able to understand and respond to oppression as it relates to their ability to obtain orgasm without intrusion from the church or state. White gay men are only "other" in this society when they choose to come out of the closet. But all black men are treated as "other" regardless of whether we sleep with men or women—our black skin automatically marks us as "other."

Look around, brothers. There is rampant killing in our communities. Drug addiction and drug trafficking overwhelm us. The blood of young black men runs curbside in a steady flow. The bodies of black infants crave crack, not the warmth of mother's love. The nation's prisons are reservations and shelters for black men. An entire generation of black youths is being destroyed before our eyes. We cannot witness this in silence and apathy and claim our hands are bloodless. We are a wandering tribe that needs to go home before home is gone. We should not continue standing in line to be admitted into spaces that don't want us there. We cannot continue to exist without clinics, political organizations, human services, and cultural institutions that *we* create to support, sustain, and affirm us.

Our mothers and fathers are waiting for us. Our sisters and brothers are waiting. Our communities are waiting for us to come home. They need our love, our talents and skills, and we need theirs. They may not understand everything about us, but they will remain ignorant, misinformed, and lonely for us, and we for them, for as long as we stay away hiding in communities that have never really welcomed us or the gifts we bring.

I ask you, brother: Does your mama *really* know about you? Does she *really* know what I am? Does she know I want to love her son, care for him, nurture and celebrate him? Do you think she'll understand? I hope so, because I *am* coming home. There is no place else to go that will be worth so much effort and love.

THE EVIDENCE OF BEING

At the beginning of the 1980s, creating poetry from a black gay experience was a lonely, trying occupation. No network of black gay writers existed to offer support, critical commentary, or the necessary fellowship and affirmation.

I had read requisite portions of James Baldwin's works, but I still hungered for voices closer to home to speak to me directly and immediately about the contemporary black gay experience. I wanted reflection. To compensate, I read all I could by gay poets such as C.S. Cavafy, Walt Whitman, Paolo Pasolini, and Jean Genet, but my hunger for self-recognition continued. I began reading lesbian poets such as Audre Lorde, Adrienne Rich, Pat Parker, and Sappho, but my hunger, only somewhat appeased, persisted.

As I approached the mid–1980s, I began to wonder if gay men of African descent existed in literature at all, beyond the works of Baldwin and Bruce Nugent, or the closeted works of writers of the Harlem Renaissance, such as Countee Cullen, Claude McKay, Langston Hughes, Alain Locke, and Wallace Thurman. Baldwin's voice was post-Harlem Renaissance: eloquent, crafted, impassioned; he created some of the most significant works to be presented by an "acknowledged" black homosexual in this century. It is not my intention to overlook his broader significance in the context of African American and world literature, where works of his are ranked among the very best this century of writers has created. However, in the specific context of black gay literature, Baldwin's special legacy serves as a role model, as source, as inspiration pointing toward the possibility of being *and* excellence. The legacy he leaves us to draw from is a precious gift for us to hold tight as we persevere.

My search for evidence of things not seen, evidence of black gay experiences on record, evidence of "being" to contradict the pervasive invisibility of black gay men, at times proved futile. I was often frustrated by codes of secrecy, obstructed by pretenses of discretion, or led astray by constructions of silence, constructions fabricated of illusions and perhaps cowardice. But I persevered. I continued to seek affirmation, reflection, and identity. I continued seeking the *necessary* historical references for my desire.

In terms of my heritage of Negritude, I found an abundance of literary texts to reinforce a positive black cultural identity, but as a black gay man there was, except for Baldwin, little to nurture me. Unbeknownst to me, Adrian Stanford's *Black and Queer* had been published by the Good Gay Poets of Boston in 1977. I would not be introduced to Stanford's work until 1985. Joseph Beam owned two copies of Stanford's *Black and Queer* and gave me one for my collection. I have treasured this gift since receiving it from Joe, who also told me Stanford was murdered in Philadelphia in 1981. In the poem "Yeah Baby," the late poet tells us (9):

> i've had them roll up in
> chauffeured limousines,
> swing open the door and beg
> "please get in."
>
> i've been approached, followed,
> waited for, hung onto
> and groped by all those staid
> white queens that
> don't like *colored boys*.

For me, the evidence of black gay men creating *overt* homoerotic poetry begins with that small, powerful book. What I am suggesting is that black gay men have been publishing *overt* homoerotic verse since 1977, a mere thirteen years as of this writing.

For the homosexuals of the Harlem Renaissance engaged in the creation of literature, it would have been *inappropriate* to "come out" of whatever closets they had constructed for personal survival. The effort to uplift the race and prove the Negro worthy of respect precluded issues of sexuality, reducing such concerns to the sentiment of the popular urban blues song—"Ain't Nobody's Business If I Do." The defeat of racism was far too important to risk compromising such a struggle by raising issues of homosexuality.

For an individual to have declared himself homosexual, no matter how brilliant he was, would have brought immediate censure from what Zora Neale Hurston wickedly called the "Niggerati," the up-and-coming literary, cultural, and intellectual leaders of the Negro community (Rampersad 1986, 132). However, the work of Locke, Cullen, Hughes, and other Harlem Renaissance men of bisexual or homosexual identities is not be dismissed in the quest for an African American gay tradition simply because it fails to reveal their homosexual desires. The works that these men created are critically important contributions and challenging legacies in the total picture of African American literature and cultural struggle. But because the mission to uplift the race predominated, there is little homoerotic evidence from the Harlem Renaissance except for selections of work by Richard Bruce Nugent. His work was considerably more daring, judged by the standards of his day, than were those of his more closeted

Renaissance contemporaries, none of whom dared risk publishing homoerotic literature for fear of falling from grace.

The evidence of Nugent's daring is best exemplified by his beautiful short story, "Smoke, Lilies and Jade," considered to be the first work by a black writer to examine homosexual desire. The story appeared in the short-lived and very controversial *Fire!!* (published November 1926), a journal created by Thurman, Nugent, Hughes, and others of their circle. Over five decades later, "Smoke, Lilies and Jade" appeared in the controversial gay anthology *Black Men/White Men* (Smith 1983), and a little over six decades later it was part of the narrative script for the film *Looking for Langston* (Julien 1988). *Fire!!* was intended to be a black arts quarterly, but only one issue appeared. "The sales of *Fire!!* were very disappointing," writes Faith Berry, in the biography, *Langston Hughes: Before and Beyond Harlem*. Copies of the issue were stored in a cellar in Harlem, but "in an irony like no other, a fire reportedly destroyed them all, leaving the sponsors with a printer's debt of more than a thousand dollars" (Berry 1983, 83).

Fire!! also contained writings by Hughes, Cullen, Hurston, and Arna Bontemps, and artwork by Aaron Douglas, to name but a few of its contributors. In Charles Michael Smith's "Bruce Nugent: Bohemian of the Harlem Renaissance," we are told (1986, 214) that *Fire!!* "created a firestorm of protest, particularly from the black bourgeoisie. The critic for the Baltimore *Afro-American,* for example, wrote acidly: 'I have just tossed the first issue of *Fire!!* into the fire!'"

Continuing this journey through African American literature, we find no evidence of black gay men openly participating in the 1960s Black Arts Movement with the exception of Baldwin, and even he was attacked because of his sexuality by Eldridge Cleaver in *Soul on Ice,* and by writer Ishmael Reed who crudely insulted Baldwin by calling him a "cocksucker," in an apparent attempt to diminish Baldwin's brilliance (Troupe 1989, 202).

The evidence of black gay men that exists from this period is mostly created from the perspective of a black nationalist sensibility in that this literature most often condemns homosexuality, ridicules gays, lesbians, dykes, faggots, bulldaggers, and homos, and positions homosexuality as a major threat to the black family and black masculinity. Such a sensibility also considered homosexuality to be caused by white racism (or by exposure to white values), and conveniently overlooked the possibility of natural variance in the expression of human sexuality.

Perhaps the only "black revolutionary" spokesperson remotely sympathetic to the struggles of homosexuals and women was Huey P. Newton, Supreme Commander of the Black Panther Party. In "A Letter from Huey to the Revolutionary Brothers and Sisters About the Women's Liberation and Gay Liberation Movements," Newton urged black men and women to align themselves with these movements in order to form powerful coalitions. He writes:

> Whatever your personal opinion and your insecurities about homosexuality and the various liberation movements among homosexuals and women (and I speak of the homosexuals and women as oppressed groups), we should try to unite with them in a revolutionary fashion.
>
> ...I don't remember us ever constituting any value that said that a revolutionary must say offensive things toward homosexuals or that a revolutionary would make sure that women do not speak out about their own particular oppression.
>
> ...[T]here is nothing to say that a homosexual can not also be a revolutionary ... Quite the contrary, maybe a homosexual could be the most revolutionary.
>
> We should be willing to discuss the insecurities that many people have about homosexuality. When I say, "insecurities" I mean the fear that there is some kind of threat to our manhood. I can understand this fear... [B]ut homosexuals are not enemies of the people (1970).

Aside from Newton and Baldwin, there was no other black male leadership, self-appointed or otherwise, attempting to see heterosexist oppression as being akin to and stemming from the same source responsible for perpetuating oppressions of race, gender, class, and economics.

Many factors have contributed to this *lack of witness,* this lack of participation by black gay men in creating literature that reflects our experiences. The long-standing constructions of fear, denial, invisibility, and racism perpetuated much of the silence that has prevailed.

Black gay men can consider the 1980s to have been a critically important decade for our literature. Literary journals, periodicals, and self-published works were sporadically produced and voraciously consumed. The 1980s gave us *Blacklight, Habari-Daftari, Yemonja* (which later became *Blackheart), Black/Out, BLK, Moja: Black and Gay, BGM,* the *Pyramid Periodical,* the *Real Read,* and a promising selection of self-published chapbooks and portfolios that, taken as a whole, suggests that an important period of fermentation and development in black gay literature has been occurring since the release of Stanford's *Black and Queer.* In addition, two significant collections of black gay literature—the ground-breaking *In the Life,* edited by Joseph Beam and published by Alyson Publications (1986), and the poetry anthology *Tongues Untied,* published in London by Gay Men's Press (1987)—served notice that a generation of black gay writers are at work dismantling silence.

Against stifling odds and breaking rank from historic constructions of repression, black gay men are developing meaningful and significant literary voices through workshops and brotherly encouragement. The most obvious example of this nurturing is the Other Countries Collective based in New York City. Through a process of workshops, collective members critique one another's writings. The workshops are designed to reinforce and stimulate, affirm and encourage. The collective published its first *Other Countries Journal* in 1988, and plans to publish others in the '90s. They also present public readings, some for audiences of primarily black heterosexuals.

By the close of the 1980s, *BLK*, a Los Angeles-based black gay news magazine, was consistently publishing, month after month, and was available nationally. This was accomplished under the leadership of its editor and publisher, Alan Bell. The New York-based literary journal the *Pyramid Poetry Periodical*, founded in 1986 by Roy Gonsalves as a triannual publication, had also achieved the distinction of consistently publishing in its present quarterly format as the *Pyramid Periodical*, and obtained national distribution under the guidance of editor Charles Pouncy. Self-published chapbooks, and volumes of verse were produced by Donald Woods (*The Space*), Alan Miller (*At the Club*), Assoto Saint (*Stations*), Philip Robinson (*Secret Passages*), Roy Gonsalves (*Evening Sunshine*), and Lloyd "Vega" Jeffress (*Men of Color*). The phenomena of black gay men self-publishing, including my own self-published works, *Earth Life* and *Conditions*, surely challenges the insidious racism and homophobia that prevail in the offices of mainstream, small press, and university publishing houses. For what other reasons would so many black gay men take on the task? If there is to be evidence of our experiences, we learned by the close of the 1980s that our own self-sufficiency must ensure it, so that future generations of black gay men will have references for their desires.

And finally, perhaps our most compelling literary achievements were documented in two films as the decade came to its close. Isaac Julien's controversial *Looking for Langston,* and Marlon Riggs' documentary *Tongues Untied,* both splendidly utilized the poetry and writings of black gay men in bold presentations of the black gay experience. *Looking for Langston,* which Julien created as a "meditation" on Hughes and the Harlem Renaissance, examines issues of race, sexuality and the role of the Negro artist during that period. In the late fall of 1989, Riggs premiered *Tongues Untied,* a black gay documentary which takes its name from the black gay poetry anthology. The work is grounded in personal testimony from Riggs about his life as a black gay man.

The 1990s promise to be a decade of fruition and continuing significance for black gay literature. Novelists such as Randal Kenan (*A Visitation of Spirits*) and Melvin Dixon (*Trouble the Water*) released first works as we neared the close of the eighties. Larry Duplechan released three novels in the eighties (*Eight Days A Week, Blackbird,* and *Tangled in Blue*). Award-winning science-fiction writer Samuel Delany's autobiography *The Motion of Light in Water* and writer Mickey C. Fleming's *About Courage* were also added to the ever-growing pantheon of black gay literature. Other writers are planning to produce self-published collections of verse, more novels are being written, theater collectives are being formed such as Reginald Jackson's Rainbow Repertory Theater in New

York City, and new films and documentaries are being planned and created as this anthology goes to press.

The late 1980s also witnessed the emergence of black gay men's groups such as Gay Men of African Descent (New York), Adodi (Philadelphia), Unity (Philadelphia), and Black Gay Men United (Oakland). These organizations structure themselves around social, cultural, and political issues. In many instances they provide emotional and spiritual support for their members: workshops covering a broad range of issues; retreats and cultural programming; and lectures by guest speakers on subjects ranging from AIDS and health care to developing personal financial resources. The existence of these groups continues the necessary work of affirming us.

What we must do now, more than ever, is nurture one another whenever and wherever possible. Attend the readings of black gay writers, buy their works, invite them to college campuses and community centers to speak and conduct workshops, and subscribe to black gay publications in order that the necessary nurturing can continue.

Much of the evidence that emerged in the 1980s is only the surface of what is yet to be revealed. We *must* focus our attention around issues of craft and discipline in order to create our very best literature. We must demand this of ourselves. There is a need to look closely at revealing the full extent to which black gay men have *always* participated in positive and nurturing roles in the structures of family within the African American community. There is a need to look closely at intimacy and the constructions of our desire and bring forth from these realms the knowledge that we are capable of loving one another in committed, long-standing, productive relationships. In our fiction, prose, and poetry there is a need to reveal more of our beauty in all its diversity. We need more honest pictures of ourselves that are not the stereotypical six-foot, dark-skinned man with a big dick.

We must begin to identify what a black gay sensibility is; identify its esthetic qualities and components; identify specific constructions and uses of language suitable for the task of presenting our experiences in the context of literature; and then determine how this sensibility and esthetic relates to and differs from African American literature as a whole.

Ours should be a vision willing to exceed all that attempts to confine and intimidate us. We must be willing to embrace and explore the duality of community that we exist in as black *and* gay men. We would be wise to develop strong, powerful voices that can range over the entire landscape of human experience and condition.

Perhaps the second Renaissance in African American literature occurred when black women claimed their *own* voices from the post-sixties, male-dominated realm of the "black experience," a realm that at times resembled a boxing ring restricting black women to the roles of mere spectators. What black women, especially out black lesbians, bravely did was break the silence surrounding their experiences. No longer would black men, as the sole interpreters of race and culture, presume to speak for (or ignore) women's experiences. Black women opened up new dialogues and explored uncharted territories surrounding race, sexuality, gender relations, family, history, and eroticism. In the process, they angered some black male writers who felt they were being culturally castrated and usurped, but out of necessity, black women realized they would have to speak for themselves—and do so honestly. As a result of their courage, black women also inspired many of the black gay men writing today to seek our own voices so we can tell our truths. Thus we are at the beginning of completing a total picture of the African American experience. Black gay men will no longer exist in a realm of invisibility.

Our immediate task, as black gay men creating our own literary tradition, is to work diligently and to utilize honesty and discipline as our allies. If we commit ourselves to strive for excellence and nothing less, we will create the *evidence of being* powerful enough to transform the very nature of our existence. And the silence and invisibility that we self-imposed, or often accepted will give way to the realization of just how fierce *and* necessary we really are. SNAP!

LOYALTY—A PRELUDE TO COMING HOME

For my so-called sins against nature and the race, I gain the burdensome knowledge of carnal secrets. It rivals rituals of sacrifice and worship, and conjures the same glassy-eyed results—with less bloodshed. A knowledge disquieting and liberating inhabits my soul. If often comforts me, or at times, is miserably intoxicating with requisite hangovers and regrets. At other moments it is sacred communion, causing me to moan and tremble and cuss as the Holy Ghost fucks me. It is a knowledge of fire and beauty that I will carry beyond the grave. When I sit in God's final judgment, I will wager this knowledge against my entrance into the Holy Kingdom. There was no other way for me to know the beauty of Earth except through the sexual love of men, men who were often more terrified than I, even as they posed before me, behind flimsy constructions of manhood, mocking me with muscles, erections, and wives.

I discovered any man can be seduced—even if the price is humiliation or death for the seducer. Late nights and desperate hours teach us to approach loneliness unarmed, or we risk provoking it to torture us with endless living sorrows we believe only the dead can endure.

But who are these dead, able to withstand the constant attack of merciless loneliness with its intense weapons, its clever trickery and deceit? Many of them are men like me, born of common stock, ordinary dreamers. Men who vaguely answer to "American," or exhibit visible apprehension when American is defined and celebrated to their exclusion. Men who more often than not are simply ignored.

We constitute the invisible brothers in our communities, those of us who live "in the life"; the choirboys harboring secrets, the uncle living in an impeccable flat with a roommate who sleeps down the hall when family visits; men of power and humble peasantry, reduced to silence and invisibility for the safety they procure from these constructions. Men emasculated in the complicity of not speaking out, rendered mute by the middle-class aspirations of a people trying hard to forget the shame and cruelties of slavery and ghettos. Through denials and abbreviated histories riddled with omissions, the middle class sets about whitewashing and fixing up the race to impress each other *and* the racists who don't give a damn.

I speak for thousands, perhaps hundreds of thousands of men who live and die in the shadows of secrets, unable to speak of the love that helps them endure and contribute to the race. Their ordinary kisses, stolen or shared behind facades of heroic achievement, their kisses of sweet spit and loyalty are scrubbed away by the propaganda makers of the race, the "Talented Tenth" who would just as soon have us believe black people can fly, rather than reveal that black men have been longing to kiss one another, and have done so, for centuries.

The black homosexual is hard-pressed to gain audience among his heterosexual brothers; even if he *is* more talented, he is inhibited by his silence or his admissions. This is what the race has depended on in being able to erase homosexuality from our recorded history. The "chosen" history. But these sacred constructions of silence are futile exercises in denial. We will not go away with our issues of sexuality. We are coming home.

It is not enough to tell us that one was a brilliant poet, scientist, educator, or rebel. Who did he love? It makes a difference. I can't become a whole man simply on what is fed to me: watered-down versions of black life in America. I need the ass-splitting truth to be told, so I will have something pure to emulate, a reason to remain loyal.

DISCUSSION QUESTIONS

1. How did the presence or absence of voices with whom to identify affect the coming out process of readers? How has this changed over time and across generations? What effect have movements to censor gay-positive material, especially for younger readers, had in your local community? What strategies have worked or not worked in dealing with such challenges to access?

2. African-American men have traditionally been regarded as sexual supermen in North American racist mythology. How has this affected struggles for black liberation in the United States? How has this stereotype intersected with homophobia? With sexism?

3. How do power and eroticism interact in a society that is at once capitalist, white supremacist, and male supremacist? What is the relationship between this and militarism? What obstacles does this put in the way of a more just and peaceable society? What strategies could overcome these obstacles?

SUGGESTIONS FOR FURTHER READING

Joseph Beam, Ed. 1986. *In the life: A Black Gay anthology.* Boston: Alyson.

Eric Garber. 1989. A spectacle in color: The lesbian and gay subculture of Jazz Age Harlem. *Hidden from history: Reclaiming the gay and lesbian past.* Martin Duberman, Martha Vicinus, and George Chauncey, Eds. New York: New American Library.

Craig Harris. 1989. Weaving the future of black gender politics: A feminist agenda for black gay men. *Gay Community News,* 17(19):7.

SEXUAL DISSENT AND THE FAMILY:
THE SHARON KOWALSKI CASE
Nan D.Hunter

This article, like the case that inspired it, discusses several intersections of issues. Sharon Kowalski and Karen Thompson's struggle touches on the way the court system assumes that people with brain injuries, and other disabilities, are incompetent to make choices about their lives. The nature of family and the way in which society draws boundaries around "acceptable" forms of family based on arbitrary criteria rather than on the qualities of relationships are considered. The essay touches on the importance of public recognition of lesbian and gay male relationships, and the assumption by many that these relationships are inherently inferior if not downright exploitative. Finally, the essay examines the level of denial made possible by the "heterosexual assumption" that is at the heart of lesbian and gay invisibility.

In the gay liberation period of the early 1970s, many activists, following positions taken by the women's movement, expressed a strong critique of the bourgeois family as a repressive institution. This critique has been muted in recent years in favor of a project of redefining "family" broadly enough to include committed relationships of lesbians or gay men, including in many cases the children of one or both of the partners. In framing a discussion of the meaning of family, it will be important to keep in mind the observations on the importance of families in African-American culture, as pointed out by Jewelle Gomez, Essex Hemphill, and bell hooks elsewhere in this collection.

No connection between family, marriage, or procreation on the one hand and homosexual activity on the other has been demonstrated.
–Supreme Court, Bowers v. Hardwick, 1986

Sharon Kowalski is the child of a divorce between her consanguineous family and her family of affinity, the petitioner Karen Thompson... That Sharon's family of affinity has not enjoyed societal recognition in the past is unfortunate.   –Minnesota State District Court, 1991

In the effort to end second-class citizenship for lesbian and gay Americans, no obstacle has proved tougher to surmount than the cluster of issues surrounding "the family." For the past twenty years, the concept

---

of family has functioned as a giant cultural screen. Projected onto it, contests over race, gender, sexuality and a range of other "domestic" issues from crime to taxes constantly create and recreate a newly identified zone of social combat, the politics of the family. Activists of all persuasions eagerly seek to enter the discursive field, ever-ready to debate and discuss: Who counts as a family? Which "family values" are the authentic ones? Is there a place in the family for queers? As battles are won and lost in this cultural war, progressives and conservatives agree on at least one thing—the family is highly politicized terrain.

For lesbians and gays, these debates have dramatic real-life consequences, probably more so than with any other legal issue. Relationship questions touch almost every person's life at some point, in a way that military issues, for example, do not. Further, the unequal treatment is blatant, de jure and universal, as compared with the employment arena, where discrimination may be more subtle and variable. No state allows a lesbian or gay couple to marry. No state recognizes (although sixteen counties and cities do) domestic partnership systems under which unmarried couples (gay or straight) can become eligible for certain benefits usually available only to spouses. The fundamental inequity is that, barring mental incompetence or consanguinity, virtually any straight couple has the option to marry and thus establish a next-of-kin relationship that the state will enforce. No lesbian or gay couple can. Under the law, two women or two men are forever strangers, regardless of their relationship.

One result is that every lesbian or gay man's nightmare is to be cut off from one's primary other, physically incapacitated, stranded, unable to make contact, without legal recourse. It is a nightmare that could not happen to a married couple. But it did happen to two Minnesota women, Sharon Kowalski and Karen Thompson, in a remarkable case that has been threading its way through the courts for six years.

Sharon Kowalski, notwithstanding the Minnesota State District Court's characterization of her as a "child of divorce," is an adult with both a committed life partner and parents who bitterly refuse to acknowledge either her lesbianism or her lover. Kowalski is a former physical education teacher and amateur athlete, whose Minnesota women's high school shot-put record still stands. In 1983, she was living with her lover, Thompson, in the home they had jointly purchased in St. Cloud. Both women were deeply closeted; they exchanged rings with each other but virtually told no one of their relationship. That November, Kowalski suffered devastating injuries in a car accident, which left her unable to speak or walk, with arms deformed and with major brain damage, including seriously impaired short-term memory.

After the accident, both Thompson and Kowalski's father petitioned to be appointed Sharon's guardian; initially, an agreement was entered that the father would become guardian on the condition that Thompson retain equal rights to visit and consult with the doctors. By the summer of

1985, after growing hostilities, the father refused to continue the arrangement and persuaded a local court that Thompson's visits caused Kowalski to feel depressed. One doctor hired by the father wrote a letter stating that Kowalski was in danger of sexual abuse. Within twenty-four hours after being named sole guardian, the father cut off all contact between Thompson and Kowalski, including mail. By this time, Kowalski had been moved to a nursing home near the small town where she grew up in the Iron Range, a rural mining area in northern Minnesota.

Surely one reason the Kowalski case is so compelling is that for millions of parents, learning that one's son is gay or daughter is lesbian would be *their* worst nightmare. That is all the more true in small-town America, among people who are religiously observant and whose expectations for a daughter are primarily marriage and motherhood. "The good Lord put us here for reproduction, not that kind of way," Donald Kowalski told the *Los Angeles Times* in 1988. "It's just not a normal life style. The Bible will tell you that." Karen Thompson, he told other reporters, was "an animal" and was lying about his daughter's life. "I've never seen anything that would make me believe," that she is lesbian, he said to *The New York Times* in 1989. How much less painful it must be to explain a lesbian daughter's life as seduction, rather than to experience it as betrayal.

Since 1985, Kowalski's parents and her lover have been locked in litigation, seeking review as far as the Supreme Court (which declined to hear the case). Thompson's stubborn struggle to "bring Sharon home" has now entered a new stage. In late 1988 a different judge, sitting in Duluth, ordered Kowalski moved to a new facility for medical evaluation. Soon thereafter, based on staff recomendations from the second nursing facility, the court ordered that Thompson be allowed to visit. The two women saw each other again in the spring of 1989, after three and a half years of forced separation. For the past two years, Thompson has visited Kowalski frequently. Kowalski, who can communicate by typing on a special keyboard, has said that she wants to live in "St. Cloud with Karen."

Since their daughter was moved to the new facility near Minneapolis, Donald and Della Kowalski have made only a handful of trips to see her. In May 1990, citing a heart condition for which he had been hospitalized, Donald Kowalski resigned as his daughter's guardian. This resignation set the stage for Thompson to file a renewed petition for appointment as guardian, which she did. But in an April 1991 ruling, Minnesota State District Court Judge Robert Campbell selected as guardian Karen Tomberlin—a friend of both Kowalski and her parents, who supported Tomberlin's request. On the surface, the court sought balance. The judge characterized the Kowalski parents and Karen Thompson as the "two wings" of Sharon Kowalski's family. He repeatedly asserted that both must have ample access to visitation with Kowalski. He described Tomberlin as a neutral third party who would not exclude either side. But the biggest single reason behind the decision, the one that he characterized as "instrumental," seemed to be the judge's anger at Thompson for ever telling Kowalski's parents (in a private letter), and then the world at large, that she and Kowalski were lovers.

The court condemned Thompson's revelation of her own relationship as the "outing" of Sharon Kowalski. Thompson did write the letter to Kowalski's parents without telling Kowalski (who was at the time just emerging from a three month coma after the accident) and did build on her own an active political organization around the case, composed chiefly of disability and lesbian and gay rights groups. Of course, for most of that period, she could not have consulted Kowalski because the two were cut off from each other.

In truth, though, the judge's concern seemed to be more for the outing of Kowalski's parents. He describes the Kowalskis as "outraged and hurt by the public invasion of Sharon's privacy and their privacy," and he blames this outing for the bitterness between Thompson and the parents. Had Thompson simply kept this to herself, the court implies, none of these nasty facts would ever have had to be discussed. But then Thompson would never have been able to maintain her relationship with her lover.

An openly stated preference for ignorance over knowledge is remarkable in a judicial opinion. Ultimately, that is what this latest decision in the Kowalski-Thompson litigation saga is about. One imagines the judge silently cursing Thompson for her arrogance in claiming the role of spouse, and for her insistence on shattering the polite fiction of two gym teachers living and buying a house together as just good friends. Women, especially, aren't supposed to be so stubborn or uppity. One can sense the court's empathetic response of shared embarrassment with the parents, of the desire not to be told and thus not to be forced to speak on this subject.

The conflict in the Kowalski case illustrates one of the prime contradictions underlying all the cases seeking legal protection of lesbian and gay couples. This culture is deeply invested with a notion of the ideal family as not only a zone of privacy and a structure of authority (preferably male in the conservative view) but also as a barrier against unlicensed sexuality. Even many leftists and progressives, who actively contest male authority and at least some of the assumptions behind privacy, are queasy about constructing a family politics with queer sex on the inside rather than the outside.

When such sexuality is culturally recognized *within* family bounds, "the family" ceases to function as an enforcer of sexual norms. That's why the moms and dads in groups like P-FLAG, an organization primarily of parents supportive of their lesbian and gay children, make such emotionally powerful spokespersons for the cause of civil rights. Parents who welcome sexual dissenters within the family undermine the notion that such dissent is intrinsically antithetical to deep human connection.

The theme of cultural anxiety about forms of sexuality not bounded and controlled by the family runs through a series of recent judicial decisions. In each case, the threat to norms came not from an assault on the prerogatives of family by libertarian outsiders, a prospect often cited by the right wing to trigger social anxieties. Instead, each court faced the dilemma of how to repress, at least in the law, the anomaly of unsanctioned sexuality within the family.

✳ In a stunning decision two years ago, the Supreme Court ruled in *Michael H. v. Gerald D.* that a biological father had no constitutionally protected right to a relationship with his daughter, despite both paternity (which was not disputed) and a psychological bond that the two had formed. Instead, the Court upheld the rule that because the child's mother—who had had an affair with the child's biological father—was married to another man, the girl would be presumed to be the husband's child. It was more important, the Court declared, to protect the "unitary family," i.e., the marriage, than to subject anyone to "embarrassment" by letting the child and her father continue to see each other. The Court ruled that a state could properly force the termination of that bond rather than "disrupt an otherwise harmonious and apparently exclusive marital relationship." We are not bound, the Court said, to protect what it repeatedly described as "adulterous fathers."

✳ In *Hodgson v. Minnesota* last year, the Supreme Court upheld a Minnesota requirement that a pregnant teenager had to notify both of her parents—even if they were divorced or if there was a threat of violence from her family—prior to obtaining an abortion, so long as she had the alternative option to petition a court. The decision was read primarily as an abortion decision and a ruling on the extent of privacy protection that will be accorded a minor who decides to have an abortion. But the case was also, at its core, about sex in the family and specifically about whether parents could rely on the state for assistance in learning whether a daughter is sexually active.

✳ In two very similar cases this past spring, appellate courts in New York and California ruled that a lesbian partner who had co-parented a child with the biological mother for some years had no standing to seek visitation after the couple split up. Both courts acknowledged that the best interests of the child would be served by allowing a parental relationship to continue, but both also ruled that the law would not recognize what the New York court called "a biological stranger." Such a person could be a parent only if there had been a marriage or an adoption.

Indeed, perhaps the most important point in either decision was the footnote in the California ruling that invited lesbian and gay couples to adopt children jointly: "We see nothing in these [statutory] provisions that would preclude a child from being jointly adopted by someone of the same sex as the natural parent." This opens the door for many more such adoptions, at least in California, which is one of six states where lesbian or gay-couple adoption has occurred, although rarely. The New York court made no such overture.

The effort to legalize gay marriage will almost certainly emerge as a major issue in the next decade. In the past year, lawsuits seeking a right to marry have been filed in the District of Columbia and Hawaii, and activists in other states are contemplating litigation. In 1989 the Conference of Delegates of the State Bar of California endorsed an amendment of that state's law to permit lesbian and gay couples to marry.

A debate continues within the lesbian and gay community about whether such an effort is assimilationist and conservatizing and whether same-sex marriage would simply constitute the newest form of boundary. Much of that debate, however, simply assumes that the social meaning of marriage is unchanging and timeless. If same-sex couples could marry, the profoundly gendered structure at the heart of marriage would be radically disrupted. Who *would* be the "husband" in a marriage of two men, or the "wife" in a marriage of two women? And either way—if there can be no such thing as a female husband or a male wife, as the right wing argues with contempt; or if indeed in some sense there *can* be, as lesbian and gay couples reconfigure these roles on their own terms—the absolute conflation of gender with role is shattered. What would be the impact on heterosexual marriage?

The law's changes to protect sexual dissent within the family will occur at different speeds in different places, which might not be so bad. Family law has always been a province primarily of state rather than federal regulation and often has varied from state to state; grounds for divorce, for example, used to differ dramatically depending on geography. What seems likely to occur in the next wave of family cases is the same kind of variability in the legal definition of the family itself. Those very discrepancies may help to denaturalize concepts like "marriage" and "parent" and expose the utter contingency of the sexual conventions that, in part, construct the family.

DISCUSSION QUESTIONS

1. What assumptions about family and sexuality underlie the courts' various decisions in the Kowalski case? What assumptions about people with disabilities?

2. People with disabilities are often assumed not to be sexual beings. Lesbians and gay men, on the other hand, are often assumed to be nothing but. How do these assumptions play themselves out in this and other cases? What do they tell us about our culture's attitudes toward sexual activity? What do they tell us about the need for discussion of sexual practices in working out programs of social change?

3. How do the readers define family? How does this definition fit with their larger social change work? What cautions might be raised about accepting the family as the basic unit of society?

4. How much control should parents have over their children's sexuality? For how long?

SUGGESTIONS FOR FURTHER STUDY ON DISABILITY

Diane Driedger & Susan Gray, Eds. 1992. *Imprinting our image: An international anthology by women with disabilities.* Canada: Gynergy.

Yvonne Duffy. 1981. Womyn loving womyn. *...All things are possible.* Ann Arbor: A.J. Garvin & Associates, P.O. Box 7525, Ann Arbor, MI 48104.

Marsha Saxton, Ed. 1987. *With wings: An anthology of literature by and about women with disabilities.* UK: Feminist Press.

Karen Thompson & Julie Andrzejewski. 1988. *Why can't Sharon Kowalski come home?* San Francisco: Spinsters/Aunt Lute.

SUGGESTIONS FOR FURTHER STUDY ON FAMILIES

Harriet Alpert. 1988. *We are everywhere: Writings by and about lesbian parents.* Freedom, CA: Crossing Press.

Frederick Bozett, Ed. 1987. *Gay and lesbian parents.* New York: Praeger Press.

Phyllis Chessler. 1987. *Mothers on trial: The battle for children and custody.* Seattle: Seal Press.

Joe Gantz. 1983. *Whose child cries? Children of gay parents talk about their lives.* Rolling Hills Estates, CA: Jalmar Press.

Gay Fathers of Toronto. 1980. *Gay fathers: Some of their stories, experience and advice.* Toronto: Gay Fathers of Toronto.

Carolyn Griffin, Marian & Arthur Wirth. 1986. *Beyond Acceptance: Parents of lesbians and gays talk about their experience,* New Jersey: Prentice-Hall.

Louise Rafkin, Ed. 1989. *Different mothers: Sons and daughters of lesbians talk about their lives.* Pittsburgh: Cleis Press.

Kath Weston. 1992. *Families we choose: Lesbians, gays, kinship.* New York: Columbia University Press.

MILITARISM AND VIOLENCE

Socialization

"Dykes to watch out for #114," by Alison Bechdel, from DYKES TO WATCH OUT FOR: THE SEQUEL *by Alison Bechdel, published by Firebrand Books, Ithaca, NY 14850. Copyright © 1992 by Alison Bechdel. Reprinted with permission.*

EXIT 10: AN ALLEGORY
Diana Chapman

This allegory is one of only two pieces in this collection not by North American writers. It comes from a British anthology, Heterosexuality, *in which lesbians and gay men look at the institution from an unexpected angle. (Alan Wakeman's graphic "What Exactly is Heterosexuality?... and What Causes It?" is from the same anthology.) While the nature of allegory is such that too much interpretation by the editors would be inappropriate, its inclusion here as an introduction to our section on socialization is meant to point out that socialization of males and females in a militarist society is conditioned by what Adrienne Rich has called "compulsory heterosexuality." The relationship between that compulsory heterosexuality and the needs of military state capitalism is strongly suggested by the following tale.*

Moving inexorably towards Earth is a spaceship. It is programmed for an orbit well above Earth to avoid the load of detritus that homo sapiens is already spewing into the atmosphere. Aboard is the Scientific Officer of a minor department of the Galactic Civil Service and It's attendant Robot. "It" since It incorporates several sexes in It's own person. For the purposes of this narrative It shall be called God.

The sad truth is that God set up Planet Earth several eons ago as part of a series of galactic experiments. It only had six days in which to do it and rather skimped the final stages. It is now returning to observe progress after an interval of time which by It's own time scale is but an evening gone, but by human time is a thousand ages.

The Robot knows its job and brings the spaceship to a docking point a suitable distance above Earth. It then activates the ship's giant scanner to search out an area of significant activity on the planet. Before long the image of a huge arena appears on the screen. God and the Robot look at it with interest. Into the arena from a door out of sight below the scanner stream a mass of men and women jostling and arguing. Ahead of them set in a great curving wall are doors marked "Exit," and each Exit has a number. In front of each Exit is a Guardian who stands on a pile of old books. On each Guardian's head is a great crested helmet, their torsos are encased in moulded corselets and they sport huge ornamented codpieces. Their feet are encased in terracotta boots.

"Exit 10: An allegory," by Diana Chapman, published in HETEROSEXUALITY, *edited by Gillian Hanscombe & Martin Humphries, published by GMP Publishers Ltd., P.O. Box 247, London N179QR. Copyright © 1987 by Diana Chapman. Reprinted with permission.*

At each side of the arena are blackboards around which the humans jostle to read the instructions chalked on them. These tell the humans through which gate they should go to participate in various activities.

Through Exit 3 for example, people are turned into philosophers, psychiatrists and used-car salesmen. Exit 7 offers war and all its attendant professions. Exit 10 is labelled: "Heterosexuality" (inc. breeding, domestic duties etc.) As the docile humans line up at the various Exits the guards check their suitability for admission by a cursory glance at their genitals. This rather rough and ready test is the basis upon which one in two of the applicants is turned away and waved towards Exit 10. The majority of those thus rejected shrug their shoulders and trudge off towards the only Exit apparently available to them.

"That's odd," says God, intently watching the screen back in the spaceship. "D'you notice, Robot, all the ones turned away and pushed towards Exit 10 are female. Why do you suppose that is?"

"If I may suggest, Omniscience," murmurs the Robot, "perhaps that is all the female is fit for. You did after all, create male first and then remove one of his ribs to provide raw material for creating the female."

"What if I did," says God testily, "I still endowed her with intelligence equal to his. If I'd only intended her as a breeding machine, domestic servant and sexual receptacle, I'd have designed her quite differently. Six arms and a built-in hydraulic lift for a start. Oh look—some of the females are arguing. Adjust the sound, Robot, this should be interesting."

In front of the Exits some of the women are arguing with the great armored Guards.

"Why can't I go through here?" demands one woman.

"Why aren't MEN sent through Exit 10?" shouts another.

The Guardian pushes up his visor and grins down at them. "You don't want none of this nonsense that goes on through here," he says. "You're not meant for it. A strong man, a good screw and lots of babies, that's all you need, and when you go through there—" he jerks his thumb towards Exit 10, "—you'll get 'em."

"What about MEN?" a woman persists. "If sex and babies are so bloody marvellous, why don't you go through Exit 10 too?"

The Guard looks puzzled. "They don't need to, darlin', they get all that anyway. Y'see, after you lot goes through Exit 10, you go into the Automatic Brainwash. That makes you forget any daft ideas you might have had like jobs and independence and that, and the Moving Pathway takes you where the men are waiting to pick you off."

"Sounds horrible," says a tall young woman.

"'ORRIBLE!" shrieks the outraged Guard. "It's yer DESTINY, and don't you fergeddid!"

"The hell with destiny," another woman shouts, and makes a rush towards a forbidden door.

The Guard grabs her, roughly. "Yer stupid cow," he yells. "Don't yer know what's good for yer? Look! Look at that!"

He jerks the woman round and her eyes follow the direction of his pointing finger. On the ground, some almost obliterated but some quite fresh, are omnious brown stains.

"That's blood that is. Blood of daft cunts like you who wouldn't go nice and easy through Exit 10. Don't argue wiv' me gel. I'm telling yer."

As he lets go of her a light voice speaks from behind.

"Trouble Sarnt?" it inquires.

The Guard stands to attention. "No, Sir. Just the usual few stridents, Sir. Don't want to go through the krek door, Sir."

"My Dear Ladies"—the speaker is slender and handsome, his voice soft and his eyes kind. "Be sensible. No reasonable person would go through any other gate but Exit 10 if they had a choice. If you only knew what lies beyond these others. The heat, the dust, the skirmishes, the smells, the PEOPLE—UGH! Whereas, on the other side of Exit 10 there is protection, love, rose gardens, gurgling pink babies, snowy nappies blowing in the zephyr—"

"Scuse me guv—" a woman breaks in, "you make it sound everso nice. I take it you had no choice, but if you had would YOU go through Exit 10?"

The beautiful man flinches. "CHRIST NO!" he shrieks and suddenly spotting a friend on the other side of the arena hastily makes his excuses and hurries away.

By this time the sun is low in the sky. Only a small group of defiant women remain in the arena. They are tired, hungry, thirsty and uncertain. Those Guards who remain are becoming irritable.

"Give 'em another five minutes," mutters one, "then we'll bloody well boot 'em through."

The women overhear this and move uneasily away in the direction of Exit 10.

"I'm not going through there," says the tall one whose name is Amazonia. "Didn't you hear what he said about the Automatic Brainwash?"

"Not much choice, is there luv?" an older woman replies. Her name is Domestica.

Suddenly one of the other women gives a shout, "Hey, look over there!"

The women turn eagerly to where she is pointing and sure enough, beyond Exit 10 and half hidden under a bougainvillea tree, is a small opening.

"Come on women!" cries Amazonia, and the little band hurries towards the unlabelled Exit. They duck under the bougainvillea and find themselves in a cool, dark space. Ahead of them rises a short flight of stone steps at the top of which is a sturdy door lit by the flames of a fire burning in a cresset. They climb the steps and read by the firelight an inscription carved into the lintel of the door. It reads: "All blokes abandon, ye who enter here."

There are murmurs from the women: "Right on!" "Suits me!" "Let's get through quick."

"Yes," cries Scholastica, a small, bespectacled woman. "Hurry, the Guards are coming."

Sure enough, pounding feet and shouts are nearing the door behind them. Amazonia gives the door a push and it swings open on well-oiled hinges. She holds it back and the women tumble through. Amazonia lets go of the door, it swings back and closes with a final clunk. On the other side the Guards beat and shout ineffectually. Amazonia and Scholastica smile at each other in relief.

"That was close," Amazonia says.

"Yes," replies Scholastica, "but there's something odd. In the arena we are led to believe that there's only one Exit for us women, yet that's not true. Not only is there another Exit but the staircase is lit, the door hinges are oiled and the lock works. Strange, isn't it?"

"It is," replies Amazonia, "and to be honest, I can't explain it. Some other time—let's catch up with the others and see what lies ahead."

They join the rest of the women who are standing in a compound surrounded by a paling fence in which a gate swings in the night breeze. Beside the gate is another flaming cresset which illuminates a neatly printed notice bluetacked onto the gate post. The women crowd forward to read it. It says: "CONGRATULATIONS. YOU HAVE NOW REACHED DEVIANT STATUS. THROUGH THE GATE LIES 'BEYOND THE PALE.' BON VOYAGE." By the moonlight the women can see a path wandering away across a moor. Clouds scud across the moon and a chilly wind blows.

"Come on women," says Amazonia. "It looks a bit bleak but at least there's no Automatic Brainwash."

Murmuring agreement, the women pass through.

Scholastica pauses to study the notice. "Funny," she mutters. "The biro is unsmudged, the paper clean and—" she lifts a corner "—the bluetack fresh." She shakes her head in a puzzled manner and hurries to catch up with the others having first carefully latched the gate.

The pilgrim band trudges steadily along the stony little path which dips and bends across the moor. They notice a gleam of light from a cottage, hear a dog barking and suddenly a fox darts across their path, an illicit chicken in its mouth.

"Lucky sod!" grunts Domestica, "me tripes are stickin' to me bleedin' backbone."

Amazonia, who is in the lead, suddenly pauses. To their left a small path runs off ending in a small flat space. In the middle of the little space sits a Well.

"If you're all as thirsty as I am," she says "that looks hopeful."

"It could be poisoned," someone says doubtfully.

Scholastica has walked over to the Well. "I don't think so," she says. "See, here's a pile of plastic cups, a disposal bin and some wooden benches." She sniffs the bucket and lowers it into the Well. There is a splash and Scholastica winds up the brimming bucket. "Here goes," she says, and tastes the water. "It's fine," she announces and finishes the cupful.

The parched women eagerly dip their cups in and drink. In the meantime Scholastica has spotted another little notice tacked to the Well side. "Please do not leave litter and put all cups into the receptacle provided. Thank you." The note is unsigned. Amazonia has strolled over and together they inspect it.

"Pity no one has left any litter," observes Amazonia. "If they had we might have some clue as to who has been this way before us. Tell me," she turns to Scholastica, "why did you hold out against going out of the arena by Exit 10?"

"I think there were two reasons," Scholastica replies. "First I had set my heart on being a molecular biologist. To be honest I was rather inspired by Rosalind Franklin, who was, you may remember, very shabbily treated by Crick and his colleagues over the discovery of DNA, and I became very resentful when those damn great Guards kept pushing me away from the Science Exit. Then it occurred to me that there must be something fishy about the way the Guards reckoned the only way they could get us to go through Exit 10 was by blocking off every other. After all, if what lay beyond no. 10 was so bloody marvellous, we'd all be fighting to go through, not have to be herded. What about you?"

"Pretty much the same. I wanted to go through the Exit marked 'War.' I think now I was mistaken, but at the time it sounded exciting and dangerous, and a lot of kudos is given to those who do well in it, but the Guard pushed me back and said that women weren't meant to be brave or earn glory, that was only for men. Women were to shut up, do as they were told and have babies. ME have babies! I LOATHE babies! So I thought, 'Hell, what AM I going to do?' then someone noticed that little Exit and I ran towards it like the rest of us."

Scholastica nods towards Domestica. "Let's ask her why she came along."

Domestica scratches her nose reflectively. "Hard to say," she says. "All me mates was going towards Exit 10. They weren't game to argue with them great Guards, and there'd be no point anyway. We weren't brainy, we didn't want to do any of them posh things, we just wanted to do what was right and proper. So I went along wiv' me mates—but when I got near to that Exit 10,—cor, what a pong!"

"You could smell something?" queries Scholastica.

"Not 'alf. Terrible. Put me in mind of my poor Mother. Dirty socks, sweaty jockstraps, semen, blood, boiling nappies—the LOT. UGH! It fair turned me up. 'Dommie, me gel,' I said to meself, 'Don't get trapped like your poor Mum was, there must be another way out.' Then I looked around and saw you lot heading towards that little Exit and I hared over and caught you up, and here I am."

"It's a bit cold and cheerless out here," says Amazonia. "Are you sure you don't regret joining us?"

"Nah!" says Dommie scornfully. "When did a bitta of fresh air ever hurt anyone? Or exercise come to that? Come on, we bin here long enough. Let's get going."

The Deviant women, for such they had now become since they passed Beyond the Pale, plod on. The path skirts settlements from which dogs bark angrily and men in nightcaps jeer from windows. The faint howl of wolves is borne on the night wind, but the air is sweet and the women don't lack courage. The path takes a dip into a forest. The little band, plunging into the trees, see firelight ahead and smell delicious smells of meat roasting and vegetables brewing. They come out of the trees into a clearing in the middle of which a great fire blazes enticingly, and on which meat fizzes and blackened cauldrons bubble. Set back amongst the trees are tents and shacks. Around the fire children frolic, dogs and cats squabble amicably and women are gathered, some tending the food, or repairing clothes. One sharpens arrows, another tunes a lyre, another skins a dead rabbit. The Deviant women pause, unwilling to disturb the household calm. One of the Campfire women looks up and sees them.

"Hello," she calls. "I say, you look fearfully done up. Come over by the fire and have some plonk—there's plenty of grub, too. Come on."

Thankfully the weary Deviants sink by the fire and accept beakers of wine. By this time their presence has attracted other Campfire women who gather round with eager questions.

"Where you from? Where are your Men? What are your names?"

The exhausted Deviants look at each other and shake their heads.

"That's enough, girls," the Campfire leader orders. "The poor dears are exhausted and starving. Food and drink first and questions afterwards."

The ravenous Deviants tuck in to bowls of delicious meat and vegetables and jacket potatoes and freshly baked bread, washed down with beakers of wine. At last, replete, they sit back. Several, regrettably, fall on their backs and doze off.

"Now," the Campfire spokeswoman looks at them inquiringly, "you must have come from the Arena?"

"Yes, we have," replies Amazonia.

"So," the Campfire leader glances round, "where are your Husbands? You shouldn't be out in the cold and dark without Men to protect you."

"None of us," replies Amazonia, "have Husbands."

Consternation breaks out among the Campfire women. "Impossible...couldn't have got this far...no women allowed without one...!"

"Shut up, dears," the Campfire leader asserts her authority. "You MUST have Husbands—or at least some kind of Man. If, as you say, you came from the Arena, and I know of no other starting point, you would have to have come out via Exit 10 and the Automatic Brainwash in which case you couldn't have avoided collecting Husbands." She pauses expectantly.

"Ah, but you see," Scholastica breaks in, "we DIDN'T go through Exit 10. We found another way."

At this further dismay is voiced by the Campfire women. "Can't be true...no other Exit for women...wouldn't want to even if there was...."

Scholastica interrupts them. "We went through a little Exit half hidden by bougainvillea, up a flight of steps and through a door which locked behind us."

At this the Campfire women utter cries of disbelief. "No such Exit...never heard of it...never saw it...not true...."

Suddenly a cool voice cuts across the other voices. "Oh yes, there is such an Exit. I noticed it, in fact I was tempted to take it but didn't have the courage. It's there alright, believe me."

At this the Campfire women are dismayed. "How awful for them...took the wrong turning...have to go back and start again...."

"Tell us," someone calls, "what happened after you went through the door at the top of the stairs?"

Amazonia and Scholastica look at each other, then Amazonia says, "We found ourselves in a little compound surrounded by a paling fence in which there was a gate. A notice told us that we had by this time become Deviants and that once through the gate we were Beyond the Pale."

"What utter nonsense!" cries the Campfire leader, "you're not Deviants! How can you say such a thing? You're nice, normal, healthy women, like us."

There is a slightly uneasy silence and Scholastica clears her throat. "I would be interested to know," she says, "how you can tell Deviants from other women?"

The Campfire women mutter and shrug their shoulders. No one, it seems, knows the answer, but the cool voice breaks in from the shadows. "I can tell you," the speaker says. "They are all six feet tall and dress exclusively in dungarees and nailed boots. They smell strongly of garlic and unwashed armpits."

"Good Heavens, Sophistica!" someone says, "how DO you know all this? Have you actually seen one?"

"My beloved Husband told me," replies the hidden Sophistica languidly. "He also says they continually indulge in monstrous sexual practices which he'd be prepared to pay to watch; and if HE's prepared to shell out to watch something it must be worth watching."

"I think Sophistica's having us on," someone says doubtfully.

Amazonia has been casting round her mind for a diversion from this thorny topic. She leans forward. "You say you go through the Automatic Brainwash and then collect a Husband. Why is that?"

"WHY? It's a prize, dear. Surely—"

"PRIZE! Bloody PENALTY more like!"

The interruption comes from a thin, worn-looking woman who has moved into the firelight. It was she who was dealing with the dead rabbit and there is blood on her apron and on the cleaver which she still holds.

"Oh Misandria," someone says, "you're so prejudiced. We all know that Fred's difficult, but he's your Husband, you must make allowances."

"Allowances," growls Misandria, "I've made allowances for thirty fuckin' years and much good it's ever done me."

"May we ask, Misandria," it is Scholastica speaking, "why you married him?"

"EH?"

Misandria is taken aback. No one has asked her to explain anything for years and words don't come easily.

"Hard to say after all this time. He was one of the Gatekeepers, I do remember that, all done up in his helmet and the rest of it. I was young then, I didn't notice the terracotta boots. Anyway, all the girls I knew were trooping through that Exit 10, so I just trailed along. No one told me there was another way out."

She pauses, searching her memory.

"You went through the Gate and then presumably through the Brainwash?" Scholastica prompts gently.

"Yer, thassit," Misandria's face clears as memory comes back to her. "There was this moving path and it took us into a tunnel with all soft lighting, rose coloured it was. As you went along there was all these pictures of them lovely men—Gary Groper, Charles Voyeur, Gregory Pecker—and it smelt nice…Channel Five I think it was. We all had earphones and there was lovely music and these soft voices, and they kept on and on saying things like, "Did the Earth move, Maria?"…"She had to lose them all to realize she loved Rhett…," and all the time there were diamonds and sapphires and rubies flashing into our eyes and when we got to the end the men were waiting to pick us off, and we were so softened up we couldn't even see 'em properly. And we couldn't see each other, us women, our mates, at all."

"Then what happened?"

"I saw him, Fred, in his armour. High as a steeple, strong as Hercules. He grabs me arm and next thing I know I've signed a bit of paper and him and me goes to his house."

She pauses and laughs. It is not a pretty sound.

"Jesus wept! He takes off his helmet and his corselet and his codpiece and what's left? I'll tell yer what's left. A plucked fowl with a couple of pickled walnuts and a chipolata between its legs. 'Make me some soup,' it whines, 'I'm getting a cold.'"

The Campfire women break into soothing noises. "There, there, that's Marriage, dear. They're only Men after all."

Misandria breaks away from their comfort with a great cry, "That's it! They ARE only men; but they make out they're higher and stronger and greater than they really are, and they put their feet on our necks and make us eat shit, and we're expected to treat them like they was fuckin' God, and they're only men."

She bursts into tears. The women crowd to comfort her but as they do a great yell of rage rents the air. Into the firelight rushes a small man. Balding with a hairy paunch, he clutches a towel round his middle. He spots Misandria in tears. "Y' stupid cunt!" he yells, "why haven't y' stoked the Aga? Where's me clean shirt? Why havent y' pressed me trews? I TOLD y' ten bloody times I was going to the club tonight and I'd wanta hot bath. D'you expect me to do it myself or summat?" He stands, quivering with righteous indignation in the suddenly silent circle of women.

Misandria walks towards him, the blood-stained cleaver still dangling from her hand.

"For two pins," she hisses, "I'd slit you from arsehole to breakfasttime. For thirty years I've lived with you, cooked for you, nursed you, cleaned and laundered for you. Dried your tears when you wept and gritted my teeth when you screwed me. Well, get this Freddie boy, it's over. I'm through, I'm quitting, from now on you're flying solo."

"Oh come on, Mizzie," the man begins to whine, "we're pals, you and me. We've had a few words now and again, but I'm yer Husband. Anyway," he adds spitefully, "y've nowhere to go."

"Oh yes I 'ave." Misandria gestures towards the watchful Deviants. "I'm goin' with them. They've got sense AND they're not cluttered with bloody men."

Fred looks, and for the first time he takes in the presence of the Deviants. He begins to laugh.

"Y' daft cow," he sputters, "d'you know what they are? Them's Deviants. Dykes, lezzies, freaks, weirdos, they couldn't get a man if they—"

"Oh shut up, you crapulous little prick."

The cool voice is strolling from the shadows into the firelight. She is tall and very beautiful. Her earrings glint in the light and a long black cloak hangs from her shoulders. She swings, her cloak swirling, towards her audience.

"Mizzie is quite right," she proclaims, "we put up with far too much from these bastards. Look at me!"—she pauses, and the Deviants murmur appreciatively. "I've had three Husbands, and so many lovers I've lost count. I've done so many handjobs I've got tennis elbow and so many blowjobs my bridgework's wearing out. I've paid their bills, cleaned up their flats, cooked their meals and then had their girlfriends weeping on my shoulder. I think, darlings, like Mizzie, I've had enough. And you—" she turns to the Deviants, "can count me in. By the way, Mizzie, bring that machete along, it might come in useful."

A cry of protest goes up from the Campfire women.

"Sophistica—you CAN'T! Think of poor Cecil. He's your Husband after all."

Sophistica raises her elegant hand. "Sweetie, he won't even notice, he's too busy shagging his new secretary. She dotes on him, poor cow, but I think he's getting bored already. I see the signs."

Silence falls. The Deviants mutter amongst themselves.

"Won't you stay with us?" asks the Campfire leader. "It's quite cozy, really, and after a time you get used to the Husbands, they're not all like Mizzie's and Sophistica's."

The Deviants shake their heads.

"I think we must be moving on, it will soon be sunrise," says Amazonia.

"Where will you go?" someone asks.

The Deviants shrug their shoulders.

Amazonia says, "We shall hope to find a place where we can set up our camp and be safe from men. Maybe we'll have to go to an island. One thing we're sure of, others have been this way before us, we are not as small a band as we seem."

The little band of Deviant women with their two new recruits make their way out of the camp and on to the path. The Campfire women wave goodbye. Some frown and shake their heads disapprovingly, some look decidedly wistful. In the East the sky lightens with the first hint of dawn.

Meanwhile, back at the spacecraft, God is looking very downcast.

"Well, Robot," It observes, "that project went wrong pretty quickly didn't it? From all the other data you've given me it seems that the male of the human species is not only treating the female appallingly, but is making Earth a living hell for all the other creatures I put on it to keep the humans company. If it weren't against Regulations, I'd abort the whole sorry thing. As it is, I have to leave them to work out their own salvation— or damnation, most probably. I see they've learnt to split the atom, so it can't be long now."

"If I might make a suggestion, Supremacy?" murmurs the Robot, "your Illustriousness will no doubt be contemplating further projects in other parts of the Universe, with hope of a better outcome than this one?"

"Indeed, yes, Robot. Had you something in mind?"

"A mere notion," said the Robot, deprecatingly. "Among the lesser species on Earth, the arachnids are adaptable and in their way successful. Using their construction as a basis, but introducing the higher faculties...."

"Go on, Robot. I can see that with eight legs, many eyes and web-spinning facility, they have possibilities. What particular advantage had you in mind?"

"Merely that the female is bigger and stronger than the male—and devours him after copulation."

"Robot," says God, "I think you've got something there. Set course for home. I'm going back to the drawing board."

DISCUSSION QUESTIONS

1. What are some of the ways in which heterosexuality is made compulsory? How does this play itself out day-by-day as the "assumption of heterosexuality?"

2. How does a militarist society benefit from compulsory heterosexuality? A capitalist one? What does this suggest about the current political efforts to promote "family values?"

3. What are the differences in the impact of compulsory heterosexuality on women and on men? What are some of the inducements used to get women and men to buy into this system?

4. What is the threat posed by lesbians to this system? By gay men? By bisexual people? How can the insights of those who are punished for not conforming to the system inform our strategies for a more just and peaceable society?

5. In what ways is violence used to keep women in line?

SUGGESTIONS FOR FURTHER READING

Margaret Andersen & Patricia Hill Collins. 1992. *Race, class and gender: An anthology.* Belmont, CA: Wadsworth Publishing.

Hester Eisenstein. 1983. *Contemporary feminist thought.* Boston: GK Hall.

Kay Leigh Hagan. 1991. Orchids in the Arctic: The predicament of women who love men. *Ms.* (November).

Hunter College Women's Studies Collective. 1983. *Women's realities, women's choices: An introduction to women's studies.* New York: Oxford University Press.

Adrienne Rich. 1980. Compulsory heterosexuality and lesbian existence. *Signs*, 5(4):631-660.

Virginia Sapiro. 1990. *Women in American society.* Mountain View, CA: Mayfield Publishing.

Edward Stein, Ed. 1992. *Forms of desire: Sexual orientation and the social constructionist controversy.* New York: Routledge.

Lenore Weitzman. 1984. Sex-role socialization: A focus on women. *Women: a feminist perspective.* Jo Freeman, Ed. Mountain View, CA: Mayfield Publishing.

MORE POWER THAN WE WANT:
MASCULINE SEXUALITY
AND VIOLENCE
Bruce Kokopeli and George Lakey

This essay has been widely reprinted since its publication in 1976. It has come to play a central role for many pacifists seeking to understand the connections between war, violence, masculinity, and feminism. Its point of view represents that strain among gay men that sees rejection of the traditional "masculine" role as an important step toward liberation for all people. The influence of "effeminism" faded, however, as the gay liberation movement took a turn toward respectability and assimilation. From the middle of the decade, a tendency to look to "masculine" gay men as providing a better role model for public consumption gained the upper hand. The effeminist strain of the movement eventually found a home in the Radical Faerie movement and in those sections of the men's movement supportive of feminism.

Because much of its analysis derives from the authors' work against the war in Southeast Asia, its inclusion in a collection devoted to exploring links between militarism and heterosexism is especially relevant. Furthermore, it incorporates a clear understanding of the relation between personal life choices and larger political consequences.

Patriarchy, the systematic domination of women by men through unequal opportunities, rewards, punishments, and the internalization of unequal expectations through sex role differentiation, is the institution which organizes these behaviors. Patriarchy is men having more power, both personally and politically, than women of the same rank. This imbalance of power is the core of patriarchy, but definitely not the extent of it.

Sex inequality cannot alone be enforced through open violence or even blatant discriminatory agreements—patriarchy also needs its values accepted in the minds of people. If as many young women wanted to be physicians as men, and as many young men wanted to be nurses as women, the medical schools and the hospitals would be hard put to maintain the masculine domination of health care; open struggle and the naked exercise of power would be necessary. Little girls, therefore, are encouraged to think "nurse" and little boys to think "doctor."

Patriarchy assigns a list of human characteristics according to gender: women should be nurturant, gentle, in touch with their feelings, etc.; men should be productive, competitive, super-rational, etc. Occupations are valued according to these gender-linked characteristics, so social work, teaching, housework, and nursing are of lower status that business executive, judge, or professional football player.

When men do enter "feminine" professions they disproportionately rise to the top and become chefs, principals of schools, directors of ballet, and teachers of social work. A man is somewhat excused from his sex role deviation if he at least dominates within the deviation. Domination, after all, is what patriarchy is all about.

Access to powerful positions by women (i.e., those positions formerly limited to men) is contingent on the women adopting some masculine characteristics, such as competitiveness. They feel pressure to give up qualities assigned to females (such as gentleness) because those qualities are considered inherently weak by patriarchal culture. The existence, therefore, of a woman like Indira Gandhi in the position of a dictator in no way undermines the basic sexist structure which allocates power to those with masculine characteristics.

Patriarchy also shapes men's sexuality so it expresses the theme of domination. Notice the masculine preoccupation with size. The size of a man's body has a lot to say about his clout or his vulnerability, as any junior high boy can tell you. Many of these schoolyard fights are settled by who is bigger than whom, and we experience in our adult lives the echoes of intimidation and deference produced by our habitual "sizing up" of the situation.

Penis size is part of the masculine preoccupation, this time directed toward women. Men want to have large penises because size=power, the ability to make a woman "really feel it." The imagery of violence is close to the surface here, since women generally find penis size irrelevant to sexual genital pleasure. "Fucking" is a highly ambiguous word, meaning both intercourse and exploitation/assault.

It is this confusion that we need to untangle and understand. Patriarchy tells men that their need for love and respect can only be met by being masculine, powerful, and ultimately violent. As men come to accept this, their sexuality begins to reflect it. Violence and sexuality combine to support masculinity as a character ideal. To love a woman is to have power over her and to treat her violently if need be. The Beatles song "Happiness is a Warm Gun" is but one example of how sexuality gets confused with violence and power. We know one man who was discussing another man who seemed to be highly fertile—he had made several women pregnant. "That guy," he said, "doesn't shoot any blanks."

Rape is the end logic of masculine sexuality. Rape is not so much a sexual act as an act of violence expressed in a sexual way. The rapist's mind-set—that violence and sexuality *can* go together—is actually a product of patriarchal conditioning. Most of us men understand that mind-set, however abhorrent rape may be to us personally.

In war, rape is astonishingly prevalent even among men who "back home" would not do it. In the following description by a Marine sergeant who witnessed a gang rape in Vietnam, notice that nearly all of the nine-men squad participated:

> They were supposed to go after what they called a Viet Cong whore. They went into her village and instead of capturing her, they raped her—every man raped her. As a matter of fact, one man said to me later that it was the first time he had ever made love to a woman with his boots on. The man who led the platoon, or the squad, was actually a private. The squad leader was a sergeant but he was a useless person and he let the private take over his squad. Later he said he took no part in the raid. It was against his morals. So instead of telling his squad not to do it, because they wouldn't listen to him anyway, the sergeant went into another side of the village and just sat and stared bleakly at the ground, feeling sorry for himself. But at any rate, they raped the girl, and then, the last man to make love to her, shot her in the head (McClusker 1972, 29).

Psychologist James Prescott adds to this account:

> What is it in the American psyche that permits the use of the word "love" to decribe rape? And where the act of love is completed with a bullet in the head! (1975, 17)

MASCULINITY AGAINST MEN: MILITARIZATION OF EVERY-DAY LIFE

Patriarchy benefits men by giving us a class of people (women) to dominate and exploit. Patriarchy also oppresses men, by setting us at odds with each other and shrinking our life space.

The pressure to win starts early and never stops. Working class gangs fight over turf; rich people's sons are pushed to compete on the sports field. British military officers, it is said, learned to win on the playing fields of Eton. Competition is conflict held within a framework of rules. When the stakes are really high the rules may not be obeyed; fighting breaks out.

We men mostly relate through competition, but we know what is waiting in the wings. John Wayne is not a culture hero by accident. Men compete with each other for status as masculine males. Because masculinity equals power, this means we are competing for power. The ultimate proof of power/masculinity is violence. A man may fail to "measure up" to macho sterotype in important ways, but if he can fight successfully with the person who challenges him on his deviance, he is still all right. The television policeman Baretta is strange in some ways: he is gentle with women and he cried when a man he loved was killed.

However, he has what are probably the largest biceps in television and he proves weekly that he can beat up the toughs who come his way.

The close relationship between violence and masculinity does not need much demonstration. War used to be justified partly because it promoted "manly virtue" in a nation. Even today we are told that the Marines are looking for a "few good men." Those millions of people in the woods hunting deer, in the National Rifle Association, and cheering the bloodiest hockey teams are overwhelmingly men.

The world situation is so much defined by patriachy that what we see in the wars of today is competition between various patriarchal ruling classes and governments breaking into open conflict. Violence is the accepted masculine form of conflict resolution. Women at this time are not powerful enough in the world situation for us to see mass overt violence being waged on them. But the violence is in fact there; it is hidden through its legitimization by the state and by culture.

In everyday middle class life, open violence between men is of course rare. The defining characteristics of masculinity, however, are only a few steps removed from violence. Wealth, productivity, or rank in the firm or institution translate into power—the capacity (whether or not exercised) to dominate. The holders of power in even polite institutions seem to know that violence is at their fingertips, judging from reactions of college presidents to student protest in the 1960s. We know of one urbane *pacifist* man, the head of a theological seminary, who was barely talked out of calling the police to deal with the nonviolent student sit-in at "his" seminary!

Patriarchy teaches us at very deep levels that we can never be safe with other men (or perhaps anyone), for the guard must be kept up lest our vulnerability be exposed and we be taken advantage of. At a recent Quaker conference in Philadelphia a discussion group considered the value of personal sharing and openness in the Quaker Meeting. In almost every case the women advocated more sharing and the men opposed it. Dividing by gender on that issue was predictable; men are conditioned by our life experience of masculinity to distrust settings where personal exposure will happen, especially if men are present. Most men find emotional intimacy possible only with women; many with only one woman; some men cannot be emotionally intimate with anyone.

Patriarchy creates a character ideal—we call it masculinity—and measures everyone against it. Many men fail the test as well as women, and even men who are passing the test today are carrying a heavy load of anxiety about tomorrow. Because masculinity is a form of domination, no one can really rest secure. The striving goes on forever unless you are actually willing to give up and find a more secure basis for identity.

MASCULINITY AGAINST GAY MEN:
PATRIARCHY FIGHTS A REAR GUARD ACTION

Homophobia is the measure of masculinity. The degree to which a man is thought to have gay feelings is the degree of his unmanliness. Because patriarchy presents sexuality as men over women (part of the general dominance theme), men are conditioned to have only that in mind as a model of sexual expression. Sex with another man must mean being dominated, which is very scary. A non-patriarchal model of sexual expression as the mutuality of equals doesn't seem possible; the transfer of the heterosexual model to same-sex relations can at best be "queer;" at worst, "perverted."

In the recent book *Blue Collar Aristocrats*, by E. E. LeMasters, a working class tavern is described in which the topic of homosexuality sometimes comes up. Gayness is never defended. In fact, the worst thing you can call a man is homosexual. A man so attacked must either fight or leave the bar.

Notice the importance of violence in defending yourself against the charge of being a "pansy." Referring to your income, or academic degrees, or size of your car is no defense against such a charge. Only fighting will re-establish respect as a masculine male. Because gay appears to mean powerless, one needs to go to the masculine source of power—violence— for adequate defense.

Last year, the Argentinian government decided to persecute gays on a systematic basis. The Ministry of Social Welfare offered the rationale for this policy in an article which also attacked lesbians, concluding that they should be put in jail or killed:

As children they played with dolls. As they grew up, violent sports horrified them. As was to be expected, with the passage of time and the custom of listening to foreign mulattos on the radio, they became conscientious objectors (El Caudillo 1975, 5).

The Danish government, by contrast with Argentina, has liberal policies on gay people. There is no government persecution and all government jobs are open to gays—except in the military and the diplomatic service! Two places where the nation-state is most keen to assert power are places where gays are excluded as a matter of policy.

We need not go abroad to see the connections between violence and homophobia. In the documentary film *Men's Lives* a high school boy is interviewed on what it is like to be a dancer. While the interview is conducted we see him working out, with a very demanding set of acrobatic exercises. The boy mentions that other boys think he must be gay. Why is that? the interviewer asks. Dancers are free and loose, he replies; they are not big like football players; and "you're not trying to kill anybody."

Different kinds of homosexual behavior bring out different amounts of hostility, curiously enough. That fact gives us further clues to violence and female oppression. In prisons, for example, men can be respected if they fuck other men, but not if they are themselves fucked. (We used the word "fucked" intentionally for its ambiguity.) Often prison rapes are done by men who identify as heterosexual; one hole substitutes for another in this scene, for sex is in either case an expression of domination for the masculine mystique.

But for a man to be entered sexually, or to use effeminate gestures and actions, is to invite attack in prison and hostility outside. Effeminate gay men are at the bottom of the totem pole because they are *most like women*, which is nothing less than treachery to the Masculine Cause. Even many gay men shudder at drag queens and vigilantly guard against certain mannerisms because they, too, have internalized the masculinist dread of effeminacy.

John Braxton's report of prison life as a draft resister is revealing on this score. The other inmates knew immediately that John was a conscientious objector because he did not act tough. They also assumed he was gay for the same reason. (If you are not masculine, you must be a pacifist and gay, for masculinity is a package which includes both violence and heterosexuality.)

A ticket of admission to Masculinity, then, is sex with women, and bisexuals can at least get that ticket even if they deviate through having gay feelings as well. This may be why bisexuality is not feared as much as exclusive gayness among men. Exclusively gay men let down the Masculine Cause in a very important way—they do not participate in the control of women through sexuality. Control through sexuality matters because it is flexible; it usually is mixed with love and dependency so that it becomes quite subtle.

Now we better understand why women are in general so much more supportive of gay men than non-gay men are. Part of it of course is that heterosexual men are often paralyzed by fear. Never very trusting, such men find gayness one more reason to keep up the defenses. But heterosexual women are drawn to active support for the struggles of gay men because there is a common enemy—patriarchy and its definition of sexuality as domination. Both heterosexual women and gay men have experienced firsthand the violence of sexism; we all have experienced its less open forms such as put-downs and discrimination and we all fear its open forms such as rape and assault.

Patriarchy, which links characteristics (gentleness, aggressiveness, etc.) to gender, shapes sexuality in such a way as to maintain male power. The Masculine Cause draws strength from homophobia and resorts habitually to violence in its battles on the field of sexual politics. It provides psychological support for the military state and is in turn stimulated by it.

PATRIARCHY AND THE MILITARY STATE

The parallels between these two powerful institutions are striking. Both prefer more subtle means of domination but insist on violence as a last resort. Both institutions provide role models for socialization: the masculine man, the feminine woman; the patriotic citizen. Both are aided by other institutions in maintaining their legitimacy—religion, education, business, sport.

The sexual politics of the family provides the psychological model for the power politics of the state. The oft-deplored breakdown of the family may, from this point of view, have positive effects. Future Vietnams may be ruled out by the growing unmasculinity of soldiers and unfeminine impatience of women.

The business allies of the military are no doubt appalled. The patriarchal family gets constant bolstering from that camp: family services are traditionally the best funded of the private social work agencies; business promoted the Feminine Mystique quite consciously.

`The interplay at the top levels of the state between violence and masculinity is becoming clearer. Political scientist Richard Barnet refers to the "hairy chest syndrome" among National Security Managers in government agencies.

> The man who is ready to recommend using violence against foreigners, even where he is overruled, does not damage his reputation for prudence, soundness, or imagination, but the man who recommends putting an issue to the U.N., seeking negotiations, or—horror of horrors—"doing nothing" quickly becomes known as "soft." To be "soft"—that is, unbelligerent, compassionate, willing to settle for less—or simply to be repelled by homicide, is to be "irresponsible." It means walking out of the club (Barnet 1977, 109).

The Mayagüez incident, in which the United States bombed Cambodia with no real effort at negotiations or other steps, was a clear example. In fact, it was so clear that Henry Kissinger felt impelled to deny that the U.S. response was to "prove our manhood."

An Angolan leader tried to touch the masculinity nerve in an appeal for U.S. help for the anti-Soviet FNLA. Holden Roberto told *Newsweek*:

> Most of the world is sniggering up its sleeve at America's detente efforts and the way the Soviets pay lip service to it while consolidating their position. Maybe, like the cuckolded partner in a betrayed marriage, the United States will be the last to learn the truth (December 29, 1975).

From all this it seems obvious to us that the struggle for a world without war must also be a struggle against patriarchy with its masculine character ideal and its oppression of women and gays. Pacifist men, by rejecting violence, have taken a healthy first step in dropping out of masculinity. Some have sought to compensate for that by being more rigorously "tough" in other ways and by participating in the oppression of women and gays. This must stop. Peacemakers need to see women and gays as the potential allies they are and develop a feminist perspective as they act for peace.

It seems equally obvious that feminists and gays must include, in our list of patriarchal enemies, the military state. The sexual politics of domination/submission is so reinforced by militarism that one cannot be eliminated without the other. Masculinity and violence are so intimately related that one cannot be defeated by itself.

ANDROGYNY: NEW PEOPLE FOR THE NEW SOCIETY

If the masculine character ideal supports militarism, what can support peace? Femininity? No, for that character ideal also has been shaped by patriarchy and includes along with virtues such as gentleness and nurturance, a kind of dependency which breeds the passive-aggressive syndrome of curdled violence.

We are encouraged by the vision of androgyny, which acknowledges that the best characteristics now allocated to the two genders indeed belong to both: gentleness, intelligence, nurturance, courage, awareness of feelings, cooperativeness, rooting one's sense of identity in *being* as well as doing and not tying it to ownership of people or things, initiative, befriending persons rather than physical characteristics, sensuality with appreciation for the erotic dimension of everyday life.

Many of these characteristics are now allocated to the feminine role which has led some men to conclude that the essential liberating task is to become effeminate. We don't agree, since some desirable characteristics are now allocated to the masculine role (for example, initiative, intelligence). Further, some characteristics are not assigned to *either* gender in this culture: having an identity independent of ownership of people and things, for example. Women are expected to be as jealous as men and as absorbed in material accumulation or consumerism.

We urge people to continue the exploration of what a peaceful and sexually liberated society will be like and what kind of people will inhabit it. Let us allow our creativity to flow beyond the definitions patriarchy has given us.

Also needed are strategies for moving toward the androgynous vision which will show us how to change our organizations, campaigns, and lifestyles. All of us in this struggle have a lot to be proud of, and none of us needs to be guilt-tripped into changing. Let's all find the support we need to keep on growing. The future is ours if we only claim it.

DISCUSSION QUESTIONS

1. What are some of the ways "nontraditional" men, either peace activists or gay men, continue to benefit from masculine privilege in their work and their personal relationships?

2. What are some of the concrete things men can do to relinquish power in mixed organizations? What would it mean for mixed groups to have women's leadership? What would it mean for groups of men to have gay male leadership?

3. How are "effeminate" men marginalized in peace or political organizations? What threat do they pose to the patriarchy? How would our strategies and forms of organization be different if we were to let go of any attachments to gender privileges, including masculine and heterosexual?

4. What does it mean to be a "male role model"? How is this discussion different in communities of color and largely white groups? What would it mean to have gay men as role models, especially in settings where young people—female and male—may not yet identify as gay or straight? If we exclude gay men as role models in such settings, what is the message we convey?

5. How might "blending in" to society as it is currently organized be an effective strategy?

SUGGESTIONS FOR FURTHER READING

Elise Boulding. 1988. Warriors and saints: Dilemmas in the history of men, women and war. *Women and the military system.* Eva Isaksson, Ed. New York: Harvester/Wheatsheaf.

Cynthia Enloe. 1989. Beyond Steve Canyon and Rambo: Feminist histories of militarized masculinity. *The militarization of the western world.* John Gillis, Ed. New Brunswick, NJ: Rutgers University Press.

Michael Kimmel. 1989. From pedestal to partners: Men's responses to feminism. *Women: A feminist perspective.* 4th edition. Jo Freeman, Ed. Mountain View, CA: Mayfield Publishing.

Paul Patton & Ross Poole, Eds. 1985. *War/Masculinity.* Sydney: Intervention.

Lindsy Van Gelder. 1987. Personal politics: A lesson in straight talk. *Ms.* (November).

THE RATIONALITY OF CARE
Sara Ruddick

In defining the practices and thinking of care, Ruddick examines the preponderance of women and suggests ways in which this then translates into an antimilitaristic stance. Preservative love, arising from the dailiness of meeting the needs of those under one's care, is contrasted with military thinking whose aims are the destruction of those bodies mothers protect. Ruddick is included in this anthology as an exploration of the links between feminist and maternalist analyses. The issues of antimilitarism and nonviolence are explored at greater length in her 1990 book Maternal Thinking: Toward a Politics of Peace *(New York: Ballantine).*

To speak with my voice: the ultimate. I didn't want anything more, anything different. If need be, I could prove that, but to whom?
    —Christa Wolf, *Cassandra*

And looking into the face ... of one dead man we see two dead, the man and the life of the woman who gave him birth; the life she wrought into his life! And looking into his dead face someone asks a woman, what does a woman know about war? What, what, friends in the face of a crime like that, what does a man know about war?
    —Anna Shaw, speech to women's peace party, 1915

I heard her voice, calling "Mother, Mother." I went towards the sound. She was completely burned. The skin had come off her head altogether, leaving a knot of twisted hair at the top. My daughter said, "Mother, you're late, please take me back quickly." She said it was hurting a lot. But there were no doctors. There was nothing I could do. So I covered up her naked body and held her in my arms for nine hours. At about eleven o'clock that night she cried out again, "Mother," and put her hand around my neck. It was already ice-cold. I said, "Please say Mother again." But that was the last time.
    —Hiroshima survivor

We surely say that a decent man will believe that ... being dead is not a terrible thing ... There is no further need of wailing and lamentations ... They're useless to women who are to be decent, let alone for men.
    —Plato, *Republic*

Most women and men support organized violence, at least in "emergencies." Certainly, women have not absented themselves from war.

Wherever battles are fought and justified, whether in the vilest or noblest of causes, women on both sides of the battle lines support the military engagements of their sons, lovers, friends, and mates. Increasingly, women are proud to fight alongside their brothers, and as fiercely, in whatever battles their state, cadre, or cause enlists them.

Nonetheless, throughout history there have been women who insist that, as women, they have distinct reasons for rejecting men's wars. This does not mean that women are innately or inevitably peaceful. As Jane Addams put it:

> The belief that a woman is against war simply and only because she is a woman and not a man, does not, of course, hold. In every country there are many, many women who believe that War is inevitable and righteous, and that the highest possible service is being performed by their sons who go into the Army ([1915] 1984, 86-87).

Nor are women afraid to fight, unable to fight, or morally superior to fighters. In the words of Olive Schreiner:

> It is not because of woman's cowardice, incapacity, nor, above all, because of her general superior virtue that she will end war when her voice is finally and fully heard ([1911] 1978, 170, 173).

Rather, to quote Addams again:

> The women do have a sort of pang about it... That curious revolt comes out again and again, even in the women who are most patriotic... Even those women, when they are taken off their guard, give a certain protest, a certain plaint against the whole situation which very few men I think are able to formulate (86–87).

Both Addams and Schreiner traced women's "curious revolt" against war to their experience as mothers. Neither Addams nor Schreiner believed that women became generally wise from being mothers. Schreiner did however attribute to women a quite specific knowledge:

> No woman who is a woman says of a human body, "it is nothing"... On this one point, and on this point almost alone, the knowledge of woman, simply as woman, is superior to that of man; she knows the history of human flesh; she knows its cost; he does not (170, 173).

In this paper, I take Addams's and Schreiner's claim seriously. From the work they have done, women have derived a distinctive kind of knowledge that might be put to antimilitarist use. More particularly, women would tell a "history of human flesh" quite differently from a military history. I put to one side the passions and fears that make many women—like many men—militaristic. My concern is only with those women who protest wars and preparation for wars.

A preliminary note about terminology: By the "whole situation," which is the object of protest, I mean organized, deliberate, "legitimate" violence, not random assaults and individual aggression or defenses against them but the social violence of which good people approve. Nor will I be concerned with the absolute renunciation of violence, a preoccupation which divides anti-militarists. My concern is with a collective decision to invest funds and energies in armies and weapons, then to rely upon the threat or use of military violence to protect the collective and enforce its will.

THE RATIONALITY OF CARE

In the past several years, feminist philosophers have developed a critique of "Reason" as it has been defined in Western philosophy. Repeatedly, throughout the history of Western philosophy, the dichotomies that define reason also define and reinforce a dichotomy between male and female. Within certain canonical texts, reason is explicitly defined as not female. Conversely, the "female" is defined as the antagonist of reason, as what is particular, passionate, changeable, bodily, and sensuous. What is reasonable—abstract, impersonal, passionless— discourse is accordingly associated with what is "male." The rational self controls not only bodily sensation, particular attachment, and passionate desires but also those people associated with the bodily, particular, and passionate. Hence, "reason" grants the right to speak in public and to rule at home.

> [G]ood order would have been wanting in the human family if some were not governed by others wiser than themselves. So by such a kind of subjection is woman naturally subject to man, because in man discretion of reason predominates (Aquinas quoted by Lloyd 1984, 36).

To say that reason is "male" is not to say that actual men are reasonable. Ideals of reason describe an attainment that excludes most people. The point is that to attain rationality requires, for men or women, a separation from and control of sensuous, particular, passionate, concrete attachments, and styles of cognition that mark the "female." "Female" persons are harbingers of disagreement and are therefore of an unruly division that threatens the rational self and rational argument.

Military thinking, the plans and justifications for war, express in exaggerated form those characteristics that render reason "male." Virtually no one denies that military thinking is imbued with masculine values. No more than a man is born reasonable is a boy born a soldier. Becoming a soldier means learning to control fears and domestic longings, which are explicitly labelled "womanly." This much has long been familiar. What is increasingly clear is that becoming a militarist means acquiring a distinctive way of thinking. Feminist critics have underlined the ways in which philosophers honor, even as they construct, conceptual connections between reason, war, and masculinity. The struggle to become reasonable "mustn't be useless to warlike men"; on the contrary, philosophers see to it that those men and (sometimes) women who are called "reasonable" have "proved best [both] in philosophy and with respect to war" (Plato, *Republic*, 543a, 521d). Even as the tendency to define reason in opposition to the feminine takes different historical and philosophical forms, even more, the requirements of military thinking vary radically, depending upon political, economic, and technological contexts of war. In our nuclear age, there is a "language of warriors," a "technico-strategic rationality," which is shared by armers and disarmers, chiefs of staff, and chief negotiators (Dyson 1984; Cohn 1990). This rationality exhibits in near caricature the kinds of dichotomization and abstraction that, in other contexts, have been characterized as male. Military theorists

> portray themselves as clear-sighted, unsentimental analysts describing the world as it is ... a world of self-confirming theorems invites fantasies of control over events that we do not have.... Through abstracted models and logic, hyperrationalism reduces states and their relations to games which can be simulated.... One of the legacies of war is a "habit of simple distinction, simplification, and opposition." ... One basic task of a state at war is to portray the enemy in terms as absolute and abstract as possible in order to distinguish as sharply as possible the act of killing from the act of murder.... It is always "the *enemy*," a "pseudo-concrete universal" (Elshtain 1985, 49-50).

In a gendered world, thinking is structured by divisions in our lives. Mostly male humans have created not only the practices of science, law, war, philosophy, psychology, and poetry but also our thinking about these practices. At the same time, certain distinctive kinds of work have been undertaken primarily by women. It is likely that out of women's work, just as out of men's, distinctive kinds of thinking would arise. Moreover, unless we learn to look at women's ways of knowing in their specificity, I fear we will drift into the very sentimental dichotomies some feminists fear. We will, for example, consider peace as a womanly, sweetly empty counterpart to men's wars rather than as the myriad kinds of nonviolent actions it must become.

In attempting to articulate ideals of reason, which are in some sense feminine but which ultimately could transcend gender, I have found it useful to draw upon a "practicalist" conception of reason that, though central to current philosophical discussion, differs from the dominant masculinist ideal. According to practicalists, reason arises from and is tested against "practice." Practices are collective human activities distinguished by the aims that identify them and by the consequent demands made upon practitioners committed to those aims. The constitutive aims of a practice determine what counts as reasonable within it, even as a "reasonable" articulation of aims and strategies render the practice coherent and communicable. Not any stretch of discourse counts as reasonable. To be "reasonable," a kind of thinking must make coherent and communicable a sense of the activities of practitioners. Yet there is no primary reason, no standard of coherence and communicability that transcends practice. Practices in some ways surprisingly alike, in others strikingly contrastive, give rise to reasons that can be compared and contrasted. Scientific reasoning is distinct from, though in many elements similar to, religious, historical, mathematical, psychoanalytic, or hermeneutic reasoning.

In practicalist terminology, the mothering of children can be understood to be a practice from which a distinctive kind of thinking arises. Maternal thinking, like scientific or religious thinking, attempts to make coherent and communicable the practice whose aims it serves. The work of mothering is, symbolically and psychologically, the central instance of what has come to be called "caring labour" (Rose 1983, 1986). "Care" is a general designation covering many practices—nursing, homemaking, and tending the elderly, for example—each of which is caring because it, like mothering, includes among its defining aims insuring the safety and well-being of subjects cared for. Instances of care cannot, however, be simply assimilated. For example, caretaking always involves "teaching" the subjects of care, and teaching itself can be understood as a kind of caring labor. But the teaching of healthy children differs from the instruction of the ill or elderly or the members of a household by a homemaker, while teaching itself is not exhaustively described in the language of care. To confuse the care of healthy children with nursing, tending the elderly, homemaking, or teaching would be bad for child, patient, homemates, older person, student, and the caretaker herself.

Amidst the varieties of caring, there are elements of the work that, though not present in all cases, are sufficiently common and central to be formative of a rationality of care, just as, despite the varieties of science or religion, we still speak of scientific or religious rationality.

The rationality of care—like scientific or religious rationality—is potentially genderless. Caretaking is a human activity. A small but weighty fraction of specifically maternal work is ineluctably female. Only women can carry and give birth to infants; where babies are nursed, only women can nurse them. But pregnancy, birth, lactation, and the care of tiny, relatively immobile infants make up a very small portion of maternal work. A scrambling, temperamental toddler in reach of poisons under the sink, a school child left out of a birthday party, a college student unable to write her papers—these children are more emblematic of the demands upon a mother than the smiling infant so briefly quiet on her lap. Of the many kinds of caring labor that are not evidently maternal, most can be done by men and women. Similarly, many women refuse caring work either because it neither interests nor suits them or because of exploitative and confining work conditions. A woman is no more "naturally" a caretaker, no more obligated to caring labor, than a man is "naturally" a scientist or obligated to become one. Both kinds of work should be open to capable and interested women and men.

Although the work of care could transcend gender, care has been profoundly womanly. This is not, in the first instance, because many women are caretakers but, rather, because most caretakers are women. Women have not only borne but have also cared for children. Although the sociological explanations are in dispute, few disagree that in most cultures the work of nursing, caring for the elderly, and even teaching, especially of small children, has been performed by women. Accordingly, to study care would be to study women, even if only a small proportion of women engaged seriously in care. As it is, however, in most cultures throughout the world, many more women than men expect to undertake and identify with caretaking work. Although many women refuse caring labor, women as a group are apparently more likely than men to acquire the abilities of care and to see the world from the vantage it affords. Hence the rationality of care and "women's ways of knowing" are inextricably entangled. When critics, psychologists, artists, and others speak of women's minds, they are speaking also—though of course not only of— the rationality of care. In most cultures now, to articulate a rationality of care is also to ascribe a distinctive intellectual vantage to women.

To speak of women's ways of knowing or of a rationality deriving from work that has, as a matter of history, been women's work is not tantamount to creating a "woman's reason" to rival the "man's." It is a reason that thrives on dichotomy that looks for a female to oppose to the male, a "natural" woman to oppose to man's "culture," a subjective mind to oppose to his objectivity. It is militarists who benefit from the equation of women with irrationality, who call Cassandra mad and defense intellectuals people of reason. The struggle to be "rational"—to see what is real in all its complexity and ambiguity—is a peacemaker's struggle. The task is to reconceive rationalities that will be instruments of nonviolent action, rather than of war.

Because "the feminine" has been defined in part by its exclusion from rationality, and because care is womanly, it becomes a struggle to articulate without sentimentality or abstract simplification a "rationality of care." Women who put pillowcases, toys, and other artifacts of "attachment" against the barbed wire fences of missile bases are prizing the symbols of care from the context where they are expected and harmless. They are "words" of a developing language which is spoken by women in public in order to resist violations of care in care's name.

The rationality of care, as I read it, is consonant with, and indeed often exemplifies, alternative ideals of reason advanced by feminists. At the same time, it contrasts with masculinist and militarist rationalities. For example, since care is constituted by the demand of subjects that they be assisted, the adequacy of distinctions and concepts is tested in terms of responsiveness to need, rather than, for example, by the prediction, control, or destruction they enable. The ability to respond to human needs without undue fantasy or projection requires a nonintrusive attention to specific particulars of persons and of connections and dependencies among them. Such attentive love differs markedly from the intellection of day dreaming, experiment, invention, and strategy, though caretakers may engage in all of these, sometimes in the service of care and certainly in other intellectual pursuits. Since the vulnerable are subject to abuse and neglect, the circumstances of care allow for violence. Caretakers are tempted by sadism, self-indulgent aggression, and self-protective indifference to the real needs of others. They must learn to see and speak truly about these temptations and about the discipline of resisting them. By contract, increasing vulnerability and aggressing against the vulnerable is an aim of the military. A benign detachment from one's own and others' vulnerability is often an aim of the man of reason.

On the practicalist view of reason, the meaning of "reason," "feeling," and their right relation are given within a practice. Caring work is imbued with disturbingly ambivalent feelings about the subject cared for and the demands of the work. Maternal love, for example, is intermixed with hate, sorrow, and regret; affection for the elderly with impatience and resentment; compassion for the ill with disgust and despair. In a practice governed by the demand to assist and protect, ambivalent and potentially destructive feelings cry out for reflective assessment. Reflective assessment of feeling is, like attentive regard, a defining "rational" activity of caretakers. As attention is itself a kind of love tested in practice, so reflective assessment is itself tested by feelings in the context of the need to assist. Rather than separating reason from feeling and both from action, the practice of care makes reflective, active feeling one of the most difficult attainments of reason. In sum, in the rationality of care, "feelings" are at best complex but sturdy instruments of work quite unlike the simple and separate hates, fears, and loves that motivate military endeavors or are put to one side in many philosophical analyses.

Yet the opposition between the rationalities of militarism and of care, though real, is not simple. I myself have contrasted the "preservative love" of mothering with military destruction. And, indeed, the contrast seems nearly a contradiction. Mothering begins in birth and promises life; military thinking justifies organized, deliberate deaths. A mother preserves the bodies, nurtures the psychic growth, and disciplines the conscience of children she cares for; the military deliberately endangers the same body, mind, and conscience in the name of victory and abstract causes. Mothers protect children who are at risk; the military risks the children mothers protect. Yet I took the term "preservative love" from J. Glenn Gray's account of it in warriors' lives (Gray 1970). For Gray, preservative love is poignantly bittersweet in battle where it flourishes because it is threatened everywhere by death. By contrast, the preservative love of care is marked by its unexciting dailiness and a matter-of-fact acceptance of vulnerability and the threat of loss. Preservative love is opposed to military destruction but the opposition is a matter of the weight and context of destruction and love within two systems of thinking.

Ideals of reason are controlling, and, within Western scientific thinking at least, the capacity to control is made a test of reason. Just-war theories control our perceptions of war, turning our attention from bodies and their fate to abstract causes and rules for achieving them. Nuclear thinking gives an illusion of control over events that are profoundly unpredictable. Both the experience of being controlled by alien thought and the value put on control within that thought leads some feminists to reject the idea of control altogether. Indeed, caretakers think about control differently from scientists or generals. When the objects of care

are human, they are not objects but subjects. Caretakers are liable to depend upon the dependence of those who depend upon them. They have to learn to relish reciprocity. It is an attainment of reason to perceive those cared for as intentional, self-generating agents, to identify as a caretaker's virtue her respect for the independent, uncontrollable will of the other. If the care is successful, a teacher or mother will protect and enable someone whose will cannot be controlled. Even a nurse or companion to the elderly can protect, as one would a flame in the wind, her subjects' ability to formulate and act on desires of their own. But none of this is tantamount to relinquishing control. Rather, the best control makes room for the limits of control. No one who has cared for a small toddler, supervised a classroom, or helped the learning-disabled in their travels will trust her own or her subjects' spontaneity. Care without control is a horror.

In sum, the opposition between militarism and care is not simple. Central concepts, while including certain commonalities, tend to be differently defined, weighted in ways appropriate to a system of thinking, and put to distinctive uses. I would now like to illustrate this general point by comparing military and caretaking concepts of the body.

THE HISTORY OF HUMAN FLESH

Both militarists and caretakers, unlike philosophers, do their work among bodies. Both are ambivalent about the bodies they work among. Each of them conceives of the body as sexual and sharply gendered. For each, death is a central bodily experience. In sharp contrast to military ideology, maternal thinking weights birth over death, offering a concept of natality as central to the rationality of care. Moreover, despite their shared preoccupation with sexuality and death, the concepts of the body, taken as a whole, differ radically.

One aim of militarist thinking is to develop descriptive and justificatory concepts appropriate to a "history of human flesh" in battle. The central business of war is a trafficking in bodies. Soldiers achieve their aims by threatening to damage bodies or actually doing so—burning, cutting, blasting, pounding, breaking flesh and bones. As Elaine Scarry puts it,

> Injury is the thing every exhausting piece of strategy and every single weapon is designed to bring into being: it is not something inadvertently produced on the way to producing something else but is the relentless object of all military activity (1985, 73).

It sometimes seems that high-tech war is a contest between weapons where damage to bodies is not only described as "collateral" but is also a genuinely lamented secondary effect of the contest (Cohn 1990). Yet we call these machines "weapons" precisely because with them we can threaten to sicken, mutilate, and burn up human bodies. Soldiers are killed and kill with weapons that are meant to be cruel. "Radiation sickness" and chemical poisons are not merely the "fall out" of "clean" explosions but predictable effects. Napalm purposely includes an ingredient that increases the adhesion of burning petrol to human skin. Explosive (dum dum) bullets, the metal cubes of claymore mines, the fiberglass fragments of cluster bombs are deliberately designed to tear bodies apart not only in pain but precisely in ways that defeat medical skill.

Although some people are military enthusiasts despite—or even because of—war's cruelty, for many others military allegiance depends upon concealing the crude realities of injuring. There is a gap—moral and conceptual—between aims of war and the "glassed eye balls, and swollen bodies, and fixed blue unclosed mouths, and great limbs tossed," which is war's outcome (Schreiner [1911] 1978, 170). Reluctant militarists must keep their eyes fixed on justice despite the absence of moral or political connections between the capacity to out-injure and the cause in which one fights. Whatever the cause, "our boys" must be seen as defenders and victims, not killers. Accordingly, military thinking proves identifiable techniques of redescription and evasion that focus the mind on strategy rather than on suffering: on sacrifice rather than on killing; and on the cause rather than the bodies torn apart in its name. Primary among these conceptual strategies is the creation of the "just warrior" using interlocking myths of masculinity, sacrifice, and heroic death.

In most armies, in most of history, the just warrior is not only male but manly. Militarists seem nearly obsessed by the division between male and female bodies. Men and women may fight together outside of state power, but once violence is "legitimately" organized, only male bodies are deemed suitable to "carry the battle to the enemy." Military requirements cannot account for such a stringent association of war with masculinity. Many weapons and battle plans do not require the upper body strength that recruiters celebrate and that men, on the average, display. "The male's greater vital capacity, speed, muscle mass, aiming and throwing skills, his greater propensity for aggression and his more rapid rises in adrenaline" may indeed make him on the average "more fitted for physically intense combat" (Marlowe 1983). Such specifically masculine strength has little to do with the computer centers, missile silos, bomber cockpits, and armored tanks at the center of modern battle plan. (Women in the Air Force are now members of command teams in missile silos; but they still cannot become bomber pilots.)

Although there is wide agreement that soldiers must be men, there are at least two competing views of manliness. For an enthusiastic militarist, the soldier who is necessarily male, is simultaneously a man who is "naturally" suited to become a soldier. There is little doubt that for many soldiers and strategists, injuring is sexualized and sexually exciting; soldiers themselves often describe their sexuality as compulsive and predatory. Military speech is imbued with masculinist heterosexual metaphors. War is a "pissing contest." "To disarm is to get rid of all your stuff." "Spasm attacks" release "70 to 80 percent of our megatonnage in one orgasmic whump." Military lectures are filled with references to "vertical erectory launchers, thrust-to-weight rations, soft lay-downs, deep penetration." An invasion of a small island becomes a "pre-dawn vertical insertion"; an outmoded missile is maintained because it's "in the nicest hole." Suspected or captured soldiers, male and female, are tortured in specifically sexual ways. Women, generally, are sexually exploited while "conquered" women are predictably raped. Even children and the elderly are not immune from sexual abuse.

Citing connections between sex, gender, and war, some militarists "explain" the inevitability of battle in terms of men's sexuality. By contrast, those who are only reluctantly militarist, minimize and lament the sexualization of injuring. In order to justify war, they employ a competing, romantic, conception of armed manliness, both hetero- and homosexual. In their planes and ships, as on their battlefields, soldiers participate in a homoerotic romance ("bonding") whose sensual intensity suffuses war memoirs and poetry. The comrade turned heterosexual is no rapist but rather a temporarily celibate though fully sexual partner of the woman and women he excites and defends. As their literature and memories attest, the potentially violent yet vulnerable, dangerous yet restrained protector and warrior is alluring to girl and grandmother, sweetheart and wife.

This restrained sexuality of the just comrade is entwined with ideas of imminent death and sacrifice. The soldier is poignantly and particularly erotic as he becomes one with cause or cadre, relinquishing individual sexual union for the "universal." His romantic death is sacrificial, at best heroic. Yet the ideology of death that serves reluctant militarists sits uneasily with the bodily realities it masks. Ideologically, military dead are warriors although soldiers are at least as able to flee death as the citizens of the villages and cities they bomb and burn. Military deaths are meaningful; the best battlefield death is a courageous, chosen testament to valor. In fact, numerous military deaths are accidental or fratricidal and an individual's death is rarely of even military consequence. A soldier's death is meant to be swift and clean; a sharp sacrifice. In fact, even as death by hemlock is messy and painful in ways philosophical fantasy must obscure, so too dying soldiers, like the assaulted victims who outnumber them, vomit, sob, shit, and scream their life away.

If military thinking must conceive of the body in ways that justify the work of killing and dying, caretakers depend upon a conception that justifies giving birth and sustaining what is born. Like militarists', caretakers' work is done through and with bodies. Mothering begins in some woman's intensely, ineluctably, often shatteringly physical experience. Much caretaking work, including early mothering, is done amidst feces, urine, vomit, milk, and blood. The subjects of care, generally, are physically at risk; their bodies must be tended as they are, not as they romantically might become. Bodies come in various shapes, have distinctive "chemistries," are liable to their own styles of being and acting.

In myriad ways, the subjects of care assert themselves: this physical being is here; whoever cares for me, cares for this.

The omnipresence of bodies does not, for the caretaker any more than for the militarist, guarantee respect for the bodily. Caretakers may deny bodily pleasure in favor of suffering, preparing the way for "heroic" birth and the "sacrifice" of children. For these caretakers, pain, danger, and illness—certainly real enough—morbidly overshadow the exhilaration of even painful childbirth, the erotic experiences of nursing and holding, the wonder of children's healthy bodies, and the frequent beauty of even frail or dying bodies. More aggressively, caretakers may conceive of bodily nature as the "enemy" rather than substance of their work. The concept of body-as-enemy arises when caretakers transform the necessary control of their subjects' behavior into dominating rule in the caretakers' interests. Dominating caretakers may be sadistic or self-interested; they may also be fearful or misguided about the meaning of care. Whatever the motives, the "nature" of the subject threatens the caretaker. A mother or teacher sets herself against what she cannot control. Her own bodily and libidinal "weakness," like that of her charges, must be conquered. Wills must be broken, desires ruled. Bodies that are "deformed," greedy, dirty, aggressive, and lustful must be brought to heel. This is the fascist moment of care.

In maternal thinking, the conception of bodily nature as an enemy partly arises from and certainly abets a fearful preoccupation with sexuality. Caretakers, especially mothers, are expected to deny and repress their own passion—especially if it is not legalized, domestic, and heterosexual—and to simplify or deny their children's. Since mothers are blamed and blame themselves for their own "unruly" sexual lives and for unusual sexual proclivities in their children, they are likely to long for bodies that are asexual, sharply gendered, and well behaved.

However, there is latent in the practice of care, an alternative conception of the sexual body. Mothers and teachers of small children witness, to some extent direct, and are frequently the object of infants' and children's erotic desires. Caretakers themselves experience and control erotic responses to their subjects. As participants in and witnesses to infant-child erotic life, caretakers could welcome eros where it begins. This would mean acknowledging surprising desires, both of their own and of the children they tend. It would mean recognizing rather than repressing expansive, complex ways of being masculine and feminine, so evident in children's and adolescents' lives.

A welcoming maternal sexuality would oppose both the predatory license of the "naturally" aggressive male soldier and the romantically mystified allure of the just warrior. Mothers could control in themselves and discourage in children the sexualization of injury and destruction. The alluring helplessness of a child who is also stubborn and disobedient can be a powerful stimulus to sadistic excitement both for a mother or teacher or for a larger child. But sadism, however understandable, cannot be visited upon vulnerable subjects. More generally, the most welcoming maternal eroticism cannot justify abusive sexual behavior in the name of natural impulse. Small children, ill or disabled adults, or anxiously sexual adolescents demand restraint. Despite the temptation to abuse or to be passive in the face of abuse, caretakers, ideally, discipline their own desires and resist any predatory sexuality by which their subjects are threatened.

While the marauding male soldier is a fearful apparition, the just defender is a quintessential hero. Mothers will not cease to desire the armed yet vulnerable warrior simply by learning to acknowledge the complexities of their own and their infants' erotic life. The lifting of repressive denial offers more modest hopes. In recognizing the complexity of any desire, mothers could subject military romance to critical reflection. Moreover, if they were allowed and accorded themselves desires of their own, mothers would be less in need of the heightened and distant eroticism the warrior figure provides. By opposing the sharpened division of masculine and feminine, so at odds with the vicissitudes of emerging sexual identities, they would undermine a linch pin of military ideology. Most importantly, enjoying in bodily pleasures, one's own and other's, makes sacrifice and transcendence less necessary or attractive.

Whatever the hopes for maternal eroticism, mothers are not embattled as they insist on the right to name and act on their desires at the same time that they struggle for an understanding of sexuality adequate to the moral complexities of care. While a transformed sexuality might fuel the appreciation of bodies, it is at least as likely that maternal conceptions of the bodily will shape the developing conceptions of sexuality.

No more than war deaths are cared-for deaths heroic. Dying bodies stumble, smell, forget, swell, waste away, fester, and shake. But whereas military ideology masks these realities, the practice of care depends upon grasping them accurately. And whereas military strategies grasp the body's vulnerabilities in order to exploit them, caretakers perceive accurately in order to comfort.

The caretaker's regard—a species of attentive love—is a discipline of intellect and action nearly the opposite of the planned cruelty epitomized in the claymore mine or napalm bomb. Any death that results from predictable and avoidable damage to a body—whether from war, poverty, social neglect, or individual abandonment—is a violation of birth's hope. Precisely because of its commitment to beginnings, its basis in trust, the concept of "natality" grasps the betrayal in violent death.

The conceptions of natality and natal death render the caretaker's conception of the body, taken as a whole, antimilitaristic. To be sure, caretakers who fear an uncontrolled "nature" and simplify sexuality play into military hands. When will, bodies, and desires appear uncontrollable, then military discipline can bring them to heel. When sexuality is denied or simplified, the predatory assaultive sexuality of soldiers can be concealed while the allure of the warrior, like the desire of the women who serve him, goes unexamined. Yet there is, in the rationality of care, a sturdy antimilitarist conception of the body. In this conception, the body is not fearful either in its pleasure or in its suffering. Birth is privileged over death, and with that privilege comes a commitment to protect, a respect for ambiguity and ambivalence, a prizing of physical being in its resilience and variety. Bodies are at least as important as the causes that use them. When they are damaged—exploded, burned, poisoned, irradiated, or cut up—no heroic phrases come to the rescue. Although "nature" is, from a caretaker's perspective, "unnaturally" cruel, caretakers assuage rather than abet the cruelty of dying. Caretakers create ways of tending, comforting, and finally, of surviving and mourning, that allow the living to include the dead among them as the real, complicated creatures they were. Real complicated peoples, caring and cared for, do not make good heroes or enemies.

A Word About Politics

It is clear that neither the practice nor the perspective of care assures an antimilitarist politics. Caretakers caught up in daily passions and exhausting details easily ignore the political uses made of their work. Ideology reinforces the temptation to abdicate responsibility. Although caretaking is assertive work, and although caretakers frequently must act in anger, caretakers are expected to defer to the opinions of the "reasonable" and powerful on whose support they in fact depend. In so far as they are political, caretakers are meant to serve as an auxiliary to causes and cadres organized by men. Not surprisingly, many relinquish the right, if not the capacity, for angry independent judgments of public good. The political effectiveness of care depends upon a wider feminist and labor politics that emboldens caretakers—especially women—to judge and organize in the name of care on their own and their subjects' behalf.

Even confident caretakers find it difficult to extend care from the intimate to the public. Women are only now learning to conceive of their *own* communities and states under the aspect of protective and nurturant care. It may seem too simple to ask of a state or cadre what it needs, what practices will really protect and nourish its citizens. But these questions compete with technological, militarist, and heroic assertions of honor and danger. To care for *alien* states or cadres and the strangers in them is still more difficult, requiring patient identification with different "others" in their particularities. Many women who begin by "rescuing our children" come to see violence when any child hungers. Some are able to see even in "the enemy" real "others" with attachments and obligations like their own. This ability may be increasingly widespread in a world that is endangered, as a whole, by the violence that any leaders plan. Nonetheless, extensive sympathetic identification remains a fragile achievement for those whose lives have been shaped by passionate loyalties to their "own."

Suppose that caretakers acted independently in the name of care. Suppose too that they succeeded in the morally and conceptually difficult task of extending the perspective of care from intimate to public. How does a caretaker's politics connect to other bases of antimilitarism? In particular, what is the relation of the politics of care to feminist peace politics? What are the antimilitarist strategies of care? What hope have we that caretakers could affect the entrenched militarism of most states?

These and other questions require a paper of their own. Let me close on a confident note.

For reasons both deep and banal, it matters what women say and do. Women have serviced and blessed the violent while denying the character of the violence they serve. Because they have played their military parts well, women's mere indifference could now matter. With the tacit collaboration of disaffected women, a smaller group of caretakers can invent a language of outrage and love. Already, women are creating care's *rational protest* in urban public squares, rural town meetings, churches and synagogues, peace camps, sanctuaries, and around kitchen tables. From the perspective of care, the imposition of suffering by military force is only one, structurally primary and potentially annihilating, instance of the violation of care. To organize in the name of care is to organize against any bigotry, exploitation, and poverty that does violence to the promise of natality.

The rationality of care seems a prime example of what Foucault called a "subjugated knowledge"—"lost in an all-encompassing theoretical framework or erased in a triumphal history of ideas (Welch 1985, 19)"— "regarded with disdain by intellectuals as being either primitive or woefully incomplete," but liable to become "insurrectionary" (Foucault 1980, 81-82). People everywhere depend upon the work of care. Yet, politically as well as psychologically, it is dangerous to acknowledge that dependence. The obligations and attachments of care conflict with other public obligations and attachments required for the success of abstract causes. As Hegel put it, "the community only gets an existence through the interference with the happiness of the family....It creates for itself in what it suppresses and what it depends upon an internal enemy—womankind in general" (Lloyd 1986, 72). To control women caretakers, contradiction between the work of care and its political abuses is construed as a proper separation of public from private, reason from emotion, male from female, each located within its own sphere. As ideals of reason prove militarist and exclusionary, as women claim speech and battlefields come home, this familiar ideology breaks down, making conceptual and political space for insurrectionary knowledges.

Certainly, a protest in the name of care is only one of many necessary analyses and politics. To make a difference does not require being the only, or even the most important, agent of change. It is sufficient that women caretakers are a potentially subversive element within the militarized societies that depend upon them. Nor do caretakers, themselves changing as they change the world, provide us with "programs" or "ideologies." Caretakers have barely begun to imagine, let alone to achieve, the conditions and disciplines of a caring "peace." What caretakers can announce is that such a peace is the only choice in the face of the nightmare that military protection and honor offers to caring love.

DISCUSSION QUESTIONS
1. To what extent is the fear of open lesbians and gay men in the military based on the fear that the love of comrades-in-arms will be transformed into the "wrong" kind of love? If it were, presuming mutual consent, what would be the result?

2. What are some examples of the ways in which power and dominance have become eroticized in our daily lives? Chapkis, in the recommended readings, suggests that "women's personal social and indeed sexual repertoire must be expanded to include the possibility of dominance and control just as that of men must come to include the possibility of surrender." What are some of the implications of this expansion?

3. What might be some of the implications/effects of men mothering?

4. What might constitute a "protest in the name of care?"

SUGGESTIONS FOR FURTHER READING
Pat Barker. 1992. *Regeneration*. New York: NAL–Dutton.

Wendy Chapkis. 1988. Sexuality and militarism. *Women and the military system*. Eva Isaksson, Ed. New York: Harvester/Wheatsheaf.

Cynthia Enloe. 1983. *Does khaki become you? The militarization of women's lives*. Boston: South End Press.

The Ten Commandments of Womanhood

NINETEEN HUNDRED AND EIGHTEEN

Thou Shalt Not Waste Time, for idleness is shame and sloth a mockery; and lo! the day cometh when thy men shall be called from the harvest and their workshops stand empty and silent.

Thou Shalt Not Waste Substance, for once, thrice and ten times shall thy country call upon thine household for gold, and woe betide the land if at the last thy purses be found bare.

Thou Shalt Not Waste Bread, for every fragment that falls idly from thy board is withheld from the mouths of thine allies' children, and the kits of thy sons and brothers in the trenches.

Thou Shalt Not Bedeck Thyself Lavishly, for the silk upon thy back and the jewel upon thy breast are symbols of dishonor in the hour of Earth's agony and thy nation's peril.

Thou Shalt Not Be Vain and Self-Seeking, for the froward and jealous heart judgeth itself in the sight of the Lord; and in the time of world travail who shall say to her sister, "I did it and thou didst it not."

Hearten Thy Men and Weep Not, for a strong woman begetteth a strong man, and the blasts of adversity blow hard and swift across the world.

Bind Up the Wounds of Thy Men and Soften Their Pain, for thy presence by the light of their campfires is sweet and grateful, and the touch of thy hand deft in the hour of need.

Keep Thou the Faith of Thy Mothers, for in the years of thy country's sacrifice for Independence and Union they served valiantly and quailed not.

Keep Thou the Family Fruitful and Holy, for upon it the Lord shall rebuild His broken peoples.

Serve Thou the Lord Thy God with Diligence, for His houses of worship shall not be empty nor His altars unvisited, in the years of His mighty chastening.

"The Ten Commandments of Womanhood: Nineteen Hundred and Eighteen" was prepared by the President of the Connecticut Congress of Mothers and issued by the Connecticut State Council of Defense during World War I.

THE ARMY WILL MAKE A "MAN" OUT OF YOU
Helen Michalowski

Helen Michalowski provided the following note when this article was reprinted in Reweaving the Web of Life. *"It is important to listen well to these men who have been through it—and made it back. All romantic and dramatic notions of glory, pride and power associated with war must be dispelled as we enter a renewed era of warmaking. Hopefully, a better understanding of the military processes which desensitize and brutalize men will encourage us to prevent the damage all around and to bridge the gulf threatening to widen between women and men."*

These accounts of military training and its reinforcement of the most violent and woman-hating aspects of our culture's ideal of masculinity should not be taken as confined to the military setting. The same messages are provided to boys and later to men in less intentional ways every day. Examples of the latter can be found in James Baldwin's very personal memoir, "Here Be Dragons." His essay reminds us that in a racist society socialization of black males and white males shows significant differences.

Military training merely draws on this tradition for its own purposes. In this way, the priority given to the military in our society has a destructive effect throughout all aspects of our lives, not least with respect to homophobia and misogyny.

Male children are set up to be soldiers. The military takes the attitudes and behaviors already developed in young males and hones them to a fine edge. The attitudes include being emotionally closed, preferring power over pleasure, and feeling superior to women. The behaviors include domination, aggression, and physical violence to oneself and to others.

The military prefers to work on young men who are still unsure of their individual identity and place in the world. In basic training young men are isolated from everyone but people like themselves where they are totally under the control of drill sergeants who conduct a not so subtle form of brainwashing.

Steve Hassna, Army Drill Sergeant:
There's Joe Trainee doing what Joe does best—being dumb. And it's not the man's fault. But it is such a shock to his—to his whole being. You

take that man, and you totally strip him, and then you make him like a big ball of clay, and you take and you make him a soldier. Whether he wants to be a soldier or not, you make him a soldier.

...They taught me in drill sergeant's [school], get the psychological advantage off the top. Remain on top; remain the aggressor. Keep the man in a state of confusion at all times, if you want to deal with him in that way, but do not let him get his thing together so he can retaliate in any way, you know what I mean? If in doubt, attack.

...I was gruff—I was gruff to the point where I was letting you know I am in command. You might as well strike anything in your mind, any feeling, that you are going to do anything but what I tell you (Smith).

Victor DeMattei, Army Paratrooper:

Basic training encourages woman-hating (as does the whole military experience), but the way it does it is more complex than women sometimes suppose. The purpose of basic training is to dehumanize a male to the point where he will kill on command and obey his superiors automatically. To do that he has to be divorced from his natural instincts which are essentially nonviolent. I have never met anyone (unless he was poisoned by somebody's propaganda) who had a burning urge to go out and kill a total stranger.

So how does the army get you to do this? First you are harassed and brutalized to the point of utter exhaustion. Your individuality is taken away, i.e., same haircuts, same uniforms, only marching in formation. Everyone is punished for one man's "failure," etc. You never have enough sleep or enough to eat. All the time the drill instructors are hammering via songs and snide remarks that your girl is off with "Jody." Jody is the mythical male civilian or 4F who is absconding with "your" girl, who by implication is naturally just waiting to leave with Jody.

After three weeks of this, you're ready to kill anybody. Keep in mind there is no contact with the outside world. The only reality you see is what the drill instructors let you see. I used to lie on my bunk at night and say my name to myself to make sure I existed (DeMattei 1978).

In basic training, the man is made an object, dehumanized, subjugated. The system starts to break down when people are seen as people.

Robert McLain, Marine:

Talk to anybody who was going through Marine Corps boot camp...the dehumanizing process is just hard to describe. I wish somebody had a record of suicides that go on at these places...[and] the beatings that go on daily. Boys are turned not into men, but beasts— beasts that will fight and destroy at a moment's notice, without any regard to what they are fighting or why they are fighting, but just fight. I have seen men fight each other over a drink of water when there was plenty for both of them (Lifton 1973).

Steve Hassna:

...I hated that thing of embarrassing a man in front of 40 people. Basic training is such a dehumanizing process to begin with that when you stand there and dehumanize a person in front of his peers, that he's got to sleep with, and in the same building, that's hard. They lose respect for the man.

...But I don't like dying. And killing. It's very weird because I started realizing again, thousands and thousands of men, 18, 19, 20, 22 years old—I'm thinking, Jesus Christ, man, they're gonna kill every swinging dick in the country! You know, there won't be a male American over 25 left standing. I can't—it just—it got to be bodies. I started to get personal with them. Instead of looking at them as Joe Trainee and that was it, I was looking at them as McNulty and Peterson and Nema and Hill and the other thousand that I can't remember. Well, when you do that...it don't set too well. Now it sets even worse because it's taken me seven years to get to the point where I can look back on that and realize—you know, I trained troops. I was a staff sergeant, E-6, with the hat, who trained troops for a year. And probably half of them are dead. And I'll never know (Smith).

The military is a blatant hierarchy. Power and privilege correspond directly with one's rank, but feelings of superiority are encouraged throughout. Especially those men in less desirable, more hazardous assignments are encouraged to feel superior. Inevitably, someone has to be on the bottom. Somebody has to be the scapegoat, the enemy.

Ernie "Skip" Boitano, 9th Division Army:

...The military has this thing where if your platoon sergeant gets down on you and you don't have any kind of karma, something going for you to get him off your back, then all of a sudden the platoon leader and the platoon sergeant start making you the kicking boy of the platoon, then all of a sudden the CO's [commanding officer] down on you. All he hears about you is bad. And the next thing you know, you're up for an article 15 and then you're up for a battalion article 15 because the colonel's heard a lot of bad things about you. He sees you goofing off and he catches you. You don't necessarily have to be doing anything anybody else wouldn't be doing, but because everybody kind of knows who you are negatively, you're it. It keeps building on top of that. It just starts with one person with a little bit of power to get down on you. He can bend someone else's ear and say, "Hey, look at this clown." It may even be that the whole platoon starts working on him. They want to get in tight with the sergeant or they want to feather their cap. So they're all working on this one poor guy. Once these people get down on you, it's downhill from there. There's no getting out from under it....Maybe that's something about people.... I know guys who tried. They went to the field all the time. They did everything they could and it never got any better. It was like somebody got picked out and they put a sign around your neck and from then on everybody just let them have it. Any time they had trouble, that person got it (Smith).

During basic training, the man's insecurity about his own sexuality is manipulated so as to link sexuality with aggression and violence.

Unnamed soldier:

...I [was] very stirred, patriotically [and thought] that I someday was going to have to, do this... That I would get my chance... I remember questioning myself...saying this may all be a pile of crap...this stuff about patriotism and yet because of this indecision...the confusion within myself, I said...I don't think I'll ever be able to live with myself unless I confront this, unless I find out, because if I [do not] I'll always wonder whether I was afraid to do it... I had the whole question of whether I was a man or not...whether I was a coward (Lifton 1973).

Wayne Eisenhart, Marine:

One of the most destructive facets of bootcamp is the systematic attack on the recruits' sexuality. While in basic training, one is continually addressed as faggot or girl. These labels are usually screamed into the face from a distance of two or three inches by the drill instructor, a most awesome, intimidating figure. During such verbal assaults one is required, under threat of physical violence, to remain utterly passive. A firm degree of psychological control is achieved by compelling men to accept such labels. More importantly, this process is used as a means to threaten the individual's sexual identity. The goals of training are always just out of reach. We would be ordered to run five miles when no one was in shape for more than two or were ordered to do 100 push-ups when they and we both knew we could only do 50. In this manner, one can be made to appear weak or ineffective at any time. At this point, the drill instructor, usually screams something in your face like "You can't hack it, you goddamned faggot."

...Once the sexual identity was threatened, psychological control achieved, and sexuality linked with military function, it was made clear that the military function was aggression. The primary lesson of boot camp, towards which all behavior was shaped, was to seek dominance. Our mission was always "close with the enemy and destroy him." To fail in this, as in all else, was non-masculine. Aggression and seeking dominance thus was equated with masculinity. Recruits were brutalized, frustrated, and cajoled to a flash point of high tension. Recruits were often stunned by the depths of violence erupting from within. Only on these occasions of violent outbursts did the drill instructor cease his endless litany of "You dirty faggot" and "Can't you hack it, little girls?" After a day of continuous harassment, I bit a man on the face during hand-to-hand combat, gashing his eyebrow and cheek. I had lost control. For the first time the drill instructor didn't physically strike me or call me a faggot. He put his arm around me and said that I was a lot more man than he had previously imagined. Similar events occurred during bayonet drill. In several outbursts I utterly savaged men. In one instance, I knocked a man off his feet and rammed a knee into his stomach. Growling and roaring I went for his throat. I was kicked off the man just before I smashed his voice box with my fist. In front of the assembled platoon the DI (drill instructor) gleefully reaffirmed my masculinity. The recruit is encouraged to be effective and to behave violently and aggressively (Eisenhart 1977).

Physical violence against troops is more central to basic training in the Marines than in other branches of the armed forces. All branches associate masculinity with insensitivity, invulnerability and violence—only more subtly.

Wayne Eisenhart, Marine and Counselor:

...In [Marine] boot camp, there was a Private Green who had a good deal of difficulty with the rigorous physical regime. He was slender and light complexioned. Private Green was a bright, well-intentioned young man who had volunteered and yet lacked the composite aggressive tendencies thought to comprise manhood. Although not effeminate by civilian standards, he was considered so in boot camp. He was continually harassed and called girl and faggot. We began to accept the stereotyping of him as effeminate, passive, and homosexual.

While in the midst of a particularly grueling run, Private Green began to drop out. The entire platoon was ordered to run circles around him each time he fell out. Two men ran from the formation in an attempt to carry him along. His eyes were glazed and there was a white foam all around his mouth. He was beyond exhaustion. He fell again as the entire formation of 80 men continued to run circles around him. Four men ran from the formation and kicked and beat him in an attempt to make him run. He stumbled forward and fell. Again he was pummeled. Finally four men literally carried him on their shoulders as we ran to the base area where we expected to rest. We were then told that, "No goddamned bunch of little girl faggots who can't run seven miles as a unit are going to rest." We were ordered to do strenuous calisthenics. Private Green, the weak, effeminate individual who had caused the additional exercises, was made to lead us without participating. He counted cadence while we sweated. Tension crackled in the air, curses were hurled, and threats made. As we were made to exercise for a full hour, men became so exhausted their stomachs cramped and they vomited. Private Green was made to laugh at us as he counted cadence. The DI looked at Private Green and said, "You're a weak no-good-for-nothing queer." Then turning to the glowering platoon he said, "As long as there are faggots in this outfit who can't hack it, you're all going to suffer." As he turned to go into the duty hut he sneered, "Unless you women get with the program, straighten out the queers, and grow some balls of your own, you best give your soul to God 'cause your ass is mine and so is your mother's on visiting day." With a roar, 60 to 70 enraged men engulfed Private Green, knocking him to the ground, kicking and beating him. He was picked up and passed over the heads of the roaring, densely packed mob. His eyes were wide with terror, the mob beyond reason. Green was tossed and beaten in the air for about five minutes and was then literally hurled onto a concrete wash rack. He sprawled there dazed and bleeding.

Private Green had almost been beaten to death in a carefully orchestrated ritual of exorcism. In him were invested those qualities most antithetical to the military ethos and most threatening to the sexual identity of the individual Marines. Masculinity is affirmed through aggression and completion of the military function. We had been ordered to run around Private Green in order to equate passivity and nonaggression with being a clear and present danger (Eisenhart 1977).

Basic training not only links sexuality with dominance, aggression and violence, it also teaches that the man's very survival depends upon maintaining these attitudes and behaviors. By associating qualities that are stereotypically considered common to women and homosexual men with all that is undesirable and unacceptable in the male recruit, misogyny and homophobia are perpetuated in the military and in society at large. It is understandable that it would take a long time and a lot of work for men to undo the effects of military training as it pertains to their own male self-image and these images of women and gays.

To my knowledge, no studies have been done to establish or refute a connection between military training/experience and violence against women; however, it seems reasonable to suspect such a connection. The purpose of basic training is to prepare men for combat. That experience certainly affects men in their relationships with other people, especially women.

Robert McLain:

...When I came back home I was very much anti-war, and yet there was a hostility in me toward other people....If someone irritated me, my first impulse was to kill the fucker....I'd catch myself and I'd think of another alternative to deal with whatever the problem was....Today there is still a lot of hate in me—a hatred that makes it difficult to form ...relationships with anyone (Lifton 1973).

Wayne Eisenhart:

...One young veteran I have worked with became completely impotent three years after discharge. Unable to maintain an erection during the last three attempts at intercourse, he was afraid to try again. At this time he purchased a weapon, a pistol, and began brandishing and discharging it. His sexuality was blocked by a frustrated idealized male role which could not tolerate intimacy. The means to affirm manhood was through face to face combat, aggressive behavior, and the seeking of dominance.

...[There] is a constant fear of being harmed by someone and a constant elimination of real or fantasized adversaries in order to maintain a feeling of adequacy and security. My personal experience directly validates this. Since I was not exposed to much combat in Vietnam, I can only conclude that this process originated for me in basic training.

Perhaps this can best be articulated if I share some observations concerning my own intrusive imagery. Generally these take the form of daydreams. They consist of brief, very violent eye-gouging, throat-ripping fantasies revealing an underlying hypermasculine ideal. There is usually a woman involved and I am always dominant and inordinately violent in defeating some adversary. These brief images leave me with a feeling of power and supermasculinity. I usually find that my muscles tense during such imagery....

As a civilian, one generally attempts to create a more authentic masculine self-image that cannot help but be influenced by the military experience. Constantly in social and sexual relationships I have found myself trying to be "heavy," feeling at times foolishly as if I were a caricature of myself. I have striven constantly to achieve dominance. In the past more so than now, I felt insecure sexually and had a very low tolerance for feeling threatened. Occasional outbursts of violence have shamed and frightened me. This all has cost me dearly in social relationships (Eisenhart 1975).

Robert Lifton, Psychologist who worked with Vietnam veterans:

A number of veterans told how, when brushed by someone on the street—or simply annoyed by something another person had done—they would have an impulse to "throttle" or kill him. And they would directly associate this impulse with patterns of behavior cultivated in Vietnam: with "wasting" whomever passed for the enemy, with the numbing and brutalization underlying that behavior, but also with the rage beneath the numbing (Lifton 1973).

Steve Hassna:

...A lot of times I'd wake up in the middle of the night and throw [my wife] out of bed and throw her behind the bunker. And start screaming. She was scared of me. She finally left me. Because I would get to the point where I was so pissed off, I'd tell her, "Don't do it again; don't push me." I didn't want to hurt nobody, but I'd get to the point where I can't relate to people no more and so I just snapped. I was going like this until I realized what it was that sent me to Vietnam, indoctrinated from childbirth, the whole thing, I stopped having these bad dreams. Because I could see it wasn't me that was fucked up, it was my government and my whole society that got me this way (Smith).

Robert Lifton, Psychologist:

Falling in love, or feeling oneself close to that state, could be especially excruciating—an exciting glimpse of a world beyond withdrawal and numbing, but also a terrifying prospect. A typical feeling, when growing fond of a woman was, "You're getting close—watch out!" The most extreme emotion of this kind expressed was: "If I'm fucking, and a woman says I love you, then I want to kill her...[because] if you get close...you get hurt."

...It is possible that he and many others continue to associate the nakedness of sex with Vietnam images of grotesque bodily disintegration—as did Guy Sajer, with memories from the German Army experience of World War II: "As soon as I saw naked flesh [in a beginning sexual encounter] I braced myself for a torrent of entrails, remembering countless wartime scenes, with smoking, stinking corpses pouring out their vitals" (Lifton 1973).

When people are divided into distinct sex roles, the function of the female is to give birth and nurture, while the function of the male is to kill and die. Powerful cultural myths support the idea that the purpose of the son is to be a blood sacrifice—Jesus sacrificed to God the Father, Isaac to Abraham.

There are some parallels between the oppression of women and men according to sex roles. The media/cultural hype is similar—women love being sex objects and men love getting their heads beaten, whether on a football field or a battlefield. The appeal to virtue is similar. Women sacrifice themselves to serving their family, while men sacrifice themselves to the Armed Service. The cover-up is similar. Until recently no one heard about rape or battered women, and no one ever talked about men who come back from war sound in body but emotionally disabled. And who ever talks about the physically disabled?

One wonders if there is a statistical difference between the incidence of women coming to women's shelters who associate with men having had military or para-military (police) experience and those who associate with men not having had this background. Let's interview women—mothers, sister, lovers—who have had before-and-after basic training relationships with men. What if any changes do they notice? Let's also interview women "dependents," particularly military wives. What is their place in the "pecking order?" What kinds of friendships get formed when the family gets transferred every one and a half to four years? Do these women feel isolated? What do they think about the "security" of military life?

Because women have not been in the military in significant numbers until recently, there does not exist a great body of material relating their experience. Let's interview women in the military. Is the training comparable? How do men in the military view and treat women they work with? Women they command? How do women in the military view other military women?

For the last several years women have been recruited to the military in unprecedented numbers; not because the military has any great interest in "equality" for women, but because the male population ages 17–21 has declined by 15%. There is a great and urgent need to deepen and broaden the popular understanding that while women certainly have the right and capability to be soldiers, for women to become like men have been would not be a step toward anyone's liberation.

We have to redefine the word "service" so that it is neither forced nor armed. Rather than women being trained to kill, let men learn to nurture life.

DISCUSSION QUESTIONS

1. What are some personal experiences readers may have had, either in the military or in other situations, that illustrate some of the dynamics Michalowski presents here?

2. To what extent is the process illustrated by the testimonies Michalowski has collected intrinsic to the military idea?

SUGGESTIONS FOR FURTHER READING

James Baldwin. 1985. Here be dragons. *The price of the ticket: Collected nonfiction 1948–1985.* New York: St. Martin's.

Gregory Herek & Kevin Berrill, Eds. 1992. *Hate crimes: Confronting violence against lesbians and gay men.* Newbury Park, CA: Sage Publications. For the parallel use of gay bashing to validate masculinity, see especially ch. 7 (Joseph Harry, "Conceptualizing anti-gay violence"), ch.10 (Eric Weissman, "Kids who attack gays"), and ch.12 (Michael Collins, "The gay-bashers").

FEMINISM AND MILITARISM: A COMMENT
bell hooks

While much of this section has expressed a classic feminist viewpoint about the relations between socialization as girls and boys and the appeal of militarism in society, bell hooks here introduces a note of caution about generalizing this across race and class. She asks whether too essentialist a view of women's opposition to, and for that matter men's propensity to, violence and war may make more difficult the task of dismantling militarism. She also points out the difference between the distinct roles men and women play under militarism—a sexual division of labor—and the generalized acceptance of the framework of militarism as good for the whole of society. If women are purely passive or detached from the system, what power do they have, ultimately, to change it?

In many ways hooks' analysis requires us to accept that racism and colonialism are in themselves forms of violence, and that people of color do not bear responsibility for them. This does not mean, she insists, that they will have no role to play in eradicating racism and colonialism. Rather, she calls for a clear and truthful analysis so that together we may do the work of social change, one that takes seriously women's political choices and power.

As a child growing up in Hopkinsville, Kentucky, with its proximity to Fort Campbell, I thought the army was composed primarily of black men. When I saw soldiers, they were black. I overheard adults talking about black men joining the army to find work, to find the dignity that comes with having a purpose in life. They would say, "better to be in the army than prowling the streets." Yet my father cautioned his daughters about entering relationships with soldiers, telling us "he knew what these men were like—he'd been in the army." There was an aspect of his experience serving in the all-black Quartermasters working supply lines during World War II that had changed him profoundly. After returning home, he showed no interest in travelling to new places, to "foreign" lands. An unexplained, unnamed aspect of that experience made him linger near home. I can remember my surprise when I discovered pictures of him in uniform, pictures taken in foreign places about which he never spoke. Yet he always kept a picture of the black men in his section of the 537th Battalion

"Feminism and militarism: A comment," by bell hooks, published in TALKING BACK: THINKING FEMINIST, THINKING BLACK, *by bell hooks, published by South End Press, Boston, MA. Copyright © 1989 by Gloria Watkins. Reprinted with permission.*

in his room. As children, we often studied the faces of those black men in uniform, looking for him. At age sixty-one, he travelled to Indiana to reunite with his army comrades, to mourn for those dead, to lament that no amount of fighting had brought an end to war.

More than ten years ago, when I first applied to enter college, one school had a special scholarship for relatives of men who had fought in World War I. It was then that I asked my grandfather, Daddy Gus, if he had fought in the war. His voice when he responded was gruff and exasperated, saying, "No. I would have none of war. Why should I have fought in any war. No I never fought nobody's war." Since childhood and into my adulthood, he had loomed large in the landscape of masculinity as a man who truly lived in peace and harmony with those around him— violence was just not his way. His persistent anti-war stance, as well as the anti-war stance of other southern black males in our community who were very vocal about their feelings about militarism (highlighting the contradiction that black men should serve in wars, die for this country, for this democracy, which institutionalized racism and denied them freedom,) impressed me. Their attitudes showed us that all men do not glory in war, that all men who fight in wars do not necessarily believe that wars are just, that men are not inherently capable of killing or that militarism is the only possible means of safety. I have thought of these black men often when I hear statements that suggest that men like war, that men wish for the glory of death in war.

Many women who advocate feminism see militarism as exemplifying patriarchal concepts of masculinity and the right of males to dominate others. To these women, struggling against militarism is to struggle against patriarchy. Rena Patterson argued in her essay, "Militarism and the Tradition of Radical Feminism":

> To prevent war is to fight male power, to expose and defy the pretensions of masculinity, and to recognize and act against the basic principles of operating in all domains of patriarchal-capitalist society.

Introducing her book of essays *Ain't Nowhere We Can Run: A Handbook For Women on the Nuclear Mentality*, Susan Koen writes:

> It is our belief that the tyranny created by nuclear activities is merely the latest and most serious manifestation of a culture characterized in every shape by domination and exploitation. For this reason, the presence of the nuclear mentality in the world can only be viewed as one part of the whole, not as an isolated issue. We urge the realization that separating the issue of nuclear power plants and weapons from the dominant cultural, social, and political perspective of our society results in a limited understanding of the problem, and in turn limits the range of possible solutions. We offer then, the argument that those male-defined constructs which control our social structure and relationships are directly responsible for the proliferation of nuclear plants and weapons. Patriarchy is the root of the problem, and the imminent dangers created by the nuclear mentality serve to call our attention to the basic problem of patriarchy.

By equating militarism and patriarchy, these feminists often structure their arguments in such a way as to suggest that to be male is synonymous with strength, aggression, and the will to dominate and do violence to others; and that to be female is synonymous with weakness, passivity, and the will to nourish and affirm the lives of others. While these may be stereotypical norms that many people live out, such dualistic thinking is dangerous; it is a basic ideological component of the logic that informs and promotes domination in Western society. Even when inverted and employed for a meaningful purpose, like nuclear disarmament, it is nevertheless risky, for it reinforces the cultural basis of sexism and other forms of group oppression. Suggesting as it does that women and men are inherently different in some fixed and absolute way, it implies that women by virtue of our sex have played no crucial role in supporting and upholding imperialism (and the militarism that serves to maintain imperialist rule) or other systems of domination. Often the women who make such assertions are white. Black women are very likely to feel strongly that white women have been quite violent, militaristic in their support and maintenance of racism.

Rather than clarifying for women the power we exert in the maintenance of systems of domination and setting forth strategies for resistance and change, most current discussions of feminism and militarism further mystify woman's role. In keeping with sexist thinking, women are described as objects rather than subjects. We are depicted not as laborers and activists who, like men, make political choices, but as passive observers who have taken no responsibility for actively maintaining and perpetuating the current value system of our society which privileges violence and domination as the most effective tool of coercive control in human interaction, a society whose value systems advocate and promote war. Discussions of feminism and militarism that do not clarify for women the roles we play in all their variety and complexity, make it appear that all women are against war, that men are the enemy. This is a distortion of woman's reality, not a clarification, not a redefinition.

Such devaluation of the roles women have played necessarily constructs a false notion of female experience. I use the word "devaluation" because it seems that the suggestion that men have made war and war policy represents a refusal to see women as active political beings even though we may be in roles subordinate to men, and the assumption that to be deemed inferior or submissive necessarily defines what one actually is or how one actually is continues a sexist pattern that would deny the "powers of the weak," as Elizabeth Janeway labels it. While I think it is important for advocates of feminist movement to continually critique patriarchy, I also think it important that we work to clarify women's political engagements, and not ignore our power to choose to be for or against militarism.

When I hear statements like "women are the natural enemies of war," I am convinced that we are promoting a simplistic view of woman's psyche, of our political reality. Many female anti-war activists suggest that women as bearers of children or the potential bearers of children are necessarily more concerned about war than men. The implication is that mothers are necessarily life-affirming. Leslie Cagan, in an interview in *South End Press News*, confirms that women participating in disarmament work often suggest that because they bear children they have a "special relationship and responsibility to the survival of the planet." Cagan maintains, and rightly so, that this is a "dangerous perspective" because "it focuses on woman's biology and tends to reinforce the sexist notion that womanhood equals motherhood." She explains:

> It may be that some, even many, women are motivated to activism through concern for their children. (It may also be a factor for some fathers who don't want to see their kids blown up in a nuclear war either!). But this simply doesn't justify a narrow and limiting perspective.
> It is limiting because it says that woman's relationship to such an important issue as the future of our planet rests on a single biological fact.

Advocates of feminism who are concerned about militarism must insist women (even those who have children) are not inherently more life-affirming or non-violent. Many women who mother are very violent. Many women who mother, either as single parents or with males, have taught male and female children to see fighting and other forms of violent aggression as acceptable modes of communication that are more valued than loving or caring interaction. Even though women often assume a nurturing, life-affirming role in their relationship to others, performing that role does not necessarily mean that they value or respect that mode of relating as much as they may revere the suppression of emotion or the assertion of power through force. Feminists must insist that women who do choose (whether or not they are inspired by motherhood) to denounce violence, domination, and its ultimate expression—war—are political thinkers making political choices. If women who oppose militarism continue to imply, however directly or indirectly, that there is an inherent predisposition in women to hate violence, they risk reinforcing the very biological determinism that has been the ideological stronghold of anti-feminists.

Most importantly, by suggesting that women are naturally nonviolent, anti-war activists mask the reality that masses of women in the United States are not anti-imperialist, are not against militarism, and until their value systems change, they must be seen as clinging, like their male counterparts, to a perspective on human relationships that embraces social domination in all its forms. Imperialism and not patriarchy is the core foundation of militarism. Many societies in the world that are ruled by males are not imperialistic. Nor is it inconceivable in white-supremacist societies like Southern Africa, Australia, and the United States, that sexist men will support continued efforts to equalize the social status of white women and white men to strengthen white supremacy. Throughout the history of the United States, prominent white women who have worked for women's rights have felt no contradiction between this effort and their support of white Western imperialists' attempts to control the planet. Often they argued that more rights for white women would better enable them to support U.S. nationalism and imperialism.

At the beginning of the 20th century, many white women who were strong advocates of women's liberation were pro-imperialist. Books like Helen Barret Montgomery's *Western Women in Eastern Lands*, published in 1910 to document fifty years of women's work in foreign missions, indicate that these women saw no contradiction between their efforts to achieve emancipation of the female sex and their support for the hegemonic spread of Western values and Western domination of the globe. As missionaries, these women, the vast majority of them white, travelled to Eastern lands not as soldiers but nevertheless armed with psychological weapons that would help to perpetuate white supremacy and white Western imperialism. In the closing statement of her work, Helen Montgomery declares:

> So many voices are calling us, so many demand our allegiance, that we are in danger of forgetting the best. To seek first to bring Christ's kingdom on the earth, to respond to the need that is sorest, to go out into the desert for that loved and bewildered sheep that the shepherd has missed from the fold, to share all of privilege with the unprivileged and happiness with the unhappy, to lay down life, if need be, in the Way of the Christ, to see the possibility of one redeemed earth, undivided, unvexed, unperplexed resting in the light of the glorious Gospel of the blessed God, this is the mission of the women's missionary movement.

Like some contemporary feminists, these white women were convinced that they were naturally predisposed to bring nurturance and care, though in this case it was to non-white countries, rather than to anti-war efforts.

It is still true that men more so than women, and white men more so than any other group, advocate militarism, spread imperialism; that men continue to commit the majority of violent acts in war. Yet this sex role division of labor does not necessarily mean that women think differently than men about violence, or would act significantly different if in power. Historically, in times of national crisis, women fight in combat globally and do not show any predisposition to be more nonviolent. Significantly, war does not simply involve the arena of combat. Wars are supported by individuals on a number of fronts. Ideologically, most of us have been raised to believe war is necessary and inevitable. In our daily lives, individuals who have passively accepted this socialization reinforce value systems that support, encourage, and accept violence as a means of social control. Such acceptance is a prerequisite for participation in imperialist struggle and for supporting the militarism that aids such struggle. Women in the United States are taught the same attitudes and values as men, even though sexism assigns us different roles. At the end of an essay discussing women's participation in war efforts, "The Culture in Our Blood," Patty Walton asserts:

> In conclusion, women have not fought in wars because of our material circumstances and not because we are innately more moral than men or because of any biological limitation on our part. The work of women supports both a society's war and its peace activities. And our support has always derived from our particular socialization as women. In fact, the socialization of women and men complements the needs of the culture in which we live... Men are no more innately aggressive than women are passive. We have cultures of war, so we can have cultures of peace.

Sex role division of labor has meant that often as parents, women support war effort by instilling in the minds of children an acceptance of domination and a respect for violence as a means of social control. The sharing of these values is as central to the making of a militaristic state as is the overall control of males by small, ruling groups that insist that men make war and reward their efforts. Like men, women in the United States learn from watching endless hours of television to witness violence without responding. To fight militarism, we must resist the socialization and brain-washing in our culture that teaches passive acceptance of violence in daily life, that teaches us we can eliminate violence with violence. On a small yet significant scale we should all monitor the television watching of children and ourselves. Since bourgeois women in the United States benefit from imperialist conquest as consumers, we must consume less and advocate redistribution of wealth as one way to end militarism. Women who oppose militarism must be willing to withdraw all support for war, knowing full well that such withdrawal necessarily begins with a transformation in our psyches, one that changes our passive acceptance of violence as a means of social control into active resistance.

DISCUSSION QUESTIONS

1. If women are nonviolent and antimilitarist by virtue of their role as childbearers, what does this mean for lesbians without children? What does it mean for straight women who choose either not to have children, or to remain single altogether?

2. How inescapable is socialization? How do we acknowledge our individual autonomy? How do we avoid blaming others who make their political choices from a different place in the structures of power? How do we build alliances with them?

3. In particular, how do we relate to women, especially women of color, who see the military as their best choice for creating a space for themselves in a racist, patriarchal society?

SUGGESTIONS FOR FURTHER READING

Cynthia Enloe. 1989. Nationalism and masculinity. *Bananas, beaches and bases: Making feminist sense of international politics.* Los Angeles: University of California Press.

Janet Radcliffe Richards. 1990. Why the pursuit of peace is no part of feminism. *Women, militarism & war: Essays in history, politics, and social theory.* Jean Bethke Elshtain & Sheila Tobias, Eds. Savage, MD: Rowman & Littlefield Publishers.

Amy Swerdlow. 1990. Motherhood and the subversion of the military state: Women Strike for Peace confronts the House Committee on Un-American Activities. *Women, militarism & war: Essays in history, politics, and social theory.* Jean Bethke Elshtain & Sheila Tobias, Eds. Savage, MD: Rowman & Littlefield Publishers.

MILITARISM AND VIOLENCE

History

SEXUAL DISSIDENTS AND THE NATIONAL SECURITY STATE, 1942-1992
Richard Cleaver

The following essay presents a brief overview of the history of lesbian and gay organizing efforts in the United States since the 1940s, with an eye to showing how the constraints of organizing inside a militarist society have shaped that history.

The author raises one caution. Formal organizations are not, and have not been, the only or even necessarily the primary way in which most individual lesbians, gay men and bisexuals have ordered their lives. Such organizations have generally been more important to white and middle-class individuals than to others who love members of their own sex. Furthermore, by the nature of class in the United States, middle-class activity is better documented than working-class activity. Throughout the period of time covered below, there has also been a working-class subculture of lesbians, gay men and bisexuals. Therefore this sketch should not be taken as relating the experience of all women who love women or all men who love men.

With the cold war over, a new attack on the entertainment industry is now afoot, which seeks to define once again what is American and what is un-American....And from the sound of what I am hearing, gay men and lesbians have become America's new Communists.—Representative Ted Weiss, June 1992.

More than half a century has passed since the Japanese attacked Pearl Harbor on December 7, 1941. At the end of this half century, the military power of the United States of America is unsurpassed. Yet U.S. military and foreign policy—they are virtually the same thing—continue to be shaped by the events of a Sunday fifty years gone. As the 20th century nears its end, our policy decisions are still made as if the greatest danger to world peace were an attack on the United States rather than an attack by the United States.

The result is a political and social system distorted by fear and ruled by secrecy. Because the distortion is justified by the slogan "national security," the system is sometimes called "the National Security State."

The same decade in mid-century that saw the creation of the National Security State also saw the beginnings of a political and social movement of lesbians and gay men. With varying intensity during the intervening five decades, this movement has itself been portrayed as a threat to the security of the nation and its institutions, especially the family. The

This article was written expressly for this collection, July–November 1992.

collapse of the "Red menace" at the end of the 1980s has forced the political actors who used to get and keep power by invoking the Soviet threat to cast about for replacements. What better candidate than those the McCarthy era persecuted as openly as Communists?

Meanwhile, the lesbian/gay/bisexual movement's goals, tactics, and language are hotly debated. A glance at history reveals that they always have been. Often the debates have been directly related to the larger ideology of the National Security State within which the movement has had to claim space.

This essay is a brief exploration of these interactions. It will survey the large-scale developments in lesbian/gay organizing since Pearl Harbor, placing them in the context of U.S. politics in general and the State's reaction to the presence of lesbians and gay men in the body politic in particular.

Two of the author's premises had better be laid out at once.

First, persecution may have played at least as large a role in forming the group identity we now name with the terms "lesbian" and "gay male" as such other, more widely-noticed factors as the increased capacity for alternative living arrangements afforded by industrial capitalism, or medical explanations of sexuality. Certainly these last were necessary prerequisites. But they do not explain why a vigorous emancipation movement for homosexuals arose in Germany as early as 1900 but could not, despite some attempts to transplant it to the United States, take root here until after World War II. Nor do they explain why a similar movement is only now beginning to appear in another modern industrial society, Japan. These questions are not academic: they point to lessons on how contemporary political and social change activists conceive of our tasks. Much more study of late nineteenth and early twentieth century interactions between U.S. militarism, gender anxiety and sexual subcultures is needed, as is cross-cultural study of sexuality and its changing meanings through modern history, before we can hope to answer these questions.

Second, the National Security State requires a high level of conformity from its subjects. As the demands of national security, militarily defined, have taken a more or less central role in the political life of this country in the past half century, so the pressure to conform has been more or less influential in shaping the strategies and goals of lesbian, gay and bisexual movement.

The National Security State

The term National Security State has most often been applied to military dictatorships in Latin America, which are usually regarded as wholly different from the United States political system. The National Security State has taken an especially vicious form in Chile under Pinochet or in Argentina during the time of the "dirty war," to pick only two examples out of many. But the underlying ideology originated in the United States and was deliberately exported to Latin America, primarily by an extensive program of officer training for Latin American military and police personnel at such institutions as the School of the Americas and the Inter-American Defense College.

Marcus Raskin has summarized three basic assumptions underlying the creation of the National Security State: "[1]the United States is under continuous siege from enemies real or potential, but mostly conjured....[2]America's place in the world is primarily achieved through military and covert means....[3]the United States can never be at peace, [but] must always be involved in some kind of military or paramilitary activity that it initiates and controls." In short, those who in the late 1940s designed the institutions that make up the National Security State "presumed a world inhabited by Enemy Others" (1992, 777).

Since World War II, the military establishment has had first claim on national resources. This in turn has required reorganizing the economy. Seymour Melman (1991) has called it "military state capitalism." The magnitude of the change has been hidden in two ways. First, the outward political forms have been observed. Second, the mantra "national security" has been drafted to account for the changes that do get noticed, as well as to cover a multitude of hidden crimes and misdemeanors.

National security, of course, has been defined in purely military terms: such notions of security as women's ability to go out after dark without fear of rape, or universal access to adequate medical care or housing, are not part of the definition. Neither unemployment, infant and maternal mortality, nor illiteracy has generally been regarded as a threat to national security as defined by the National Security State.

In 1959, C. Wright Mills described the consequences with perfect clarity:

> Peace is no longer serious; only war is serious. Every man and every nation is either friend or foe, and the idea of enmity becomes mechanical, massive, and without genuine passion. When virtually all negotiation aimed at peaceful agreement is likely to be seen as "appeasement," if not treason, the active role of the diplomat becomes meaningless; for diplomacy becomes merely a prelude to war or an interlude between wars, and in such a context the diplomat is replaced by the warlord (206).

THE FOUNDATIONS OF THE NATIONAL SECURITY STATE

To build the National Security State, previously unknown institutions of government were needed. The National Security Act of 1947 created a "National Military Establishment" (renamed the Department of Defense in the 1949 amendments to the Act) that brought the old War and Navy Departments under a single "Secretary of Defense." The Act also established three new institutions: the Joint Chiefs of Staff, the Central Intelligence Agency and the National Security Council.

This bureaucratic expansion made a large standing army possible for the first time. Our political tradition had previously viewed permanent professional armed forces of more than token size with suspicion, ever since the billeting of a standing army on the colonies had been denounced as one of George III's royal crimes. The Army was filled by the first true peacetime draft, under the Selective Service Act of 1948, which was made permanent by the Universal Military Training and Service Act of 1951. Finally, the Armed Services Procurement Act of 1947 gave the National Military Establishment the authority to negotiate, and monitor compliance with, "defense" contracts—the foundation for Melman's military state capitalism.

These acts of Congress were supplemented by executive branch regulations. Among these was Executive Order 9835 of March 1947, which set up a loyalty screening process that eventually extended well beyond Federal employment and into the broad arena of "defense" contractors. President Truman's order was superseded in April 1953 by the newly-inaugurated President Eisenhower's Executive Order 10450. This expressly included "sexual perversion" as grounds for denying employment. As many as 12.6 million Americans were subject to loyalty and security tests under these regulations, that is to say more than 20% of the workforce (D'Emilio 1983, 46).

In *Pentagon Capitalism* (1970), Seymour Melman has chronicled the extension of Department of Defense control over more and more of what is rather erroneously called "private" industry (a "well cultivated fiction," in Melman's phrase). Because they were singled out under the "sexual perversion" heading, this extended government control had a particular impact on lesbians and gay men at the very historical moment when they were struggling to come to a political understanding of themselves and their place in this newly militarized society. The issue of Civil Service discrimination was to become a rallying point for homophile activists a decade later.

Two other developments in the building of the National Security State need to be mentioned.

February and March 1950 produced NSC 68, "a top-secret strategy paper prepared under the auspices of the secretaries of state and defense" (Barnet 1990, 285). This document posed the mission of the U.S. military as the reversal of political developments of the late 1940s in Eastern Europe and Asia, a doctrine known as "rollback." NSC 68 finally put into official—if secret—policy the need to put the United States on a permanent wartime footing. It also spoke clearly of the need for shaping public opinion so as to guarantee that Congress would appropriate funds for this mobilization.

Another cornerstone of this edifice, one that still affects lesbians and gay men, was the McCarran-Walter Act of 1952. This act regulated immigration and naturalization, and was a followup to Senator Pat

McCarran's 1950 Internal Security Act, which stigmatized "member[s] of immoral classes." Both acts were passed over President Truman's veto. McCarran-Walter prevented the admission to the United States (even temporarily) of subversives and people "afflicted with a psychopathic personality," a phrase which was considered to cover homosexuality. McCarran-Walter deliberately made a juridical connection between the danger of Communist infiltration and the danger of sexual infiltration, a connection that stood in U.S. law until 1989 and that continues to hamper travel to the United States by lesbians and gay men, now under the pretext of AIDS prevention.

THE FOUNDATIONS OF LESBIAN AND GAY MOVEMENT

While efforts to create political pressure groups to address the problems of homosexual people (to use the common pre-war language) were made in this country during the 1920s and 1930s, none survived long. The mass mobilization of World War II, in place by 1942, created a new context for organizing. Salvatore Licata (1981, 166) has put it this way: "The government's identification and labeling of thousands of individuals marked a new institutional position. For the first time, homosexual men and women became a statistically and socially designated minority." The continuous history of organized homophile or lesbian/gay or queer movements (to note in passing some of the terms used in those movements) dates from 1945, when World War II veterans began to organize around discrimination arising from the so-called "blue discharges."

In late 1945, two events occurred that sparked resistance among homosexual women and men who had served in the armed forces during World War II. The Metropolitan Veteran's Benevolent Association was founded in New York City by four gay men as a kind of mutual aid society to help in the transition to civilian life. This organization, which lasted until 1954, eventually involved as many as 50 members.

Meanwhile, in October 1945, the *Pittsburgh Courier*, an African-American newspaper with a nationwide readership, began a campaign to look into "blue discharges"—discharges that were other than honorable (though not dishonorable). These were printed on special blue paper, with notations disclosing the reasons for withholding honorable status. Discharge status, then as now, was important in determining eligibility for various benefits. It also had strong implications for employability. African-Americans had a disproportionately high rate of blue discharges. The *Courier* pointed out (Bérubé 1990, 233) that the discharge was often retribution for "bona-fide resentment to racist treatment." The campaign was explicitly inclusive: the newspaper declared it was "fighting for the rights of the 37,000 white veterans involved as well as for those of the 10,000 Negroes involved." Many of these veterans, black and white, had received blue discharges for being homosexual.

Political activity of this kind by homosexuals as homosexuals, focusing on a particular, concrete grievance that could be challenged within existing ideas of equal justice, was new in this country. It had been made possible by the experiences of women and men who desired same-sex relations during the wartime mass mobilization. These experiences, as Allan Bérubé has described them in *Coming Out Under Fire*, were quite varied, some positive, some negative. Within the newly expanded military establishment there was a range of attitudes toward such women and men, ranging from the most rigorously punitive to the most liberally psychiatric.

The "blue discharge" was only one result of this confusion, but during the immediate postwar period, when mass demobilization was assumed to be the goal, it was the principal grievance. Once the decision to maintain a large peacetime military establishment had been made, it became necessary to create a more consistent and smooth-running set of policies on all aspects of military discipline. The needs of small military forces with limited missions and accordingly limited budgets are no longer adequate in times of mass mobilization, especially when that mobilization is considered to be a permanent state of affairs. (This permanent war footing also required a greater conformity among civilians—indeed, it blurred the distinction between military and civilian personnel.) Thus the haphazard approaches of wartime and immediately thereafter had to be brought in line with a single policy uniformly enforced. This process was completed in 1950 by the Uniform Code of Military Justice. With respect to "homosexuality" the policy has remained unchanged. "Homosexuality," says Department of Defense Directive 1332.14, "is incompatible with military service."

SELLING MILITARISM

The postwar move to favor the military establishment in the nation's priorities was resisted, although after fifty years it is difficult for many of us to imagine a time when such a shift was considered an ominous departure from American values. It is important to emphasize that militarism, understood as the system of political, economic and personnel structures that make up the National Security State, is a new development in U.S. history.

We should distinguish here between militarism and imperialism. For much of our history, expansion was possible with a very small standing Army raised without conscription. Often imperialist designs were accomplished with no overt military action at all. This is not to deny that imperialism is a longstanding feature of U.S. history. The United States themselves, after all, are constructed on land stolen from the first inhabitants of this continent. Certainly once President Jefferson completed the Louisiana Purchase, the expansion of United States control over additional territory became a constant of U.S. policy.

If, however, we consider *overseas* expansion by the United States as the beginning of U.S. imperialism—it was during that thrust in the 1890s when the term "imperialism" became a staple of political discourse in this country—it is noteworthy that it came at the same time that many people were alarmed about the "feminization" of the American man now that the Western frontier had been declared closed. Teddy Roosevelt's cult of manly vigor, recapitulated in the Kennedy years, illustrated this trend. The Boy Scouts of America, which at the time of this writing is embroiled in controversy over its exclusion of gay men and atheists, was another institutional expression of this fear (Hantover 1980; Macleod 1983). Worry about the "feminization" of the American male has surfaced more than once in the interim: it was again a staple of the feature pages of U.S. newspapers in the late 1980s.

Policy makers who pushed for the changes that became the structure of the National Security State during and immediately after World War II (most of them appointed officials of the Executive branch who had seen their power grow immensely under emergency wartime arrangements) worried about the danger of failure. The danger was twofold.

First, public opinion was overwhelmingly in favor of a swift and nearly total demobilization. Second, the end of the war meant a return to prewar power disputes between Congress and President. A Republican Congress was elected in 1946 on a platform of thrift and smaller government. The Democratic Truman administration knew that to get Congress to go along with plans for a permanent military establishment, they would (in the words of Senator Arthur Vandenberg) have to "scare the hell out of the country."

The effort succeeded all too well, as *U.S News and World Report* noted in 1948:

> War scares, encouraged by high officials only a few weeks ago, so alarmed the...U.S. public that top planners now are having to struggle hard to keep Congress from pouring more money into national defense than the Joint Chiefs of Staff regard as wise or necessary. It is proving more difficult to turn off than to turn on a war psychology (Borosage 1970, 46-7).

Very true: forty-five years later it still has not been turned off.

HOMOSEXUALITY AND THE POLITICAL USES OF FEAR

The scare strategy was launched as society was changing. Women who had never expected to work for wages had found well-paid jobs in war industries, and the independence that went with them. Despite a strong propaganda effort after the war to persuade women that they really wanted to go back to domesticity, not all did. A racially-segregated military had fought for Democracy against Fascism, and many African-Americans decided it was time the fine phrases of the war rhetoric became a new daily reality in the United States. Economic hardship accompanied the reconversion of manufacturing, rekindling memories of the Depression and increasing union membership.

In addition, many women and men who left home during the war had discovered that desires they thought were theirs alone were shared by many others. The gay bars, the military-sponsored "soldier shows" involving cross-dressing, the social circles formed for protection and mutual support, and the gender-segregated landscape of their lives during the war all contributed to a firmer, more broadly based sense of identity and community for people who were learning to call themselves "gay."

Despite postwar efforts to put the genie back into its bottle, such knowledge could not be unlearned. Furthermore, it was shared by many women and men who returned to heterosexual relations after demobilization. When Alfred Kinsey published *Sexual Behavior in the Human Male* in 1948, the point of no return was passed. The publication was greeted by howls of outrage. The scare was on along the sex front.

Three points need to be made about this use of fear.

First, the threat of social disintegration (in the eye of certain beholders) has classically created a reaction from those who benefit by the existing social arrangements. One equally classic response has been to use the threat of an external enemy to deflect internal social conflict. Such a "rally round the flag" campaign was at full force in the late 1940s and early 1950s. Fear was the primary tool of such campaigns.

Second, although the official enemy was the Soviet Union, a choice made more plausible by events in central Europe and east Asia during the late 1940s, for day-to-day fear such a distant enemy was less useful than an internal one. Most of the energy of organized anti-Communism went toward ferreting out secret infiltrators or dupes of the Communist Party. The result was a cloak-and-dagger atmosphere of which the sensational trials of Alger Hiss and of Ethel and Julius Rosenberg were only the most visible expression. The prominence of Communist party activists in the social change coalitions of the 1930s made such an atmosphere very easy to create, since there were many people in the country who had had some contact with such coalitions.

Third, it is important to note that fear of Communism has never quite been able to stand alone. Red scares are not uncommon in our country's history, but in a culture as impatient with explicit ideological discussion as ours, panics over Red infiltration have really only taken off when anti-Communism could be combined with other fears closer to home. Through most of our history this has meant some form of agitation against immigrants, often of an explicitly anti-Catholic or anti-Semitic kind.

Earlier Red Scares, however, came during or just after periods of high immigration. The late 1940s and early 1950s were not such a period, so traditional Nativism was of little utility except in such circles as the resurgent Ku Klux Klan and the John Birch Society. Many of the most vociferous anti-Communists were Catholics, traditionally the target of

Nativist attacks. Furthermore, some who were working diligently to build the National Security State, like Edward Teller, were immigrants themselves. Anti-Semitism, too, although still widely practiced, for example in real estate covenants and club memberships, had become slightly less respectable after the liberation of the Nazi death camps.[1] The McCarran-Walter Act, mentioned above, did trade on the connection of Communism and foreigners, and the deportation power has often been used to punish dissidents, not only during the McCarthy period.

Given the attempts to enforce a return to a gender-based prewar division of labor, and given the increasing visibility of homosexuals as a result of the wartime mobilization, the budding gay world was a prime candidate for twinning with Communists as an internal threat.

It was certainly large enough, if the Kinsey reports could be trusted. The figures seem reasonable so soon after the mass wartime mobilization; the numbers for women were probably too small if anything. Half of men and nearly a third of women reported some erotic response to members of their own sex. More than a third of men and a sixth of women reported sexual contact to orgasm with members of the same sex. How many men who had turned to their buddies for sexual comfort on a remote Pacific island saw in those figures some safely buried past incident rising up to haunt a happy suburban married life? What might happen if the contact were discovered by wife, employer or business partner?

What did happen to those who were discovered was indisputable: they were purged as ruthlessly as Communists, probably in larger numbers. Although the "blue discharge" issue brought to light as early as 1945 how difficult it was for many people known to be homosexual to find work, homosexuals as co-conspirators with Communist infiltrators inside the government did not become a public issue until 1950.

THE PEURIFOY DIVERSION

It was raised on February 28 of that year by John Peurifoy, Deputy Undersecretary of State in charge of internal security. Three weeks earlier, a heretofore relatively obscure Wisconsin senator named Joseph McCarthy had made a sensational charge before a Wheeling, West Virginia, Republican women's club. Brandishing a piece of paper whose actual

---

[1] Those in the concentration camps who bore the pink triangle (gay men) or the black triangle (lesbians) did not benefit from these revelations. Most were regarded by all sides as common criminals and none received any compensation for decades. In fact, the constitutional court of the Federal Republic of Germany in 1957 upheld the constitutionality of the Nazi "novella" of June 28, 1935, which added homosexual thoughts to the acts traditionally forbidden under German law. It was the (Communist) German Democratic Republic that first repealed the anti-gay law, in 1968. The Federal Republic followed in 1969. It is worth noting that current (1992) U.S. military policy also stigmatizes homosexual thoughts, rather than requiring evidence of any particular behavior for discharge purposes.

contents are still unknown, he declared that it contained the names of 205 (or 57: accounts differ) Communists working in the State Department.

Peurifoy, summoned to testify about this before a Senate committee, may have dropped his bombshell as a way of turning aside McCarthy's charge. Asked about the dismissal of State Department employees for security reasons since 1947, Peurifoy said that there had been 91; but most of them were homosexuals, rather than Communists.

If Peurifoy hoped to indicate that the State Department was not really a haven for Communists, the tactic failed. His distinction between different undesirables was overrun by the politicians.

In April, Guy Gabrielson, Republican national chairman, sent a letter to party workers which warned (according to *The New York Times* [Katz 1978, 141]), "Perhaps as dangerous as the actual Communists are the sexual perverts who have *infiltrated* our government in recent years [italics mine]."

On June 7, the Senate ordered a full-scale inquiry that resulted in the report, "Employment of Homosexuals and Other Sex Perverts in Government." This document was released on December 15, 1950. The committee's view of its mandate was hardly impartial. It listed as one of its tasks "to consider reasons why employment [of homosexuals] by the Government is undesirable" (Arno 1975, 1). Note that they considered "why," not "whether."

The report admitted that the presence of homosexuals in Government employment had not caused concern in the past. "The subject as a personnel problem until recently has received little attention from Government administrators and personnel officers" (Arno 1975, 1). The Committee blamed such a scandalously laissez-faire attitude on "the false premise that what a Government employee did outside of the office on his own time, particularly if his actions did not involve his fellow employees or his work, was his own business" (Arno 1975, 10).

The report took the view that it was dealing with a conspiracy. Not only are homosexuals security risks as individuals (a highly inaccurate account of a case from pre-World War I Austria-Hungary providing their only evidence) but they have an ominous propensity to favor one another as company: "if a homosexual attains a position in Government where he can influence the hiring of personnel, it is almost inevitable that he will attempt to place other homosexuals in Government jobs" (Arno 1975, 4). Note the similarity of this charge to Guy Gabrielson's use of the term "infiltration." In both cases there is an implication of outsiders moving into a previously unsullied environment. Gabrielson's tentative "perhaps" found no echo, however, in the Senators' certitudes. "One homosexual can pollute a Government office" (Arno 1975, 4).

In July, *New York Post* columnist Max Lerner took a closer, and for the time unusually skeptical, look at the scare. His July 17 column recounted an interview with the Republican floor leader of the Senate, Nebraska's

Kenneth Wherry, sometimes called "the Merry Mortician" from one of his pre-Congressional jobs. Wherry told Lerner (Katz 1978, 146–8), "You can't hardly separate homosexuals from subversives. Mind you, I don't say every homosexual is a subversive, and I don't say every subversive is a homosexual. But a man of low morality is a menace in the government, whatever he is, and they are all tied up together." Interestingly enough, Wherry repeatedly refused to tell Lerner exactly what kind of man he was after. "You can handle it without a definition," he said at one point. Later he insisted, "I'm not going to define what a homosexual is." Whoever "they" were, however, "we should weed out all of them—wherever they are on the government payroll." Wherry appealed to the interviewer on this point, "But look, Lerner, we're both Americans, aren't we? I say, let's get these fellows out of the government."

Wherry's vagueness was perhaps not wholly genuine. The less clear we are about the enemy within, the easier it is to sweep out anyone at all. Gabrielson had used the same tactic of indirection: "The country would be more aroused over this tragic angle of the situation if it were not for the difficulties of the newpapers and the radio commentators in adequately presenting the facts, while respecting the decency of their American audiences"(Katz 1978, 141). Like Joe McCarthy brandishing his mysterious list of Communists, not even the number of whom was clear, refusing to define clearly the nature of the threat made the threat more, not less, credible. We are more afraid of what we don't know than what we do.

The Peurifoy incident and its aftermath set the terms of the debate over access to government employment for a quarter century to come. The debate provided the fledgling organizations of gay people with a specific injustice they could use to rally support. At the same time, it fostered a climate that chilled the groups' willingness to be too insistent. We will examine the result below. Before we do, however, it is appropriate to look a bit more closely at why this tactic was so enduringly successful, especially since at the close of the war, as at several points since, homosexual people had some reason to believe that social conditions might be changing in their favor.

LOYALTY AND SEX PERVERSION

That sexual dissidents should be scapegoated alongside political dissidents is less surprising than it first appears. By the early 1950s, the security of the State had come to be defined as the highest good, and loyalty, defined as the opposite of dissent, had become the standard of citizenship. Once these values become paramount, any group of people who are seen as representing the Enemy Other can be attacked.

In most documents of the period and since, the main reason given for denying lesbians and gay men public employment (along with the many private-sector jobs requiring security clearances) has been the danger of blackmail. Yet the argument is curiously feeble. Blackmail only becomes a danger when homosexual behavior has already been defined as beyond the pale. The steps taken in the late 1940s and 1950s made blackmail more worthwhile, not less, since they increased the negative consequences of discovery. Defining "sexual perverts" as undesirable in any job affecting national security at the same time as the proportion of all jobs falling into that category increased, made exposure much worse than it need have been. The very people and policies that raised the alarm about blackmail were the ones that worked to make blackmail more likely.

This counterargument was made almost from the start, and not only by gay people themselves. Perhaps because of its transparency, the blackmail argument has never been regarded as sufficient among hard-core opponents of lesbians, gay men and bisexuals. It has served, rather, to preface a more complex argument which has been repeated and refined throughout the period of the National Security State, if sometimes only within right-wing circles.

These circles are fixated on two continuing concerns: the disaster that would result from any change in the gender, racial, or class arrangements of society, and the need to rely on the use of force to impose those arrangements inside and outside the United States. In short, the specter of blackmail and disloyalty is a tool of the supporters of militarism.

One of most widely circulated of the early antihomosexual broadsides was by one Countess R.G. Waldeck. Her article "Homosexual International" was apparently reprinted in several places: the version used here appeared in *Human Events*, a right-wing weekly, on September 29, 1960. Her major argument was that an international conspiracy of homosexuals has existed through time, a "homosexual international" that works secretly to subvert governments.

> Welded together by the identity of their forbidden desires, of their strange, sad needs, habits, dangers, not to mention their outrageously fatuous vocabulary, members of this International constitute a world-wide conspiracy against society. This conspiracy has spread all over the globe; has penetrated all classes, operated in armies and in prisons; has infiltrated into the press, the movies and the cabinets; and it all but dominates the arts, literature, theater, music and TV.
>
> And here is why homosexual officials are a peril to us in the present struggle between West and East: members of one conspiracy are prone to join another conspiracy. This is one reason why so many homosexuals from being enemies of society in general, become enemies of capitalism in particular (453).

One of the things that most upset the Countess was the relative ease with which homosexuals seem to cross class lines in pursuit of pleasure. "This dangerous mixture of anti-social hostility and social promiscuity inherent in the vice inclines them towards Communist causes" (455).

Waldeck also associates homosexuals with foreign courts, a traditional bugbear of American political rhetoric. It is worth remembering, since the State Department was one of McCarthy's principal targets, that the linkage of diplomacy with whispering secrets in the perfumed salons of Europe has often been used in this country to ridicule negotiation in solving international conflicts. Real Americans, more manly and direct than Europeans, rely on warfare instead.

The Countess's arguments were to resurface in the rhetoric of the Right beginning in the late 1970s, as we shall see. By that time, they were a bit shopworn; in the 1950s, they were generally, though not entirely, effective in repressing any movement toward greater sexual diversity.

The establishment of the National Security State brought a slowing of social progress. Instead the period saw conformity strengthened, discipline imposed—both of these being thought of as antidotes to Communist "licentiousness" especially as regards the family—and society organized more efficiently for military purposes.

The issue of family structure was of particular importance at a time of conflict over the expulsion of women from wage work to make way for returning male soldiers. Returning women soldiers were expected to want to marry. Those who did not, especially if they wished to remain in the military, were ruthlessly purged. Allan Bérubé and John D'Emilio have written vividly on this in "The Military and Lesbians during the McCarthy Years" (1984).

EFFECTS ON GAY MOVEMENT

Naturally, the increasingly rigid climate of conformity had its effect on the budding organizations of gay people (women and men both used the term to refer to themselves at this period). Some organizations disappeared entirely, although the members often joined newer groups, like those in the Metropolitan Veteran's Benevolent Association who became the League and then, in 1955, the Mattachine Society of New York (MSNY). It may be that the association of civil rights and Communism had some effect on the short lifespan of the Knights of the Clock, an explicitly interracial group founded in Los Angeles in 1950. This group, disbanded in 1953, was described in a 1956 survey of organizations of homosexuals as follows: "Its aims were to promote fellowship and understanding between homosexuals themselves, specifically between other races and the Negro, as well as to offer its members aid in securing employment and suitable housing. Special attention was given to the housing of interracial couples of which there were several in the group" (Cutler 1956, 93).

At the time, such anti-racist activity around the country was routinely denounced as Communist, and met with violence and arrest. How this affected the Knights is unclear; very little information is available about the group and the attention it has received is skimpy. Three members, however, went on to become founders of *ONE*, about which more later.

The groups that did survive faced bitter struggles over goals, tactics and even the definition, and self-definition, of their constituencies. Some of the struggles were openly about Communist influence. Others reflected the pressures of organizing in the intensely conformist atmosphere of the newly militarized society.

Of these struggles, that within the Mattachine Foundation, which led eventually to its replacement by the Mattachine Society, has been well documented elsewhere (e.g. Adam 1987, D'Emilio 1983, Licata 1981, Marotta 1981, and more personally Timmons 1990). For our purposes it must suffice to note that Harry Hay, whose brainchild Mattachine was, had been a Communist Party worker in California. This was known to the other original Foundation members, some of whom indeed had some involvement in left groups themselves.

As the group grew, however, and as the anti-Communist climate worsened, newer members were shocked to learn of this connection and mounted a concerted movement to purge the group of Communist influences. This culminated in a "constitutional convention" held in April 1953. Changes made then headed the organization in a more innocuously conformist direction, although contradictions remained. By the mid-1950s, Mattachine insisted, "POLITICALLY, the Mattachine Society is strictly non-partisan. It espouses no 'isms' except Americanism, for it realizes that such a program is possible only in a free nation such as the United States of America. It opposes Communism....It believes in EVOLUTION, not REVOLUTION"(Cutler 1956, 43).

To a certain extent, the emphasis on purging Communist influence was a cover for other issues, closer to home and thus harder to discuss openly. Some of these were nothing more, or less, than personality conflicts. Others were organizational.

But some of the disputes revolved around fundamental differences in understanding who the people coming together were and what goals they were organizing to achieve, issues that remain charged and divisive today. One of the most Marxian things about Mattachine was the founders' assertion that homosexuals constituted a minority group within society, a class that could and should struggle alongside others for a new society. This analysis remained a feature of the purged Mattachine, at least in theory.

Such a view was by no means universal among Mattachine members, much less gay people in general (it still isn't). In its membership pledge, the Mattachine hinted at a less progressive view: "While it is my conviction that homosexuality in our society is not a virtue but rather a handicap, I believe that I can live a well oriented and socially productive life." This was to be achieved, according to the pledge, by reforming one's own conduct, "try[ing] to observe the generally accepted social rules of dignity and propriety at all times...in my conduct, attire and speech" (Cutler 1956, 14).

This strategy of making lesbians and gay men more acceptable in order to win freedom—which of course is a separate issue from how "variants" conceive of themselves, although a related one—loomed large in most statements of purpose during the 1950s. Mattachine spoke of educational activities "toward the members of the variant minority, emphasizing the need for the definition and adoption of a personal behavior code which will be above criticism from anyone. This will eliminate most—if not all—the barriers to integration." The Daughters of Bilitis, whose "Aims and Purposes" described it as "A women's organization for the purpose of promoting the integration of the homosexual into society," gave first place to "[e]ducation of the variant...to enable her to understand herself and make her adjustment to society in all its social, civic and economic implications"(Cutler 1956, 104).

In a society that saw itself as the Leader of the Free World, so perfect that all other societies were to pattern themselves after its example, there was little place for any program of social change. The conformity imposed by a permanent war footing instead placed the burden on individuals to shape up and fit in. It is hardly surprising that the same debate should have reemerged with bitter force in the 1980s, a similarly triumphalist—and anti-Communist—period in U.S. history.

The language used at the time reveals some of the skittishness felt by some in the new movement. The term "homophile" avoided the sexual connotations of the word "homosexual." Similarly, many writings from the period use the term "sex variant," downplaying the magnitude of differentness. Both terms represent a concession to conformity that was to be rejected with scorn by a later generation of "gay" and "lesbian" activists.

Such euphemisms were not universally adopted, however. There was already, in fact, a debate over what would in time come to be called lesbian and gay pride, a debate which still continues.

A prominent location for the rhetoric of pride was the pages of *ONE* magazine. *ONE* grew out of the ferment in the early Mattachine. Although it certainly had no clearly definable "house line," many articles spoke disparagingly of the timidity of other groups. In August 1958 it printed "I Am Glad I Am Homosexual" by Hollister Barnes. The article began with a reference to the horror expressed by some participants in the April 1953 Mattachine convention on hearing another attender say, "I am proud of being a homosexual." Barnes goes on to denounce the anti-sexual attitude of those who would today be called "assimilationists," while speaking approvingly of an attitude of defiance toward social pressures that "has an almost anarchistic quality that is yet as American as the 'hot dog.' It is in the spirit of that old Colonial flag, emblazoned with a rattlesnake and the motto, 'Don't tread on me.' This is the individualism of the queen, flaunting makeup and a bracelet or two in the face of an amused or embarrassed public" (7).

The author goes on to ask, "Are such persons [those who claim to be proud] really serious in their views? Do they mean what they say, or are their words but a form of compensation for hurts and insults they may have endured? That we should ask such questions shows the very depth of the infection we have suffered through centuries of religious and other propaganda." The article ends on a defiant note. "Let no one think we don't mean business, or intend to enforce our rights."

Allowing for differences in language, this 1958 manifesto could be the product of a 1990s Queer National. It is poles apart from the official line of the homophile organizations, but it suggests that the line was not universally subscribed to.

Another major struggle in the 1950s had to do with women's autonomy. From the beginning, lesbians participating in Mattachine, *ONE* and other groupings found, as their sisters continue to find, that men's concerns and needs grabbed first place on the organizational agenda. As a result, the number of women participating was often much smaller than that of men, although in many cases the women who did participate played vital, and visible, roles.

The founding of the Daughters of Bilitis in San Francisco in 1955 gave women a room of their own in the homophile house. Predictably, men in putatively mixed groups complained about women "splitting" the movement, and DOB's magazine, *The Ladder*, often devoted space to explaining why women needed to organize on their own. Nevertheless, in the relatively small world of homophile organizations, DOB remained a visible and well-connected participant, and membership overlap between it and mixed groups was not unknown.

Unknown at the time, "informants had actually infiltrated DOB in the 1950s and were supplying the FBI and CIA with names of the organization's members. The FBI file on DOB stated, as though the mere fact in itself were evidence of the organization's subversiveness, 'The purpose of [DOB] is to educate the public to accept the Lesbian homosexual into society.'" (Faderman 1991, 149). Male and mixed organizations also were subjects of FBI scrutiny, not only in the 1950s but for decades thereafter (Gregory-Lewis 1977, D'Emilio 1982). Although the existence of such surveillance is rarely discussed openly, it is hardly inconsistent with conditions of organizing under the National Security State.

The 1950s, then, were not unlike more recent decades in the struggle. By 1955, at the latest, virtually all the questions that still shape lesbian and gay politics had been raised. Were those beginning to build this movement "homosexual," "homophile," "variant" or "gay," and did the latter term include "lesbians?" Were these people, whatever they called themselves, a minority, or maladjusted—and who could answer that question better, themselves or "objective" experts? Should they be trying to make themselves as inconspicuous as possible, or to build support among the powerful, or to insist on their rights as citizens of a democracy? What kind of organizations would best achieve what kinds of goals? These are questions of identity, of strategy, of language, all of them still hot in the movement today. Many disputes were submerged under the necessity of trying to keep organizations alive in a period of extreme hostility; but once some degree of organizational stability had been achieved, they would break out in fierce debates in the 1960s.

MILITARISM IN THE KENNEDY YEARS

The election of 1960 was framed as the coming of age of the generation that had fought World War II. President Kennedy brought with him a cult of youthful vigor and virility. He also brought a more confident militarism than the somewhat ambivalent approach of the fiscally conservative Eisenhower administration.

The picture of Kennedy as a militarist is at odds with 1990s nostalgia. There is not space in this paper to give a detailed refutation of the myth; those who need further convincing should consult Marcus Raskin's essay, "The Kennedy Hawks Assume Power from the Eisenhower Vultures" (1970). Here we must be content with indicating two features of Kennedy militarism that set it apart from the previous decade.

The first was his enthusiastic embrace of counterinsurgency warfare. This was signaled by his appointment of Maxwell Taylor, a disgruntled general of the Eisenhower era, as his personal military advisor, and later as ambassador to South Vietnam.

Taylor believed the United States had configured its military strategy too heavily toward fighting a full-scale war directly against the USSR, at the expense of equally pressing concerns elsewhere. A corollary to this was his view that the United States was too cautious in using military force to deal with these other arenas of conflict. His evidence for this was the 1954 fall of Dienbienphu, a French stronghold in (significantly) Vietnam. The French had asked for U.S. intervention to help keep their colony; Eisenhower had refused. Guided by the Dulles brothers—Allen, the head of the CIA, and John Foster, Secretary of State—he thought covert action would be sufficient and require less taxation.

Taylor knew the latter to be true. "Without making a specific estimate, one may be sure that the total bill will exceed any peacetime budget in United States history," he wrote (Raskin 1970, 90). "But," as Raskin explains, "in exchange for this bill, we would, [Taylor] thought, be able to deter general war and win local war quickly."

The embrace of counterinsurgency (which would reemerge in the 1980s, with refinements based on experience, as Low Intensity Conflict, the main doctrine of the U.S. military establishment in the post-Cold War period) was institutionalized in three National Security Action Memoranda signed by Kennedy in 1962. The first, NSAM 124 (January 18, 1962) established a cabinet level Special Group (Counterinsurgency). The second, NSAM 177 (August 7, 1962) empowered the Attorney General (the

President's brother Robert[1]) to train foreign police "in appropriate less developed countries where there is actual or potential threat of internal subversion or insurgency." This policy continues today, for example under the guise of "drug wars" assistance to Colombia, where the police are complicit in the murder of gay men and lesbians under their so-called "social purification" campaign. The third memorandum, NSAM 182 (August 24, 1962) created an "Overseas Internal Defense Policy." The term "overseas internal defense" is interesting (it turns up again, this time as "foreign internal defense," in a Pentagon Training and Doctrine pamphlet in 1986). The implication is that intervention in the internal affairs of other countries is an integral part of the "defense" of the United States. And if that is so abroad, why not even more so here at home?

The second feature of Kennedy-style militarism can be seen in the choice for Secretary of Defense, Robert McNamara. McNamara came from Ford Motor Company, with a reputation as a good manager: Richard Barnet (1977, 119) called him "the leading specimen of *homo mathematicus.*" His tightening of Pentagon procedures, especially in the area of procurement, had far-reaching effects on the whole of the U.S. economy, as Seymour Melman's *Pentagon Capitalism* explores in detail. This attitude of efficiency, part and parcel of the new broom atmosphere of the Kennedy administration, gave militarism a boost. Raskin again:

> War was a natural extension of bureaucratic decision making. It was the life of the state—purposive, rational, and not wasteful. Weapons were not for show; they were for use—unless threat proved to be enough. This view represented a significant change from the policies of the Eisenhower administration, which saw threat value in the brandishing of nuclear weapons but did not envision fighting wars with them. Indeed, there were no war options under the Eisenhower administration once nuclear weapons were introduced against the Soviet Union. (The war plans of Eisenhower's administration were described by Herman Kahn as a wargasm.) While [Secretary of State John Foster] Dulles talked like a brinksman, his military policies did not match his words. The great change in switching over to the Kennedy national security theory was that policy makers thought that nuclear weapons could be used as an instrument of war fighting. Thermonuclear war was no longer "unthinkable" as Eisenhower had said, or mad (1970, 72-3).

McNamara embodied the assumption that the problems of cold-war international relations were technical problems to be solved by competent management. The resulting antidemocratic attitude was clear: "We have more facts than you, and for reasons of national security we cannot share them with you. Leave matters of war and peace to the experts."

This did not mean that the people were not given a role in the brave new world. The most famous phrase of Kennedy's inaugural address laid

---

[1] Robert Kennedy had served in the 1950s as counsel to Senator Joseph McCarthy's Permanent Subcommittee on Investigations for two separate periods.

the role out: "Ask not what your country can do for you; ask what you can do for your country." For many young people, some of them homosexually inclined, these words sounded a clarion call to action. In a few more years, of course, it would be action of a stripe not envisioned by any President.

The slogan's altruistic ring concealed its continuity with the previous decade's emphasis on suppressing dissent for the greater good of a threatened society: that is, for the enlistment of the whole populace in the war against Communist subversion. The fear of Communism, and of the social unrest that was Communism's domestic sidekick, was still very much a feature of the early 1960s. This was, after all, the age of the backyard bomb shelter, a powerful emblem of fear and of "family values."

The cult of action went hand in hand with a style that emphasized vigor and manliness. Only later was the Kennedy brothers' obsession with heterosexual prowess to be common knowledge. The TV footage of touch football games in Hyannis Port contrasted with the more sedate golfing vacations of the Eisenhower years. Combined with their coverup of the young President's debilitating back problems, except when they could be framed as a manly dismissal of pain, the media thereby created an image of the administration as a center of athletic masculinity. This too goes hand in hand with a tendency to devalue open, democratic debate: football teams are notoriously not democracies. Swift action in response to a challenge leaves no time for politics.

The other side of this coin is a contempt for negotiation as a weak, and especially a feminine—and when proposed by men in government, an effeminate—course of action. An essay by a former junior administration official, Marc Feigen Fasteau, "Vietnam and the Cult of Toughness in Foreign Policy," (1975) describes this attitude in detail, particularly as it was played out in the bitterest legacy of Kennedy militarism, the United States invasion of Southeast Asia. This complex of counterinsurgency warfare, then as now usually referred to rather reductively as the "Vietnam War," actually involved overt or covert (to people at home) U.S. military activity not only in Vietnam but in Laos, Cambodia and on a smaller scale in Thailand, Burma and the Philippines. As it shaped every kind of activity in the United States for nearly a decade in the late 1960s and early 1970s, so it was to shape the homophile movement and its lesbian and gay liberation successors.

THE HOMOPHILE MOVEMENT DURING THE AGE OF THE BOMB SHELTER

The atmosphere of vigor and manly activity that surrounded Kennedy militarism had its effect on the homophile movement, especially in regard to the debates on purposes and tactics. Hearing the call to action and looking to the example of the civil rights movement (with which the Kennedy administration maintained uneasy relations at best), some lesbians and gay men pushed for a more active approach to anti-homosexualism (to use a term from the period), as opposed to an educational and behavior-modification focus. The goal of such action, unlike the early movement's interest in creating a distinct gay culture, was that of making it possible for gay people to "ask what you can do for your country." Barbara Gittings, editor of *The Ladder* and founder of DOB New York, later described the change: "During the movement of the 1950s, homosexuals looked inward, focusing on themselves and their problems; and they sought tolerance, understanding. In the 1960s, we looked outside ourselves for the roots of the trouble" (Teal 1971, 39).

Part of the difference was generational, although survivors of the fifties, like Gittings, continued to take part on all sides of these debates. Kennedy had appealed to youth, and homosexual youth took him up on it.

Their elders did not welcome them with open arms. Fearful that the presence of young people in their groups would lay them open to charges of "recruiting," if not outright child molesting, the more established homophile organizations would not allow young people to join them. One such young man was Randy Wicker. Even after reaching the required age for joining MSNY, he maintained the Homophile League of New York he had founded in the meantime: this gave him a base for actions MSNY considered too militant. By mid-decade, young people had founded a number of new groups, including the first Student Homophile League, founded at Columbia University in October 1966 and chartered by the university in April 1967.

In 1964, the various east coast groups came together as ECHO (East Coast Homophile Organizations) which approved increasingly activist measures, not without controversy: DOB New York felt it necessary to withdraw from formal affiliation over the change in strategy, although many if not most DOB members continued to work with ECHO as individuals.

During this period, *The Ladder* (whose editors were on the activist end of the question) printed a series of back-and-forth articles between DOB member Dr. Florence Conrad (1965) and Mattachine Society of Washington president Dr. Franklin Kameny (1965). The debate was ostensibly over the role of research as a goal for homophile organizations, but in reality it was about tactics. Conrad felt that homophiles could not speak for themselves to the general public and be taken seriously. Objective experts were needed to lend authority to the movement's civil libertarian goals. (The two did not disagree on this characterization of the movement's goals, and both used the Black civil rights movement to bolster their arguments.) Kameny insisted that offering members of homophile groups as objects of study by academic experts in hopes of increasing tolerance in the wider society was a waste of time. His point was that homosexuals themselves were the experts and didn't need more information. Proclaiming this forthrightly was necessary not only to gain the ear of possible straight allies, but also to gain and keep homophile organizations' respect among the closeted. Kameny did not shrink from using the word "militancy" to describe his position.

Kameny had founded the Mattachine Society of Washington (MSW) after losing a suit against the government for reinstatement in a civilian job as an astronomer for the Army Map Service, from which he had been dismissed in 1957. The year Kameny lost, 1960, Fannie Mae McClackum won her case in the United States Court of Claims, eight years after she was dismissed from the Air Force Reserve. She did so, however, on the basis that no proof of her being lesbian had been offered (Faderman 1991, 155).

Civil service policies in general and the issue of security clearances for lesbians and gay men in particular were important rallying points for organizing in the 1960s. This is not surprising, since Kennedy militarism had defined citizenship in terms of what one could do for one's country, and the needs of the country in terms of countering "Communist" insurgencies, it was logical for lesbians and gay men to seek validation of their full participation in society by trying to join the military establishment. Using "patriotism" as proof of political worthiness has a long tradition; it was to surface again in the early 1990s in connection with the war against Iraq.

MSW began picketing the Civil Service Commission, and in 1965 ECHO instituted what became a yearly Fourth of July picket at Independence Hall in Philadelphia. This sparked a heated debate about the value of picketing, which was seen by its opponents as a confrontational and extreme form of action, more likely to alienate potential straight allies than to win sympathy.

The West Coast saw a parallel development of militant politics. In 1961, José Sarria, a popular drag entertainer whose act consisted largely of scenes from opera edited to create a clear flavor of what would soon come to be called "gay pride," ran for San Francisco supervisor in 1961. His candidacy was a reply to several recent city elections in which candidates had run on anti-homosexual, "save San Francisco for family values" platforms. Also in San Francisco, the Society for Individual Rights was founded in 1964 as an activist alternative to the homophile groups. The Council on Religion and the Homosexual took to the city's streets around the same time. By then local San Francisco politicians felt it wise to appear at gay groups' candidate nights.

Similar approaches were being adopted in southern California. In particular, a group of young people later referred to as "Morris's minions," after activist Morris Kight who played a leadership role from the mid-sixties on, devised a number of actions designed to increase gay visibility and protest police brutality. A group called PRIDE, which stood for Personal Rights in Defense and Education, organized a series of demonstrations in 1967 around an incident of police brutality at a bar called the Black Cat.

As the decade wore on, gay activism on both coasts took on an explicitly antiwar flavor. Kight formed the Dow Action Committee in 1966 to protest the manufacture by Dow Chemical of the napalm used against civilians in Vietnam. Many of the same people participated in the Peace Action Council demonstration of June 23, 1967, against President Lyndon Johnson. Meanwhile, the Homophile League of New York staged a protest at the Whitehall Street military induction center on Thanksgiving 1967.

This change from efforts to win admission to the military establishment to militant protest against it marked a turning point as the movement entered its next phase.

The shift within the homophile movement reflected developments within U.S. society as a whole, most notably the growing opposition to U.S. military involvement in Southeast Asia. There is no space here to describe this in detail. It will have to suffice to note that as in the legend, Camelot (as the Kennedy years were described at the time) degenerated into social strife whose effects are still being played out, and whose meanings are still at issue, a quarter of a century later.

On August 7, 1964, Congress had passed the so-called Gulf of Tonkin resolution, which gave President Johnson a blank check to use military force. He raised the number of U.S. military "advisors" during that year from 16,000 to 23,000. The following year saw Operation Rolling Thunder, an attempt to force North Vietnam to withdraw support for the National Liberation Front in the South by carpet bombing civilian as well as military targets in the North. The failure of this tactic led to the calling up of U.S. reserve units later in 1965, and eventually dramatic increases in the number of young men conscripted into the regular Army, as the number of ground troops committed to South Vietnam took on the dimenstions of a U.S. invasion.

Richard Nixon was elected president in 1968 at least in part on the strength of his claim that he had a secret plan to end the war, combined with the fact that the Democratic candidate was Hubert Humphrey, a liberal cold-warrior (he had introduced legislation in Congress in the early 1950s to prepare camps for interning suspected Communists) who as Vice-President was implicated in Johnson's war policies. Once President, Nixon not only increased the violence used inside Vietnam, but expanded the war into neutral Cambodia as well.

These policies were the foreseeable outcome of Kennedy administration militarism, which saw Vietnam as a kind of laboratory for Maxwell Taylor's ideas. Indeed, Taylor had described it as such in testimony to Congress in 1963: "Here we have a going laboratory where we see subversive insurgency, the Ho Chi Minh doctrine, being applied in all its forms" (Klare & Kornbluh, 1988, 12). The Fasteau article mentioned above describes the investment of personal masculinity in the policy by the men who devised it. This investment prevented them from abandoning the "experiment" even when it became obvious, as it quickly did, that it was a failure. The failure was a result of false assumptions; but the policy makers' commitment to heterosexist masculinity made them unable to recognize the falsity.

Ironically, this took place at a time when women and sexual dissidents were increasingly refusing to accept the dictates of that same heterosexist masculinity.

THE GAY LIBERATION ERA

During the night of June 28-29, 1969, patrons of a bar called the Stonewall Inn, on Sheridan Square in New York's Greenwich Village, refused to play their assigned roles in the ritual of a pre-election vice-squad raid on gay bars in the neighborhood. Instead, they barricaded police inside the bar. Disturbances continued in the neighborhood for two more nights. The incident has come to be called the Stonewall Rebellion, and is now sometimes described as the beginning of "the gay rights movement."

This attribution is in the nature of myth rather than history; as we have already seen, civil rights were already the goal of a longstanding movement. Its mythic nature is thrown into relief by the equally ahistorical reluctance of later activists to recognize that the people who resisted at Stonewall were hardly the kind of people they would have chosen as representatives of "the gay community," had they been in a position to choose. The resisters were mainly people of color, both African-American and Latina/o; they were very young (many too young to be in a bar); many were homeless and supported themselves by prostitution; and many were cross-dressers. Furthermore, the nearly unanimous opinion of the respectable, middle-class homophile activists at the time was that the Stonewall richly deserved to be raided.

Nevertheless, the resistance did become a myth, and as such a cultural and political fact. The main significance of the event was as a catalyst for tendencies already present in the homophile movement. After Stonewall, things moved very rapidly and the number of movement activists increased geometrically, as well as geographically.

The language changed to reflect the new Stonewall sensibility. The homophile movement quickly became the gay liberation movement. (*Come Out!*, a radical gay paper of the time, called the term homophile "a genteel bastard word.") The change also reflected the broader social climate. While the term "gay" had been in use for quite some time, becoming generally current among both women and men by the end of World War II, it had remained in the nature of insider argot, and the general unfamiliarity of non-gay people with its private meaning served as a kind of camouflage.

The new activists, however, had no patience with anything clandestine, nor had they any patience with such terms as "homophile," "homosexual,"or "sex variant." Claiming, not altogether accurately, that these were terms imposed by the oppressor, they insisted on transforming private language into public proclamation. This was of a piece with their general strategy of openness and defiance, summed up in the slogan, "Out of the closets and into the streets!"

This in turn was a reflection of the larger shift on the Left from "liberal" approaches to "revolutionary" ones. This shift was based on a distinction between working for the betterment of others—the "liberal" approach—and fighting for one's own liberation—the "revolutionary" approach (Marotta 1981, 100).

Immediately after Stonewall, a group of the more militant activists who seceded from the established New York homophile organizations came together with newly radicalized young gay people to form the Gay Liberation Front (GLF). Other groups with the same name sprang up around the country (this author helped found one at Amherst College). The name was a frank tribute to the radical politics of the times: it echoed the National Liberation Front, the official name of those forces opposing the U.S.-supported government in South Vietnam. Thus it aligned the new movement with The Movement, the opposition to the war in Southeast Asia. As noted before, many GLF activists had already participated in that movement, and they worked to elaborate a political theory that would connect the oppression of gay people with that of Blacks, Vietnamese, and other groups in the United States and abroad.

The name also demonstrated the indebtedness of these activists to what was coming to be called the "women's liberation" movement. In the immediate post-Stonewall period the gay movement spoke a clearly anti-patriarchal language. Gay men thought of themselves as embodying a new kind of identity at odds with masculinity as it was then defined. The first issue of *Come Out!* presented GLF's analysis this way:

> Because our oppression is based on sex and the sex roles which oppress us from infancy, we must explore these roles and their meaning....Does society make a place for us...as a man? A woman? A homosexual or lesbian? How does the family structure affect us? What is sex, and what does it mean?
>
> What is love? As homosexuals, we are in a unique position to examine these questions from a fresh point of view (Marotta 1981, 101).

This was consistent with contemporary counterculture styles of dress and deportment, which had a distinctly "effeminate" quality even among non-gay males. The internal reality and the structure of power were another matter, as would soon appear.

Also inherent in the Gay Liberation Front idea was the need to build coalitions with other groupings of the oppressed. At that historical moment, coalition building meant working out relations with the Black Panther Party, which had become a symbol of liberation struggle within the United States. The history of the often turbulent and contradictory relations of Gay Liberationists and Panthers in various parts of the country deserves to be explored more thoroughly. For our purposes the important thing to note is that, at least in some places, the two groups worked together, if not always comfortably. The most visible sign of this was an open letter from Huey Newton, Supreme Commander of the Black Panther Party, which supported such collaboration and went so far as to say that "a person should have freedom to use his [sic] body in whatever way he wants to....[T]here's nothing to say that a homosexual cannot also be a revolutionary. And maybe I'm now injecting some of my prejudice by saying that 'even a homosexual can be a revolutionary.' Quite the contrary, maybe a homosexual could be the most revolutionary" (given in full in Teal 1971, 170-1). Appearing first in *The Black Panther* on August 21, 1970, the letter was quickly reprinted in underground and gay papers everywhere.

This strategy of coalition building was not unchallenged. Tensions over the issue led, in New York, to the founding of a new group by activists who withdrew from GLF (although in practice individuals continued to relate to more than one group). This new formation called itself the Gay Activists Alliance (GAA). Its constitution, approved December 21, 1969, listed four basic rights. These were (1) the right to our own feelings, (2) the right to love, (3) the right to our own bodies, (4) the right to be persons. These were to be secured by focused action "repudiating...violence (except for the right of self-defense) as unworthy of social protest, disdaining all ideologies, whether political or social, and forbearing alliance with any other organization except for those whose concrete actions are likewise so specifically dedicated" (Teal 1971, 127).

Arthur Evans, one of the GAA founders, explained this last limitation in an interview published in 1972:

"We have to have our identity. We don't have our identity yet. The gay community isn't a community yet." [Evans] adds that until gays achieve this sense of being a people, they cannot form alliances with other oppresssed peoples. Those GLF groups that call for gays to unite with the other oppressed in society fail to recognize this, he believes (Tobin & Wicker 1975, 197).

The course adopted by GAA was widely criticized at the time as less militant than that of GLF. In fact, Evans's point of view is nothing more or less than what is now known among progressives influenced by Latin American liberation theology as "conscientization," using Brazilian educator Paulo Freire's term. In any case, GAA soon became much more publicly visible than GLF. It also perfected an important array of tactics of nonviolent direct action, most notably the "zap."

The zap consisted of quick, unexpected and very audible appearances at political meetings, on television, and the like. The problems associated with zapping targets not usually considered political fair game were carefully debated in advance. In one notable case, *Harper's* magazine was visited October 27, 1970, after it published an article by Joseph Epstein containing some especially offensive anti-gay passages. Such tactics, though their history is forgotten, still characterize such groups as ACT UP and Queer Nation.

Not surprisingly, the choice of nonviolent action was questioned by some. This too reflected a growing romance of armed struggle flourishing on the Left. While armed groups of gay liberationists seem never to have materialized, and while GAA itself carefully excepted self-defense from its discipline of nonviolence (something most nonviolent activists would not have approved) debate raged over whether adopting nonviolence merely reinforced stereotypes of the passive homosexual.[1] In assessing this debate, it is important to note that agents of the Alcohol, Tobacco and Firearms Division of the U.S. Treasury Department urged a government informant they had hired to infiltrate the movement in Washington, D.C., to "incite commune members to make bombs and molotov cocktails" (Gregory-Lewis 1977a, 12).

There was yet another kind of division among early gay liberationists, described by Toby Marotta (1981) as cultural vs. political. In a nutshell, the division was between those activists who chose to develop a new counterculture that would eventually supplant the oppressive system currently in place, and those who felt that taking on the power structure right now would lead to the beginnings of change. This division, overt or hidden, persists to the present. Both positions had their strengths and drawbacks, as the 1970s would demonstrate.

There was a nationalist position as well. One expression of it was a plan, never realized, to take over sparsely populated Alpine County in California to provide a kind of gay homeland. Such ideas were not new: an article by Leo Ebreo in the December 1965 issue of *The Ladder* (4–8) drew a series of parallels between Zionism and the homophile movement. Significantly, it was titled, "A Homosexual Ghetto?" Both the name and the idea were to become current in several U.S. cities in the ensuing decade.

The tone of the early 1970s can be summarized as one of lively ferment. There was a mood of optimism that saw the proliferation of groups and publicity as evidence that gay liberation was around the corner. Gay liberationists saw themselves as a kind of vanguard among the anti-capitalist anti-militarist and anti-masculinist circles in which most of them moved.

ALARUMS & DIVERSIONS IN THE SEVENTIES

There were, of course, sobering times to come, not only in the gay liberation movement but on the Left as a whole. Many of the problems that soon began to appear were shared by the peace movement as well. Some reflected the logical development of parallel progressive movements,

---

[1] The debate on nonviolence has surfaced more than once since, and is taken up later in this collection.

principally second-wave feminism. Some other problems were self-generated, often because long-range implications of choices made were not adequately examined, or movement history and its lessons ignored. Naturally, some were matters of personality and some are inherent in the life-cycle of any social change movement. Only a few of these will be noted here, largely as they continue to affect movement choices today, and as they reflect the particular constraints of trying to make change inside a patriarchal and militarized capitalist state.

Before doing so, however, it is worth raising a question we do not yet have enough information to answer. That is the extent and effects of goverment-sponsored infiltration of the gay liberation movement. There is a reasonable tendency to regard such questions as a form of paranoia. On the other hand, the success of the FBI's counterintelligence program (known as COINTELPRO) in destroying the Black Panther Party is well-documented. In a two-part series that appeared in *The Advocate* in 1977 Sasha Gregory-Lewis revealed that gay liberationists were regarded as allies of other "subversive" elements that the Federal government is known to have targeted. This is not the only evidence of such activity; we noted earlier the FBI's surveillance of the Daughters of Bilitis. This whole area deserves much more study. Care must be taken, however: the fear of infiltration, or charges about individuals and groups, can be just as damaging as the reality. Lillian Faderman reminds us of Betty Friedan's 1973 claim (in *The New York Times*) that "lesbians were sent to infiltrate the women's movement by the CIA as a plot to discredit feminism" (Faderman 1991, 212).

Government spying on citizens, however well we have been trained to ignore its operation in the United States, is a standard feature of the National Security State. People of all political stripes have tended, regrettably, to personalize this issue. For some, the FBI's obsession with keeping files on subversives (with special attention to their sexual practices) was merely a quirk of J. Edgar Hoover's. For others, the continuity over time of certain operatives working together for the CIA and other agencies implies a conspiracy of individuals outside the normal channels of government.

The more mundane reality is that the definition of "security" as State security, rather than the safety of individual citizens or groups of citizens, lies at the heart of the National Security State as an institution. Once this definition has been accepted as the highest responsibility of the organs of state, and once a large bureaucracy has been put in place to carry out that responsibility, and once rooting out subversive activity by citizens of the State has been assigned to this bureaucracy—all three of which developments were complete before 1950 and remain largely unchallenged today—then spying on dissident groups, the use of provocateurs to incite anti-State acts, and disinformation about the whole become not aberrations or subversions but routine tasks of government.

In the early 1970s the debate over women's autonomy, simmering ever since the middle 1950s, boiled over. Women in gay liberation groups named the problems they encountered in working day by day with gay men, and raised the need for those men to share power within the groups. This in turn often meant looking at who defined which issues were to be addressed in political organizing. Ultimately the nature of lesbian oppression, its relation to gay men, and the self-definition of the gay liberation movement were at the heart of the disputes.

During the first months after Stonewall, women's consciousness-raising groups within GLF and other groups decided to withdraw and organize independently. This was hardly surprising, since the same dynamic was taking place throughout the Left as part of the dramatic resurgence that has come to be called the second wave of feminism.

The tensions of working in mixed-gender groups led Del Martin, one of the founders of DOB who had long asserted the need for separate women's organizations, to declare her independence in *The Advocate*. Her article, published in Fall 1970, covered many of the grounds for this. "After 15 years of working for the homophile movement—of mediating, counselling, appeasing, of working for coalition and harmony...I have...been forced to the realization that I have no brothers in the homophile movement." She bid goodbye to

> all those homophile organizations with an open-door policy for women. It's only window dressing for the public and in the small towns of suburbia, for mutual protection. It doesn't really mean anything and smacks of paternalism....Goodbye to all the 'representative' homophile publications that look more like magazines for male nudist colonies....Goodbye to the gay bars that discriminate against women.....Goodbye to the Halloween Ball, the drag shows and parties....Goodbye to the male homophile community. 'Gay is good,' but not good enough—so long as it is limited to white males only. We joined with you in what we mistakenly thought was a common cause... (Teal 1971, 187-8).

Martin's declaration encapsulates many of the levels of difference women were finding with their gay liberationist brothers. "Common cause" too often meant that issues affecting men came first on the agenda, while issues identified by women were left for later. Much of gay men's style offended lesbians, whether it involved drag—which many women experienced as mockery—or, as it would in a few years, veneration of the most repressive of masculine icons. The overt sexual expression among gay men, which became more pronounced after Stonewall, was also distasteful.

Over the decade of the 1970s, more and more lesbians came to make the same declaration of independence from gay men. Those who continued to work in mixed groups, at least occasionally, often found that they had to face bitter opposition even to gain explicit acknowledgement of their presence, as when many local organizations spent enormous time and energy debating whether to change their name from Gay such-and-such to Gay and Lesbian such-and-such. In many cases, the women who achieved such a name change were so burned in the struggle that the renamed organization in fact had few, if any, lesbians participating.

For a time, some gay liberationist men took the side of lesbians. Many of these men, as the *Come Out!* article cited above indicated, had come to see themselves as dissidents against the straight male structures that women were also fighting against. They refused to identifiy themselves as "men" under the current definitions. Some called themselves "effeminists." While this strain of gay male activism has continued to the present, it has become fairly marginal except for the Radical Faerie movement (which had more complex historical roots).

Instead, as the decade continued, gay male style took a different turn, one that might not have been expected given the Stonewall soil in which it flowered. This style became well enough known outside gay male circles that it produced a new stereotype of the gay man as a white, urbane trend-setter with plenty of disposable income. Like all stereotypes its general applicability is doubtful. The new style was to be found largely in the new "gay ghettos" that took shape during the 1970s in a few cities: San Francisco, New York and Los Angeles preeminently; to a lesser extent in Boston, Chicago, Philadelphia, Washington, D.C.; and correspondingly less in even smaller urban areas such as Seattle. Most gay men, however, did not and do not live in these neighborhoods, although those with enough money may visit them on vacation and bring elements of the style home with them. Furthermore, these "liberated zones" were and are largely white, and are by no means free of the racism that pervades U.S. society. Gay men of color have had to struggle for space in the movement, and many have decided the effort is not worthwhile. Nor have the lives of gay men who live in small towns and on farms been given much attention in describing gay life in this country. And all of the above ignores the reality of lesbian presence within the "gay community." The result is a falsified public image of "the gays" as white, male, affluent and urbanized.

This image is consistent, however, with a major development among men in the 1970s: the commercialization of gayness. Without consciously choosing a nationalist strategy, gay men fled from repression at home to safe haven in the cities already named. This became possible after Stonewall had produced a critical mass of people able to claim space (political, social and geographic) in the cities with a history of homophile organizing. It opened up both the need—as an economic base for the new migrants—and the opportunity for gay-run enterprises. As is to be expected in a capitalistsociety, the growth of gay male enterprise led to mass market culture—not necessarily in scale but in structure. Mass market publications, such as *The Advocate* became, replaced the "underground" press, which in any case was disappearing or being transformed in other parts of society as well. There also appeared a number of slick entertainment monthlies, which combined erotic photographs with fiction, cultural commentary, and travel notes. This new mass circulation press spread the style to places without large organized gay populations, and also helped spawn a travel industry keyed to the special needs of gay men. Gay bars began to have windows, and the music, dance, and fashions of gay men eventually percolated to the mainstream culture.

How did the Stonewall era produce such a capitalist's dream so soon? This is a complex question, and a thorough discussion is beyond the scope of this history, but a few points are worth noting.

To begin with, there was a falling off of political activism in the society at large, especially with the winding down of direct U.S. military involvement in Southeast Asia, which had been the rallying point for many white activists. In many cases, this was related to a rising concern for personal fulfillment, which often resulted in a stance that suggested no political change was possible until individuals had achieved an inner perfection. Revulsion in the wake of the political corruption that led to Richard Nixon's resigning the Presidency in 1974 reinforced this attitude. Furthermore, for gay men, the superficial comforts brought by the carving out of safe space in the cities and the attendant commercial trappings of gayness (for those who could afford them) created an illusion of success. As Jane Meyerding has pointed out (1992), systems such as racism allow those with relative privilege to ignore continued oppression in their midst. Thus an illusion came to be mistaken for real social change.

Something more like a real model for change was taking place among lesbians. This constitutes the other major development of the 1970s: the building of Lesbian Nation. This was the outcome of the declarations of independence made by lesbians like Del Martin. Identifying politically with the women's movement rather than the gay liberation movement, many lesbians worked out a theory of patriarchy that put lesbians in a privileged position as agents of its overthrow. "Feminism is the theory, lesbianism is the practice," went the slogan. The result came to be known as lesbian-feminism.

For many, this meant as far as possible detaching their lives from the toils of the patriarchy and living among women. Some were able to do this literally, by moving to rural areas. (Some men, especially effeminists, began doing this as well, communicating among each other by such means as the quarterly *RFD*.) Others had to negotiate women's space in places where they could make a living.

The difficulty of doing that on women's wages was considerable. This meant that through most of the 1970s lesbian culture was not as commercialized as gay male culture. Nevertheless, as in all cases of nation-building, the process created strong pressures to conform to a certain style, just as gay male style tended to become more clearly recognizable. Women's music and women's bookstores became financially stable, even if their stability was precarious in comparison to gay men's community businesses. By the end of the decade the beginnings of commercialization could be observed in the Lesbian Nation.

Whatever the reasons for the developments of the 1970s, two of their results can be distinguished.

First, there was a break in the continuity of the communities' historical memory. The tendency to dismiss, or forget, the two decades of lesbian and gay life before Stonewall was perhaps less among lesbians than among gay men, but young people of whatever sex operated all too often in a historical vacuum.

Second, both subcultures created pressure to conform to their own norms. This was consistent with what was happening in the rest of the society, as the election of Ronald Reagan in 1980 was to show. Its particular meaning among gay men—less so among lesbians—was that the sense of sexual dissidence and the revolutionary aspirations that characterized the period just before and after Stonewall were left behind in favor of a civil rights or integrationist approach that resembled the positions of the middle 1960s. A certain complacency could be detected, until a backlash erupted at the end of the decade.

THE BACKLASH

In 1976, the voters elected an anti-candidate, Jimmy Carter, as their next president. Carter was outspokenly a "born-again" Christian, and just as outspokenly not a member of the traditional political establishment. Although Carter, a Democrat, was more liberal than the two Republican presidents who succeeded him, he may be seen in retrospect as the harbinger of a new prominence of conservative Christians in U.S. politics.

The religious Right (as it came to be called) built its power as the voice of those who were bewildered by social change. The eternal verities regarding sexuality, family structure, and the God-given nature of man and woman no longer seemed to apply. What's more, lesbians and gay men inside the churches began to demand that the churches no longer contribute to victimizing them and instead recognize lesbians and gay men as full and equal participants in their institutional life.[1]

---

[1] The use of Christian terms is deliberate. Although a few Jews have made common cause with the religious Right, which in turn has tolerated their presence to make the movement appear less sectarian, the movement is overwhelmingly Christian, and for the most part unabashedly proclaims its goal to be a "Christian America." (To the author's knowledge, there is no non-Christian presence in the religious Right, Muslim, Buddhist or otherwise, besides this token Jewish one.) Lesbian, gay male and bisexual Jews have also agitated within the institutional structures of Judaism in the United States, but the differences in the way power and authority are structured in Jewish tradition, not to mention the difference in political power

This state of affairs led, within a year of Carter's inauguration, to a series of well-funded and widely publicized attacks on the political gains made since Stonewall. The campaigns sought to repeal equal protection ordinances in various cities. The backlash may thus be seen as a measure of the success of lesbian and gay organizing. Although these ordinances did no more than guarantee that the basic rights of lesbians and gay men be respected, the Right tried, with varying success, to characterize them as threats to children, feeding on traditional fears about "homosexuals."

Rhetorically, the campaigns concentrated on the schools, since gay rights ordinances protected lesbian and gay male teachers from employment discrimination. The first of these efforts was mounted in 1977 in Dade County, Florida, by singer and former Miss Oklahoma Anita Bryant. Her "Save Our Children" campaign was not just a local effort. Among other powerful national figures, Senator Jesse Helms (R-NC) lent Bryant the use of his staff. Her success in repealing the county's anti-discrimination protection for lesbians and gay men led to further such efforts around the country, which still continue fifteen years later. A statewide ballot proposition in California the following year, called the Briggs Initiative after its sponsor, would have forbidden hiring lesbians and gay men as teachers. These two attacks and those that followed brought many new activists, female and male, into local organizations, beginning a swing back to political activism that was to be more visible in the 1980s.

This attack against the perceived power of "militant homosexuals" was by no means isolated. It was part of a larger effort to turn back the political clock in the wake of the social unrest of the late 1960s and early 1970s. This effort had several facets, but one in particular claims our attention here: the campaign to preserve the National Security State.

CURING THE VIETNAM SYNDROME

For those sectors of society who depended on the National Security State for identity and livelihood—a group which included not only defense contractors and politicians, but many intellectuals as well, especially foreign policy "experts"—the 1970s were a frightening time. First, the antiwar movement had stolen from them the monopoly on interpreting foreign affairs, and cast grave doubt on the Cold War bipartisan consensus they had done so much to build. Second, by the mid 1970s, insurgents in Vietnam, Laos and Cambodia succeeded in taking state power, despite all the force and destruction the U. S. military could bring to bear.[1]

---

wielded by the branches of Judaism as compared with Christian denominations, mean that such struggle is properly detached from that within the churches.

[1] Contrary to the myth fostered since the end of U.S. military presence in the former Indochina, that destructive power was enormous, including more tonnage of bombs than in the whole of World War II.

This defeat seems to have been devastating to the self-esteem, and masculinity of the Cold Warriors. In fact, when President Gerald Ford, in 1975, sent in a force of Marines to rescue the U.S.S. Mayagüez off Cambodia, incurring more casualties than there were personnel on the ship, Secretary of State Henry Kissinger felt obliged to state explicitly at a press conference that the operation had nothing to do with proving the nation's manhood.

Reacting to this political climate, which was marked by a widespread suspicion among voters that military intervention in other Third World countries might lead to a repetition of the experience of the war in Southeast Asia and its attendant social unrest, national security managers and their supporters in the media coined a phrase, "the Vietnam syndrome," that implied that such anti-militarism on the part of the general public was a kind of mental disease rather than a responsible political position.

When Jimmy Carter became president in 1977 and began to propose that human rights ought to be the touchstone of U.S. foreign policy, the Cold Warriors panicked. Carter confirmed their worst fears when he negotiated a treaty to return the Canal Zone to Panamanian sovereignty. This provided an opening for Ronald Reagan to push for the White House on the slogan, "We bought it, we paid for it, it's ours, we're not giving it back."[1] The argument was short on substance but rich with emotional appeal: Richard Barnet has aptly characterized the foreign policy of the period as "the politics of feelings" (1990, 352ff.), a phrase that applies equally to the Bryant and Briggs campaigns.

Finally, the decade closed with two international developments that were nightmares for the Cold Warriors, and one that was a godsend. The nightmares were the Iranian and Nicaraguan revolutions, neither inspired nor supported by the Soviet Union but both declared to be so by the Right (since non-white people could never have overthrown U.S. client governments on their own initiative). The godsend was the Soviet invasion of Afghanistan, which gave the Cold Warriors a chance to say they told the rest of us so.

By the time these events took place, a group of "experts" was already in place to explain them. The Committee on the Present Danger, established in March 1976, was made up of both Democrats and Republicans committed to restoring U.S. military dominance in the world, and not incidentally their own tarnished place in U.S. society. Many of its members, like Eugene Rostow, had been responsible for the U.S. invasion of Southeast Asia; its "driving figure" (Barnet 1990, 368) was none other

---

[1] It also suggests an explanation for the long-term goal of the U.S. invasion of Panama in 1989, as well as the subsequent abolition of the Panamanian military. This latter step especially provides grounds for renegotiating the Panama Canal treaties to permit a permanent U.S. military presence there.

than Paul Nitze, author of NSC 68 back in 1950. The Committee laid out the critique of Ford's and Carter's foreign policy that was to bring Ronald Reagan to the presidency. It also, not unexpectedly, brought many Committee members jobs in his administration.

Two members of the Committee's board of directors, Norman Podhoretz and Midge Decter, addressed themselves to the dangers of "homosexuality" around this time. Podhoretz wrote an article in the October 1977 issue of *Harper's*, entitled "The Culture of Appeasement." Somewhat shortened, this became a chapter in his 1980 book, *The Present Danger*; in that form its more obviously homophobic passages were deleted. In the longer version, we see the kind of linkages the Right made between homosexuals—in this article, only men—espionage and Communism, in much the same terms as Countess Waldeck had used in "Homosexual International," quoted above. The *Harper's* article drew parallels between the young university Communists in Britain during the 1930s (what Waldeck had called "the Pink Decade") and Americans' antiwar sentiments during the 1970s. For Podhoretz,

> [t]hat Auden and Burgess[1] were both homosexuals clearly had something, perhaps everything, to do with their need "completely and finally to rebel against England"....For whatever else homosexuality may be or may be caused by, to these young men of the English upper class it represented...the refusal of fatherhood and all that fatherhood entailed: responsibility for a family and therefore an inescapable implication in the destiny of society as a whole(Podhoretz, 1977, 30-1).

The refusal of responsibility became even more sweeping, however, in the United States under Carter: "an indispensible element was added to the antidemocratic pacifism of the interwar ethos: a generalized contempt for middle-class or indeed any kind of heterosexual adult life" (Podhoretz 1977, 31).

Midge Decter's "The Boys on the Beach," which ran in *Commentary* in September 1980, expanded on this theme. Her piece, a nostalgic reflection that contrasted the nice gay men she had known on Fire Island before Stonewall with the rude militants that came after, concludes that women need to be protected and supported by men, but that men will not do their duty unless forced to do so. Toleration of open gayness gives men permission to shirk this duty. That is why homosexuality is a threat to the family. This was precisely the position being taken at that time by Phyllis Schlafly in her successful campaign to defeat the Equal Rights Amendment.

These arguments by members of the Committee on the Present Danger exposed urbane intellectual audiences to arguments being made by the religious Right. The conservative Christians' obsession with homosexuality was strong enough that they turned away from the Sunday

---

[1] W.H. Auden, the poet, was a conscientious objector during World War II. Guy Burgess was a spy for the Soviet Union, active into the 1950s.

School teacher Carter in favor of a divorced and remarried man from Hollywood who was not much of a church-goer, Ronald Reagan, because Carter had *once* received a delegation of lesbian and gay lobbyists at the White House.

The Committee on the Present Danger and the new Christian Right, together with their allies, set the agenda for the Reagan administration. The agenda amounted to rearmament, actual and moral. The Right saw these remedies for a moral decay they believed had taken over during the 1970s, blurring the age-old truths of gender. Once Reagan was elected president, the stage was set for a military buildup that increased economic disparities at home, made possible a series of military exploits abroad, and left the country bankrupt. This political brew needed only a final ingredient to spill over into active repression of lesbians and gay men.

The ingredient was a disease, Acquired Immune Deficiency Syndrome, which Moral Majoritarians and their allies quickly hailed as God's (or, in the case of more secular-minded "experts" like Patrick Buchanan, Nature's) retribution against the sins of Sodom. Public health could now be invoked ito justify repression, so that some members of Congress, most notably Representative William Dannemeyer, R-CA, were able to propose "quarantine" (read concentration camps) for "AIDS carriers" (read lesbians, gay men, and bisexuals). Dannemeyer, and his Senate colleague Jesse Helms, R-NC, were adept at framing their proposals in such a way as to frighten other members of both Houses into silent acquiescence.

The rhetoric of the backlash played up how little was known about AIDS, allowing the Right to draw on the power of the fear of the unknown (as they had in the McCarthy era). Hence opposition to education about AIDS became one of their main tactics. The visibility of "militant homosexuals" especially the availability of good information about our lives, came under attack. for similar reasons. Also useful was the spreading of fear that homosexuals were "infiltrating" (say) the school system. Thus, as Representative Ted Weiss noted in the epigraph to this article, the tone of the early 1950s was restored to halls of government.

AT THE END OF THE HALF-CENTURY

Other materials in this anthology cover many of the debates and issues of the 1980s and early 1990s. Rather than going over the events of the most recent decade, then, a few observations will serve to close this survey.

In the gay male community, AIDS has overshadowed most other issues. Three consequences are worth noting here. First, the day-to-day realities of coping with massive death and disease have required new networks of support and different forms of community building. This has gone some way toward reversing the individualistic, commercial trends of the previous decade. Second, it has led to a broadening of the gay male agenda and the coalitions that organize to further it. For example, the need for a system of universal health care, which most middle-class gay men had not previously considered, came home to them as private health insurance failed to answer their needs. Third, the epidemic spurred reconsideration of forms of political action, especially nonviolent direct action, that in the late 1970s and early 1980s had been neglected or even ridiculed. This development is covered in Barbara Epstein's article in this collection.

Another arena of activism has also been characterized by strong working relations between lesbians and gay men. This is the issue of access to the U.S. military. In a decade when the administration was attempting to narrow the Federal government's responsibility for its citizens to the arena of military security, this once again became an important issue. It especially affected students, since funds to pay for increasingly expensive higher education were more and more contingent on cooperation with the military. The effort to obtain free access to the military for lesbians and gay men was contested by antimilitarists; the resulting "right to fight" debate is covered elsewhere in this collection.

Other issues also arose as the 1980s became the 1990s. Many of these were current flowerings of perennials: the self-definition of the movement (should it include bisexuals? tranvestites and transsexuals? advocates of intergenerational sex?), its goals (civil rights? revolutionary change? assimilation?) and its tactics (legislation? direct action? caucuses within the Democratic and Republican parties? advertising campaigns?), even the language to be used (queer? lesbian, gay and bisexual?). Some debates were more novel, although in fact the underlying questions have mostly come up before. Is homosexuality innate or chosen? Biologically determined or something else? What is the nature of its history (the so-called constructionist/ essentialist debate)? What does it mean to build our politics around identity?

So: where does the political movement of sexual dissidents in the United States stand at the end of its first half century? One thing is certain: our work is still carried out, as it has been all along, within a militarist system. That fact will continue to affect our strategies, our ability to build coalitions, our choice of issues. Any other conclusions can only be tentative. Here we will content ourselves with observations.

The first has to do with the continuing tensions to be found in the history of queer organizing in this country. Naturally, since that history has been relatively short, it is not surprising to see the same points of dispute arise repeatedly. Furthermore, some of these represent real and irreconcilable differences that we will just have to learn to accept and live with: richness to be celebrated, not heresy to be eradicated.

Nevertheless, it may well be that some disputes reappear because they are not really addressed head on, with an eye to their ultimate political consequences. To take one example: much political capital is invested in the idea that being a lesbian or gay man is no more a choice than being Black. Does our liberation project really depend on that? After all, several freely-chosen identities, notably religion, are at least as well protected by law, if not better, than ones we think of as innate, like race or gender.

Second, our political discussions must take into account the context in which we organize. We generally assume that our political system is, if not benign, at least somehow within the liberal tradition (using the term in its broader sense). This author believes, to the contrary, that the establishment of the National Security State has transformed the content of the liberal political institutions, and put State security at the center of our national priorities. Therefore, our movement must challenge that priority to succeed.

This does not mean dropping our current agenda. At the very least, the viciousness of recent attacks on "militant homosexuals" is sufficient proof that our existence is a challenge in itself. It does require that we be conscious of the structures we are up against. In particular, we must recognize that the militarism by its nature encourages conformity and false "bipartisanship." Putting our eggs in those baskets is a mistake. Assimilation won't make us more acceptable to our enemies. It will only make us seem more insidious, thus strengthening one of their traditional charges.[1] Citizenship has been redefined as deferring to the needs of a continuing military establishment. Neither path leads toward liberation.

The U.S. election of 1992 was described as the first after the end of the Cold War. The significance of this may be overrated. Certainly the election rhetoric against sexual dissidents was still as warlike as anyone could wish. The national security establishment is scrambling to find new enemies to justify its continuance, a sign that the National Security State as a structure is, or has become, independent of the Soviet threat used to create it.

Throughout the period covered by this essay, we have been treated as enemies of the State, by Patrick Buchanan and Rev. Pat Robertson at the 1992 Republican convention no less than by McCarthy and Wherry in 1950. What will the turn of the century bring for sexual dissidents living in this National Security State?

---

[1] Findings of a study by Stewart Page and Mary Yee, "Conceptions of male and female homosexual stereotypes among undergraduates," published in the *Journal of Homosexuality* (Fall 1985) suggest to me that some people are more hostile to lesbians and gay men who do not conform to stereotypes of mannishness and effeminacy, since such people call traditional gender into question more strongly than stereotypical lesbians and gay men.

DISCUSSION QUESTIONS

1. What role has persecution played in the formation and maintenance of the category of "homosexual"? What will, or might, happen once homophobia is eradicated?

2. What role has the strategy of assimilation played in lesbian and gay men's organizing? How has it been effective? Ineffective?

3. What are some of the reasons for women's resistance to working with men? How has sexism changed in mixed-sex organizations? How has it stayed the same?

4. What lessons for contemporary activists does this history suggest?

SUGGESTIONS FOR FURTHER READING ON MILITARISM

Richard Barnet. 1977. *The roots of war: The men and institutions behind U.S. foreign policy.* New York: Pelican.

Noam Chomsky. 1987. *On power and ideology.* Boston: South End Press.

Sidney Lens. 1987. *Permanent war: The militarization of America.* New York: Schocken Books.

Leonard Rodberg & Derek Shearer, Eds. 1970. *The Pentagon watchers.* New York: Doubleday.

John W. Dower. 1986. *War without mercy: Race and power in the Pacific War.* New York: Pantheon.

WAR CULTURE:
WAR, LANGUAGE, RAPE, AND AIDS
Michael Bronski

Immediately following the Iraqi invasion of Kuwait on August 2, 1990, the United States carried out a massive deployment of troops to Saudi Arabia, under the name "Operation Desert Shield," with the declared aim of protecting Kuwait from an Iraqi military advance. This buildup, which included troops from other countries as well but in significantly lower numbers, led inevitably to an attack on Iraq by the coalition forces on January 16, 1991.

Lesbians and gay men were divided in their response to the war. A long-time lesbian activist, Leslie Cagan, was one of the chief coordinators of nationwide action against the war. The National Gay/Lesbian Task Force (NGLTF) came out against the war as well, but received sharp criticism from many of its constituents for doing so. Some lesbian and gay activists saw the war as an opportunity to prove their patriotism and thus achieve some gains once the war was over, notably a reversal of the military's policy against "homosexuality." Some, on the other hand, saw the military decision to retain lesbian and gay male members of the armed forces only long enough to prosecute the war, with the intention of discharging them immediately thereafter, as final proof of Pentagon intransigence on the policy.

"Soon To Be a Major Motion Picture." All right, you really haven't seen these words flashed across CNN news coverage from Iraq, or on the cover of *TV Guide*'s self-congratulatory pieces on television war coverage, or even on recruiting posters: "Uncle Sam Wants *You* To Be the Next Chuck Norris." But you know that they are lurking there; a soft-focus, hazy, pentimento waiting to reveal itself. But capitalism works only so fast and we will have to wait several months before *Desert Storm: The Movie* makes it to the big screen. Movies are not being entirely left out of the media loop—*Top Gun*, the classic 1980s boy and his supersonic jet romance, has been quickly slipped into cable TV slots; World War II movies, to remind us what a "good" war is, are being shoveled into any available VHF programming; and new films like the appalling *Flight of the Intruder* are doing well at the box office due to war mania. McLuhan"s global village is getting smaller and smaller and while TV is clearly the "hot medium" here—rendering the press, at times, almost superfluous—it is not just visual images which are shaping popular thoughts and sentiments about the war. Language—on television, radio, in the print media and on the street corner—is a major influence on how this war is being constructed, and a casual reading shows that it is as much about sex, gender, and disease as anything else.

As the world slides into the second week of the U.S.-led war against Iraq there are still almost no reports of casualties. Ironically, yet weirdly right in a sort of metaphoric way, we do hear about Barbara Bush. The day before the deadline for the start of her husband's war the First Lady managed to steer her sled into a tree and break her leg. In a script turn that would have been rejected by the writers of *Cop Rock*, Barbara was removed from the scene of the accident in the manly arms of Arnold Schwarzenegger, a one-time Mr. Universe, right-wing fund raiser, and now head of the President's Council on Physical Fitness. While neither the government nor the newscasters are telling the public how many deaths have occurred so far, we do—in both print and electronic media—receive the occasional cheery notice of Barbara Bush's improving condition.

This, of course, is all mordantly ironic, like something you might find on *Twin Peaks*. But it also underscores how deeply gender differentiated the reporting on the war against Iraq is. War has always been a masculine province. Even when a woman is blamed for war—Helen of Troy is clearly the prototype here—it has been the men who decide battle plans and who gets killed. Over the centuries war has assumed a gendered language that by relying on sexual innuendo and insinuation both reflects and justifies sexual stereotypes and hatreds. This war is no different.

Perhaps the most striking, though historically overused, sexual metaphor to be found in news reports every day is that of "rape." "The rape of little Kuwait" and "the rape of innocent Kuwait" are phrases which have appeared in almost every newscast since the invasion of that country by Iraqi troops. And while there have been reports of Kuwaiti women being raped by Iraqi Special Forces, the phrase "the rape of Kuwait" refers simply to the entree of hostile foreign soldiers. But it is with this image of rape—sexual violation of an innocent, passive, essentially feminine persona—that early news coverage primed the U.S. public (as well as much of the rest of the world) to accept the upcoming war.

If Kuwait had not been portrayed as "innocent" (in sexual terms, that translates as not trampy or sluttish) or "passive" (unable to defend itself) or "feminine" (not man enough to fight back), there would be little public sympathy for U.S. policy. Who wouldn't rush to defend a lady in distress?

The use of the rape metaphor is hardly new. It has been used in recent and past history, and always as a nationalistic self-justification; you never heard about the "rape of poor little Panama" or the "rape of innocent Grenada" in the U.S. press. Susan Brownmiller, in her 1975 *Against Our Will: Men, Women, and Rape*, details the uses of the rape metaphor especially in regard to the German invasion of Belgium during World War I.

To help stir up anti-German sentiment, the Allies reported (and turned into nationalistic propaganda) the rape of Belgian women by German soldiers. The piteous idea of these "helpless" women became so identified with the German invasion that Belgium itself, pictured in countless posters as a beautiful woman at the feet of the dreadful Hun, became identified as the victim of rape. (The fact that Belgian women were raped—as were women of other countries by the Allied troops—was of little interest to the propagandists. War, after all, isn't *about* women, it's about men.)

Of course, "rape" is hardly the only gendered and sexualized word being used as a metaphor for the war today. It is common to hear again and again in the same newscast how American and British missiles "penetrated" Baghdad and how much damage they caused.

After a few nights in which there were no missile attacks on Israel, the Cable News Network (CNN) anchor asked the Jerusalem bureau reporter how it felt to finally spend a night "unmolested by the sounds of air raid sirens and explosions." The phallic implications of projectile missiles are obvious enough without the Defense Department and newscasters using language to make it sound like an orgy. On one level it makes obvious the point of who is stronger and who is weaker. But on another level it reinforces sexual behaviors and stereotypes in our everyday culture and reality. This is something in which those in power also have a great deal of interest.

Take the twisting pronunciation of Saddam Hussein's name. Sometime during the press conferences held this past September, George Bush changed his pronunciation of the Iraqi leader moniker from "Sa-daam," (with its stress on the second syllable) to "Sodom" (as in "and Gomorrah.") Not only does this call up biblical images of the evil, decadent, and untrustworthy cities of the plain, but in the past weeks it has actually taken on a more sexualized, homophobic meaning and intent. Two pro-war demonstrators at a Boston rally carried signs that read "Sadaamy" with a caricature of a missile aimed squarely at a man's buttocks.

In fact, the notion of sodomy as the ultimate humiliating rape overrides all of the sexualized suggestions of Saddam Hussein's name. This clearly plays into the age-old traditional Western fantasy of Eastern sexuality. The Crusaders of the Middle Ages brought back tales of the Sultan of Egypt and Syria, Saladin, and his predilection for buggering boys. They relied upon accepted Christian responses to these "unnatural acts" to stir up support for their wasteful, imperial, expeditions. (Ironically, noble Crusade leader Richard the Lion-Hearted was a well-known boy buggerer himself; hypocrisy and media spin are limited by neither country nor century.)

Interestingly enough, during the first week of actual combat, Bush changed his pronunciation again. This time he shifted to a broad, American flat-land "Saad-dam" (accent on the first syllable). This suggests less the soon-to-be-destroyed by fire and brimstone city than the prince of darkness himself: and you thought that jihads were declared only by Muslims.

While the metaphors being used to describe this war are all similar, each has important singular nuances and differences. They are protean; their meanings change depending upon situation and intent. Hussein has "sodomized" Kuwait—an unnatural act, "rape," associated with a corrupt Middle-Eastern sexuality not unlike that described by the Crusaders. Hussein's shelling of Israel is only a "molestation"—something more than copping a feel on a bus but less than a violent assault. The incessant, continual bombing of Baghdad by the U.S.—which is causing at least as much pain, suffering, disease, and death as experienced by Kuwait since the Iraqi invasion, a fact completely blacked out of the media by the U.S. government—is healthy, "normal," manly penetration.

But sexuality enters into military metaphors in other ways, one of these being how we conceptualize and use the very word "war."

Although it is perfectly clear to the entire world that there is a war going on in the Persian Gulf—and for that matter, given the large group of nations involved, the massive amounts of munitions being exploded, the drastic destruction to the environment, and the possibly high numbers of casualties and deaths it is, for all intents and purposes, World War III—you might not know it since the "W" word is hardly mentioned at all. *Time* and *Newsweek*, of course, were quick to print gripping, bold, black and red "WAR" covers that practically jumped off newsstands and into the hands of passerbys eager for information. And daily tabloids like the *Boston Herald* and the *New York Post* were certainly willing to retire for a few days their favorite 18-point headline "13 Year Old Girl Raped on Way Home From Sunday School," to scream "WAR!!!" the minute they could. But a quick perusal of the *New York Times* and other more "respectable" papers shows that the more obvious bellicose language is missing from the headlines. The United States is not involved in something as drastic as "war" in these stories but rather a "conflict," or a "situation in the Persian Gulf" or (and at least this word slouches towards conveying the seriousness of the situation) a "crisis in the Middle East."

And to be fair to the *Times*, there technically isn't a war going on. At least not a declared war, at least not officially declared by the United States. It is true that Congress authorized (by a very small margin; hardly a mandate) President "I'm no wimp" Bush to commence air attacks on Iraq, but there was no technical declaration of war. This should be no surprise because although the word "war," as well as an endless list of war metaphors are an intrinsic part of everyday English usage, the wheres, whens, and why-fors of how they are actually used is quite circumscribed. Everyone agreed on World War I and World War II—they were "wars" and were called so when they were happening. And while the Korean War was certainly labeled as such (and continues to be thought of in the popular imagination as war,) according to official State Department policy it was actually a "police action," not a war at all. This selective labeling is even more interesting when you consider Viet Nam.

Like the Korean War and the War in the Persian Gulf, Viet Nam was never officially declared a war by the U.S. While it was happening it was called "the Viet Nam War" or "the war in Viet Nam." But as time lapsed popular sentiment turned against the blatant war-mongering and patriotic sloganeering (especially when huge numbers of veterans attempted to fit back into U.S. society), the popular language used to describe the war changed. What should have been called "the war *against* Viet Nam" was called "the war in Viet Nam" in the mid-1970s, by the early 1980s (when it was clear that it was a complete national policy fiasco) it was being called "the Viet Nam experience," which makes it sound like some slightly exotic, "orientalized," Club Med trip.

The use of the word "war" and its attendant metaphors is not random. They are used, either consciously or unconsciously, for specific effect and purpose, not so much as descriptions, but rather to convey additional moral, imaginative, or judgmental information. The ubiquitous "war between the sexes" is, in fact, a cover-up of the fact that men, generally, have social power over women. Under the administration of Lyndon Johnson a "war on poverty" was declared in an attempt to raise the standard of living for U.S. citizens whose income fell below the (already very minimal) federal standards of living. Under the Nixon and Reagan administrations, the deserving poor became criminal perpetrators and the "war on poverty" became, essentially, "the war on drugs" complete with—in an odd, post-cold war borrowing—a "drug czar."

In all of these cases the word "war" is used to actually define a social situation to the advantage of whoever is doing the naming. A "war on poverty" makes the federal government look as though it is helping the lower classes; the "war on drugs" is an attempt to convince the middle and upper classes (none of whom, of course, do drugs) that the more rambunctious lower (i.e. criminal) classes will be kept in their place and punished. When used by the U.S. government on issues of social policy, "war" is almost always used to put the other—either people or abstract ideas—on the defensive. A declaration of war is a sign of dedication and a determination to take drastic action. In simple terms, a declaration of war is a declaration of moral righteousness and certainty; in the eyes of those who declare them, all wars are "good wars."

This is, of course, true of the War in the Gulf (or, to be a little more exact, The War Against Iraq) but in a topsy-turvy Alice-In-Blunderland reversal, actual wars (although undeclared) are labeled something else and the traditional military designations are used to designate social policy stances.

Listening to the constant barrage of news reports relating bombings, air raids, casualties and invasions it is impossible not to be reminded of how the language used to describe war is also used to describe AIDS.

Susan Sontag, in both *Illness as Metaphor* and *AIDS and Its Metaphors*, discusses in detail the role of military metaphor in mystifying and understanding health and disease, but the last weeks have pointed out, again and again, how deeply rooted and entwined in both culture and language these dual concepts are.

The conceptualization of AIDS as a war is not a new idea. Taking physical well being to be the criterion—a presumption, surely—it is understandable that we would come to view anything which might weaken or change that condition as an "enemy" of health. And the presence of an "enemy" means that a warlike situation is possible. The metaphor of war is an oddly comforting one and in Western culture it seems almost a reflex response.

In his book on the immune system, *The Body at War*, Dr. John M. Dwyer details in military terms how the body's defenses work. In five chapters with titles like "The War and the Warriors," and "Where Are the Generals?" he maps out a battle plan of how the human body fights the enemy of disease.

The conceptualization of the body as battleground is, however, not without problems. Health, in our culture, is not a neutral condition—there is a separate set of moral, emotional, and sexual judgments that are seen as directly related to *physical* well being—and by militarizing the physical self, we stand the risk of losing any number of social or psychological wars. In his book *Mortal Embrace: Living with AIDS*, Egyptian writer Emmanuel Dreuilhe takes the idea of the military metaphor and AIDS to an extreme. People who die of AIDS are "killed in action"; PWAs are "soldiers on the front lines"; when he enters a gay bar now, he feels "like a soldier on leave"; a body racked by PCP is a "bombed out ruin"; sex in the late 1970s occurs in "the pre-war period"; "the saber cuts of Kaposi's sarcoma" leaves scars on a PWA's face; discovering that you are HIV+ leaves you "shell shocked." Every page is packed with the language of war and battle.

It is easy to see how, in a homophobic culture in which gayness and death are already linked, AIDS feels like a war, both personally and socially. But as writer John Preston has said: "I have a problem thinking of AIDS as a war because the fact is that everyone eventually dies—of something—and so to frame the discussion, one's life, in those terms is to always lose the war. There is *no* way that you can win. But as a gay man in my forties who has seen many of my contemporaries die, I do *feel* as though I am in the middle of a war and that gay male life is sometimes a battlefield."

After finishing with war news last Friday, the anchor on Boston's Public Television station, WGBH, announced that the Centers for Disease Control released figures showing that 100,000 people had died of AIDS in the past decade. (This number is probably grossly underestimated, given the number of AIDS-related deaths that go unreported.) Juxtaposed with the reports of war-related fatalities (also grossly underreported by both sides), such information helps viewers reconfirm the metaphorical connections between war and AIDS. And it isn't a great leap to link those two specific realities together. The endless reporting of the allegedly meager fatalities connected with the war compared to the simple news item approach to the milestone of 100,000 dead of AIDS calls into question the priorities of social and foreign policy as well as news reporting. Part of the reason ACT UP/New York decided to do its January 23 political actions—which it called the Day of Desperation—was to highlight the fact that the news coverage of the War Against Iraq was essentially blotting out all attention to AIDS.

This has to be, to some degree, a conscious intention of the President's war policy. It is not just the AIDS epidemic that Washington would like the public to forget, but the savings and loan scandal (in which first son Neil Bush is a prime suspect), the collapse of the banking system, the need for more read-my-lips taxes, the oncoming recession/depression, and the complete lack of any distinctive social or foreign policy are all subjects that the President and his advisors would like us to forget. "War can be a diversion for a bad ruler," wrote Roman historian Tacitus, and that certainly goes a long way in explaining this one.

And there are other conditions that, at least in the minds of activists, link the War Against Iraq and AIDS. By far the primary one is how the cost of the war will impact not only money for AIDS care and research but social and health programs in general. Current estimates claim that the War Against Iraq is costing a half billion dollars a day and it is money that might have been used for drug research, education, or care, or a whole host of less incendiary things. It may seem a little disingenuous to compare the two—the government would never spend that much money on health care anyway—but it does point out where priorities lie.

There is no question that the priorities of the Federal government, and any of its research or health institutes, have never been with AIDS. An October 18 headline in the *New York Times* that stated "Bush Unconvinced More AIDS Money Will Curb Epidemic" tells it all. In the 1950s the government declared a "war on cancer," and it has been a particularly badly run war if the results after 30 years are anything to go by. Declaring war is something that has never even been suggested for AIDS. Of course, the big difference between those afflicted by cancer and those by AIDS is one of victim status. Cancer victims are generally "innocent" while AIDS victims—as PWAs are still called in the popular press—are clearly "guilty."

An ACT UP spokesperson said of the Day of Desperation, "We want people to know that the government spends over one billion a day on this war and only five billion in ten years to fight AIDS." In plain terms, there was no need for a war against AIDS because AIDS itself is a government declared war against undesirables.

The overwhelming emphasis in the news on the War Against Iraq has made a radical change in everyday language and thinking. The constant barrage of military metaphors and defensive thinking has clouded all other issues. Although ACT UP's "Day of Desperation" was an imperative stance to take in the wake of media war obsession, the response in the press showed how far the situation had gone. When ACT UP activists staged a protest that interrupted the "CBS Evening News," they were described as "terrorists" who "invaded" the inner sanctum of the media. The language of war was quickly adopted to describe and demonize the civil disobedience actions of an AIDS activist group. It is no accident that this is also the same language used to describe the "AIDS virus" and how it enters a "healthy" body. The issue of AIDS became, once again, invisible in the wake of war mania.

The metaphors of war and the military are so intrinsic to Western culture that it is impossible to completely avoid them. But it is possible to understand how they function. It is a matter of understanding that the "war between the sexes" is actually about women struggling for freedom, and that a "war on drugs" is more about social control of the inner city than helping people lead sane and healthy lives. When we think about the War Against Iraq it is important to remember that "the Mid-East crisis" is really an undeclared war that entails the repeated, incessant bombing of a city. It is also important to recognize that when broadcasters refer, as Dan Rather did the other day, to "Saddam Hussein's war against the United States" it is a gross distortion of reality. It is also important to remember that being HIV+ or having ARC or AIDS-related illnesses, does not mean that our bodies are "at war" or a "battlefield." And while losing enormous numbers of friends may make us feel as though we are in the middle of a war, we should never lose sight of reality, no matter how enticing the metaphor might be. It is important to remember that in U.S. culture, gay and lesbian people are still "the enemy" and when war metaphors are so easily used they are eventually going to be used against us.

Discussion Questions

1. What are some other examples of everyday use of war language? What is the hidden message they convey?

2. In what ways has society considered HIV+ people "guilty" of sickness as compared to other illnesses? In what other ways does U.S. culture "blame the victims?"

3. What do the readers think of the ACT UP strategies outlined here?

4. How important is language on the formation of social change movements?

5. What forms have discussions of "PC" (political correctness) taken in the readers' communities? What are some strategies for addressing the myriad conflicts that arise in trying to discuss issues of race, class, sex, and sexuality?

SUGGESTIONS FOR FURTHER READING
Michael Bronski. 1984. *Culture clash: The making of a gay sensibility.* Boston: South End Press.

Carol Cohn. 1990. Clean bombs and clean language. *Women, militarism, and war: Essays in history, politics and social theory.* Jean Bethke Elshtain & Sheila Tobias, Eds. Savage, MD: Rowman & Littlefield Publishers, Inc.

Douglas Crimp. 1988. *AIDS: Cultural analysis, cultural activism.* Cambridge: MIT Press.

Steven Epstein. 1988. Nature vs. nurture and the politics of AIDS organizing. *OUT/LOOK* 3, 1(3):46-53.

Rebecca Isaacs & Allan Bérubé. 1991. OUT/LOOK dossier: Lesbians at war with the military. *OUT/LOOK* 13, 4(1):14-27.

Cindy Patton. 1985. *Sex and germs: The politics of AIDS.* Boston: South End Press.

Catherine Saalfield & Ray Navarro. 1991. Shocking pink praxis: Race and gender on the ACT UP frontlines. *Inside/out: Lesbian theories, gay theories.* Diana Fuss, Ed. New York: Routledge & Chapman Hall.

MILITARISM AND VIOLENCE

Violence

THE CONTEXT OF ANTI-GAY VIOLENCE: NOTES ON CULTURAL AND PSYCHOLOGICAL HETEROSEXISM
Gregory M. Herek

The cultural context of heterosexism is described in this important essay by Gregory Herek. Herek gives countless examples of the ways in which heterosexism is manifested on the social and individual levels, including religion, the law, the mental health field, the mass media, and psychological prejudice. The essay stresses the need for interventions in order to transform heterosexism, including education, institutional changes, increasing visibility of lesbians and gay men, and confronting anti-gay violence.

Hate crimes against lesbians and gay men in the United States must be understood in context: anti-gay violence is a logical, albeit extreme, extension of the heterosexism that pervades American society. *Heterosexism* is defined here as an ideological system that denies, denigrates, and stigmatizes any nonheterosexual form of behavior, identity, relationship, or community. Like racism, sexism, and other ideologies of oppression, heterosexism is manifested both in societal customs and institutions, such as religion and the legal system (referred to here as *cultural heterosexism*) and in individual attitudes and behaviors (referred to here as *psychological heterosexism*).

The present article has four goals. First, it describes cultural heterosexism in the United States today as the backdrop against which anti-gay violence occurs. Second, it explores how key components of the cultural ideologies of sexuality and gender foster heterosexism and, ultimately, anti-gay violence. These components of ideology are conceptualized here as underpinning anti-gay hostility by creating conditions in which gay people remain largely invisible while the concept of homosexuality is imbued with various symbolic statuses (e.g., deviance, sickness, evil). Third, the article describes how these symbolic statuses, rather than interactive experiences with gay persons, form the basis for most heterosexuals' attitudes and how, as a result, those attitudes function primarily to fulfill psychosocial needs. Finally, the article considers how societal transformations now in progress might affect cultural heterosexism and its underlying ideologies. The overall question to be addressed is not so much *why* homosexuality is stigmatized in American society, but rather *how* heterosexism is transmitted through cultural institutions and individual experience.

INSTITUTIONAL MANIFESTATIONS OF CULTURAL HETEROSEXISM

Cultural heterosexism is like the air that we breathe: it is so ubiquitous that it is hardly noticeable. Even a cursory survey of American society reveals that homosexuality is largely hidden and, when publicly recognized, is usually condemned or stigmatized. This alternation between invisibility and condemnation is readily apparent in four major societal institutions: religion, the law, psychiatry and psychology, and mass media.

In prescribing guidelines for moral living, modern Christian and Jewish religious institutions stress the inherent virtue of committed marital relationships through which children are conceived and raised in the faith. Marriages are heterosexual by definition; homosexual behavior is widely condemned; same-sex relationships and families are not recognized. Some denominations and congregations recently have adopted more accepting positions concerning homosexuality. They have opposed discrimination, allowed gay people to join the clergy and, in rare cases, blessed gay relationships. Others, however, have reaffirmed and even intensified their rejection. The Catholic Church, for example, officially opposed extending civil rights protection to gay people in a Vatican statement which also was widely interpreted as condoning anti-gay violence: "When civil legislation is introduced to protect behavior to which no one has any conceivable right, neither the Church nor society at large should be surprised when other distorted notions and practices gain ground, and irrational and violent reactions increase" (Congregation for the Doctrine of Faith, 1986, paragraph 10). In the third paragraph of that document, homosexual feelings are described as "ordered toward an intrinsic moral evil," which leads to the conclusion that homosexuality "itself must be seen as an objective disorder."

Gay men and lesbians also remain largely outside the law. Except in two states (Wisconsin and Massachusetts) and a few dozen municipalities (e.g., San Francisco, New York City, Chicago), legal protections do not exist for gay people in employment, housing, or services. [*Eds. note: Since this article was written, five additional states have enacted laws to protect lesbians and gay men from discrimination: California, Connecticut, Hawaii, New Jersey and Vermont.*] Gay relationships have no legal status, and lesbian and gay male parents often lose legal custody of their children when their homosexuality becomes known. The right of states to outlaw homosexual behavior was upheld by the U.S. Supreme Court in 1986 (*Bowers v. Hardwick*, 1986). In a clear illustration of the linkage between legal philosophies and religious teachings, Justices White and Burger refused to find a constitutional right for adults to engage privately in consenting homosexual behavior, based on the fact that legal proscriptions against sodomy have very "ancient roots" and that condemnation of homosexuality "is firmly rooted in Judeo-Christian moral and ethical standards."

In contrast to other institutions, the mental health field has made homosexuality highly visible; this visibility, however, has been within a discourse of pathology. Despite Freud's refusal to label homosexuality a sickness, mainstream American psychiatry and psychoanalysis spent much of the 20th century seeking its "cure." When finally subjected to rigorous scientific testing, however, the linkage of homosexuality with psychopathology proved to be wrong. Consequently, the American Psychiatric Association finally dropped homosexuality as a diagnosis from its Diagnostic and Statistical Manual in 1974. Since then, the American Psychological Association (APA) has led other scientific and professional organizations in removing the stigma so long associated with homosexuality. Nevertheless, the International Classification of Diseases (ICD) continues to label homosexuality as a mental illness, and the language of pathology still infuses popular perceptions.

A fourth institution that reflects and perpetuates cultural heterosexism is the electronic mass media. Mirroring society, media portrayals of homosexuality are relatively infrequent and typically are negative when they occur. Vito Russo's 1981 study of Hollywood films, for example, demonstrated that most homosexual characters die before the end of the movie, usually from suicide or murder. In children's cartoons, characters whose homosexuality is implied through their violation of gender roles long have been targeted for ridicule, contempt, and violence. Even when gay characters have been portrayed positively in more recent films and television programs, they almost always appear in a story *because* they are gay (i.e., because their homosexuality is important to the plot). Thus all characters are heterosexual unless explicitly identified as homosexual, in which case the story focuses on their sexuality rather than their day-to-day nonsexual lives.

As these examples show, homosexuality is alternately rendered invisible and condemned by cultural institutions. Psychological heterosexism parallels this process: most heterosexuals perceive the world entirely in heterosexual terms until confronted with evidence of homosexuality, at which time they respond with some combination of discomfort, confusion, condemnation, hostility, and disgust. In the next section, the ideological systems that underlie this dual negation are explored.

CULTURAL IDEOLOGIES OF SEXUALITY AND GENDER

A cultural *ideology* is defined here as a system of beliefs, values, and customs that form the basis for group members' shared perceptions of social reality. It reflects a consensual worldview and the institutions based on it, both of which evolve continuously through social interaction. Heterosexism is one component of the broader and overlapping ideologies of sexuality and gender. Although these ideologies vary across groups within American society, the twin themes of denial and stigmatization concerning homosexuality recur repeatedly. In this section, the roots of those themes are considered for each ideology.

Heterosexism, Sexuality, and Socioerotic Identity

Since the 19th century, Western societies have come to define who people *are* in terms of what they *do* sexually, giving rise to social categories based on sexual behavior and preference. The social roles and psychosocial identities deriving from these categories are referred to here as *socioerotic identities.* Historically, socioerotic identities became incorporated into the Western worldview as various economic and social changes permitted individuals to leave traditional kin-based lives in order to seek out others with sexual proclivities like their own. This trend coincided with shifts in social consensus about the primary goal and cultural focus of sexuality: from reproduction to intimacy and personal happiness, and from family and community to the individual.

Social categories developed to describe those who transgressed the boundaries of existing marital and reproductive roles—namely, homosexuals and bisexuals. These are master statuses to which all other characteristics of an individual are subordinated in others' perceptions. From the first, the modern concept of "the homosexual" developed more in opposition to "normalcy" than to heterosexuality per se, and was stigmatized as sinful, illegal, and sick.

In theory, all members of society can be categorized according to their socioerotic identity. However, just as White Americans typically do not think of themselves as White, and men usually can think of themselves as human beings rather than as males, so heterosexuals can think of themselves as husbands or wives, fathers or mothers. Those identities largely negate the experiences of gay and bisexual people, however. Like members of other minorities, they must define themselves in terms of the characteristic (sexual orientation) that relegates them to unequal status and sets them in opposition to the dominant group. Socioerotic identity, based as it is entirely on sexuality, is inherently problematic for at least two reasons. First, it constitutes a public manifestation of what society prescribes should be private—namely sexuality. Second, because homosexual behavior is regarded negatively by society, an identity based on such behavior is inevitably stigmatized.

Privatization and Invisibility: The Personal-Public Dichotomy

In a questionnaire study of heterosexuals' attitudes toward lesbians and gay men (Herek 1987), one college student wrote: "Homosexuals would be more acceptable if they wouldn't flaunt their homosexuality." Another student wrote: "Gay people have a right to live their own lives as long as they keep it to themselves and don't display the fact in public." Expressing a sentiment widespread in American society, these comments reflect an important component of sexual ideology: the belief that sexuality belongs only in the personal or private sphere of life. This aspect of sexual ideology perpetuates homosexuality's invisibility and creates a basis for stigmatizing it when it becomes visible.

The cultural dichotomy between public and private spheres of life, with sexual intimacy and pleasure relegated to the latter, has developed fairly recently in historical terms. Ostensibly, all sexuality is privatized. Private heterosexuality, however, has public counterparts through which it is implicitly affirmed. The institution of marriage publicly legitimizes heterosexual partnerships through such mechanisms as wedding rituals, tax and inheritance laws, employee benefits programs, and immigration and naturalization policies. The institutions of parenthood and the family are heterosexually identified: the birth of children (which implicitly is interpreted as affirming the parents' heterosexuality) is recognized by the larger community through birth announcements, gift-giving, religious rituals, tax deductions, and other customs.

Homosexuality, however, has no corresponding public institutions. Because same-sex marriage is illegal, gay relationships and families remain hidden. When gay people engage in behaviors that parallel those allowed to heterosexuals, they make public what society prescribes should be private. They are accused of "flaunting" their sexuality and thereby are perceived as deserving or even "asking for" retribution, harassment, or assault.

For example, displaying a photograph of one's (heterosexual) spouse in the workplace implicitly conveys information to others about one's private sexual behavior. Yet because that spouse has a public identity as husband or wife, most onlookers (if they even notice the photo) do not think of the person pictured primarily in sexual terms. Rather, their interest centers upon the partner's physical appearance, social status, occupation, and personality. They do not perceive the photograph's display to constitute an inappropriate intrusion of the private sphere into public life. When the photograph is of a same-sex partner, in contrast, everyone is likely to notice. The partner's gender overwhelms all other information about her or him. The sexual component of the relationship is no longer mundane and implicit; the private-public barrier is perceived to have been violated. The seemingly innocent act of displaying a partner's photograph fundamentally changes one's status and relationships.

Sexualization and Stigmatization

Heterosexism derives in part from cultural negativity toward particular forms of sexuality. As Rubin (1984, 280-281) summarized, "normal" sexuality "should ideally be heterosexual, marital, monogamous, reproductive, and non-commercial. It should be coupled, relational, within the same generation, and occur at home. It should not involve pornography, fetish objects, sex toys of any sort, or roles other than male and female."

Gay sexuality violates many of these rules. It is not reproductive by definition and not marital by statute. Many gay relationships are not sexually exclusive. Some homosexual men have staked out "cruising areas" for sexual behavior that are semipublic. Because of the culture's abiding suspicion of and hostility toward such "merely" pleasurable sexuality, gay sexuality is "'bad,' 'abnormal,' or 'unnatural'" (Rubin 1984, 281).

Not only are gay people reduced to their socioerotic identity, but that identity is equated with deviance and abnormality. Further, it is stereotyped as pathological, predatory, compulsively promiscuous. At best, gay people are perceived as basing their identity and lifestyle upon a trivial pursuit, namely, sexual pleasure. At the worst, homosexuality is stigmatized as inherently sick or dangerous, and worthy of punishment through legal (through the criminal justice system) or extralegal (in the form of anti-gay hate crimes) means.

Heterosexism and Gender

Whereas biological sex is about physiology, gender is about behavior. The ideology of gender is a set of shared beliefs, values, and customs concerning "masculinity" and "femininity." Children internalize the rules for behavior prescribed by this cultural ideology in the course of defining their gender identity (i.e., their core sense of self as a man or woman). Because they are learned at a very early age, the meanings attached to masculinity and femininity subsequently seem "natural" rather than socially constructed.

Although gender identity is distinct from socioerotic identity (the sense of self as heterosexual, homosexual, or bisexual), the two are closely related. Heterosexuality is equated ideologically with "normal" masculinity and "normal" femininity, whereas homosexuality is equated with violating norms of gender. Although no inherent connection exists between sexual behavior and gender conformity, gay men are widely stereotyped as highly effeminate, and lesbians as hypermasculine. This ideological linkage between sexuality and gender has at least three consequences.

First, gay people are stigmatized not only for their erotic behaviors, but also for their perceived violation of gender norms. Second, because homosexuality is associated with deviation from something so "natural" as masculinity or femininity, its labeling as abnormal receives further justification. Heterosexuals with deep-seated insecurities concerning their own ability to conform to cultural standards for masculinity or femininity may even perceive homosexuality as threatening their sense of self as a man or woman.

Third, a dual pattern of denial and condemnation is associated with gender which parallels that previously described for cultural heterosexism. People who do not conform to gender roles—regardless of their actual sexual orientation—are often labeled as homosexual and stigmatized or attacked. Fear of such labeling leads heterosexuals and homosexuals alike to monitor their own behavior carefully to avoid any appearance of gender nonconformity.

PSYCHOLOGICAL HETEROSEXISM

The foundation of *psychological heterosexism*—the individual manifestation of anti-gay prejudice—is laid down early in life. Long before children know anything about homosexuality or heterosexuality per se, they learn to prize what their parents and peers define as "good" and "normal." They learn moral values, attitudes toward the body and sexuality, and the distinction between private and public. They develop a gender identity and internalize negative feelings and stereotypical beliefs about those who violate gender roles. They learn to value acceptance from peers and adults, and acquire strategies for winning it. They learn the benefits and costs associated with multiple social roles, including those of the "normal" and its counterpart, the deviant. They learn the social attitude associated with race, gender, and those who are different or "queer," long before they understand that *queer* is an epithet for homosexuals.

Because of homosexuality's cultural invisibility, relatively few children are likely to have personal contact with someone who is openly gay while learning these concepts. Consequently, rather than defining homosexuality as a characteristic associated with flesh-and-blood human beings, most people respond to it primarily as a symbol: the embodiment of such concepts as "sin," "sickness," "predator," "outsider," or whatever else an individual considers to be the opposite of her- or himself, or set apart from her or his community. Whereas attitudes toward people with whom one has direct experience function primarily to organize and make sense of that experience, attitudes toward symbols serve a variety of expressive needs. At least three functions are served by psychological heterosexism.

First, anti-gay prejudice may serve a *value-expressive* function, helping individuals to affirm who they are by expressing important personal values. For example, a fundamentalist Christian may express hostile attitudes toward gay people as a way of affirming her or his own Christianity. She or he opposes homosexuality because such opposition is an integral part of being a good Christian, which is of central importance to feeling good about oneself. The same individuals would express similar hostility toward other groups if they were similarly defined in religious terms. Violence also may serve a value-expressive function for the perpetrator. For example, members of hate groups such as the Ku Klux Klan appeal to moral authority in their anti-gay rhetoric.

Anti-gay prejudice can also serve a *social-expressive* function by helping individuals to win approval from important others (e.g., peers, family, neighbors) and thereby increase their own self-esteem. As with the value-expressive function, lesbians and gay men are treated as abstract concepts. With social-expressive prejudice, they are the epitome of outsiders; attacking them solidifies one's own status as an insider, one who belongs to the group. Expressing anti-gay attitudes or violently attacking gay people thus leads to being accepted and liked, which are of central importance to the individual. For example, some assailants in anti-gay street assaults view the attack primarily as a way of demonstrating their loyalty and increasing group solidarity. Perpetrators in male-male rapes and sexual assaults also have been observed to be motivated by needs to maintain status and affiliation with peers.

Anti-gay prejudice also may serve a *defensive* function by reducing the anxiety that results from unconscious psychological conflicts (e.g., those associated with one's own sexuality or gender). The defensive function is summarized in the popular notion that people who express anti-gay prejudice actually are revealing their own latent homosexuality. For people with defensive attitudes, lesbians or gay men symbolize unacceptable parts of the self (e.g., the feminine man, the masculine woman). Expressing anti-gay hostility is a strategy for avoiding an internal conflict by externalizing it to a suitable symbol which then is attacked. Anti-gay assaults, for example, may provide a means for young males to affirm their masculinity (consciously or not) by attacking someone who symbolizes an unacceptable aspect of their own personalities (e.g., homoerotic feelings or tendencies toward effeminacy). Similarly, some perpetrators in male-male sexual assaults apparently wished to punish the victim as a way of dealing with their own unresolved and conflictual sexual interests.

Anti-gay hostility thus functions to define who one *is* by identifying gay people as a symbol of what one is *not* and directing hostility toward them. With the value-expressive function, prejudice defines the world according to principles of good and evil, right and wrong; by opposing the embodiment of evil (gay people), one affirms one's own goodness. With the social-expressive function, prejudice defines the ingroup and outgroup; by denigrating outsiders (lesbians and gay men), one affirms one's own status as an insider. With the defensive function, prejudice defines the self and the "not-self"; by attacking gay people, one symbolically (and unconsciously) attacks the unacceptable or bad aspects of self.

Psychological heterosexism can serve these functions only when cultural ideology converges with psychological needs. Anti-gay prejudice can be value-expressive only to the extent that an individual's self-concept is tied to particular values that have become socially identified as antithetical to homosexuality. It can be social-expressive only insofar as an individual's social group rejects gay people and the individual strongly needs to be accepted by members of that group. It can be defensive only when lesbians and gay men are culturally defined in a way that links them to an individual's own psychological conflicts.

Gay people can fulfill these symbolic roles only so long as they remain abstract concepts for the prejudiced heterosexual person, rather than flesh-and-blood human beings. Having a close friend, coworker, or family member who is openly gay can eventually change a prejudiced person's perception of homosexuality from a value-laden symbolic construct to a mere demographic characteristic, like hair color or political party affiliation. By coming out to others, lesbians and gay men disrupt the functions previously served by anti-gay attitudes. When heterosexuals learn that someone about whom they care is gay, formerly functional prejudice can quickly become dysfunctional: the untruth in stereotypes becomes obvious, social norms are perceived to have changed, and traditional moral values concerning sexuality are challenged by their juxtaposition against the heterosexual person's past experience with, knowledge about, and feelings of love for the specific gay man or lesbian. Thus, as with other forms of prejudice, interpersonal contact between gay people and heterosexuals under favorable conditions is one of the most effective ways of reducing psychological heterosexism.

Coming out, however, is difficult and possibly dangerous. It requires making public an aspect of oneself that society perceives as appropriately kept private. It can mean being defined exclusively in terms of sexuality by strangers, friends, and family. It also can mean being newly perceived as possessing some sort of disability or handicap, an inability to be what one should be as man or woman. In the worst situations, it means being completely rejected or even attacked by those to whom one has come out.

Many gay people remain in the closet because they fear these negative interpersonal consequences, as well as discrimination and stigmatization. Additionally, having continually to overcome invisibility is itself a frustrating experience; allowing others to assume that one is heterosexual often is the path of least resistance. Consequently, most heterosexuals' attitudes and behavior toward gay people remain uninformed by personal interactions and instead are driven by the cultural ideologies of sexuality and gender.

TRANSFORMATIONS IN HETEROSEXIST IDEOLOGY: IMPORTANT RECENT TRENDS

The feminist and gay movements, coupled with the struggles for civil rights for racial minorities, have had a profound impact on socioerotic self-definitions, perceptions of the public and the private, and gender roles during the past twenty-five years. Additionally, lesbians and gay men have achieved increasing visibility through community action and by individually coming out. Since the early 1980s, the AIDS epidemic has influenced this process in ways that perhaps will not be recognized for years. In the final section of this article some of these changes and their possible implications for cultural and psychological heterosexism are briefly considered.

Heterosexism and Sexuality
From Private to Public

Through intense political struggle, lesbians and gay men have begun to make what previously was the private world of homosexuality a focus for public discourse. This discourse has itself evolved. The liberationist approach of the early 1970s, which celebrated a polymorphously perverse sexuality, has yielded to a paradigm that defines homosexuals as members of a minority community similar to ethnic groups. Lesbians and gay men now are often perceived as a quasi-ethnic minority group struggling for civil rights. Consequently, gay people are beginning to attain the rudiments of a public identity that is based on community membership as well as individual sexual behavior.

This public identity also has begun to include relational and parental roles. Lesbian and gay male relationships, long hidden from heterosexual society, have become increasingly visible. Growing numbers of openly gay people are raising children, thereby defining parenthood as a component of their gay identity. Some official recognition has been accorded to gay families. A New York Supreme Court, for example, ruled that a gay lover constitutes family for purposes of rent control laws. Former New York Mayor Koch expanded benefits such as funeral leave to include gay city employees. In 1989, San Francisco Mayor Art Agnos signed a domestic partners bill that created a mechanism for members of an unmarried couple (gay or heterosexual) to register their relationship legally, and extended to domestic partners the same considerations provided by the city to married partners. Opposition to societal recognition of gay families has been vigorous. The 1989 San Francisco domestic partners bill, which closely resembled an ordinance vetoed seven years earlier by then-Mayor Feinstein, was defeated by city voters in a subsequent referendum. Both the mayoral veto and the referendum were heavily influenced by religious groups.

The AIDS epidemic has given further visibility to gay relationships and communities. Media coverage has included reporting on the devoted care that gay men with AIDS have received from their lovers and gay families, often while their biological relatives rejected them because of their homosexuality. Such portrayals, along with increasingly frequent personal interactions as more gay people come out in response to the epidemic, undoubtedly have changed public perceptions of gay relationships—

showing both that they exist and that they can include such socially valued attributes as self-sacrifice and commitment.

Thus recognition and legitimation of gay communities, relationships, and families have begun to infiltrate American society. Gay men and women have increasing access to public identities that allow them to affirm their sexual orientation on the basis of community membership and relational commitment but without violating privacy barriers or being "merely" sexual. Public debate is expanding to include a discourse on community and family as well as sexual self-expression.

The Legitimizing of Socioerotic Identities

Because it is a public manifestation of what society prescribes should be private, socioerotic identity heretofore has been inherently stigmatized. This may change, however, as heterosexuals increasingly feel forced to make their own socioerotic identities explicit. Individual Whites often become aware of their own racial identity for the first time when they are surrounded by highly visible racial minority cultures. Similarly, as gay relationships and families become increasingly visible, individual heterosexuals may experience greater pressure to assert and prove their socioerotic identity rather than simply defining themselves in terms of marital and familial status. As a result, socioerotic identity may become less trivialized and accorded greater importance by heterosexual society. Ironically, it may simultaneously become less salient to lesbians and gay men who will have relational, familial, and community-based identities newly available to them. To the extent that homosexuality remains stigmatized, this process may have a negative consequence, at least in the short term: pressures to affirm one's heterosexuality may become even more intense for adolescents and young adults, especially males. In the absence of effective prevention programs, this pressure may foster an increase in anti-gay attacks by young males strongly concerned about their own sexuality and social acceptance.

Heterosexism and Gender

An early goal of the gay movement was to foster sexual liberation, which required, in part, the breaking down of rigid gender roles. Although the range of experiences available to each gender has expanded somewhat, the importance of gender conformity remains relatively unchanged: people who seriously transgress gender roles (e.g., "drag queens" and "bar dykes") remain at the low end of the hierarchy of acceptability (among gay people as well as among heterosexuals). But a change has occurred, albeit not the one originally foreseen by gay liberationists: the traditional equation of homosexuality with gender norm violation appears to be weakening.

As heterosexual Americans have begun to have more contact with openly gay people, the inaccuracy of stereotypes associating a homosexual orientation with the adoption of cross-gender mannerisms and behavior has become more evident. As conceptualizations of gay people become more complex and differentiated, global stereotypes (such as the "sissy" and the "bull dyke") are being replaced by multiple subcategories of various "types" common in gay communities (e.g., "lipstick lesbian," "homo politico," "clone"). Heterosexuals may well continue to dislike effeminate men and masculine women (as do some gay people), but may not equate this with dislike of all homosexuals. As a result, gay people whose outward behavior conforms to cultural conceptions of masculinity and femininity may achieve greater acceptance (Rubin 1984).

Symbolism and Attitudes

As a consequence of the gay political movement, heterosexuals now can have positive attitudes toward gay people that are psychologically functional in ways not previously possible. Because of its identification with movements for racial equality and women's rights, as well as the rights of privacy and free speech, the movement for gay civil rights increasingly has become a respectable progressive political cause. Consequently, heterosexuals who identify themselves as liberals, feminists, and civil libertarians can express support for gay rights as a way of affirming their social identities (a value-expressive function). This equation of the gay community with notions of political progressivism receives impetus when bigoted individuals and hate groups identify gay people as targets comparable to Black and Jews. Ironically, such attacks may permit positive attitudes toward gay people to serve both value-expressive and social-expressive functions as many members of society express their distaste for such bigotry and distance themselves from the groups that promulgate it. If uncoupling of gender and sexuality becomes widespread, the cultural basis for defensive anti-gay prejudice also may diminish as gay people become less suitable symbols for externalizing anxiety about one's own gender identity.

Additionally, AIDS has affected the symbolic status of homosexuality in American culture in both negative and positive ways. By linking stigmatized sexual behavior with death, the popular view of AIDS in the United States reinforces both a moralistic condemnation of homosexuality and individual feelings of defensiveness. Gay people (lesbians have not been differentiated from gay men in popular discourse on AIDS) are viewed by many as receiving just punishment for their sins, and homosexuality is equated with death. Yet, the AIDS epidemic also has led many heterosexuals to confront their own attitudes toward homosexuality for the first time. Because AIDS has made gay people more visible, more heterosexuals have had to articulate their own feelings about homosexuality, often in relation to a gay loved one.

CONCLUSION

Anti-gay violence and victimization in the United States today cannot adequately be understood apart from cultural heterosexism. By alternately denying and stigmatizing homosexuality, this ideology fosters the individual anti-gay prejudice that makes victimization of lesbians and gay men possible. The analysis presented here highlights the necessity of a comprehensive approach to eliminating anti-gay violence. Interventions that focus specifically on violence and victimization clearly are needed. These efforts, however, will not be sufficient to eliminate the ultimate causes of anti-gay violence. Making lesbians and gay men visible and removing the stigma that has so long been attached to a homosexual orientation will require institutional changes. Societal transformations have begun in the past few decades that eventually may shake the foundations of cultural and psychological heterosexism. Perhaps most important of these has been the widespread emergence of lesbians and gay men from invisibility into public life. By discouraging and directly punishing this emergence, anti-gay violence functions to perpetuate heterosexism as well as express it. Eradicating heterosexism, therefore, inevitably requires confronting violence against lesbians and gay men. Eliminating anti-gay violence, in turn, requires an attack upon heterosexism.

DISCUSSION QUESTIONS

1. What individual and collective steps can be taken to continue to move us in the direction outlined in this essay?

2. How is anti-gay violence addressed in your community? How are lesbian and gay men's organizations speaking out against gay bashing? How responsive is the police department in your area to the needs of lesbians and gay men?

SUGGESTIONS FOR FURTHER READING ON ANTI-GAY AND -LESBIAN VIOLENCE

Gary David Comstock. 1991. *Violence against lesbians and gay men.* New York: Columbia University Press.

Gregory Herek & Kevin Berrill, Eds. 1992. *Hate crimes: Confronting violence against lesbians and gay men.* Newbury Park, CA: Sage Publications.

Mab Segrest & Leonard Zeskind. 1989. *Quarantines and death: The Far Right's homophobic agenda.* Atlanta: Center for Democratic Renewal.

MURDER WILL OUT—
BUT IT'S STILL OPEN SEASON ON GAYS
Donna Minkowitz

Complicating the problem of violence against lesbians and gay men is the nature of official responses to the problem, which Donna Minkowitz discusses here. At its most extreme, it can be seen in Senator Jesse Helms's unsuccessful attempts to remove hate crimes based on sexual orientation from the Hate Crimes Statistics Act, which mandated that the FBI keep records on the number of hate crimes in the United States. Including sexual orientation in such statistics, Helms claims, is tantamount to endorsing homosexuality. This is similar to the argument used to suppress information about lesbian and gay teen suicide, described in Shira Maguen's article later in this section.

On January 10, 1992, Erik Brown, 21, and Esat Bici, 19, were sentenced to twenty-five years to life for the July 2, 1990, murder of Julio Rivera, a gay man from the South Bronx. The two youths had bragged to friends about killing the 29-year-old bartender "because he was gay," but nobody, gay and lesbian activists included, really expected them to go to jail for it. Most antigay murders are never prosecuted, and those that are typically result in acquittals or light sentences. No wonder Brown's and Bici's families, friends and attorneys were outraged. Suddenly, a district attorney and a judge had diverged from the criminal justice system's time-honored view of gay-bashing as an offense on a par with jaywalking.

Bici's aunt, Aferdita Suljovic, shouted homophobic execrations for twenty minutes outside the courtroom as Rivera's friends and the media filed out: "It's about time we started picking on them! They have special privileges, but we're *real people*—people that didn't lose any chromosomes! Because [Queens D.A. Richard] Brown wants to keep his job, you know who's gonna be voting for him—pretty in pink!" Brown's and Bici's friends taunted, "Put your lipstick on, honey!" as Rivera's ex-lover walked by in tears. (During the trial, they had baited gay spectators with whispers of "Faggot.") Like Brown's and Bici's defense lawyers, they didn't seem to grasp that open expressions of disdain for gay people might hurt the defendants' case.

At the sentencing hearing, Bici's lawyer, Barry Rhodes, acknowledged for the first time that the defendants "went out to commit an assault, to beat someone up," but asked for leniency on the grounds that they hadn't planned for the victim to actually *die*. Rhodes, who'd earlier informed a reporter that "Bici is normal—he likes girls," laid ultimate blame for the tragedy at the feet of gay and lesbian activists, whom, in a gorgeous example of doublespeak, he termed a "lynch mob." Hearing the phrase, I could only think of the way Rivera died, butchered by Bici, Brown and co-defendant Daniel Doyle with a hammer, knife and plumber's wrench after the three had gone out looking for a "homo" to "tune up"—as Doyle put it—after a skinhead party. Combing a popular gay cruising area in Jackson Heights, Queens, for a likely victim, they lured Rivera into a secluded alcove in a schoolyard and then beat him viciously.

Harold Harrison, Erik Brown's attorney, also made gay people out to be the real criminals in the case. The jury, he declared, "ended up carrying out the desires of the gay rights activists" pressing for "the furtherance of the 'No Gay-Bashing' doctrine they espoused." Harrison actually argued that the trial had been unfair because defense attorneys were not allowed to exclude gays and lesbians from the jury.

During the trial itself, both defense lawyers relied heavily on homophobic arguments. Harrison and Rhodes frequently alluded to Rivera's active sex life, implying that, as a promiscuous gay man, he deserved what he got. Rhodes asked Alan Sack, Rivera's ex-lover, what precautions he had taken while holding Rivera's blood-covered body, so that the attorney could elicit the word "AIDS" in response. An eyewitness who saw Brown and Bici fleeing the scene of the crime was asked, "Weren't you cruising that night?" Even in jury selection, Harrison and Rhodes had appealed to potential juror's homophobia by asking if they'd ever heard of Dykes on Bikes, a lesbian social group completely unconnected to the case.

It's customary for defense lawyers in gay-bashing cases to use homophobia as their main trial strategy. But what was unusual about the Rivera trial was that the judge, jury and prosecutors declined to aid them in this effort. In a 1983 case in Washington, D.C., two college students were found guilty of torturing a gay man (taking a knife to his testicles and nearly killing him) in a public park. Yet the judge sentenced them to 400 hours of community service, on the ground that they had acted in response to a sexual proposition from the victim. In a 1988 trial of an antigay murder in Broward County, Florida, the judge chucklingly asked the prosecutor, "That's a crime now, to beat up a homosexual?" It's not uncommon for antigay killers to brag about the deed—as Brown and Bici did—and get acquitted anyway. In a 1986 Kalamazoo, Michigan, case, 17-year-old Terry Kerr had boasted to friends about killing a "fag." Prosecutors said he'd kicked Harry Wayne Watson "until blood sprayed from his face" and then gone home and returned with a sledgehammer to administer the fatal blows. But a jury acquitted Kerr because he claimed he was reacting to a sexual advance from Watson. The presiding judge in the case, Robert Borsos, later said, "I would have found first degree murder if it had been a bench trial."

Defense attorneys who use homophobia as a tactic have good reason to believe they will find friends on the bench or in the jurors' box. At a 1988 sentencing hearing for the convicted killer of two gay men, Dallas Judge Jack Hampton referred to the victims as "queers" and said he was handing down a light sentence because "I put prostitutes and queers at the same level....And I'd be hard put to give somebody life for killing a prostitute." The "prostitute" comparison is telling. To authorities like Hampton, both women and gay people deserve a beating if they're sexually active. Victims of gay-bashing often receive the same judicial treatment as rape victims; both sets of complainants are said to be "asking for it."

Even prosecutors are often reluctant to ask for harsh sentences in gay-bashings and frequently decline to argue that antigay bias was the motive. Even more disturbing, some have made egregiously homophobic statements to the press. In a January 6 letter to the editor of the New York *Daily News,* Nassau County D.A. Denis Dillon described gays and lesbians as engaging in "deviant disordered sexual practices which contravene Catholic moral teaching," and he applauded the organizers of the St. Patrick's Day parade for keeping out "militant homosexuals." Dillon is currently supervising the prosecution of Angelo Esposito, accused in the December 28 antigay slaying of 26-year-old Henry Marquez near a gay bar in Bellmore, Long Island. How can Dillon be expected to deliver a strong prosecution if he says gay people are immoral? Similarly, the district attorney of Niagara County, Peter Broderick, declared in a 1989 radio interview that lesbians and gay men are "sick people" and "queers." If prosecutors think that such statements are appropriate, no wonder gay-bashers do.

But the biggest obstacle to prosecuting antigay murders is often the police. Even in New York City, one of the few cities where cops deign to keep records on antigay crimes, police consistently undercount homophobic attacks, refusing in many instances to label them as bias crimes. A bias label brings heightened scrutiny that often gives police and other officials greater incentive to pursue the case. In 1990 the N.Y.P.D. classified 102 cases as antigay, but at least three times that number had been reported to them, according to data compiled by the New York City Gay and Lesbian Anti-Violence Project. In more that two-thirds of the cases, police disputed victims' belief that the attacks were bias-motivated. In the Rivera case, it took nine months to classify the murder as a bias crime, and they never assigned a full-time detective to the murder. They let valuable early leads slip out of their hands because, among other reasons, they were reluctant to give credence to the statements of a gay prostitute who linked the three skinheads to the crime. The Anti-Violence Project and Queer Nation had to demonstrate for four months and heckle Mayor David Dinkins at a fundraiser before any arrests were made.

Police in other cities are often worse. In Dallas, recruit Mica England was told she could not be hired as a police officer because she is a lesbian. (A Texas state court recently ruled that the department could no longer use such criteria in hiring.) Thomas Woodard, a bisexual deputy sheriff in Orange County, Florida, was fired when supervisors heard of his relationship with a man. And do we even have to mention the callousness of the Milwaukee police, who nonchalantly returned a bleeding 14-year-old boy to the clutches of Jeffrey Dahmer because, apparently, they assumed violence between gay lovers was natural? When police are openly homophobic, how can they be relied on to solve antigay hate crimes? In a 1989 study, 73% of gay-bashingsurvivors surveyed had declined to report the attack to police; most said their reason was fear of encountering antigay treatment from police officers. In fact, police homophobia nationwide is the main reason there are no meaningful national statistics on antigay murders. The Hate Crimes Statistics Act, recently passed by Congress, mandates that the F.B.I. keep records on crimes motivated by homophobia (among other biases), but the F.B.I. receives all its data on nonfederal crimes from local police departments. Since most departments still refuse to keep records on antigay offenses, the only homophobic crimes the F.B.I. can be expected to chart with any accuracy are federal ones—a category into which very few gay-bashings fit. And only a few cities have gay and lesbian antiviolence organizations with sufficient resources to tally the crimes themselves. In New York, the Anti-Violence Project reported thirteen murders in 1990 and sixteen in 1989, at least two-thirds of which the project defines as definitely bias-motivated. Very few of them received any attention from the media or from politicians.

Unlike the vast majority of homophobic killings, however, the murder of Julio Rivera resulted in arrests, convictions and substantial jailtime for the killers. The reason can be expressed in one word: activism. Led by Matt Foreman of the Anti-Violence Project, by Queer Nation and by Alan Sack, activists bit onto this case and would not let go, harrying police, prosecutors and the Mayor for more than a year and a half to treat this crime with the seriousness it deserved. Finally, this past January, they saw the fruits of their labor: Judge Ralph Sherman stated from the bench that "courts of this state should send out a message that our society cannot, will not and must not tolerate these crimes of senseless intolerance—by imposing the maximum sentence." What does it say about the current situation of gay people in America that we must count it as a mammoth victory when someone actually serves time in jail for killing us? Ending gay-bashing itself—the most common kind of bias attack, according to the Justice Department—is still another matter.

DISCUSSION QUESTIONS

1. Why might those responsible for keeping order in society have a contradictory response to violence against lesbians and gay men? How is this related to their response to violence against women in general, and against people of color and the homeless?

2. Does the persistence of laws forbidding sodomy in many states contribute to this problem?

3. What are some other local groups who are victimized by police and courts? How might we begin to build joint campaigns with them? How will we need to frame the issues?

4. How might the militarized organization of police forces contribute to their hostility to lesbians and gay men? What alternative ways of organizing public safety duties might be tried?

SUGGESTIONS FOR FURTHER READING

Kevin Berrill & Gregory Herek. 1992. Primary and secondary victimization in anti-gay hate crimes: Official response and public policy. *Hate crimes: Confronting violence against lesbians and gay men.* Gregory Herek & Kevin Berrill, Eds. Newbury Park, CA: Sage Publications.

Hayden Curry & Denis Clifford. 1984. *A legal guide for lesbian and gay couples.* Reading, MA: Addison-Wesly.

John Gonsiorek & James Weinrich, Eds. 1991. *Homosexuality: Research implications for public policy.* Newbury Park, CA: Sage Publications.

National Center for Lesbian Rights. 1992. *Recognizing lesbian & gay families: Strategies for obtaining domestic partnership benefits.* NCLR (1663 Mission St. 5th Floor, San Francisco, CA 94103).

Richard Mohr. 1988. *Gay/Justice: A study of ethics, society and law.* New York: Columbia University Press.

TEEN SUICIDE:
THE GOVERNMENT'S COVER-UP
AND AMERICA'S LOST CHILDREN
Shira Maguen

Violence is not always direct. This article deals with indirect violence on two levels. The first is the toll that homophobia takes on young people for whom exploring the meaning of their sexuality is too painful to face any longer. Although youth suicide is widely talked about, rarely has the difficulty of growing up in a heterosexist society been explored when considering the problem.

Indeed, attempts to examine it are often deliberately repressed, as this article points out. This is the second level of violence: right-wing attacks on any discussion of heterosexism and its toll. In the current political climate, dedicated heterosexists have considerable power. We also note that then-Secretary of Health and Human Services Louis Sullivan, mentioned in the article as having yielded to pressure from Rep. William Dannemeyer, espoused in public speeches during his tenure the view that lesbians and gay men have no right to be considered a minority group deserving of recognition and protection under the law.

Mark Wood, a gay teenager from Seattle, Washington, committed suicide after he got an honorable discharge from the Marines. After talking to his minister, the 18-year old went into the chapel, knelt at the altar, and shot himself.

Gay and lesbian teenagers are killing themselves in staggering numbers. They are hanging themselves in high school classrooms, jumping from bridges, shooting themselves on church altars, cutting themselves with razor blades, and downing lethal numbers of pills.

A conservatively estimated 1,500 young gay and lesbian lives are terminated every year because these troubled youths have nowhere to turn. They are scared and alone. They face a government bureaucracy that could help but that instead has fallen under the influence of right-wing fundamentalists who care more about conservative political correctnessthan about saving lives. The gay and lesbian community—always wary of child-abuse accusations—offers little assistance. School boards, parents, and teacher associations all dance around the issue, putting public image above human lives.

"The government does not have the best interest of children at heart," says Virginia Uribe, founder of Project 10, a Los Angeles Unified School District program that provides on-campus counseling for gay and lesbian youth. "They are coming from a deep core of prejudice against gay and lesbian teens. [Representative] William Dannemeyer [R-CA] has failed young people completely and indirectly contributes to their deaths. [Secretary of Health and Human Services] Louis Sullivan has sold out to religion and lost his sense of principle. He bears a great responsibility for these kids. It's disgusting."

The facts and figures surrounding gay teen suicide and the government cover-up of them are indeed disgusting. According to a 1989 study first commissioned and then squelched by the Department of Health and Human Services (HHS), gay youth are two to three times more likely to attempt suicide than heterosexual youth, and up to 30% of those teenagers who do commit suicide are gay or lesbian.

An even more recent study, published in *Pediatrics* magazine last June—a report also ignored by the government—states that 30% of gay youth attempt suicide near the age of 15. The *Pediatrics* study, conducted by Dr. Gary Remafedi of the University of Minnesota at Minneapolis/St. Paul and Dr. James Farrow and Dr. Robert Deisher of the University of Washington also showed that almost half of the gay and lesbian teens they interviewed say they attempted suicide more than once.

According to the 1989 HHS report, conducted by Paul Gibson, a San Francisco social worker, "Suicide is the leading cause of death among gay male, lesbian, and bisexual youth" in the United States. It is also the second leading cause of death overall for teens in the United States, killing more than 5,000 annually, according to the National Center for Health Statistics in Washington, D.C.

The Gibson report was one of 50 papers commissioned for the report of the HHS secretary's Task Force on Youth Suicide. As soon as the report and its gay and lesbian suicide section were leaked in Washington an immediate conservative backlash erupted. Dannemeyer sent a letter to HHS assistant secretary James O. Mason, asking him to denounce the report. "The last thing these individuals [gays and lesbians] need is a perception of accommodation from the Bush administration," Dannemeyer wrote on Aug. 9, 1989. Dannemeyer wrote another letter to President George Bush a month later, stating, "If you choose to affirm traditional family values, my next suggestion would be to dismiss from public service all persons still employed who concocted this homosexual pledge of allegiance and…seal the lid on these misjudgments for good."

Following an October 5, 1989, meeting with Dannemeyer about the report, Sullivan responded in a letter to the California representative, saying that although youth suicide is an important issue, the views in the Gibson paper with respect to gay youth "undermine the institution of the family." In his report, Gibson merely proposed a series of recommendations, stressing that gay teens should be accepted by parents, organized religion, and society as a whole.

"Our government has announced that information about gay and lesbian anything with respect to adolescents is simply going to be ignored, and in this case it's a very deadly choice," says Teresa DeCrescenzo, director of Gay and Lesbian Adolescent Social Services (GLASS), a Los Angeles-based agency that is the only such organization in the United States licensed to provide long-term residential treatment that offers services for gay and lesbian youth. "I think there is a combination of neglect and downright obstructionism on the part of the federal government."

Following the exchanges between Danneymeyer and Sullivan, no federal action was taken on the Gibson report. "As far as we know, the entire youth suicide report continues to collect dust at HHS because of the controversy around the section on gay youth suicide," says Robert Bray, public-information director of the National Gay and Lesbian Task Force (NGLTF), a political group. "It is an unconscionable tragedy that has been ignored by health officials in Washington because of homophobia. So while public health officials, including Louis Sullivan, play political football with the issue of gay and lesbian youth suicide, kids are killing themselves."

Gibson agrees, saying, "It's unfortunate that Secretary Sullivan chose to politicize one of the basic human health issues."

When *The Advocate* attempted repeatedly to set up an interview with Sullivan, one of his press secretaries, Kim Bleine, reported back, "It is not a subject that the secretary wishes to comment on." Dannemeyer's press secretary, Paul Mero, did not return any of 12 messages left over a period of two weeks.

"Change has to come from a federal level," says Denis Penn, an Orange County, California, social worker whose lesbian daughter attempted suicide. "Local governments are under too much pressure from their communities." Gibson complains that "to ignore my report isn't going to change the fact that lesbian, gay, and bisexual youth exist. To ignore the report is not going to make these problems go away."

Instead of taking the report's recommendations, the federal government, which would usually issue press releases and hold a news conference to publicize the new information, remained silent and ordered that a more watered-down report on gay teen suicide, which was also among the 50 commissioned papers, be issued. The report, by Dr. Joseph Harry, associate professor of sociology at Northern Illinois University in De Kalb, deals mainly with older gays and lesbians—young people in their twenties or thirties—and contains only recommendations for further research rather than proposals to help prevent suicide. The Harry report does state that "homosexuals of both sexes are two to six times more likely to attempt suicide than are heterosexuals."

The attitudes of Dannemeyer, Sullivan and other conservative government officials are felt by gay youth on a day-to-day basis. "The government perpetuates homophobia," says Vanessa Williams, an 18-year old Indianan who seriously contemplated suicide after several attempts to get support from school officials were rebuffed. "They told me, 'Hang in there,'" she says. "The message that I get from the government is that it's OK to be homophobic and it's OK to gay-bash. It disturbs me that I get that message from my government. I deserve to be respected and protected too."

Bray of NGLTF finds the government's actions deplorable. "Never in our wildest imaginations did we ever consider that the subject of gay and lesbian teenagers would strike such fear and terror into our highest public health officials in this country to the point where they'd totally ignore all attempts to keep young gay people alive," he says. "It's entirely political, and it's a conscious decision."

Others point to federal inaction as exacerbating the problem on a local school board level. "I think that the problem at the federal level is just the lack of any kind of real commitment to family and a lack of commitment to education," says Robert Birlie, spokesperson for a Bay Area network of gay and lesbian educators. As a result, he adds, "there is very little going on in the school systems."

Uribe says, "Many school systems across the country have suicide-prevention units but 99.9% of them make no mention of the heightened risk of being gay or lesbian. There needs to be trained staff—psychologists, counselors—that these students have access to."

SCARED AND ALONE

Many of the adults who directly work with gay youth remain clueless about basic information on homosexuality. Because of this many of the young gays and lesbians interviewed for this article either dropped out of school or changed schools several times.

Julian Ulseth, a Minneapolis teen, never finished high school because of constant teasing. His mother, Judith, tried to find a private school that would accept him. One school agreed to take Julian but then rejected him. "They called one day when I wasn't home, and Julian told them he was gay," she says. "They later called back and said they could no longer accept him."

The Harvey Milk High School, a public school for gay and lesbian youth in New York, opened in 1985, but there are no comparable schools in the rest of the nation. On-campus support groups, like Project 10 in Los Angeles, do exist but are rare and are constantly being attacked by conservative politicians.

"The recommendations of the report and public school programs such as Project 10 simply add legitimacy to the heretofore crime of child molestation," Dannemeyer wrote in his previously cited 1989 letter to Bush.

Many gay and lesbian youths would welcome some understanding in the school system. Leonard Jenkins, an Ohio teen, came out to his teachers when he was 14. "His teachers told him he had nothing to live for," recalls his mother, Rada. "Another teacher told Leonard that he would rather for his son to come home any day with cancer than to have what Leonard had. The kid was 14, just coming out, and he was scared to death. It's no wonder there is so much suicide among these young people.

"Even the counselors had no idea [about homosexuality]," she says. "It was like bringing them out of a cave in the Dark Ages." Leonard, who was a straight-A student, found a rope, went in the band room, and tried to hang himself. Although unsuccessful, he was then hospitalized for nearly three months. It was only after the family moved and Leonard attended a different school where he remained closeted that he was able to graduate.

Social worker Penn also remembers her lesbian daughter relating several homophobic incidents at school. One day her daughter was at her locker when she heard two males saying, "Hey, is that her over there? Is that the lez? What do you say we take her out in the hills and show her the right way to do it?" Penn says, "When she told the school psychologist she was gay, they didn't believe her because she's small and very feminine."

Williams felt the same kind of helplessness. The Indiana teen says, "At school everywhere I went I would get laughed at as soon as I walked through the door. People would say stuff like 'Hey, boy.' If I got called a lesbian or a dyke, when I went to the administration or dean and asked for support, I never got that support. I think that if someone would have stood up for me and said, 'It's not OK to make fun of gays and lesbians,' it would have helped a lot."

"When kids learn things at school, that is gospel to them," says Mary Griffith, whose gay son killed himself by jumping off a freeway overpass in Portland, Oregon, after feeling there was no one left to turn to. "When they can sit there and learn with the other kids that their life is positive in the same way that their nongay peer's life is positive, then I think it can make a big difference. I know it would have made a difference in my son's life."

Remafedi, who conducted the *Pediatrics* study, confirms that kids are getting the wrong message in school, whether from from fellow students or counselors. "Virtually no professionals in the country receive any kind of special training on homosexuality, let alone the issues surrounding adolescent homosexuality," he says. "Many of the professionals that we work with are reluctant to refer gay and lesbian kids to social support groups. On one level they believe that by doing so, they might entrench the person's homosexual identity. They are worried about parents' reactions or what their supervisors might think."

AMERICA'S DESPERATE KIDS

Many teens also meet with the disapproval of their parents, who may blame their children for choosing to be gay.

GLASS program director Sharon Kidd describes one of her most frustrating cases, that of Nikki (not his real name), a 16-year-old boy from Nebraska. Nikki, a flamboyant youth who sometimes cross-dresses, was scorned and rejected from his early teens by parents who "were very unhappy with his sexual preference," says Kidd.

After a two-year hospitalization resulting from attempts at suicide and self-multilation, Nikki, by now a ward of the state of Nebraska, found his way to Los Angeles. "He was heavily into drugs and turning tricks to support his habit, living on the streets," Kidd says. Getting him into GLASS involved battling with homophobic Nebraska officials, who asked Kidd if she "changed" the sexual orientation of the youths in her program. But Nikki may be too troubled for GLASS's unlocked facility to handle. The night of August 17, he attempted suicide again, slashing his arm with a razor and scrawling something unintelligible in blood on the bathroom floor before passing out. After a hellish night in which Kidd struggled unsuccessfully to have him confined 72 hours for his own safety and for psychological evaluation, he ended up back on the streets. A day later he was in the hospital again, this time being treated for a drug overdose. Says Kidd: "He's worth saving. Society has screwed them up. It's almost as if they [troubled gay teens] need to be hospitalized."

"If parents could only stop making children fit their ideals and allow children to be themselves," says Judith Ulseth. "We kept saying to our son, who is very feminine, 'What is wrong with you?' We kept blaming him. We did not understand that that was just the way he is."

Many teens simply want their parents to listen and be supportive. "They'd pretend they were supportive, but whenever I'd mention anything gay or lesbian, the first thing out of their mouths would be 'Is that all you can talk about?'" says Williams, who came out at eleven.

"It's so much harder to come out as a teen knowing possibly your parents aren't going to accept you," says Scott (not his real name), who attempted suicide at 13. "One year in high school I had my car headlights broken three times. How do you explain that to your parents? There were so many things to worry about. If I sent away for information, who was going to get the mail? I looked in the phone book for places to call and they were all long-distance. How would I explain that to my parents?"

Many teens and experts identify this feeling of isolation from parents and the reactions from society as a principal cause of suicide. Says Williams: "I felt really alienated from the rest of the world. I didn't really have friends that I could relate to. I didn't want to die. What I wanted was attention. I wanted someone to look at me and give me that attention and realize that I was being overlooked."

DeCrescenzo says, "They have strong feelings and yearnings, and they get absolutely no support for developing their identities—from their schoolteachers, from their religious organizations, from their peers—so they go into hiding. When you go into hiding, you tend to feel more self-doubt, which very quickly turns into self-loathing and suicide attempts. All the messages these kids get from society say that they are no good."

Julian Ulseth also had a very difficult time growing up. "My son started suffering at 5," says Judith Ulseth. "He's a natural athlete. He could ride a two-wheeled bicycle before he was 4, but when someone said that he skated like a girl, he became so self-conscious that he couldn't even run without falling."

Julian tried to hang himself at 13 and later ran away. At 14 he came out to his mother. She says, "It was shocking, but it was an answer. It opened doors in my mind that I had tried to nail shut. We were trying to deny it." He would often lock himself in his room and was constantly upset. Then one night after he had an argument with his parents, he cut his wrists and swallowed a bottle of codeine. He then called his mother, who bandaged his wrists and made him vomit. Julian began receiving counseling shortly thereafter. He did not finish school but moved out with a friend and got a job.

Chris Jones, an 18-year-old Midwesterner, has made six suicide attempts. "I was under the impression that since I was gay, I wouldn't be able to do anything substantial with my life," he says. In sixth grade he took an overdose of aspirin. In eighth grade he tried jumping out of a tree, but another branch broke his fall. When he was a sophomore in high school, he tried taking prescribed pills, but there were not enough pills in the bottle to kill him.

Jones says his parents never understood what he was trying to do. "It amazed me that all the attempts went unnoticed," he says. Later in his sophomore year, Jones asked a friend to borrow a gun. "I tried to pull the trigger six times, but all of the bullets were blanks," he says. In his fifth suicide attempt, he tied a bag around his body and lit a candle inside, hoping it would use up the oxygen. His final attempt took place last January, when he was no longer living at home. The friends he was living with called an ambulance, and the police arrived as well. Jones was in the hospital for nearly three weeks.

Society's negative messages take a heavy toll on gay and lesbian youth. "Everyday I had to deal with some type of abuse," says Scott, who grew up in Ohio. "I was trying to define who I was, and there were absolutely no role models. The only gays I ever saw, like in the pride parades, were real flamboyant. It really confused me, and I kept thinking, *That's not me.* Then the mass media kept feeding me constant images of murder and AIDS. When you hear all the negative messages from your friends, your parents, and TV, you begin to think, *What is wrong with me?* It builds up, and then you want to just end everything. You figure it's the only way out. At one point, everything just climaxed. I was standing on a bridge about to jump off. Now I'm glad I didn't. I want all gay teens who are in that situation to know that it will get better."

HELL ON EARTH

Bobby Griffith was not as lucky. After spending his teen years in agony because he did not feel accepted as a homosexual, he killed himself one night after going dancing, two months after his 20th birthday. He left a club at about midnight and walked to the freeway. He stood on the overpass and eventually jumped. His mother remembers seeing him for the last time a few months earlier. She says, "He looked like he had already given up. He was just going through the motions, but he wasn't really there. His spirit seemed to be all but gone. It was the end of a constant grieving process over himself and the way life was toward him. He was worried that he would go to hell. I guess hell couldn't have been any worse that what he was living here on earth."

Stacey Yother, now 24, who is studying to be a clinical psychologist, remembers being suicidal at the age of 13. At 15 she began carrying razor blades in her shoe, and she was hospitalized at 16 following an unsuccessful suicide attempt. She says, "Society told me that as a lesbian I was expendable. I was at the point where even a public service announcement would have given me the right to live. One person coming out would have really helped."

"I think that the message these kids get from society is that they don't deserve to live," says Doris Wood, whose gay son Marty committed suicide in a chapel. "Somehow we have to counteract that."

Another of Wood's sons attempted suicide by taking a drug overdose at the age of 16 and it was not until three years later that he came out to her. "It makes me so furious when people talk about youth suicide and don't mention the increased risk of gay suicide," she says, citing several talk shows NBC's *Good Morning America* and Cable News Network's *Crier & Co.* are two recent samples of shows that have done segments about teen suicide without mentioning gay and lesbian youth.

ARE THEY OUR CHILDREN TOO?

Support programs for gay youth exist in very few parts of the nation, and there are even fewer programs run by gay and lesbian organizations aimed at preventing teen suicide. "These kids have been ignored by not only by the straight community but also by the gay community," DeCrescenzo says. "It's long since past time that the gay community stepped up and said, "'We'll take care of our own.'"

"The adult gay and lesbian community has the obligation to also step in and say, 'Yes, we'll do our share too,'" says Chris Gonzalez, director of Indiana Youth Group (IYG), a gay youth support program. "The time is right for us to start networking across the nation. These kids are dying, they're being killed on the streets, they're drugging themselves to death, they've been thrown out of their homes. The time has come for us as a gay and lesbian community to stand up for these young folks. It's obvious no one else is going to do it."

Bray agrees, saying, "Gays and lesbians around the country have to realize that these are our kids, the future of our movement, and it is mandatory that we not only advocate on their behalf to our lawmakers but to support them personally and individually." Many of the teens who attempted suicide speak of the need for role models. "I needed positive gay and lesbian role models like teachers and lawyers," says Willams.

Some teens turn to organizations such as the Boston Alliance of Gay and Lesbian Youth, a support group; Queer Nation, a direct-action group; and Parents and Friends of Lesbians And Gays (P-FLAG), a support group that has chapters across the nation. The P-FLAG chapters hold meetings on a regular basis to help families deal with homosexuality within the family.

"I wish I would have found a group earlier," says Jones, who received counseling from IYG. "It's helped me so much. It's given me the courage to go back to school." Williams says IYG, which has the nation's first gay and lesbian youth hot line run by peers, has given her a feeling of belonging to a community.

"One of the things we were getting on the hot line a lot more than we had originally anticipated was suicide calls," says Gonzalez. By this autumn, IYG, which is funded by the United States Conference of Mayors, will have eight chapters across Indiana. Gonzalez continues, "National statistics say that gay males are eight to nine times more likely to commit suicide [than straight kids] and lesbians are two to three times more likely. We have seen that to be pretty true within our program and the youth we work with."

To date, IYG has received thousands of calls, and 60% of the teens calling have contemplated or attempted suicide at some point. "A lot of them are at the end of their rope, and they don't know whom to turn to," says Gonzalez. "Straight youth have organizations like church groups and Boy Scouts to pump their self-esteem back up. Gay and lesbian teens don't have that support. It's especially hard because many teens are calling from areas across the nation that have no resources or support groups. IYG cannot turn them anywhere for help, so they just keep calling back several times." Because of IYG's commitment, the largest public school system in Indiana invited the group to give an information session last February for counselors, psychologists, and psychiatrists to increase awareness about gay and lesbian youth issues.

P-FLAG has started the Respect All Youth project to educate teachers and publishes informative newsletters on a regular basis dealing with gay and lesbian youth and their increased risk of suicide. In the future, P-FLAG hopes to use these papers to develop materials to train teachers from the National Education Association and the Parent Teacher Association.

"We are offering a workshop called Affording Equal Opportunity to Gay and Lesbian Students" says Carolyn Wallace, a National Education Association spokeswoman. "The workshop will be available for each state that wants to train school officials."

In addition, the Lesbian and Gay Public Awareness Project, an organization that works to reduce discrimination against gays and lesbians through the media, has several ads that it publishes in mainstream newspapers and magazines. One ad has a picture of Bobby Griffith as well as one of his diary entries before his suicide. "Are you abusing your child without knowing it?" the ad asks.

In all too many cases the answer seems to be yes, and researchers such as Remafedi feel time is running out. "This is an urgent public health problem," he writes in the *Pediatrics* study.

Don Keyes writes in the only report about gay and lesbian suicide from the National Institute of Suicidology, "In twenty years we have not progressed very far....The 1990s need to show a greater stride in dealing with gay youth or our legacy will be a path laden with the victims of our neglect."

DISCUSSION QUESTIONS

1. How can parents, teachers and adult friends create a climate where young people can explore their sexuality without fear? Where schools are unwilling to engage these questions, what alternative strategies are available?

2. What were readers' own experiences around discovering and giving meaning to their sexuality as young people? In particular, to what extent were we free to explore directions that we may ultimately have decided did not fit with our sexual identity?

3. What local efforts to make space for lesbian, gay and bisexual youth are going on in our community? To what extent are these efforts based on the empowerment of young people? What issues are queer youth raising and addressing in this area?

4. How can activists organize to oppose efforts to silence information about young people's sexuality? How has such organizing been inhibited by our own discomfort in talking about sexual activity? What place should

ideas about sexual practice and its importance in human life have in our general thinking about social change goals and strategies?

SUGGESTIONS FOR FURTHER STUDY ON YOUTH

Aaron Fricke. 1981. *Reflections of a rock lobster: A story about growing up gay.* Boston: Alyson Publications.

Ann Heron. 1983. *One teenager in ten: Testimonies by gay and lesbian youth.* New York: Warner.

Katherine Whitlock. 1989. *Bridges of respect: Creating support for lesbian and gay youth.* Philadelphia: AFSC.

SUGGESTIONS FOR READING ON AGING

Marcy Adelman, Ed. 1986. *Long time passing: Lives of older lesbians.* Boston: Alyson Publications.

Raymond Berger. 1982. *Gay and gray: The older homosexual man.* Boston: Alyson Publications.

Baba Copper. 1990. The view from over the hill: Notes on ageism between lesbians. *Lesbian cultures and philosophies.* Jeffner Allen, Ed. New York: State University of New York.

Monica Kehoe. 1986. Lesbians over 65: A triply invisible minority. *Historical, literary, and erotic aspects of lesbianism.* Monica Kehoe, Ed. New York: Harrington Park Press.

Keith Vacha. 1985. *Quiet fire: memories of older gay men.* Trumansburg: Crossing Press.

MY LIFE YOU ARE TALKING ABOUT
Minnie Bruce Pratt

The ugliness, the stupid repetition
when I mention my children, or these poems,
or myself as mother.   My anger when someone
tries to make my life into a copy of
an idea in her head, flat, paper thin.

How can I make any of this into a poem?
What do I mean by *this*?   For instance:

Me standing by the xerox machine, clack, slide, whish.   Another
teacher, I've known her for five years, asks what I've been writing,
lately,

and I say: *These poems about my children,*

holding up the pages.   Her face blanks.   I'd never seen that
happen, the expression, a blank face—vacant, emptied.

She says: *I didn't know you had children.*

So I say: *That's what these are about.   Not many people know*
            I have children.   They were taken from me.

She says: *You're kidding.*

I say: *No, I'm not kidding.   I lost my children because I'm*
            a lesbian.

She says: *But how could that happen to someone with a Ph.D.?*

I lean against a desk.   I want to slap her with anger.

Instead,
I answer: *I'm a pervert, a deviant, low as someone on the street,*
              as a prostitute, a whore.   I'm unnatural, queer.   I'm a
              lesbian.   I'm not fit to have children.

I didn't
explain: A woman who's loose with men is trash; a woman
              with a woman is to be punished.

Because this woman was supposed to be a feminist and
understand something.

I walk away, carrying off the poems,
useless words, black tracks on flimsy paper.
So much for the carry-over of metaphor
and the cunning indirection of the poet (me)

who lures the listener (her) deeper and deeper
with bright images, through thorns, a thicket,
into a hidden openness (the place beyond the self:
see any of the preceding or following poems).

So much for the imagination.   I don't say:
You've known for years who I am.   Have you
never imagined what happened to me day
in and out, out in your damned straight world?

Why give her a poem to use to follow me
as I gather up the torn bits, a path made
of my own body, a trail to find
what has been lost, what has been taken,

when, if I stand in the room, breathing,
sweating a little, with a shaky voice,
blood-and-bones who tells what happened,
I get her disbelief?   Or worse:

A baby-faced lesbian, her new baby snug in her closed arms,

smiles, matronizing, smug, and asks had I ever thought of
having children?

Have you ever thought of having children?

What I thought as the pay-phone
doctor's voice pronounced jovial
stunning pregnancy, advised philosophy
(why he had five, this one's only my
second) was: Where would my life be
in this concept *mother-of-two?*
There was no one around to see.
I could cry all I wanted while
I sat down and got used to the idea.

At a friend's house for dinner, we talk about my boys, her
girl, the love affairs of others, how I like morning bed with
my lover.   She complains how sex is hard to get with a three-
year-old around, glances at me as if to say: You have it so
easy.   Does say:

Well, if you had children.

In his crib the first baby bangs
his head on the side, little worm
wailing lost earth.   He burrows,
pushes through, in, out my vagina,
while in another room, I cringe
at the push of his father's penis.

Other side of the door, the two boys
half-grown, rest gangly in their sleep.
In bed, her hand slides, cold, doubtful
from my breast.   She frets: *What are they
thinking?*   While I whisper, hot, heat
in my breath, how I lost them for touch,
dangerous touch, and we would not believe
the mean knifing voice that says we lose
every love if we touch.   We pull close,

belly to belly, kiss, push, push,
no thought in writhe against ache,
our sweaty skin like muddy ground
when we come back to being there in bed,
and to the sleeping presence of children.

In a classroom, we wind through ideas about women, power,
the loss of children, men and ownership, the loss of self,
the lesbian mother.   They have heard me tell how it has been
for me.   The woman to my left, within hand's reach, never
turns her face toward me.   But speaks about me:

It's just not good for children to be in that kind of home.

I am stripped, naked, whipped.
Splintered by anger, wordless.
I want to break her, slash her.
My edged eyes avoid her face.

I say: *Why do you think this?*

I do not say: What have you lost? What have you ever
                  lost?

Later I say: *This is my life you are talking about.*

She says: *I didn't mean it personally.*

Over the phone, someone I've known for years asks what am I
writing now?

I say: *I'm working on some poems about my
                  children.*

She says: Oh, how sweet.   How sweet.

A QUESTION OF SURVIVAL
Audre Lorde

The struggle against violence is broad and indivisible. Audre Lorde, in this commencement speech given at Oberlin College on May 29, 1989, points out that our vision of ending violence must include a broad program of social justice work. There are social forms of violence, such as racism and economic exploitation, that also harm persons. While we need to concentrate our efforts, we must not let such concentration either limit our sense of power or suppress parts of our deepest selves.

I congratulate your all on this moment of your lives. Most people don't remember their commencement addresses. Next year, when someone asks you who spoke at graduation, I wonder what you will say. I remember she was a middle-aged Black woman. I remember she had a nice voice. I remember she was a poet. But what did she say? After all, there are no new ideas. Only new ways of making those ideas real and active through our lives. What you most of all do not need right now is more rhetoric. What you need are facts you don't ordinarily get to help you fashion weapons for the war in which we are all engaged. A war for survival in the 21st century, the survival of this planet and all this planet's people.

THANKS TO JESSE JACKSON

The US and the USSR
are the most powerful countries in the
world
but only 1/8 of the world's population
African people are also 1/8 of the world's population.
1/2 of the world's population is Asian.
1/2 of that number is Chinese.

There are 22 nations in the Middle East.
Not three.

Most people in the world
are Yellow, Black, Brown, Poor, Female

Non-Christian
and do not speak english.

By the year 2000
the 20 largest cities in the world
will have two things in common
none of them will be in Europe
and none in the United States.

You are all so very beautiful. But I have seen special and beautiful before, and I ask myself where are they now? I look for the imprint of their earnestness upon the worlds we share. What makes you different? Well, to begin with, you are different because you have asked me to come and speak with you from my heart, on what is a very special day for each of you. So when they ask you, who spoke at your commencement, remember this: I am a Black feminist lesbian warrior poet doing my work, and a piece of my work is asking you how are you doing yours? And when they ask you, what did she say, tell them I asked you the most fundamental question of your life—Who are you, and how are you using the powers of that self in the service of what you believe?

You are inheriting a country that has grown hysterical with denial and contradiction. Last month in space five men released a satellite that is on its way to the planet Venus, and the infant mortality rate in the capital of this nation is higher than in Kuwait.

We are citizens of the most powerful country on earth—we are also citizens of a country that stands upon the wrong side of every liberation struggle on earth. Feel what that means. It is a reality that haunts each of our lives and that can help inform our dreams. It's not about altruism, it's about self-preservation. Survival.

A 28-year-old white woman is beaten and raped in Central Park. Eight Black boys are named, arrested and accused. A 17-year-old mentally retarded white girl is raped in New Jersey. Five white boys, nameless, are protected by police for more than a month while the victim is questioned and tested. These are nightmares that affect each of our lives. I pray for the body and soul of every one of these young people trapped in these compound tragedies of violence and social reprisal. None of us escapes the brutalization of the other. Violence against women escalates, cutting across race, class, and region.

Using who we are, testifying with our lives to what we believe is not altruism, it is a question of self-preservation. Black children did not declare war upon this system, it is the system which declared war upon Black children, both female and male.

Ricky Boden, 11, Staten Island. Killed by police. 1972. Clifford Glover, 10. Queens, New York. Killed by police. 1975. Randy Evans, 14, Bronx, New

York. Killed by police. 1976. Andre Roland, seventh grader, found hanged in Columbia, Missouri, after being threatened for dating a white girl.

You are strong and intelligent. Your beauty and your promise lie like a haze over your faces. I beg you, do not waste it. Translate that power and beauty into action wherever you find yourself to be, or you will participate in your own destruction.

I have no platitudes for you. Before most of you are thirty, ten percent of you will be involved with space traffic and ten percent of you will have contracted AIDS. This disease which may yet rival the Plague of the Dark Ages is said to have originated in Africa, spontaneously and inexplicably jumping from the green monkey to man. Yet in 1969, twenty years ago, a book entitled *A Survey of Chemical and Biological Warfare*, written by John Cookson and Judith Nottingham, discusses green monkey disease as a fatal blood, tissue and venereally transmitted virus which is an example of a whole new class of disease-causing organisms, and of biological warfare interest. It also discusses the possibilities of this virus being genetically manipulated to produce "new" organisms.

But I do have hope. To face the realities of our lives is not a reason for despair—despair is a tool for your enemies. Facing the realities of our lives gives us motivation for action and the power to change. For you are not powerless. You know why the hard questions must be asked. It is not altruism, it is self-preservation—survival.

Each one of us here is privileged. We have beds and we do not go to them hungry. We are not part of those millions of homeless people roaming America today. Your privilege is not a reason for guilt, it is part of your power, to be used in support of those things you believe. Because the greatest error of privilege is to absorb without use....

Become aware of who pays for you to live the way you do. Cheap labor is never cheap for the person who performs it. It is made cheap for the benefit of those who consume the products of that labor. South African coal is the cheapest coal in the world because black coal miners slave and die in South African coalpits for less than thirty cents a day. And that cheap South African coal is putting miners in Kentucky and Virginia out of work, and breaking the coal miner unions in this country.

Look at the tags inside your robes, in your shirts. On the back of your cassette recorders. Most of us here in this room would never be able to afford these commodities if it were not for the grossly underpaid labor of women of color around the world who slave to produce them. So when you use your pocket-radios and your computers, be conscious that young women in Sri Lanka, Thailand, Malaysia are going blind assembling your electronics. When you go through your closets looking for something to wear, be aware that adolescents in the Philippines and Jamaica are losing their health to the heat and dust of textile sweatshops sewing the fine silks and cottons. I am not saying don't wear these clothes, don't use these electronics. I am saying be aware of who supports these technologies. Be aware that we have a responsibility to the people who expend that "cheap" labor that makes our lifestyles possible. Not out of altruism, but for our own survival.

The poorest one-fifth of this nation became seven percent poorer in the last ten years, and the richest one-fifth of the nation became eleven percent richer. How much of your lives are you willing to spend merely protecting your privileged status? Is that more than you are prepared to spend putting your dreams and beliefs for a better world into action? That is what creativity and empowerment are all about. The rest is destruction. And it will have to be one or the other.

It is not enought to believe in justice. The median income for Black and Hispanic families in this country fell in the last three years, while the median income of white families rose one-and-a-half percent. We are all eleven years away from a new century, and a leader of the Ku Klux Klan can still be elected to Congress from the Republican party in Louisiana. Little 14-year-old Black boys in the seventh grade are still being lynched for dating a white girl. It is not enough to say we are against racism.

It is not enough to believe in everyone's right to her or his own sexual preference. Homophobic jokes are not just fraternity high jinks. Gay bashing is not just fooling around. Less than a year ago a white man shot two white women in their campsite in Pennsylvania, killing one of them. He pleaded innocent, saying he had been maddened by their making love inside their own tent. If you were sitting on that jury, what would you decide?

It is not enough to believe anti-Semitism is wrong, when the vandalism of synagogues is increasing, amid the home-grown fascism of hate groups like the Christian Identity and Tom Metzger's American Front. The current rise in jokes against Jewish women masks anti-Semitism as well as woman hatred. What are you going to say the next time you hear a JAP story?

We do not need to become each other in order to work together. But we do need to recognize each other, our differences as well as the sameness of our goals. Not for altruism. For self-preservation—survival.

Every day of our lives is practice in becoming the person you want to be. No instantaneous miracle is suddenly going to occur and make you brave and courageous and true. And every day that you sit back silent, refusing to use your power, terrible things are being done in our name.

Our federal taxes contribute three billion dollars yearly in military and economic aid to Israel. Over 200 million dollars of that money is spent fighting the uprising of Palestinian people who are trying to end the military occupation of their homeland. Israeli soldiers fire tear gas canisters made in America into Palestinian homes and hospitals, killing babies, the sick and the elderly. Thousands of Palestinians, some as young as twelve, are being detained without trial in barbed-wire detention camps, and even many Jews of conscience opposing these acts have also been arrested and detained.

Encouraging your Congresspeople to press for a peaceful solution in the Middle East, and for recognition of the rights of Palestinian people, is not altruism, it is survival.

In particular, my sisters and brothers, I urge you to remember, while we battle the many faces of racism in our daily lives as African-Americans, that we are part of an international community of people of color, and people of the African diaspora around the world are looking to us and asking, how are we using the power we have? Or are we allowing our power to be used against them, our brothers and sisters in struggle for their liberation?

Apartheid is a disease spreading out from South Africa across the whole southern tip of Africa. This genocidal system in South Africa is kept propped into place by the military and economic support of the United States, Israel and Japan. Let me say here that I support the existence of the State of Israel and I support the existence of the U.S.A., but this does not blind me to the grave injustices emanating from either. Israel and South Africa are intimately entwined, politically and economically. There are no diamonds in Israel, yet diamonds are Israel's major source of income. Meanwhile, Black people slave in the diamond mines of South Africa for less than thirty cents a day.

It is not enough to say that we are against apartheid. Forty million of our tax dollars go as aid to South African and backed UNITA forces to suppress an independent Angola. Our dollars pay for the land-mines reponsible for over 50,000 Angolan amputees. It appears that Washington is joining hands with South Africa to prevent independence of Namibia. Now make no mistake, South Africa, Angola, Namibia will be free. But what will we say when our children ask us, what were you doing, mommy and daddy, while American-made bullets were murdering Black children in Soweto?

In this country, children of all colors are dying of neglect. Since 1980, poverty has increased thirty percent among white children in America. Fifty percent of African-American children and thirty percent of Latino children grow up in poverty, and that percentage is even higher for the indigenous people of this land, American Indians. While the Magellan capsule speeds though space toward the planet Venus, thirty children on this planet Earth die every minute from hunger and inadequate health care. And in each one of those minutes, $1,700,000 are spent on war.

The white fathers have told us, "I think, therefore I am." But the Black mother within each of us—the poet inside—whispers in our dreams, "I feel, therefore I can be free." Learn to use what you feel to move you toward action. Change, personal and political, does not come about in a day, nor a year. But it is our day-to-day decisions, the way in which we testify with our lives to those things in which we say we believe, that empower us. Your power is relative but it is real. And if you do not learn to use it, it will be used, against you, and me, and our children. Change did not begin with you, and it will not end with you, but what you do with your life is an absolutely vital piece of that chain. The testimony of each of our daily lives is a vital missing remnant in the fabric of our future.

Every Friday, women in black gather opposite Prime Minister [Yitzhak] Shamir's home in Jerusalem. Their simple handmade posters say "End the Occupation." Their numbers are growing, in Haifa, in Jerusalem, in Tel Aviv. Despite being reviled and spat upon, cursed as traitors, they continue to testify with their living to their belief in justice.

There will always be someone begging you to isolate one piece of yourself, one segment of your identity above the others and say, "Here, this is who I am." Resist that trivialization. I am not *just* a lesbian. I am not *just* a poet. I am not *just* a mother. Honor the complexity of your vision and yourselves. We learn to use each other's differences as creative tools for change by learning how to acknowledge and orchestrate the conflicting parts within ourselves, learning how to integrate the many different pieces of our identity into action behind our beliefs. So that at any point we can say, this is how what I am doing, or intend to do, fits into the whole— whether it is teaching mathematics, building bridges, writing books, raising children, designing spaceships or digging ditches.

There are so many different parts to each of us. And there are so many of us. If we can envision the future we desire, we can work to bring it into being. We need all the different pieces of ourselves to be strong, as we need each other and each other's battles for empowerment as fuel for a liveable tomorrow....

That surge of power you feel inside you now does not belong to me. It does not belong to your parents, not to your professors, although we have helped to call it forth. That power lives inside of you. It is yours. You own it, you nourish it, and you will carry it out of this room. And whether you use it or whether you waste it, you are responsible for it.

Good luck to you all. Together, in the conscious recognition of our differences, we can create the 21st century, we can make real the possibility I see reflected in your faces here today. A LUTA CONTINUA.

DISCUSSION QUESTIONS

1. "Every day of our lives is practice in becoming the person you want to be." What are some examples of this practice? How do we take that practice beyond individual conversion into collective action?

2. How do we identify the power that we have, especially at a time when past gains seem to be taken away from us? What day-to-day strategies do we use to maintain our commitment and energy for continuing the struggle?

3. What steps can you and your organization take to educate yourselves about all of the struggles Lorde has outlined? Why is it important to make these kinds of connections?

SUGGESTIONS FOR FURTHER READING

Anita Cornwell. 1983. *Black lesbian in white America.* Tallahassee, FL: Naiad Press.

bell hooks. 1992. *Black looks: Race and representation.* Boston: South End.

Audre Lorde. 1982. *Zami, a new spelling of my name: A biomythography.* New York: The Crossing Press.

STRATEGIES AND VISIONS

Responding to Violence

NO, I'M NOT KIDDING! IF YOU CAME OUT
PUBLICLY, DO YOU KNOW WHAT THAT WOULD
DO FOR OUR IMAGE?

Donelan cartoon from THE ADVOCATE 346 (July 8, 1982), p. 13. Copyright ©
1982 by Gerard Donelan. Reprinted with permission.

COMING OUT
AS NONVIOLENT DIRECT ACTION
Sean McShee

"Coming out," that is, disclosing to others that one is a lesbian, gay man, or bisexual person, has long been a foundation of our lives and of our political strategies. Its importance has rarely been fully appreciated by non-gay people. This very brief essay, taken from the action handbook for the mass civil disobedience at the Supreme Court on October 13, 1987, places coming out in a context with which peace and activists may be more familiar.

In the tradition of the Gay & Lesbian Movement we have developed a new form of non-violent direction action—coming out. In so doing, we bear our witness to the truth of our desires. By rejecting the illusion of normalcy, we unmask heterosexist domination as both the brute force of "queer-bashers" and a subtle system of institutionalized power relations.

We come out of the closet because inside is the suffocating certainty of isolation while outside is the risky exhilaration, the hope of community, love and power. Many of us have learned this through multiple coming-outs as incest survivors, PWA's/PWARC's, leather freaks, disabled people, alcoholics/drug addicts, voyeurs/exhibitionists, witches, christians and many other identities.

By acting directly we create alternatives; we affirm the possibility of a different future now. Every time we object to faggot/dyke jokes, dare to be affectionate in public, cross dress, do leather, set up AIDS/ARC programs that meet our needs, create our own institutions and communities, we break out of this dreadful set of alternatives that passes for free choice in this society. It is not the lesser of two evils, but rather the evil of the two lessers; the solution is to create more alternatives.

To act this way is to take risks. While these risks are not the same as the risk of arrest and jail, they do involve the very real danger of physical assault, rejection by family and "friends," loss of job and many more.

The risks that we take are real and call for courage, but we must not look to our militaristic society for images of courage. Instead, we must draw images of courage from our lives as lesbians and gay males: the courage of drag queens and prostitutes, of women who walk alone at night, of PWA's/PWARC's and school teachers, hairdressers and teenagers, themselves.

1. What are some coming-out stories lesbian, gay male and bisexual readers wish to share? What effect did the coming out experience have, in living and in politics? Is there a comparable process in the lives of non-gay readers? How does it compare and how is it different?

2. How does this compare with other types of nonviolent direct action in which readers have participated?

3. Coming out is never a once-and-for-all step. What are some times and places when readers have not felt safe in taking it? Why not? How can allies help create safe space for coming out?

SUGGESTIONS FOR FURTHER READING

Nancy & Casey Adair. 1978. *Word is out: Some stories of our lives.* New York: Delta.

Ruth Baetz. 1988. *Lesbian crossroads.* Tallahassee, FL: Naiad Press.

Hall-Carpenter Archives. 1989. *Inventing ourselves: Lesbian life stories.* London: Routledge.

Hall-Carpenter Archives. 1989. *Walking after midnight: Gay men's life stories.* London: Routledge.

Coming out stories: Reflections on a lifelong process. 1990.*Gay Community News*, 18(14):8 (October 14).

Sarah Holmes. 1988. *Testimonies: A collection of lesbian coming out stories.* Boston: Alyson Publications.

Julia Penelope & Susan J. Wolfe, Eds. 1989. *The Coming out stories.* Freedom, CA: The Crossing Press.

John Reid. 1976. *The best little boy in the world.* New York: Ballantine Books.

Frances Rooney. 1991. *Our lives: Lesbian personal writings.* Toronto: Second Story Press.

Stonewall stories. 1989. *Gay Community News*, 16(46):14 (June 11).

FUELED BY FURY—FIGHTING HOMOPHOBIA IN NORTH CAROLINA
Mab Segrest

Mab Segrest describes in some detail both the conditions faced by lesbians and gay men in North Carolina and some practical responses. She offers a clear and concrete analysis of the specific geographic, demographic and political situations in which lesbians and gay men must organize against homophobic attacks. Building on this analysis, she describes the realities of building coalitions with others in North Carolina as a strategy for resistance and change. This description may help readers in other localities examine ways to plan and carry out joint work.

✳ A teenager tells his mother he's gay and she puts him in a mental hospital.

✳ A woman under investigation for lesbianism by the Marines calls a friend to tell her she "can't live like this"—then drives her truck off the road into a tree, killing herself.

✳ Drunken assailants throw an eighteen-year-old who has defended a gay man against verbal harassment into a lake, drowning him.

✳ Four men armed with various high-powered weapons open fire on their gay neighbors with the "intent to commit murder."

✳ The State health department seeks to create "special facilities" for people who violate HIV control measures, and to give public officials authority to confine them directly without a court order.

✳ Lesbian and gay parents lose custody of their children simply because of the parents' sexual orientation.

✳ Police selectively apply the state's sodomy law to entrap gay men into soliciting for "crimes against nature," by coming on to them, then arresting them.

✳ A gay man who has just received a 95% performance rating is fired from his job at a restaurant when the boss finds out he is gay and in violation of the company policy on homosexuality.

These are a few of the incidents of homophobic violence and harassment reported to the North Carolina Coalition for Gay and Lesbian Equality (NCCGLE) in 1991. NCCGLE has just released its report *Homophobia and Human Rights in North Carolina*, chronicling 680 incidents

"Fueled by fury—Fighting homophobia in North Carolina," by Mab Segrest. This article is reprinted from the Resist Newsletter #247. Resist is a non-profit foundation funding grassroots social change projects since 1967. For more information, contact Resist at One Summer St., Somerville, MA 02143. Copyright © 1992. Reprinted with permission.

of violence, harassment, or discrimination. While the large majority of these incidents are harassing calls to lesbian/gay hotlines, over 60 of them constitute "hate crimes" by the U.S. Justice Department's definitions. They range from the violent criminal acts of individuals to the sanctioned policy of police, the courts, and the legislature. They are part of a widespread pattern of violence and discrimination towards lesbians and gay men in North Carolina.

MOST QUEER-HATING STATE IN THE U.S.

Progressive people outside of the South are not surprised, of course, to hear of this level of repression and brutality in the home state of Jesse Helms, arguably the most powerful homophobe in the country. Helms launched a powerfully effective attack on the National Endowment for the Arts for supporting homoerotic art, was one of few Senators to oppose the Hate Crimes Statistics Act (because it included lesbians and gay men) and has advocated quarantining people with AIDS. What *may* surprise people is the grounds for optimism that many gay and lesbian people in North Carolina feel, and the degree to which we have been able to use queer indignation at Helms to begin to become the "powerful homosexual lobby" for which he gives us such credit. Two years ago, NCCGLE took on the task of shaping a strategy to counter what the National Gay and Lesbian Task Force (NGLTF) informed us was the highest level of reported incidents of homophobic violence and discrimination of any state in the U.S. In fact, North Carolina has reported the most incidents each year since the Task Force began compiling data in the mid-eighties. During this period, racist violence has also flourished here. Both homophobia and racism are fed by repressive economic policies and practices that decrease opportunities for education and invite scapegoating. Klan and neo-Nazi groups, likewise, have targeted lesbians and gay men, and people of color, as well as Jews. The lack of a strong official response from state officials and law enforcement has allowed hate violence to escalate.

Gay agencies such as the North Carolina Human Rights Fund began to document homophobic activity in the early 1980s under the leadership of Leo Teachout. Teachout moved the documentation project to GROW, a gay community agency in his home town of Wilmington, before passing it on to NCCGLE two years ago. In 1990, NCCGLE began to take seriously the task of not just counting, but countering homophobic violence and discrimination.

The greatest challenge, as in all work against hate violence, has been finding a way to respond to crises without being driven by them; to raise issues of violence within the targeted community in ways that foster empowerment rather than terror, and within other communities and the media in ways that do not play to an image of gay people as tragic victims. We have also struggled to find the balance between necessarily responding to people who are being hurt—overcoming our own denial and habituation—and saving energy as well for long-range organizing; the balance between our knowledge of the murder, fear, and repression experienced by many lesbians and gay men in this state, and our awareness that, year by year, the climate has improved dramatically.

In fact, some of the most painful disagreements among gay and lesbian activists have come when we have come down on different sides of this fragile balance. Are those of us who emphasize the violence, in order to mobilize against it, fear-mongering? Are those of us who emphasize the progress hiding our heads in the sand? Throw in a little internalized homophobia, and a painful game of "good queer/bad queer" creates schisms and bad feelings that can linger too long.

INSTITUTIONALIZATION OF HATE

Part of the necessary long-term proactive strategy that can move us forward is an analysis of the specific causes of homophobic violence. We put Jesse Helms at the top of the list, with his ability to manipulate racism and homophobia to separate most white people from their own best economic interest. North Carolina's anti-union sentiment, carefully cultivated by corporations and the state government, makes it the "home of the working poor." Helms votes repeatedly against the economic interests of the working people, white and black. But come election time he exploits "hot button" issues like "pornographic art," scaring many white people into voting for him. In the 1990 Senate race against black Democratic challenger Harvey Gantt, one of Helms' "attack ads" showed a white man's hands crumpling a job-dismissal slip with a voice-over blaming the "Kennedy quota bill."

Helms is aided by the support of a strong religious presence in North Carolina, an overdose of fundamentalist Christianity and a predominance of Southern Baptists, that until recently was unopposed by any more moderate voice within the church.

Homophobic activity in North Carolina is further strengthened by a solid institutional base in state government. There is the legitimizing presence of the state's sodomy law, which carries penalties of up to ten years for consensual sexual activity. The legislature in North Carolina is much more powerful than either the municipalities or the Governor. Most changes at the city or county level have to be ratified by the General Assembly, which makes it difficult to pass anti-discrimination ordinances at the local level. Rural legislators often dominate the agenda, and many of them are, to put it politely, porcine. Recently, they appropriated $9 billion (a multi-year grant) for highway construction while slashing education reform; and in years past they reduced the penalty (from a felony to a misdemeanor) for farmers who knowingly permit slavery on their land—in a bill originally introduced by migrant advocates to protect workers' rights.

Likewise, court officials (judges, DAs) have little or no education in the damaging effects of homophobia. "Kiss your children goodbye" is the advice that lesbian mothers get from their lawyers in custody cases.

North Carolina is also one of the most militarized states in the U.S. Twenty percent of the troops sent to the Persian Gulf left from North Carolina bases. The military itself perpetuates homophobia with its purges; in 1991, at least two lesbians whose units returned home from the Gulf War attempted suicide because they were under investigation for homosexuality. One of the women, who drove her truck into a tree, succeeded. Dyke-baiting is also used against women in the military to force sexual favors: "Put out, or I'll tell them you're a queer," as one Marine explained.

The state's geography is also relevant. North Carolina is a big state—it takes all day to drive from the mountains to the coast. There is no one huge city, like Atlanta or Chicago. The most progressive presence is in the central Piedmont, a series of cities that begins with Raleigh-Durham and extends down the interstate to Charlotte, then west over to Asheville in the Blue Ridge mountains. "Down East" (from the Piedmont to the Atlantic Coast) is in many ways a different country, isolated, rural, repressive, militarized. Most gay/lesbian organizing is concentrated in the cities of the Piedmont and in Asheville. Part of our challenge is to figure out ways to reach into those isolated places, as we also build up the base in the cities.

I spent over a year working in the little Carolina town of Shelby after Nazis there attacked an adult book store, shooting five men in the head, and killing three of them. The book store had been known as a "hangout for homosexuals." It was hard to find any other visible gay or lesbian presence in that town. I was told that if I went to the K-mart parking lot after 1 a.m. on Thursdays, I would see gay people congregating.

My experience in Shelby gave me the feeling that in small towns, getting gay men and lesbians to "come out" and organize autonomously is probably less important or sensible than encouraging broader anti-homophobic efforts in which gay people can participate without necessarily announcing themselves. However, I also learned how difficult that can be.

Can we only offer lesbian and gay refugees access to large cities, or can we affect those smaller places from which so many of us fled? I am convinced of the importance of developing models of lesbian/gay organizing in rural, conservative states like North Carolina. Political power in the United States has already shifted out of the large cities of the Northeast. White flight has sent many people into the suburbs, and devastation of major industries has moved capital and people from the "Rust Belt" to the "Sun Belt," following cheap labor. The dynamics are different in these areas outside the metropolis. While advances in urban meccas are vital for the whole country, we here cannot just mimic San Francisco or New York, nor can all our national lesbian and gay strategies afford to be chauvinistically urban, assuming a "trickle down" effect into smaller cities, towns, and rural areas.

In North Carolina we also face issues common to organizing efforts anywhere. How do we balance the concerns of lesbians with those of gay men? For instance, in most of the documentation of past years, violence and discrimination against lesbians was hardly visible. And how do we counteract the racism, classism, sexism, and myriad of other forces that divide us?

FUELED BY FURY

Until the last five years or so, there has been little organized, visible lesbian/gay presence across North Carolina to shape a consistent response. This is not to say that there have not been effective lesbian and gay organizers and organizations here, for at least twenty years. It's just that our efforts are finally beginning to pay off, and a movement is growing across the state in many of our major cities, inspired by the 1987 March on Washington, and fueled by fury at Jesse Helms and the AIDS crisis.

Senate Vote '90, under the leadership of lesbian activist Mandy Carter, mounted an aggressive anti-Helms electoral effort with a PAC that we decided to keep outside of Democratic Party structures. It raised $170,000 from within and outside the state, and Helms' opponent Harvey Gantt simply and forcefully turned aside Helms' attempts at gay-baiting like no other politician at the state level had ever done. This electoral work increased our visibility and opened up more political space in which to organize. It is being continued with a new statewide PAC, called PRIDEPAC.

In Asheville, Charlotte, Winston–Salem, Greensboro, Raleigh, and Durham relatively new organizations are mobilizing behind anti-discrimination projects and hotlines as well as electoral activity. For the first time, we have "out" gay and lesbian activists in most of the state's major cities, ready and willing to speak publicly on our concerns. But, beyond a strong network of AIDS service organizations, there is little infrastructure that connects these groups: Metropolitan Community Church ministers (who preach to predominantly gay congregations) within North Carolina, for instance, do not meet together, nor do gay/lesbian campus groups, or groups that run lesbian and gay hotlines.

In the last two years it has become clear that if we really want to significantly decrease homophobic violence and discrimination in North Carolina, we have to organize for the long haul. We need to build up an infrastructure as we go along, developing leadership and organizational strength. Community-based agencies within each city must become the front-lines, both for documentation and for support of victims. They must be encouraged to consciously extend services to outlying rural counties. At the state level, we need to encourage campus networks, bring hotlines together to learn from one another and systematize data collection efforts, hold trainings on advocacy for victims, and encourage health projects to take on peer counseling. Lesbian/gay organizations across the state and the people working with them need the opportunity to share their analyses and evolve strategies. We can bring people together at workshops, on conference calls, and through computer hookups.

Countering these unifying efforts is a tendency towards turf issues and fragmentation into many smaller organizations. This problem is exacerbated because gay activists receive recognition in these smaller organizations that we are denied in heterosexual society.

CAMP NEW HOPE RETREAT

Last November, NCCGLE held a weekend retreat at a camp near Chapel Hill to further this work. It was funded in part by Resist. I had organized a similar workshop the year before while in the staff of North Carolinians Against Racist and Religious Violence, NCARRV. (NCARRV continues to play a pivotal role in including homophobia in state and national campaigns against hate crimes.) Thirty activists from organizations across the state met together for a weekend to learn about issues of advocacy, safety campaigns, working with community agencies, documentation and education. A plenary session asked the question, "Are we accountable to the most vulnerable among us?" with presentations by gay teens, a lesbian who monitors homophobia in the military, the director of a homeless shelter with a large black gay clientele, and a lesbian from a small town. By Sunday, we began laying out the elements of a strategy on each of the issues: enough program ideas, to be sure, to keep us all busy for ten years.

For instance, Kevin Berrill from NGLTF gave a workshop on safety campaigns, explaining how whistles were used in cities like San Francisco. Carol Ryner, the Sensei from a local Karate school, gave a demonstration of self-defense techniques. But Janelle Lavelle, who lives in a working-class section of Greensboro, was not satisfied with a program that might encourage an assailant to leave her alone, but attack the elderly woman living next door. "What about a whistle campaign for the whole neighborhood?" someone asked, and she nodded that it might work.

Perhaps the most important aspect of the weekend was the kind of interaction that occurred among the participants. The year before, my scheduling had been too ambitious, and by the end of the weekend people were inspired but totally exhausted. The second time around, with encouragement from the planning committee, we left time for relaxation and fun. We devoted the first evening to "icebreaking" exercises, and we broke up the sit-and-talk sessions with songs and physical games. We cooked together on Saturday night, then Kevin from NGLTF gave a wonderful "fireside chat," a perspective on the national importance of our work in North Carolina, which is the only statewide effort in the U.S. specifically directed against homophobic violence. Later, a local lesbian singing group performed, and after that many people stayed up and talked on the porch, watching the moon.

The next day, when it was time to strategize, people had energy and commitment. We put a big state map on the pine floor of the meeting room and divided up the state into six areas, with organizers from cities in each of the areas committing their organizations to begin outreach. We also decided to shift the emphasis in future workshops. Participants felt that more people would attend a general retreat on organizing skills for lesbians and gay men (with homophobic violence as only one of the central issues) then would come to a workshop specifically about violence.

I suggested that we use the camp for a yearly gathering to network and discuss strategies—a kind of "gay Highlander" (the Tennessee center for radical education that served as a strategy center for the civil rights movement and that helped to nurture, among other activists, Rosa Parks.) When participants left after lunch, they took with them a sense of connection and commitment and a feeling that the work was possible.

Since then, Liz from Asheville has started a hotline for the Southern Appalachian Gay and Lesbian Alliance; NCCGLE published our 1991 report, emphasizing issues of gay/lesbian youth and the military, priorities established by our discussions at the retreat; and a campus network met in the spring and is planning a fall gathering.

Many other ideas await the development of increased organizational capacity. Increasing our funding base must be a NCCGLE priority. Most lesbian/gay organizations, if they are staffed, rely on excellent volunteer support and grants from a few national sources such as Resist, the Chicago Resource Center, the Fund for Southern Communities, and the new OUT Fund of Funding Exchange. NCCGLE is working to educate progressive foundations within North Carolina on lesbian/gay issues, hoping to bring in much needed financial support.

We also need to develop alliances with primarily heterosexual groups that share our concerns. Many city gay/lesbian organizations have begun to do this through appealing to human relations commissions for hearings on homophobic violence. In two cities these hearings have resulted in ordinances that include sexual orientation as a protected category for city workers. We think that we will have a better chance in the legislature if we familiarize politicians in their own communities with the concerns of their lesbian/gay constituents.

Anti-homophobic forces within churches are also beginning to mobilize—an important antidote for the fundamentalists who can get busloads of parishioners to the legislature to rail against HoMoSexshuls. Much of this movement came in the wake of a Pride march in 1986 that drew strong fundamentalist opposition and pricked the conscience of both ministers and lay people about the need for a more loving response.

Last December, the North Carolina Council of Churches passed a strong resolution condemning anti-gay violence and calling for churches to examine the ways they have contributed to the suffering of lesbians and gay men. This year, remarkably, one liberal Southern Baptist Church voted to allow the "holy union" of a gay male couple, and another voted to license a gay minister. (Not surprisingly, these two progressive Baptist churches were subsequently expelled from the Southern Baptist Convention. So far, they have not backed down from their pro-gay stance. Both churches made their decisions with their eyes open, after extensive deliberation, so the fact that they were willing to risk expulsion speaks to their level of commitment.) In a state like North Carolina, these changes in the church may do more to reach into small towns and rural areas than any other development.

We have evolved an analysis of causes, developed strategies to respond, and have begun to galvanize a network of people willing to take them on. Now we are refining our organizational structure, getting tax exempt status, and recruiting a larger, more diverse board. We hope to have enough grant money to hire at least a half-time organizer this summer.

Last May, British neo-Nazi John Tyndall, speaking to a far right rally in Clemmons, North Carolina, remarked: "Our human refuse follows us around the country the same as your uniform garbage does. Screeching lesbians, fluffy poofers [i.e., gay men], university scum, and AIDS-ridden undesirables are always there to speak out in the name of liberalism, anti-racism and democracy."

With some effort, we may prove him right.

DISCUSSION QUESTIONS

1. What are the similarities between geographic, demographic and political conditions in North Carolina and your locale? What are the differences? What are some local forces that prevent progress? What are some local groups with whom we could build coalitions?

2. What will be some of the obstacles in building local coalitions? How can we overcome them, or turn them into opportunities for further education?

3. What resources do we have at our disposal? In particular, after reading Segrest, what resources occur to us that we have not thought about or tapped?

4. How might strategies look different based on short-term versus long-terms needs and implications?

SUGGESTIONS FOR FURTHER READINGS

John Boswell. 1980. *Christianity, social tolerance and homosexuality.* Chicago: University of Chicago Press.

Beverly Wildung Harrison. 1985. Misogyny and homophobia: The unexplored connections. *Making the connections: Essays in feminist social ethics.* Boston: Beacon Press.

John McNeil. 1988. *Taking a chance on God: Liberating theology for gays, lesbians, and their lovers, families, and friends.* Boston: Beacon Press.

Urvashi Vaid. 1988. *NGLTF media skills workshop for gay and lesbian activists.* Washington: National Gay and Lesbian Task Force, 1517 U Street, NW, Washington, DC 20009. (202) 332-6483.

AND QUEER CONTROL-FREAKS SHALL LEAD THEM
Jane Meyerding

Jane Meyerding places the queer street patrols beginning to appear around the country within the context of non-violent action despite the "bash back" rhetoric. Likewise, aggressive and shocking action, in this case destroying the papers of an anti-gay group by pouring blood on them, is explored as nonviolent action in spite of the media's labeling. Meyerding examines language, meaning and implication, urging us to evaluate our analysis and social change tactics carefully.

Freedom is never achieved by the mere inversion of an oppressive construct... Freedom is achieved when an oppressive construct...is vacated by its members and thereby rendered null and void.

—Jeffner Allen, "Motherhood: The Annihilation of Women,"p. 61

We need to take control. First, of ourselves, then of other situations in which we choose to engage.

One way to assert control is through the words we reclaim or redefine. Some words we need to empty out and blow up like balloons until they either are big enough to hold all of ourselves or they explode.

The word "normal," for example. We need to demand recognition of the fact that it is absolutely positively normal to be unique.

NONVIOLENCE IS IN ACTION

Steve Karpf, in an article in *Gay Community News* (August 11–17, 1991), describes a situation where a group of gay-bashers attacked a group of gay men, beating two of them while the others failed to intervene. "The thing that people need to understand," Karpf cites Joyce Collier as saying, "is that people do not always respond to things the way they would like to."

Lesbian and gay people don't always manage to react to gay-bashing in a way that takes control away from the bashers, who, as Karpf points out, are "looking for a victim," who are "looking specifically for someone they see as an easy target." When we do manage to respond effectively, as the success of street patrols in the nation's cities demonstrates, we do so by using the tactics of nonviolent action to take control of the situation away from the bashers, in large part by asserting our definitions over theirs. We act out our rejection of the "victim" definition they seek to impose on us. And in fact we go much further than that.

Many gay and lesbian activists would reject my description of street-patrol tactics as "nonviolence." Some, I suppose, would be offended by it. But just look at the facts. In Karpf's article and in "The Fabulous Fight Back," Sara Miles' description of her work with San Francisco's Street Patrol (*OUT/LOOK* 17, Summer 1992) the activists base their anti-bashing behavior on analytical and tactical agreements that are all but indistinguishable from the old "nonviolent discipline" documents we used to draw up before major actions in the '60s. "Everything that a patrol group does on the street is part of a three tactic process: observation, deterrence and intervention," writes Karpf, and "the first reaction" to ongoing violence "is to de-escalate the situation...."

Miles wrote a wonderfully powerful and enraged elegy for a friend gunned down by homophobes. It reads in part,

> A community that defines itself by the degree of its victimization is a community without power. To glorify persecution, declaring that a victim status confers a special nobility upon us, is obscene. We cannot find self-worth by measuring the extent to which we are hated; cannot find strength by claiming our weakness makes of us a chosen people; cannot inherit the earth by being gunned down to bleed our lives away on the winter street.
>
> Suffering is not good for the soul. Suffering evil does not make us good, will not prepare us to actively resist wrong. The despised, the rejected, the outcast, the murdered, the martyred—there are other names for what we need to do with our lives (1992, 54).

She was told she was "advocating violence," she says, when she concluded, "I suggest we take back our souls from the sorry, the sad, and the saints. Let us refuse martyrdom and regain rightful rage. And then, I suggest, let us act on it." The action she takes, however, is not violence. She joins the Street Patrol, a group operating according to "Street Patrol Rules" that are as good a "nonviolent discipline" as I've seen since 1967. Their discipline works, too. When the Patrol spots a bashing in progress, they immediately put into practice the tactics in which they have trained themselves:

> The patrol posts up six feet away, poised delicately in their biker gloves, [fuschia] berets glowing under the streetlight....Jo and I talk to the basher. We talk it down, hands not raised but ready, voices steady, firm. And then we are standing, still talking, in between the basher and the bashee, our bodies a wedge pushing the attacker out. "It's OK," we say, "It's OK, let's go now. Enough."

That's nonviolence in action. That is nonviolent action.

By taking nonviolent action, we take such radical control of the situation that we kick victimization completely out of the picture. No more victims; not us, not them. It's one of the beauties of nonviolent action that its effects often go so much further than we immediately need them to. Although we may be quite exclusively focused at the moment on preventing a bashing, of ourself or someone else, our use of the tactics of nonviolent action give the situation such a charge of *difference* that the momentary control we achieve there will continue to affect everyone involved long after would-be bashers and their intended victims go their separate ways. When we use nonviolent action to assert the *difference* we are choosing to live, we weaken the structures that make this society a complex of victimizer-victim dualities.

INACTION IS NOT NONVIOLENCE

I think it's fantastic that lesbian and gay people are discovering the power and good sense of nonviolence. They do so, of course, because it is what works. Unfortunately, many who use the tactics with gusto never go on to make the connection between what works and why it works. They fail to develop an understanding of nonviolence theory.

Among lesbians, it often is downright "incorrect" to advocate nonviolence by name. Jeffner Allen, for example, has proposed the need for what she calls "a lesbian violence" in her essay "Looking At Our Blood: A Lesbian Response to Men's Terrorization of Women" (in her book *Lesbian Philosophies: Explorations*). In doing so, she draws on the tradition of the Amazons and the debates over tactics in the British suffrage movement, and contrasts these with nonviolence, which she describes as "a patriarchal construct," a form of "heterosexual virtue" laid down for women by the very group that routinely engages in terrorism against women, most notably by the practice of rape.

In this essay Allen can accurately and clearly refute the false dichotomy of love and hate: "The opposite of hate is 'not caring' *[akedia]*, apathy, sloth." But she is unwilling to recognize the equally false dichotomy between violence and nonviolence. Instead of recognizing that the opposite of violence is passivity/inaction (another version of "not caring"), she chooses to redefine "violence" until it is big enough to include the meanings she wants it to carry: "A lesbian creation and exercise of freedom, befriending and loving what is gentle and dear, is violence."

Allen's project of redefinition is similar to the kind of redefinition crucial to the taking of control that I advocate at the beginning of this article. And therefore her conclusions are especially relevant for me. "I want to live, in rupture with heterosexual virtue and its fragmentation of my existence, a genuine wholeness, harmony, and exuberance"—what lesbian (or gay man) does not feel the resonance of that declaration?

I am concerned, however, by the gap between Allen's analysis and the little she says about tactics. "We must decide which actions are necessary for women's survival and freedom," she writes. "If we are to live free from terror, the most effective actions are those that make impossible men's acts of terrorism." Yes. But what are those actions? Allen mentions giving "priority to the freedom of my body in a world of female friendship" and urges women to "create, actively and collectively, a world of female friendship whose strength, harmony, and exuberance celebrate the similarities and differences of each individual." That sounds great, and Allen tells us it will make "any entrapment within the structure of male terrorism...intolerable." Seems pretty intolerable to me already, but I agree that such a world of female friendship would enable many other women to make choices that would free them from male domination. Most of us are unable to change until we feel we have a place to change to.

But creating worlds is a project for the long haul. What does Allen have to say about tactics in the here-and-now? She suggests that we "take seriously...the idea of an organized violent uprising of women against men," the creation of an "all-female army," and a "lesbian war...." Now, granted that she's talking about "a lesbian violence whose means and ends are apart from those men have provided for me," a kind of "violence" that "is not anti-life or pro-death, for it exhibits absolutely no equation between violence and destruction." I'm not sure what that means, actually, but I don't get really confused until Allen sets out the difference between "men's war" and "lesbian war." Men's war sustains the boundaries of men's territories, and lesbian war sustains the boundaries of the territory Allen wants to claim.

I do see the difference between national boundaries on the one hand and the bounds of bodily integrity on the other. What confuses me is why Allen chooses to make the two kinds of "war" sound as much alike as possible. What ever happened to her insight that we achieve freedom only "when an oppressive construct...is vacated by its members and thereby rendered null and void"? For millennia, the chief enforcer of oppression has been organized violence, both physical and otherwise. Is the solution for women really simply a new version of the same-old, now with a fresh camouflage of feminist philosophy? Why does Allen assume that promoting a redefinition of violence, broadening it to legitimize anything she wants to do in her undeniably worthy cause, will be any practical help in moving us toward freedom? Don't we need to retain that word "violence" in order to be able to name the violations against which we enact our resistance?

THE THRILL OF VIOLENCE

What we need most of all, I propose, are tactics that, in the words of Sara Miles, will "prepare us to actively resist wrong." And here, I admit, violence has a rarely matched allure. We are so deeply imbued with patriarchal assumptions that we aren't really sure we're *doing something* unless we are doing something violent. Join that mind-set to a general ignorance of nonviolent activist tactics, and you get a real let-down after the armed struggle stops—as witness Geuda Cohen. Back in the 1940s, Cohen was a member of the "Stern Gang," a Jewish group using violent tactics (bombs, assassination), as well as other illegal tactics (robbery) against the British mandate government in Palestine. Her book *Woman of*

Violence describes her experiences, including the difference in her life after the battle was won:

> Today I go by the rules. I observe the legal code. I don't steal. Why, then, don't I have the feeling of purity that I used to have? Today I'm good, but I'm different. I'm good because I keep away from evil. It wasn't that way then. Then I was good because I fought with evil, because I wanted to exterminate it. Its presence bothered me until I couldn't rest. When it bothers me nowadays, I take my leave of it and slam the door in its face. But when it bothered me then, I slammed the door behind me and set out after it.
>
> In doing so, I dirtied myself. That was inevitable. Evil is dirty. We were very close, evil and I, and when you wrestle with someone you can't avoid touching him. Sometimes it was hard to tell us apart. My hands weren't clean; on the contrary, they stank, but had I used my fingers to hold my nose, evil would have slipped through them.

The opposite of violence is passivity, is slamming the door between ourselves and evil, leaving us merely "good" and idle on the "clean" side of that dichotomy. We need to keep our rage and outrage available, keep it out where its power is accessible. Ignoring evil is not an option for queers with a radical commitment to transgressing boundaries of differentiation and dichotomy. Whenever we find ourselves being "good" in isolation we need to remember W. H. Auden's call to

> Ruffle the perfect manners of the frozen heart,
> And once again compel it to be awkward and alive...

I believe there are manifest and compelling reasons why sustained violent action is not an adequate or reliable (or morally acceptable) choice for the work of combined self-defense and social change we need to undertake. As Richard Cleaver says, "If things are as desperate as they feel these days, we paradoxically don't have the time *not* to figure out what action will really keep control in our own hands, keep the initiative away from those who seek our destruction (or at the very least, our invisibility), and not expose our weaknesses to their strengths." And that's why we urgently need to develop, learn, teach, and practice the tactics of sustained nonviolent action.

Because it is the long haul we're talking about, after all. Auden used a moral vocabulary when he wrote, from the perspective of an anti-fascist gay man on the eve of World War II, that

> ...Evil is always personal and spectacular,
> But goodness needs the evidence of all our lives...

Most of us, I think, whether we believe it is possible now or not, prefer inclusivity over exclusivity as the basis for our lives. Our ideal is acceptance, of us by others and of others by us—a process that begins with our acceptance of ourselves. Coming out is a wonderful example of nonviolent action. By coming out, we claim our power to be, to choose, to name our selves, and we are energized by the power we claim. There's definitely a physical thrill of energy, even if the experience is scary, and it feels great.

How do we keep hold of that energy, that power? We share it. As Auden says about the "goodness that needs the evidence of all our lives,"

...even to exist, it must be shared as truth,
As freedom or as happiness...

We stay in the closet because other people have the power to hurt us. When we come out, we are declaring that we have the power to transcend that hurt, that *we have power*. That's the crucial point.

THE SKILL OF SOCIAL CHANGE

We have power, and we need to learn how to use it. In developing our tactics, we need to choose according to several criteria: what works is primary, but we also need to consider durability. We need tactics that work for more than a minute. And by that I mean two things.

First, we should prefer tactics that, in addition to resolving or improving the situation where they are used, have the greatest possible positive consequences beyond the immediate moment.

Second, we should also prefer those tactics that we realistically can expect ourselves to continue employing. We should be looking for ways of acting, for constellations of political action, that can become ways of living.

Nonviolent tactics were described by Gene Sharp as "political jiu-jitsu." They work because they throw the opponent off balance, and they do that through the "victim's" refusal to allow victimization. Basically, nonviolent action techniques allow people who have been defined as powerless to mobilize their power in opposition to—and much to the surprise of—those who believe they have the power to impose their definitions on others. Sara Miles quotes Street Patrol member Mike as saying at a group training session, "Remember, you get style points for appearing harmless yet kicking butt. And, of course, for accessorizing your uniform." That, including the humor, is quintessential nonviolence theory, despite the reference to kicking butt. The Patrol's actual tactics, as described in the article, rely almost entirely on nonviolent intervention, for sound practical reasons. You take them by surprise. You disarm them by the unexpectedness of the situation you create, as if (it seems to them) by magic, through your knowledge and practice of the jiu-jitsu of nonviolent action. You walk into one power equation and transform it into another that no longer allows the "victim" definition to apply, not to you and not to anybody else.

For those of us who do not want to live in a world dichotomized into "us" and "enemy"—despite our enraged recognition of the injustice and danger prevailing so much of the time in so much of our world—the theory and tactics of nonviolence offer the possibility of sustained, practical, effective action. We can become active in ways that affirm the best that is in us and that help bring into being the kind of world we want to build.

I have used street patrol groups as the main example of nonviolent action here because they are the main example going at the moment. (Of, for, and by Queers, that is. There's a lot of strong, creative nonviolent action going on among animal rights/animal liberation folks these days. A good source for information is the monthly magazine *The Animals' Agenda*. And for examples and discussions of nonviolent action by and for people with disabilities, check out *Disability Rag*.) Unfortunately, the members of these street patrol groups suffer a high level of burn-out. One major reason for that, I presume, is that their action is not linked with and supported by a network of people versed in the theory of nonviolent action. We need those links, that network, to sustain us over the long haul. Isolated acts and isolated activists can be energized by contact with a community that understands and affirms what they are doing as part of a larger effort towards social change. Indeed, all of us would be energized by a recognition that the actions we take in various arenas—from sit-ins to Shanti, from Dykes on Bikes to lesbian publishing, from self-definition to self-defense, from outrageous attire in public places to righteous rage in public faces—can be comprehended within a single analysis of political action.

As that brief list of ongoing work makes clear, we Queer folk seem to have a natural talent for nonviolent action, although it arises from the same "natural" source as, for example, "women's intuition." We live our lives at an angle to the "normal," as it is defined and imposed by the dominant culture, and that gives us a head start in developing the ability to perceive a "third way" in situations described by the dominant culture as "either/or." Queer humor, drama, irony, and playfulness have been leading us into (and getting us out of) social and political confrontations for ages. When I realize how congruent these basic (and, let's face it, fabulous) survival skills are with the theory and practice of nonviolent action, I understand why so many of the most powerful practitioners of nonviolence in the United States have been lesbians (e.g., Barbara Deming) and gay men (e.g., Bayard Rustin).

Fortunately, the skills of nonviolent action are transferable. Once we begin to incorporate them into our responses—both individual/immediate and collective/planned—we will find ourselves with the capacity to "act out" on other issues, also. We will be better equipped to interrupt racism, for example. Learning how to take action, learning that we *can*, enables us to do so. And other people, seeing us in action, will learn that they can do it, too.

EXPERIMENTING WITH POWER

Even quite "shocking" nonviolent direct action can have this energizing effect, as Betty Johanna and I re-discovered in 1978. Back then, the two of us were engaged in a series of experiments exploring the power of nonviolent direct action as practiced by individuals rather than organized masses. "The 'direct' in 'nonviolent direct action' refers," we explained,

> to the direct application of personal energy to change, disrupt, or un-do the work of the institution being acted against....The intent of nonviolent direct action is to continue the disruption as long as possible. In other words, nonviolent direct action done as a form of civil disobedience is sabotage which the saboteurs choose to persist in until they are arrested and forced to stop. Above-ground sabotage.

The action Betty Johanna and I took that inspired us to write down our philosophy in 1978 was to destroy initiative petitions and financial records of a Seattle anti-gay group by pouring blood on them. (The group was attempting to repeal the portion of Seattle's civil rights ordinance protecting lesbians and gay men.) Blood is very offensive to a lot of people (even back then it was), and a lot of people who were working against the bigoted initiative by less drastic means were concerned that our action would have a negative effect on the campaign. Not only did the blood upset them, they were highly critical of our "handling" of the media. It was and is a common misconception among activists that nonviolent action is basically a "media stunt" and therefore a failure if not covered extensively on the 5 o'clock news. The statement Betty and I wrote to explain our action, said our critics, was a total loss because it was not written in a form the media would be able to understand and use. It was not a press release, it was words that came as close to the passion of our action as we could manage.

In response to that criticism, Betty and I wrote "To Reach Beyond Words," an article in which we tried to explain how we felt about both nonviolent action and activist preoccupation with the media. That article said, in part:

> Nonviolent direct actions feel right to us because we think they are the least patriarchy-identified forms of resistance: they are acts of personal responsibility-taking, are acts which any womon or group of womyn can choose to do, are directed towards individuals rather than institutions or masses, are non-hierarchical, are challenging rather than threatening, and are capable of reaching people where words can not. This un-patriarchal-ness is why they can be so effective: they are *different*, they are unexpected, they are challenging because people don't have habitual responses/defenses built up against them. Because they are shocking in their abnormality, they get through a lot of barriers patriarchy has taught—or forced—us to hide behind, barriers that divide us and therefore help patriarchy survive.
>
> Probably some of the most common *initial* responses to nonviolent direct actions, however, are shock, outrage, and anger. These are normal—in patriarchy—reactions to anything that touches and challenges us in a personal way. We all live with insecurity, and so many of us have (or, more often, *think* we have) a stake in the status quo. In our own experiences, we have often met non-radical people (including some downright conservatives) who have responded to nonviolent direct actions by saying: "I can't approve of what you/they did, but..." And what

they go on to say is proof that the action has at least started them thinking, has opened a door in their minds. Many politically active people who were critical of our action...told us that, despite their reservations, they felt challenged by the action—challenged to re-evaluate the seriousness of homophobia,...to look for ways they could be more active in resistance, and/or to re-examine the politics of "mass actions" as the only effective strategy....Almost everyone is shocked by direct actions at first (and especially by property damage.) But we have seen how often—despite continuously inaccurate and deceptive media coverage—the essential truth of the action does get through, even to people who would rather not hear it....

The mainstream media, however,...present us with "just the facts," facts chosen and presented according to the standards of patriarchal culture and the prevailing local male-elite political atmosphere. Nonviolent direct action, of course, is very basically in opposition to those standards and politics. Therefore, even when individual reporters covering an action are "liberal" (e.g., pro-"gay rights,") they cannot—are not allowed to—ever come anywhere near truly accurate coverage of such actions. Every action must immediately be labeled, and the only labels available are those of patriarchal culture. For example, pouring blood on papers...was shockingly abnormal by patriarchal standards and therefore was labeled "violent," whereas [the initiative's] attempt to degrade/destroy the lives of hundreds of thousands of lesbians and gay men was in accordance with the rules of patriarchal politics and therefore was *not* violent....

The mainstream media speak or write in the language of patriarchy. Because the only words any of us know belong to that language, it is the intention of nonviolent direct action to reach beyond words—to speak directly from life to life. We can't tell you exactly how it works, but we have seen it happen over and over again....

EXPERIENCING POWERLESSNESS

Another thing that happens over and over again, in my own experience, is hatred. Waves of hatred that knock me down and almost out of my life. Flaming rages of hatred that sear a passage from my gut to my mouth. What does it to me is seeing someone who is deeply entrenched in both injustice and reasonableness—but not usually those at the top of the unjust and "reasonable" structure. When I hear George Bush, the anger I feel is intense but not overwhelming. I'm used to him. The hatred that overwhelms me is sparked by those closer to home.

One day several years ago I found the entrance to the building in downtown Seattle where my dentist had her office surrounded by anti-abortion demonstrators and police. I waded through the crowd and was stopped by a uniformed policeman at the door. Five minutes later, I was across the street trying to control my shaking hands enough to put a quarter in the slot of a payphone, trying not to cry, trying to repress the tremendous flood of hatred that made me feel I was about to fly apart into a thousand pieces of deadly shrapnel. I wasn't angry at the Bible-waving demonstrators, although I disagree with them profoundly, and despite the fact that their discourse encouraged me to think they'd be as firmly anti-*me* as anti-abortion if they knew "what" I was. My hate was for the policeman who had refused to listen to me, who was just following orders, and who never laid a finger on me, who hardly even glanced at me, as he barred my way into the building. And for myself, because I had no way to respond. My hate was the flip side of another feeling: powerlessness.

It has taken me years to realize that my reaction to figures of authority —especially to policemen and others who work within the "criminal justice system," but even, to my own surprise and annoyance, occasionally to a professor whose class I am taking or a clerk through whom I am trying to wrest information from some public bureaucracy—is not entirely under my control. Sometimes I react not so much out of the current situation but out of past experiences of powerlessness. For me, it is much harder to "wrestle with" evil when it confronts me in the form of routine and "reasonable" procedures than when it launches an overtly violent attack. I feel powerless because I am "resource-less"—I have no options, no tactics with which to respond—and therefore I respond to the evil with a kind of helpless fury that wrings me out and disempowers me.

Thanks to past experience and nonviolence training, I usually am far more competent when faced with impending physical violence, whether in the form of a raised club or a raised and angry voice. I am not rendered helpless by the threat or the presence of that violence, because I have resources with which I can respond. Although my response may not always be sufficient to take effective control of the situation, at least I am able (usually) to do something, to take some action aimed at shifting the equation of power away from violence.

The time the cop stopped me on my way to the dentist, on the other hand, I felt lousy. I was full of fury but powerless, with no useful access to the energy of my anger, no resources for self-protection and effective self-expression. When I feel that kind of lousy, I am both a ready-made victim and a potentially dangerous human being. The hatred I feel when I am powerless is directed in virtually equal parts towards the outer object of hate and towards myself. I hate myself for my helplessness, and I hate the one who has made me so acutely aware of it. Fortunately for all of us, there are resources available to help us learn how to respond to physical and political violence, and many of those resources are listed in this book. What I, for one, need to add to the long history of creative nonviolent action represented by those resources is some work on how to gain access to the energy of the hatred I feel when I find myself caught in the experience of powerlessness.

So how do we start? Why not a monthly pot-luck and tactics party? Every month one person is excused from cooking and instead contributes the suggestion of a tactic to explore or a new way to use a tactic from a previous occasion. When we begin to see daily acts of resistance in the light of nonviolence theory—as incidents of political jiu-jitsu, albeit on a small scale—we can begin to understand how powerful we are. The power is there within us. All we need to do is name it, recognize it for what it is— and that we've been using it for years without that recognition—and then find creative, effective ways to let it out to work in the world. To unleash it. To ACT UP.

Nonviolent action is a way the "powerless" can take control of, and transform, the situation imposing that definition on them. It is the way we can resist and refuse that definition while simultaneously refusing merely to invert the situation into one where we aim to impose powerlessness on another. When we use nonviolent tactics in response to oppression or aggression, we reject both passivity and the prevailing belief that strength equals violence. Because we know better. We know that strength equals access to power, and that we—that all of us—can act with strength once we learn to make our power available to ourselves.

Most of all, we know that we are both normal and unique, and that even the most hateful of those who hate us are the same. It is absolutely positively normal to be unique. And as everybody knows, it is the unique, normally, that is precious. That is to be cherished. Until everyone becomes able to join us in celebrating the joy of our uniqueness, and their own, we will need to cultivate the control-freak side of ourselves. Lesbian songwriter/singer Alix Dobkin did a great reworking of the Almanac Singers' "Talking Union." Her version ends: "...we ain't got it easy, but we got it." How true. But so is the original version's ending (with a couple of interpolations of my own):

...if you don't let red-baiting [or modern variants thereof] break you up,
   And if you don't let stoolpigeons break you up,
And if you don't let vigilantes [or provocateurs] break you up,
   And if you don't let race hatred break you up—

You'll win....What I mean, take it easy, but take it.

AUTHOR'S NOTE
Heartfelt thanks to Richard Cleaver and Betty Johanna for their contributions to this essay.

DISCUSSION QUESTIONS
1. How is the desire or value of inclusivity lived in our personal and political actions?

2. What criteria does Meyerding outline for evaluating change strategies? How can these be applied to the strategies suggested in this and the next section?

3. How has gender disempowered both women and men and what are some strategies for claiming our power?

4. Audre Lorde has explored the power of the erotic as a profoundly creative source. How does our striving for deep human feeling impact our political organizing?

SUGGESTIONS FOR FURTHER READING
Jeffner Allen. 1986. Looking at our blood: A lesbian response to men's terrorization of women. *Lesbian Philosophies: Explorations.* Palo Alto, CA: Institute for Lesbian Studies.

Jeffner Allen. 1986. Motherhood: The annihilation of women. *Lesbian Philosophies: Explorations.* Palo Alto, CA: Institute for Lesbian Studies.

Deming, Barbara. 1968. *On Revolution and Equilibrium.* New York: A.J. Muste Memorial Pamphlet Series (339 Lafayette Street, New York, NY 10012.)

Gregory Herek. 1992. Psychological heterosexism and anti-gay violence: The social psychology of bigotry and bashing. *Hate crimes: Confronting violence against lesbians and gay men.* Gregory Herek & Kevin Berrill, Eds. Newbury Park, CA: Sage Publications.

Steve Karpf. 1991. Getting defensive: Queer patrols hit the streets. *Gay Community News,* 19(5).

Audre Lorde. 1984. Uses of the erotic: The erotic as power. *Sister outsider.* Trumansburg, NY: The Crossing Press.

Jane Meyerding. 1979. Feminism and pacifism: Doing it our way. *WIN Magazine* (February 8).

Sara Miles. 1992. The Fabulous Fight Back. *OUT/LOOK* 17, 5(1):54-59 (Summer).

STRATEGIES AND VISIONS

Some Additional Strategies

REMARKS FOR THE STONEWALL REBELLION'S 20TH ANNIVERSARY, JUNE 25, 1989
Harry Hay

Harry Hay is often considered the founder of the modern lesbian/gay movement in the United States. Hay was active in the Communist Party in the 1930s and 1940s, but struck out on his own in the early 1950s, when he drew together a handful of gay men in Los Angeles in an organization called the Mattachine Society. In the following, Hay distinguishes it from the more mainstream organization that resulted from a purge of former Communists, including Hay himself, at the group's 1953 convention, by calling the former "the First Mattachine" and the successor "the Second Mattachine."

After moving to northern New Mexico, where he became fascinated by Native American spirituality and sexual diversity, Hay returned to California as one of the founders of the Radical Faerie movement. He drew on his Marxist background to elaborate a view of homosexuals as a distinct minority in society, and went on from there to adopt the position that gay men and lesbians constitute an essentially different kind of person from straight men and women, with a long and rich history that has been deliberately suppressed. In recent years, he has warned against forming too close alliances with other social movements, in favor of maintaining a distinctive style of action and a complete autonomy. This is the view he expresses in this speech.

For most of us, whose traditions derive from Judaic-Christian sources, Homosexuality—presumed an affront to Great Mother Earth—was transmogrified into a crime to be hated by all because it was a crime against the Community. In Feudal Western Europe, controlled by the hated Holy Inquisition, from whence most of our ancestors had emigrated, homosexuality as the *pecado nefando*...latin for The Unforgiveable Sin!...which all good people of the Western Nations, Christians and Jews alike, were early drilled into hating once they understood—in each succeeding generation—that the universal scourges of disease and mass starvations were God's yearly punishments because they let filthy Sodomites survive in their midst!

To accomplish, and then maintain, this constant suppression of the Homosexual Scapegoat, Church and State worked overtime to create a total blanket of *invisibility and silence* over the social aspects of most

Homosexual life—beyond the 2% of the population which comprised the Aristocracy and the Upper Classes. So successful was this blackout that the Mollés, the Societés Joyeux and the Societés Mattachine, as certain 12th through 15th century Homosexual Affinity Groups were called, in European cities, and the numbers of Mollé or Mollie Clubs, as some Homosexual Affinity Groups were known in 16th thru early 19th century Britain, were largely unknown to the later 19th century scholars like John Addington Symonds and Edward Carpenter as they began to emerge—let alone to the many echelons of the modern Homosexual Communities themselves.

The appearance in the late 19th and early 20th centuries of Psychology, as a new medical discipline, brought to our WASP American Hetero-male-dominated Society new mind-sets for socializing generations of their young. The thinking of Freud and Jung indeed has tended to teach whole generations of young 20th century Gays and Lesbians how to actually rationalize society's detestation of Homosexuals *into their own self-hatred*, as Michael Denneny explains in a most insightful article in the Winter 1989 issue of *OUT/LOOK*. Michael Denneny pithily goes on to say "Gays were oppressed by society but—more importantly—society through use of its cultural power got Gays to oppress *themselves*...not only a neat trick but perhaps the most efficient means of oppression."

Aspects of this internalized self-hatred had been fixed in place for centuries by a British law commanding DEATH BY HANGING for anyone convicted as a practicing Homosexual, a law which—passed in 1533—was not changed from DEATH BY HANGING to merely LIFE IMPRISONMENT until 1861...the first year of our American Civil War and only fifty-one years before I was born. That socially-internalized invisibility of self-hating Gays and Lesbians was still paramount here in the United States when I founded my first Mattachine Society in Los Angeles in 1950. Our first job as we saw it was to invent and then begin to establish a positive Gay Public Image. It took me two and a half years to find five Gay men to sit down together and look at each other and find each other Good People. The first time, in November of 1950, when five of us—and then ten of us—Gay men and women—did sit down in a room in Silverlake we discovered each other...*and so ourselves*...a people of a new dimension, a people who carried—*each of them*—a new vision in their hearts of how people could be loving with each other in social as well as in personal ways...a people who dreamed to develop such an added dimensional vision as a positive Gay Identity in the teeth of the jingoist newly-hatched Korean War, *in the teeth of Senator Joe McCarthy's witch hunt against Gays in Government*. Bringing this self-actualizing discovery into collective motion, was itself, as [Boston activist and historian] Charley Shively might put it, AN ACT OF REVOLUTION!

AND IT WORKED!

Within a year-and-a-half, in the Spring and Summer of 1952, our First Mattachine Society, now five discussion groups in Los Angeles, a couple in the San Francisco Bay area, and one in San Diego—defied the Los Angeles City Establishment by challenging an entrapment case. Our fighting Waterfront Trade Union Lawyer caught the arresting cop in a lie on the witness stand, we caught the jury being tampered with, and the City of Los Angeles declined to mount a new trial. *The Queers had won something for the first time in American History!* And wouldn't you know—that the establishment greeted that victory with a total CONSPIRACY OF SILENCE? Not one blessed word of that case was ever printed by the Hetero press...NOT ONE WORD WAS EVER SPOKEN ON THE AIR!

In 1957 my First Mattachine Society's successor—*ONE Magazine*—won a landmark case before the United States Supreme Court—which forced the U.S. Post Office to permit dissemination of our books and periodicals through the mails.

But the three questions the First Mattachine founders proposed:

—who are we Gay and Lesbian people?

—where have we been coming from?

—what might we be constituted to contribute?

were too radical for even the bulk of the Mattachine Society's own socially internalized Gay self-hate in the 1950s and 1960s: the first wave of Assimilationists took over. And though new groups—like San Francisco's Second Mattachine, then the Washington, DC, followed by the Denver and then the New York Mattachine Societies all appeared one by one, though the women's DAUGHTERS OF BILITIS mushroomed in San Francisco, Los Angeles, New York, and Philadelphia, the Dorian Society flowered in Seattle, like similar small groups in Boston and other cities, the prevailing focus was Middle Class, respectable, and subdued... "we were just the same as everybody else except in bed," and "we had absolutely nothing in common with each other except our sexual inclinations." And yet—and yet—one day, early in 1953, we got a letter from New South Wales which said, "We know that here in far Australia nothing may happen in our lifetimes—but we wanted to say that just the name MATTACHINE whispers 'hope—along the wind!'" (In desolate times, "Hope along the wind" is magic in itself.) And again—in the letters section of Gay Journals like *ONE Magazine*, like *Mattachine Review,* like the Lesbian Magazine *The Ladder,* and others which began to proliferate in the early sixties, new rebel Gay voices—criss-crossing the country—were beginning to be heard—variations of First Mattachine's new vision of Gay People as carriers of the Dream of a new social dimension. *New powder trains were being laid!* And when your MAGNIFICENT STONEWALL REBELLION errupted here in New York City in June of 1969, revealing in a flash our next new concept...Gay—*as a socially viable collective identity*...those Powder Trains lit off across the country like the 4th of July! By January of 1970, we had Gay Liberation Fronts in many regions of the country.

The 1970s were full of Gay ferment—Gay/Lesbian Liberation proliferated by leaps and bounds...maybe even leaping a little too far AND

BOUNDING EVEN A LITTLE TOO FAST! For the Sleeping Giant, that Hetero-male-dominated American Society whose fundamentalist hatred of Homosexuals had succeeded in persuading us, as Michael Denneny said, to oppress ourselves for 300 years, turns out to be still running the show, and calling the turns.

A very prestigious Nationwide Public Opinion Poll, querying significantly-selected areas across the country, asked—in 1975—whether their respondents thought that Homosexuality was right or WRONG? Eighty-three percent of those queried said that they thought it was wrong. Asking that same question, in exactly the same places, in 1985 revealed that those finding it wrong had dropped from 83% to 81%. Supreme Court Justice Byron White, writing the majority opinion in the 1986 Hardwick decision, *knew about that 81%.* The Congress who sits on the Nation's pursestrings and refuses to properly fund our struggles against the AIDS epidemic know about that 81% too. For all our zaps, our Marches and Gay Pride Parades, our Movies and Documentaries, our Star-studded Telethons and extensive Radio interviews, and electing popular candidates and getting laws changed, 81% still think Homosexuality IS WRONG!

Before I go further—let me blurt out furiously that the Question *is a wrong one!* Ever since the Holocaust, and the Nuremberg trials, we don't send Public Opinion Polls into neighborhoods to inquire of respondent

> if they think *"Jews are WRONG!"*
> if they think *"Blacks are WRONG!"*
> if they think *"having blue eyes is WRONG!"*

The question should be: "What is this new dimension these people have to contribute?"

So just why is that 81% so persistently still in place? Well—FOR TWO REASONS. First, because we let them (our HETERO PARENTS, FRIENDS, and POLITICIANS) tell us *as we like to hear it* (through our Gay Window) "Oh yes, your Father and I suspected you were Gay. We just want you to know that we love you ANYWAY." Listen to that sentence again—through the Hetero window, "Oh yes, your father and I know that you've gone wrong, but we love you ANYWAY!" The ANYWAY is the mask that hides the homophobe—the Parent, the Friend, the Politician—who have learned nothing from your *coming out* to them, but who have agreed to accommodate your guilt and sin, as relatives learn to accommodate your Sister having married a Goy, or a Black. The "ANYWAY" reveals these Heteros—the parent, the friend, the politician to be—themselves—part of the 81% who think we are wrong! Perhaps it is time to say to that non-thinking accomodation—that knee jerk TOLERANCE—*no more! Not enough!*

The second and perhaps the more important reason for the stubborn persistence of the 81% is that our predominantly Gay-hating Hetero society is still mind-set upon keeping us gagged by their conspiracy of Silence. When—in October of 1987—our Gay and Lesbian Nation mounted the largest Protest March the United States had ever seen (even Jesse Jackson greeted our numbers at 750,000)—TIME/LIFE/NEWSWEEK, admittedly the largest Magazine and Media Conglomerate, saw fit NOT TO publish one word on the event. In this fashion America's 81% were being deliberately misinformed. This year the TIME/LIFE/NEWSWEEK Conglomerate plans to attempt a merger with Warner Communications, the largest Television Producer and Syndicator. And the potential of that further Monopolizing was hinted at when conglomerate members like the *Los Angeles Times* and the *New York Times*—reporting on the Women's powerful March of 300,000 pro-choice men and women on April 15, 1989— spoke of this 300,000-person event as THE LARGEST THAT WASHINGTON DC HAD SEEN since the Martin Luther King 20th Anniversary March of 1983—(it is sad to say that NOW didn't demur)—totally ignoring—NAY, DELIBERATELY OBLITERATING our GAY/LESBIAN March of more than twice that number in October of 1987! Here is the conspiracy of Silence at its most devastating! Here is how the 81% are really lied to and manipulated. And while we are on the subject of manipulation, I would propose that nowhere have we been treated to *a clearer public exposition of* that widespread—and so still prevailing—Hetero-male detestation of homosexuals that the recent Brou-ha-ha in Congress over House-Speaker Tom Foley's attempt to extricate himself from the closet politics of dirty little minds in the Bush White House, in the Congress, and among the blabbermouths of the Hetero-male press generally!

Dear Brothers and Sisters, Dearest Gay Family: on this 20th anniversary of the STONEWALL REBELLION, might we not agree that—in reviewing this sorry array of recent caricatures—we've been kidding ourselves long enough? The Heteros have been telling us since we were small that we are not the same as they: could we not at last begin to take the hint—breaking the conspiracy of Silence surrounding us to appreciate the very different people we are from them, *and always have been! Isn't it time we began to appreciate that it is one of Mother Nature's GREAT GIFTS TO US—to be DIFFERENT? I, for one, have always felt it was a GIFT TO BE GAY!*

If we really intend to break and dissipate the Conspiracy of Silence with which we have been surrounded, I suggest we are going to have to invent new ways to—for one thing—neutralize our compulsions for Hetero Middle Class DRAG...more of us shall have to become visible...and some of us shall have to become MORE visible...like me, f'r instance....

Many of you will remember that our Radical Faerie March-on-Washington-1987 Zuni-style skirts...worn over our jeans...proclaimed us "Men-not-for-killing—and Men-not-for-War." And, of course, we all equally know—concerning Gay and Lesbian major doings—that one simply can't be seen in the same outfit twice. So [today I'm wearing] variation #2.

Last night's Radical Faerie Judy Garland Memorial re-enactment in the Village and the outbreak of ACT UP this year across the country is a good start on our breakout from the Silence Conspiracy. But I would suggest that some of the tactics, such as *Confrontation, are better suited to Hetero belligerence*—to masses of angry workers—or majorities of impatient students. Successful Guerilla Resistances of History knew that the burden of their thrusts were not to clobber...they were to inform: they knew that the keystones of their accuracies were not FURY...they were the theatrical magics of surprise! They swooped in—made their points—and then vanished. *Faeries—equally—in their admittedly small groups—inform more lucidly and trenchantly by appearing when and where they are not expected*...and vanishing before the Heat arrives.

CONFRONTATION, again, lays itself wide open to the improvisatory violence and violations of infiltrating provocateurs—as LA and San Francisco may have to learn to their sorrow. ACT UP could—in such situations—find itself being sued to a "fare-thee-well"...frittering away funds that were better used for Health and Hospices. If we use confrontation at all, we might better employ it—*TO REVEAL* the harm the Government dishes out, *TO REVEAL* the wickedness and THE DEADLY CONSEQUENCES of forked-tongued Politicians...then conclude the revelations with the employment of *SACRED CLOWNS* who, in all times and in all cultures, bestow the Faerie magic of healing laughter to transform us all—once more—victims and spectators alike—back into a caring community.

So also, on this lovely Twentieth Anniversary Day...my Gay and Lesbian Family, my Beloved Family of Conscious Choice...let me, IN MY RADICAL FAERIE ZUNI-STYLE SKIRT, VARIATION #2, be one of your SACRED CLOWNS—bringing to you...

   ...*the ALL-HEAL of laughter* ...

   ...*the blessings of my irrepressible giggle*...

   ....*the ALL-HEAL of LOVE!*...

DISCUSSION QUESTIONS

1. If lesbians and gay men are essentially different from heteros (in Hay's terminology), what does that mean for strategies of liberation? How do the strategies Hay proposes differ from others being used or proposed today? How do they coincide?

2. When Hay suggests tactics like those of ACT UP and Queer Nation are "better suited to heteros" and proposes "theatrical magics" in their place, what practical distinction is he making?

3. Hay describes Radical Faeries as "Men-not-for-killing—and Men-not-for-War." Thinking back to articles by Michalowski and hooks, what makes gay men unsuited for warfare? Or are they?

SUGGESTIONS FOR FURTHER READING

Barbara Grier. 1976. *Lesbiana: Book reviews from The Ladder*. Tallahassee, FL: Naiad Press.

Jonathan Katz. 1976. Henry Hay: Founding the Mattachine Society. *Gay American history: Lesbians and gay men in the U.S.A.* New York: Harper and Row.

Del Martin & Phyllis Lyon. 1972. *Lesbian/woman*. New York: Bantam Books.

Stuart Timmons. 1990. *The trouble with Harry Hay*. Boston: Alyson.

DIRECT ACTION:
LESBIANS LEAD THE MOVEMENT
Barbara Epstein

The prominence of lesbians in the nonviolent direct action campaigns of the 1980s represents a new visibility. It has also brought a new and different flavor to nonviolent direct action. Barbara Epstein narrates some of the history of this development, and describes some of its underlying political philosophy. The activity described here suggests that women have a clear role to play not only in their own liberation but in other social change movements as well.

One of the editors, Richard Cleaver (who was a member of the planning committee for the 1987 Supreme Court civil disobedience mentioned by Epstein) would like to stress the leadership role lesbians played in that particular action: the planning committee was mainly lesbian, and the two staff people hired to carry out preparations were both lesbians with a long history of nonviolent direct action. The success of the action, at which more than 800 people were arrested, represented a wide range of styles, concerns and political viewpoints, and was due almost entirely to lesbian leadership. Furthermore, the action gave extra impetus to the spread of the direct action network ACT UP around the country.

Throughout the late sixties and early seventies, separate women's organizations played the major role in the development of feminism. But in the late seventies and the eighties, a new variant of feminism has begun to emerge out of the direct action movement. Though the major organizations of the direct action movement have consisted of both men and women, there have also been separate women's groups and actions, and while sexism has hardly been eradicated, feminism has been taken more seriously in this than in any previous movement of men and women in the United States.

Many women who had been part of separate women's organizations in the early seventies were, by the end of that decade, becoming interested in applying their feminist perspective in a broader context, and were drawn to the anti-nuclear movement because of its link with environmentalism, and its openness to a visionary perspective. The effort to link feminism, environmentalism and nonviolence has enriched all three perspectives, and in particular, has produced a variety of feminism that

"Direct action: Lesbians lead the movement," by Barbara Epstein from OUT/LOOK 1(2): 27-32. Copyright © 1988 by Barbara Epstein. Reprinted with permission.

has the potential to transcend some of the limitations of earlier strands of feminism.

The variety of feminism that has flourished in the direct action movement—rooted in radical feminism and linked to women's spirituality—has given the movement vitality and has also posed important intellectual and political questions. At the same time, radical feminism and feminist spirituality have reinforced the anti-intellectualism of the movement, creating barriers to any systematic examination of the issues that they raise.

These currents of feminism have been particularly associated with lesbians, who have played a major role in the direct action movement, often providing leadership not only for the separate women's actions and organizations within the movement, but, especially in its most recent phase, for the movement more generally. The role of lesbians in the movement highlights a question that concerns the movement as a whole: whether a minority subculture can provide the spark for political mobilization that transcends its own boundaries.

A NEW FORM OF PROTEST

The largest separate women's actions within the direct action movement have been: the two Women's Pentagon Actions, in 1980 and 1981, which brought thousands of women to Washington to encircle the Pentagon and to express their opposition to the war through theater and ritual; the Seneca Women's Peace Camp of the summer of 1983, which paralleled the British Greenham Common encampment with a massive women's presence adjacent to the Seneca Army Depot in upstate New York (a facility used by the Department of Defense to store nuclear weapons); and a Mother's Day Action at the Nevada Test Site, north of Las Vegas, in 1987, which drew thousands of women from around the country, many of them linked indirectly if at all to the counter-cultural core of the direct action movement. There have also been countless smaller women's actions linked with the direct action movement, some on occasions such as Mother's Day and some simply part of the ongoing efforts of groups of women associated with the movement.

The first Women's Pentagon Action came out of the conference "Women and Life on Earth: Ecofeminism in the 1980s," held in early 1980, which brought together women involved in the anti-nuclear and environmental movements and women who, with the decline of organized radical feminism in the mid-seventies, had become involved in feminist spirituality. For many of these women, the conference represented a re-entry into politics, this time into a women's enclave that was part of a larger mixed movement. The conference attempted to bridge political and spiritual concerns, and it called for a politics opposed to militarism, patriarchy, and other forms of oppression, a politics that would rely on direct personal expression, empowered by symbolism and drama. The first Women's Pentagon Action, planned to embody the vision expressed by the conference, was called for November of that year.

On Sunday, November 17, 2,000 women gathered in Washington. Workshops on a range of feminist topics provided an opportunity for the women to become familiar with one another before the action. Monday morning began with a march through Arlington Cemetery. As the women approached the Pentagon, they were joined by drummers and four women carrying large female puppets, each symbolizing a different stage of the demonstration: one was in black, for mourning; another in red, for rage; a third was yellow, for empowerment; and the fourth puppet, in white, symbolized defiance.

The impact of the action was due not to its numbers (which were not particularly large), but to its aesthetics, which broke away from the traditional rally format of speakers and audience, allowed greater participation and personal expression, and made a more striking impact. Some of the ideas employed at the Women's Pentagon Action were adopted by women's groups elsewhere in the country, the most popular being the idea of using weaving as a metaphor of women's power against hated institutions (and as a way of injecting color into actions). The plan to weave shut the doors of the Pentagon with brightly colored yarn came from a Vermont affinity group, the Spinsters, who had used it in demonstrations against a local nuclear plant.

Three years later, feminists in the Finger Lakes area of upstate New York discovered that the Cruise missiles being sent to the Greenham base in England actually were shipped from a location close to home—the Seneca Army Depot in Seneca Falls. Given the fact that Seneca had been the site of the first feminist convention in the United States in 1848, this seemed an ideal place to establish a women's peace camp—a sister presence to the women's encampment at Greenham Common. Money was raised and a piece of land adjacent to the Army Depot was bought; ownership was placed in the hands of the thousand or so women who participated in organizing the camp. The encampment itself began at the end of May, 1983; over that summer, about 15,000 women came through the camp at one point or another.

Many of the women in the camp were lesbians, and the camp had a pronounced counter-cultural tone. The camp, located in a conservative rural area, met with considerable hostility, and the local police protected the rights of those connected with the camp with great reluctance. At one point, roughly a hundred women embarked on a fifteen-mile "walk for peace" (for which a parade permit had been obtained) from the historic home of Elizabeth Cady Stanton in Seneca Falls to the encampment. As they passed through the town of Waterloo, the women were met by an angry crowd of several hundred people, many of them waving American flags, blocking the way. The women sat down in the road; some people in the crowd began to threaten violence. The sheriff ordered the crowd to disperse and arrested the fifty-four women who were still sitting in the road, charging them with disorderly conduct.

Since the mid-eighties, the feminist counter-culture, which had been the base of the feminist presence in the direct action movement, has become less visible. But the appeal of direct action has expanded to groups of women closer to the mainstream. In 1987, a Mother's Day Action was held at the Nevada Test Site, a stretch of land in the Nevada desert where the U.S. tests most of its nuclear weapons. The action was organized largely by the women of the American Peace Test, a group that had originated as the direct action committee of the Nuclear Weapons Freeze Campaign and amicably had left that organization when it became clear that the Freeze would not sponsor direct action. The action was also sponsored by the Nevada Desert Experience, a Catholic anti-war group that has maintained a presence at the test site for many years. Because of the cost of traveling to the site, and the relatively mainstream sponsorship of the action, the 2,000 women who came to the action were older and straighter than participants in previous women's actions. While the counter-culture was present, it was not dominant. Roughly 700 women were arrested after climbing over the fence to the test site.

THE LESBIAN CONNECTION

Lesbians have played a particularly salient role in the direct action movement, especially in its more recent phases. In the late seventies, groups of lesbians, mostly from the country, participated in the Clamshell Alliance, which mounted a series of demonstrations against a nuclear power plant under construction in Seabrook, New Hampshire. There, they were more ready than others to engage in militant and outrageous actions. Some women saw them as an inspiration; others found them an embarrassment. The same was true of the Livermore Action Group (LAG), which, in the early eighties, organized a series of protests against nuclear weapons research at Lawrence Livermore Laboratory in the San Francisco Bay Area. The Feminist Cluster of LAG, which consisted of all-female, mostly lesbian, affinity groups, gave feminism a strong presence in the organization, and at times pushed the limits of nonviolence.

During the jail stay that followed the large 1983 protest at Livermore, Bibles were handed out to the women; two members of the Feminist Cluster, discovering negative references to homosexuality, took their copies into the bathroom where they burned the offending pages. They were discovered by a guard and given additional time. The debate that ensued among the protesters, over whether and how to support these women, reflected strong and quite divided feelings over what they had done, and over the tendency of the more militant women to stretch the limits of nonviolence in the name of feminism.

Quantitatively, lesbians have been a major element in the direct action movement. About one third of the women from LAG who were jailed for two weeks in 1983 were lesbians; there was a similar percentage the year before. Lesbians have made up a much larger share of those participating in women-only actions; they made up a large majority of those participating in the two Women's Pentagon Actions, and in the Seneca Peace Camp. Lesbians have maintained a much larger presence than gay men in the direct action movement; though gay direct action groups have begun to organize around the AIDS issue, there have been no men's actions paralleling those of women.

Lesbians have also played a large and increasing role in the leadership of the direct action movement—and not only of its women's component. This has been especially true in the rural and semi-rural areas where lesbians who were active in the movements of the sixties and seventies have settled. In northern New England, especially Vermont and western Massachusetts, groups of lesbians have played major roles in anti-nuclear actions. In Key West, Florida, a group of lesbians centering around the pacifist writer Barbara Deming have provided the core for ongoing actions at the Key West Naval Base and at Cape Canaveral. In St. Augustine, Florida, a group of lesbians who own and live together in adjacent houses have organized Seeds for Peace, a group which has been the moving force in peace and environmental actions in the area.

Lesbians have also come to play a major role in direct action in many cities, and on a national level. In Boston, a group of women, mainly lesbians, has provided leadership for the Pledge of Resistance (an organization opposed to U.S. intervention in Central America) as well as for anti-war direct action more generally. In April 1986, when a large demonstration was held in Washington against the CIA, it was mainly lesbians who organized and led its direct action component in which 600 men and women were arrested. For the 1987 March on Washington for Lesbian and Gay Rights, it was lesbians from the direct action movement who provided the nonviolence training for civil disobedience at the Supreme Court.

Many of the women who organized these actions say they are not surprised to find themselves, and other lesbians, in positions of leadership in movements for nonviolent direct action. Once one has come out of the closet, they say, taking other kinds of risks is easier. Their marginality gives them a stake in fundamental social change and their grounding in feminism gives them an understanding of the interconnectedness of many issues—an understanding that is usually less developed among gay men.

Some argue that lesbians and gay men have always played important roles in movements for social change—in the peace movement, the left, and the civil rights movement. But previously, when lesbians and gay men were prominent, it was as individuals. In the direct action movement, and to some extent in the peace movement more generally, networks of lesbians have begun to play a major role.

FEMINIST PHILOSOPHIES & DIRECT ACTION

The philosophy that guides the direct action movement links feminism with ecology and a utopian social vision, and attempts to bridge politics and religion (or spirituality). This philosophy has been constructed primarily by women whose background and frame of reference is the women's movement, in most cases specifically radical, or cultural, feminism. The two main varieties of feminist world-view that have emerged in the context of the movement are anarcha-feminism and ecofeminism. Both have been strongly influenced by feminist spirituality, but in both cases there has also been tension between more spiritual and more political/intellectual currents.

Anarcha-feminism was introduced to the direct action movement by a group of anarchists who originally came together as student activists at Stanford, subsequently fanned out to Santa Cruz and San Francisco, and collectively became involved in the Abalone Alliance in time to have major impact on the Diablo Canyon blockade of 1981. Peggy Kornegger, the author of an influential anarcha-feminist piece, argued that radical feminism and anarchism were natural allies. Both perspectives, she pointed out, were based on critiques of dominance; both sought to replace power relations with equality. She argued that women's consciousness-raising groups—small, leaderless groups based on face-to-face relations—embodied anarchist principles, and that because of their history of powerlessness and lack of legitimacy, women were readily drawn to anarchist philosophy.

Other anarcha-feminist authors echoed and developed these themes. Carol Ehrlich wrote that the fundamental goals of anarchism and radical feminism were the same: "not to 'seize' power, as the socialists are fond of urging, but to abolish power." Kytha Kurin argued that in order to achieve its own goals, the radical feminist perspective must move beyond gender separatism and become, along with an ecological perspective, the guiding philosophy of a movement of men as well as women.

By the latter part of the seventies, many feminists were coming to regard separatism as an inadequate strategy; part of the attraction of anarcha-feminism was that it addressed this problem without rejecting the radical feminist analysis that had been associated with that strategy. But anarcha-feminism was not equipped to address another problem of the women's movement, described, in the title of Jo Freeman's famous essay, as "The Tyranny of Structurelessness." The piece argued that every group has leaders, that informal leaders are less accountable and therefore more dangerous than formally recognized ones, and that anti-leadership ideology had weakened the women's movement by providing a rationale for crippling attacks on the key activists who had helped the movement find direction.

Meanwhile, a related tendency calling itself ecofeminism was developing on the east coast. The term was first used by the French author Françoise d'Eaubonne in 1974 in her book *La Féminisme ou la Mort*, and was adopted by the group of women who, in 1980, held the conference "Women and Life on Earth: Ecofeminism in the 1980s." Ynestra King, a coordinator of the conference, was working toward a synthesis of ecological and feminist perspectives.

Ecofeminism has been the basis for a more substantial intellectual tradition than anarcha-feminism, and as a result has maintained a presence even as the movement with which it was originally associated has gone into decline. Several books written in the late seventies, including Susan Griffin's *Woman and Nature* and Mary Daly's *Gyn/Ecology*, began to develop a perspective based on the attempt to join radical feminist and ecological concerns. In the eighties many more works have appeared that identify themselves with ecofeminism, particularly Carolyn Merchant's *Death of Nature*, Charlene Spretnak's collection, *Politics of Women's Spirituality*, and an issue of *Heresies* devoted to feminism and ecology. Margot Adler's account of witchcraft in the United States, *Drawing Down the Moon*, and Starhawk's *Dreaming the Dark: Magic, Sex and Politics*, both straddle the worlds of paganism, feminist spirituality, and ecofeminism. In 1986, a conference entitled "Ecofeminist Perspectives" in Los Angeles attracted 1500 activists and scholars, suggesting that there is a growing audience for the approach.

Ecofeminists argue that patriarchy, the domination of women by men, has been associated with the attempt to dominate nature. Men have attempted to justify their attempts to dominate nature by associating it with women; this objectifies both women and nature by placing them in the category of the "other," and involves a denial of both human links with the natural world, and men's feminine side. Ecofeminists believe the despoliation of the environment, violence, and militarism are rooted in the culture of domination; they argue that these problems have become major threats to the human race, and must be overcome.

Anarcha-feminism and ecofeminism both intersect with paganism or witchcraft and feminist spirituality. Together witchcraft and feminist spirituality have had a strong impact on the direct action movement as a whole. Margot Adler's *Drawing Down the Moon* and Starhawk's *Dreaming the Dark* both emphasize the radical and feminist implications of witchcraft, and have drawn many young radical feminists into its orbit. Feminists were drawn to witchcraft for several reasons: its association with goddess figures; its anti-hierarchical implications and respect for nature; a desire to find a religious tradition that did not involve worshipping a transcendent male god; and, in part, because of its theatrical potential and shock value.

In spite of the fact that the direct action movement is not primarily concerned with issues that are specific to women, and that it is a movement of both men and women, feminism has provided the glue for the movement as a whole and the leaven for the distinctive political philosophy that has emerged within and around it.

Intellectually, the role of feminism has been pivotal. It has been key to placing the concepts of empowerment and personal transformation at the center of the direct action movement's concept of its mission. Many people—both men and women—have been drawn into the movement because it is based on consensus and on the broader effort to implement a radical egalitarianism generally referred to as "feminist process."

Feminism—specifically the version that is rooted in radical feminism and women's spirituality—has been the main basis for an approach in the direct action movement to define its goals and evaluate its successes differently than many earlier movements have. Feminism has been the key influence in leading the movement to regard its mission as the transformation of consciousness: the self-transformation of those within the movement, as well as the construction of a community in which new values can be realized and which can provide a lasting base for political action.

DISCUSSION QUESTIONS

1. Lesbians and gay men, as both Barbara Epstein and Harry Hay have indicated, have played prominent (if unacknowledged) parts in campaigns of nonviolent direct action. What might this tell us about the nature and possibilities of nonviolent direct action?

2. In many direct action coalitions, Christian activists have played a prominent part. Epstein has noted some of the tensions this can produce when open lesbians and gay men also participate.What are some ways this problem can be overcome in planning an action? What pieces of this work are the job of lesbians and gay men themselves, and what pieces are better done by non-gay allies? Why?

3. Epstein points out the importance of women's spirituality in shaping the actions she describes. How has that affected the political demands and strategies of the movement? How is this view influenced by essentialism, if at all?

4. What criticisms of ecofeminism and anarcha-feminism did bell hooks offer in a previous section? What new light does Epstein shed on them?

SUGGESTIONS FOR FURTHER READING

Sarah Lucia Hoagland. 1988. *Lesbian ethics: Toward new values.* Palo Alto, CA: Institute for Lesbian Studies.

Stephanie Poggi. 1986. Homophobia on what's left of the Left. *Gay Community News* (June 7).

FEMINIST POLITICIZATION:
A COMMENT
bell hooks

Much contemporary lesbian, gay male and bisexual political activity is based on identity. While no collective action can take place unless we have some sense of who "we" are, bell hooks here points out that creating identities is the beginning, not the end, of politics. Some identities carry with them privilege as well as oppression; some identities are more fluid than others by their nature; most if not all of us carry with us multiple identities, with one or another taking the front seat at different times.

Lesbians, gay men and bisexual people, like other oppressed groups, must strategize for change. This means we must think in terms of power, not powerlessness. We begin the process of claiming power from the soil of personal experience. But, as hooks puts it, "politicization necessarily combines this process (the naming of one's experience) with critical understanding of the concrete material reality that lays the groundwork for that personal experience."

Always a part of my inner listening self closes down when I hear the words "the personal is political." Yes, I understand them. I understand that aspect of early feminist consciousness-raising that urged every listening woman to see her problems, especially problems she experienced as the outcome of sexism and sexist oppression, as political issues. To begin on the inside and move outside. To begin with the self as starting point, then to move beyond self-reflection to an awareness of collective reality. This was the promise these words held. But that promise was all too easily unfulfilled, broken. A culture of domination is necessarily narcissistic. To take woman to the self as starting point for politicization, woman who, in white-supremacist, capitalist patriarchy, is particularly made, socially constructed, to think only me—my body—I constitute a universe—all that truly matters. To take her—this woman—to the self as starting point for politicization is necessarily risky.

We see now the danger in "the personal is political." The personal most known as private, as that space where there is no intervention from the outside, as that which can be kept to the self, as that which does not extend beyond. Knowing the way this culture conceives the personal, the promise was to transform the meaning by linking it with the political, a word so associated in the minds of even small school children with government, with a world of affairs outside the body, the private, the self. We see now the danger. "The personal is political." No sense of connection between one's person and a larger material reality—no sense of what the political is. In this phrase, what most resonates is the word personal—not the word political. Unsure of the political, each female presumes knowledge of the person—the personal. No need then to search for the meaning of political, simpler to stay with the personal, to make synonymous the personal and the political. Then the self does not become that which one moves into to move beyond, or to connect with. It stays in place, the starting point from which one need never move. If the personal and the political are one and the same, then there is no politicization, no way to become the radical feminist subject.

Perhaps these words are too strong. Perhaps some of you remember the poignancy, the depth, the way this slogan reached into your life, grasped hold of your experience—and you did move. You did understand better the link between personal experience and political reality. The ways individual women were able to concretely find the deep structure of this slogan, use it to radicalize consciousness, need not be denied. Still, to name the danger, the ways it led feminist politics into identity politics, is crucial for the construction of a social space, a radical front wherein politicization of consciousness, of the self, can become real in everyday life.

This slogan had such power because it insisted on the primacy of the personal, not in a narcissistic way, but in its implied naming of the self as a site for politicization, which was in this society a very radical challenge to notions of self and identity. The challenging meaning behind the slogan, however, was not consistently conveyed. While stating "the personal is political" did highlight feminist concern with self, it did not insist on a connection between politicization and transformation of consciousness. It spoke most immediately to the concerns women had about self and identity. Again, the radical insistence on the primacy of a politicized self was submerged, subsumed within a larger cultural framework wherein focus on identity was already legitimized within structures of domination. Obsessive, narcissistic concern with "finding an identity" was already a popular cultural preoccupation, one that deflected attention away from radical politics. Feminist focus on self was then easily linked not to a process of radical politicization, but to a process of de-politicization. Popularly, the important quest was not to radically change our relationship to self and identity, to educate for critical consciousness, to become politically engaged and committed, but to explore one's identity, to affirm and assert the primacy of the self as it already existed. Such a focus was strengthened by an emphasis within feminist movement on lifestyle, on being politically correct in one's representation of self rather than being political.

Exasperated with identity politics, Jenny Bourne begins her essay, "Homelands of the Mind: Jewish Feminism and Identity Politics," with the assertion:

> Identity politics is all the rage. Exploitation is out (it is extrinsically determinist.) Oppression is in (it is intrinsically personal.) What is to be done has been replaced by who am I. Political culture has ceded to cultural politics. The material world has passed into the metaphysical. The Blacks, the Women, the Gays have all searched for themselves. And now combining all their quests, has arrived the quest for Jewish feminist identity.

Bourne's essay speaks to the crisis of political commitment and engagement engendered by relentless focus on identity. I wholeheartedly affirm her effort to expose the ways identity politics has led to the construction of a notion of feminist movement that is, as she sees it, "separatist, individualistic, and inward-looking." She asserts: "The organic relationship we tried to forge between the personal and the political has been so degraded that now the only area of politics deemed legitimate is the personal." However, I think it essential not to mock or ridicule the metaphysical but to find a constructive point of connection between material struggle and metaphysical concerns. We cannot oppose the emphasis on identity politics by inverting the logic and devaluing the personal. It does not further feminist movement to ignore issues of identity or to critique concern with self without posing alternative approaches, without addressing in a dialectical manner the issue of feminist politicization—the link between efforts to socially construct self, identity in an oppositional framework, one that resists domination, and allows for the greatest degree of well-being.

To challenge identity politics we must offer strategies of politicization that enlarge our conception of who we are, that intensify our sense of intersubjectivity, our relation to a collective reality. We do this by reemphasizing how history, political science, psychoanalysis, and diverse ways of knowing can be used to inform our ideas of self and identity. Politicization of the self can have its starting point in an exploration of the personal wherein what is first revolutionized is the way we think about the self. To begin revisioning, we must acknowledge the need to examine the self from a new, critical standpoint. Such a perspective, while it would insist on the self as a site for politicization, would equally insist that simply describing one's experience of exploitation or oppression is not to become politicized. It is not sufficient to know the personal but to know— to speak it in a different way. Knowing the personal might mean naming spaces of ignorance, gaps in knowledge, ones that render us unable to link the personal with the political.

In *Ain't I a Woman*, I pointed to the distinction between experiencing a form of exploitation and understanding the particular structure of domination that is the cause. The opening paragraph of the chapter on "Racism and Feminism: The Issue of Accountability" begins:

> American women of all races are socialized to think of racism solely in the context of race hatred. Specifically in the case of black and white people. For most women, the first knowledge of racism as institutionalized oppression is engendered either by direct personal experience or through information gleaned from conversations, books, television or movies. Consequently, the American woman's understanding of racism as a political tool of colonialism and imperialism is severely limited. To experience the pain of race hatred or to witness that pain is not to understand its origin, evolution, or impact on world history.

Many women engaged in feminist movement assumed that describing one's personal experience of exploitation by men was to be politicized. Politicization necessarily combines this process (the naming of one's experience) with critical understanding of the concrete material reality that lays the groundwork for that personal experience. The work of understanding that groundwork and what must be done to transform it is quite different from the effort to raise one's consciousness about personal experience even as they are linked.

Feminist critiques of identity politics which call attention to the way it undermines feminist movement should not deny the importance of naming and giving voice to one's experience. It must be continually stressed that this is only part of the process of politicization, one which must be linked to education for critical consciousness that teaches about structures of domination and how they function. It is understanding the latter that enables us to imagine new possibilities, strategies for change and transformation. The extent to which we are able to link radical self-awareness to collective struggle to change and transform self and society will determine the fate of feminist revolution.

Focus on self in feminist movement has not been solely the province of privileged white women. Women of color, many of whom were struggling to articulate and name our experience for the first time, also began to focus attention on identity in static and non-productive ways. Jenny Bourne focuses on individual black women who promoted identity politics, calling attention to a statement by the Combahee River Collective which reads: "The most profound and potentially the most radical politics come directly out of our own identity as opposed to working to end somebody else's oppression." This statement asserts the primacy of identity politics. Coming from radical black women, it served to legitimize the emphasis in feminist movement on identity—that to know one's needs as an individual is to be political. It is in many ways a very problematic statement. If one's identity is constructed from a base of power and privilege gained from participation in and acceptance of structures of domination, it is not a given that focus on naming that identity will lead to a radicalized consciousness, a questioning of that privilege, or to active resistance. It is possible to name one's personal experience without committing oneself to transforming or changing that experience.

To imply, as this statement does, that individuals cannot successfully radicalize their consciousness and their actions as much by working in resistance struggles that do not directly effect their lives is to underestimate the power of solidarity. It is only as allies with those who are exploited and oppressed, working in struggles for liberation, that individuals who are not victimized demonstrate their allegiance, their political commitment, their determination to resist, to break with the structures of domination that offer them personal privilege. This holds true for individuals from oppressed and exploited groups as well. Our consciousness can be radicalized by acting to eradicate forms of domination that do not have direct correspondence with our identities and experiences. Bourne states:

> Identity politics regards the discovery of identity as its supreme goal.
> Feminists even assert that discovering an identity is an act of resistance.
> The mistake is to view identity as an end rather than a means....Identity is
> not merely a precursor to action, it is also created through action.

Indeed, for many exploited and oppressed peoples the struggle to create an identity, to name one's reality is an act of resistance because the process of domination—whether it be imperialist colonization, racism, or sexist oppression—has stripped us of our identity, devalued language, culture, appearance. Again, this is only a stage in the process of revolution (one Bourne seems to deny has any value), but it must not be denigrated, even if people of privilege repeat this gesture so often that is has no radical implications. For example: the slogan "black is beautiful" was an important popular expression of resistance to white supremacy (of course that expression loses meaning and power if not linked to a process of politicization where black people learn to see ourselves as subjects rather than as objects, where as an expression of being subjects we act to transform the world we live in so that our skin no longer signifies that we will be degraded, exploited). It would be a grave mistake to suggest that politicization of self is not part of the process by which we prepare ourselves to act most effectively for radical social change. Only when it becomes narcissistic or when, as Bourne states, it naively suggests that "structural, material issues of race, class, and power, would first be resolved in terms of personal consciousness" does it diminish liberatory struggle.

When I chart a map of feminist politicization, of how we become more politically self-aware, I begin with the insistence on commitment to education for critical consciousness. Much of that education does start with examining the self from a new, critical perspective. To this end, confession and memory can be used constructively to illuminate past experiences, particularly when such experience is theorized. Using confession and memory as ways of naming reality enables women and men to talk about personal experience as part of a process of politicization which places such talk in a dialectical context. This allows us to discuss personal experience in a different way, in a way that politicizes not just the telling, but the tale. Theorizing experience as we tell personal narrative, we have a sharper, keener sense of the end that is desired by the telling. An interesting and constructive use of memory and confession is narrated in the book, *Female Sexualization: A Collective Work of Memory*, edited by Frigga Haug. Collectively, the women who speak work not just to name their experience but to place that experience in a theoretical context. They use confession and memory as tools of intervention which allow them to unite scientific knowledge with everyday experience. So as not to place undue emphasis on the individual, they consistently link individual experience to collective reality. Story-telling becomes a process of historicization. It does not remove women from history but enables us to see ourselves as part of history. The act of writing autobiographical stories enabled the women in the Haug book to see themselves from a different perspective, one which they describe as a "politically necessary form of cultural labor." They comment, "It makes us live our lives more consciously." Used constructively, confession and memory are tools that heighten self-awareness; they need not make us solely inward-looking.

Feminist thinkers in the United States use confession and memory primarily as a way to narrate tales of victimization, which are rarely rendered dialectically. This focus means that we do not have various and diverse accountings of all aspects of female experience. As we struggle to learn more about how women relate to one another, to men and to children in everyday life, how we construct strategies of resistance and survival, it is useful to rely on confession and memory as documentary sources. We must, however, be careful not to promote the construction of narratives of female experience that became so normative that all experience that does not fit the model is deemed illegitimate or unworthy of investigation.

Rethinking ways to constructively use confession and memory shifts the focus away from mere naming of one's experience. It enables feminist thinkers to talk about identity in relation to strategies of politicization, feminist thinkers must be willing to see the female self anew, to examine how we are gendered critically and analytically from various standpoints. In early feminist consciousness-raising, confession was often the way to share negative traumas, the experience of male violence for example. Yet there remain many unexplored areas of female experience that need to be fully examined, thereby widening the scope of our understanding of what it is to be female in this society. Imagine a group of black women working to educate ourselves for critical consciousness, exploring our relation to radical politics, to left politics. We might better understand our collective reluctance to commit ourselves to feminist struggle, to revolutionary politics or we might also chart those experiences that prepare and enable us to make such commitments.

There is much exciting work to be done when we use confession and memory as a way to theorize experience, to deepen our awareness, as part of the process of radical politicization. Often we experience pleasure and joy when we share personal stories, closeness, intimacy. This is why the personal has had such a place in feminist discourse. To reaffirm the power of the personal while simultaneously not getting trapped in identity politics, we must work to link personal narratives with knowledge of how we must act politically to change and transform the world.

DISCUSSION QUESTIONS

1. What are some of the varied identifications we carry with us? How do we know which is most prominent in a given situation?

2. Which of our identities carries privilege? How do we deal with that privilege? What responsibilities does it bring?

3. How can we build into our process of naming and memory the necessary stages of critical understanding?

4. What has "the personal is political" meant to us? How have we experienced or been made aware of its limitations? What possibilities for liberation does this slogan still hold?

SUGGESTIONS FOR FURTHER READING

Jenny Bourne. 1987. Homelands of the mind: Jewish feminism and identity politics. *Race and Class*, 29:1-24 (Summer).

Cheryl Clarke. 1983. Lesbianism: An act of resistance. *This bridge called my back: Writings by radical women of color.* Cherríe Moraga & Gloria Anzaldúa, Eds. New York: Kitchen Table: Women of Color Press.

Combahee River Collective. 1983. A black feminist statement. *This bridge called my back: Writings by radical women of color.* Cherríe Moraga & Gloria Anzaldúa, Eds. New York: Kitchen Table: Women of Color Press.

Frigga Haug, Ed. 1987. *Female sexualization: A collective work of memory.* London: Verso.

NAVY MEMO ON LESBIANS SPARKS OUTRAGE

> *The exclusion of "homosexuals" from the U.S. military is one of the most lively issues of lesbian and gay men's political activity as this anthology is being prepared. Harold Jordan discusses some of the implications of the issue in the next piece; this article, reprinted from the Central Committee for Conscientious Objectors' journal* The Objector, *provides a glimpse into the military's internal debate on the issue.*

> *On January 29, 1993, as this collection was being readied for the printer, President Clinton announced that he was instructing Secretary of Defense Les Aspin to prepare an order, to be issued July 15, 1993, lifting the ban on lesbians and gay men serving in the military. In the meantime, Congress is to hold hearings and the military establishment permitted to offer its views.*

> *Clinton's announcement left many questions unanswered, and raised a storm of protest from the military and its supporters. It will remain to be seen how the coming changes in policy, if Congress does not block them altogether, will affect the practices laid out in this memo.*

In July 1990 the Navy Command in Norfolk, Virginia sent a memo to all surface fleet commanders and officers concerning homosexuality among women in the Navy. When the memo was leaked to the press it caused an outrage because it confirmed that the Navy's top command still held outdated and dangerous views about homosexuals in general, and particularly about lesbians.

The memo confirms that women are prosecuted for homosexuality more frequently than men, and that witchhunts are part of a Navy policy to "uncover" lesbians. The memo also suggests that sexual harassment by lesbians of other women is a more severe and devastating problem than harassment by men, and urges more vigorous enforcement of policies prohibiting this behavior.

Disturbingly, the memo also provides a stereotype of a lesbian as a hardworking, aggressive career woman who has risen to the top of her profession. This characterization targets all successful female Navy sailors and officers for witchhunts.

The memo is reprinted on the following pages.

"Navy memo sparks outrage," from THE OBJECTOR *(September–November 1990): 5. Copyright © 1990 by Central Committee for Conscientious Objectors –Western Region. Reprinted with permission.*

SUBJECT: EQUAL TREATMENT OF MALE AND FEMALE HOMOSEXUALS.

1. With the influx of women on our ships and throughout the Navy in general, it is necessary to address the sensitive issue of female homosexuality and ensure equal treatment of male and female homosexuals. We must recognize that enforcement of the Navy's policy towards homosexuality in the service is important because, for sailors in their berthing and work spaces, overt and covert homosexual activity impacts in a very negative way on morale.

2. There is a perception by many that female homosexuality is somewhat tolerated, while male homosexuality is dealt with swiftly and sternly. Several possible reasons for this perception exist. Unless a woman admits to being homosexual, it is often very difficult to prove. Male homosexual behavior or activity in the Navy has long been unacceptable, and is usually quickly reported by peers or subordinates. The male homosexual who has been reported, recognizing his untenable position, is then more likely to admit to his homosexuality and accept administrative processing. This is not necessarily the case for women. Experience has shown that the stereotypical female homosexual in the Navy is more aggressive than her male counterpart, intimidating those women who might turn her in to the chain of command. As a result, the ability to obtain credible evidence during an investigation of female homosexuality is often stymied, and all that remains are unsubstantiated rumors leading to accusations of a "witchhunt" as investigators unsuccessfully search for evidence.

3. Experience has also shown that the stereotypical female homosexual in the Navy is hardworking, career-oriented, willing to put in long hours on the job and among the command's top professionals. As such, allegations that this woman is a homosexual, particularly if made by a young and junior sailor with no track record, may be dismissed out of hand or pursued half-heartedly.

4. Whatever the reasons for this perception that female homosexuality is tolerated in the Navy, it is wrong. Recent statistics from NMPC indicate that for Fiscal Year (FY) '85 through FY '89, the number of women discharged for homosexuality as a percent of FY end strength was roughly double that of men. While this requires careful analysis, it certainly discloses one thing—female homosexuality in the Navy is not being ignored because it is too hard to deal with.

5. More important than any misperception concerning tolerance for female homosexuality is the clearly adverse impact homosexual activity or behavior has on the men and women who must live and work in close proximity to the homosexual and each other. Particularly for young, often vulnerable, female sailors, subtle coercion or outright sexual advances by

more senior and aggressive female sailors can be intimidating and intolerable, impacting negatively on work performance and mental state.

6. We must recognize that women who are targets for female homosexuals experience a unique form of sexual harassment which can be even more devastating and difficult to cope with than the more traditional harassment from men. We must do everything we can to put a stop to sexual harassment of any type.

7. The Navy standard is clear and gender neutral. Homosexuality is incompatible with Naval service and impairs mission accomplishment. Homosexual conduct must be dealt with evenly and firmly. Likewise sexual harassment in any form will not be tolerated. Women must be assured they do not have to exist in a predator-type environment. They should not have to experience improper advances from either sex.

8. It is all well and good to restate these maxims, but for the young sailor who faces sexual harassment, homo or heterosexual, the words are empty without an open and accessible chain of command. Take a close look at the chain of command with an eye towards the type of problems I have just discussed. Use I-Division classes as a forum for discussion of sexual harassment and homosexuality. Be up front about the issues. Emphasize the right of our sailors to be free from sexual harassment, which includes their ability to report such incidents without fear of reprisal. Demonstrate equality in the treatment of male and female homosexuals. The problem won't just go away, so we must deal with it sensibly, and fairly, with due regard for the privacy interests of all.

DISCUSSION QUESTIONS

1. To what extent are the memo's arguments against lesbians in the Navy veiled attacks on the presence of women in the Navy? How do arguments against gay men in the military differ?

2. During 1991 and 1992, the Navy was rocked by a series of scandals related to sexual harassment of women members by males, most notably at the convention of a private support group for naval aviation known as "Tailhook." What is the relationship between hostility to women and gay men and the climate of masculinity in the armed forces?

SUGGESTIONS FOR FURTHER READING

Allan Bérubé & John D'Emilio. 1985. The military and lesbians during the McCarthy years. *The lesbian issue: Essays from SIGNS.* Estelle Freedman, Barbara Gelpi, Susan Johnson, & Kathleen Weston, Eds. Chicago: University of Chicago Press.

Martin Bauml Duberman. 1991. Sex and the military: The Matlovich case. *About time: Exploring the gay past.* New York: Gay Presses of New York.

Kate Dyer, Ed. 1990. *Gays in uniform: The Pentagon's secret reports.* Boston: Alyson Publications.

E. Lawrence Gibson. 1978. *Get off my ship: Ensign Berg and the U.S. Navy.* New York: Avon.

Karen Jewett. 1992 Lesbian colonel fights discharge. *The Objector,* 12(3).

Linda K. Kerber. 1990. May all our citizens be soldiers and all our soldiers citizens: The ambiguities of female citizenship in the new nation. *Women, militarism & war: Essays in history, politics & social change.* Jean Bethke Elshtain & Sheila Tobias, Eds. Savage, MD: Rowman & Littlefield.

Lawrence Murphy. 1988. *Perverts by official order: The campaign against homosexuality in the U.S. Navy.* New York: Harrington Park Press.

LESBIANS AND GAY MEN AND THE MILITARY
Harold Jordan

The so-called "right to fight" debate is not new; it surfaced from time to time throughout the 1980s as various members of the military sought to use the courts to force a change in the military's policy that "Homosexuality is incompatible with military service." There have always been some lesbian, gay male and bisexual activists whose opposition to U.S. militarism made them reluctant to put energy into such attempts at change. The following essay discusses recent developments in the campaign to change the military policy and the debate over the right to fight, particularly with respect to peace organizations' role in the movement.

The essay is an updating of a talk given by Harold Jordan, Coordinator of the National Youth and Militarism Program of the American Friends Service Committee (AFSC), to co-workers in the AFSC's national office. Jordan, a paralegal, also serves as co-chair of the Military Law Task Force of the National Lawyers Guild.

The issue of lesbians and gay men and the military has finally come of age. The recent election of a president who has pledged to rescind the military ban on homosexuality has brought this issue into the public eye in a way that has never happened before. However, it would be wrong to assume that President Clinton has in any way led the movement for the reform of these discriminatory policies. The fact that the candidates were compelled to address this issue is the result of years of struggle, waged mostly by lesbian and gay advocates.

Among the more significant pressure points are these three:

(1) the lesbian and gay anti-ROTC student movement has made the military's official discrimination an issue on campuses nationwide;

(2) lesbian and gay service members and veterans have increasingly challenged the military's hypocritical practice of largely ignoring the sexual orientation of service members during wartime, but processing more gay and lesbian discharges during peacetime; and

(3) some civil rights and legal advocacy organizations have made an issue of lesbian witch hunts and have shown the link between officially-condoned homophobia and sexual harassment.

These struggles have raised deeper questions, which are hotly debated in the lesbian/gay movement and to a lesser extent the peace movement. What does it mean to advocate "civil rights" in the context of an oppressive institution (i.e., the military)? Can liberation be equated

This article was written expressly for this collection, September–December 1992.

with gaining the "right to fight?" Should a lesbian/gay rights organization speak out on war and peace issues or other issues that are not generally seen as "gay" issues? What would be the broader social impact of a presidential executive order rescinding the military's discriminatory policy?

I would like to address these issues by examining three topics: the conditions faced by lesbian and gay men in the military; the organizing and support work being done around lesbian/gay military issues in the civilian community; and the moral and political dilemmas that arise when addressing civil rights in the context of the military.

LIFE IN THE MILITARY: PRESENT REALITIES

Lesbians and gay men face a very difficult and uncertain experience when they become members of the U.S. military. Large numbers of lesbian and gay youth enter the military every year despite the fact that enlistment policies explicitly state that "homosexuality is incompatible with military service." It is estimated that more than 40,000 lesbian and gay service members participated in Operations Desert Shield and Desert Storm. Department of Defense statistics show that approximately 17,000 service members were discharged for "homosexuality" during the 1980s (fiscal years 1980-1990).[1]

Lesbian and gay young people join today's military for the same reasons as other young people: money for college; basic benefits (employment, health care, etc.); to escape from bad family or personal situations; and so on. They hold the same range of political attitudes as other young people who join the services. As with non-gay youth, political attitudes and accurate knowledge about the military are usually not factors in decision-making about enlisting.[2] These youth tend to view the military simply as an employment option, and do not assume that their sexual orientation will become an issue.

Probably most lesbian and gay service members had not discovered their sexual orientation before they enlisted. The key factor is age. The military population is young: the median age of new enlistees is less than 19. An older group would likely contain more people who were sure of

---

[1] The Navy leads the way in investigations and forced separations for "homosexuality." During the 1980s, it discharged 51% of the service members separated for this reason, although it numbers only 27% of the active duty armed forces.

[2] There are signs that youth attitudes are beginning to change. Recent Pentagon studies document a noticeable decline in youth interest in enlisting, mostly since the winter of 1990.

their sexual orientation or more explicit about it. Quite often, this process of discovery happens during the period of military service, if at all.[1]

The survival of lesbian and gay service members is very precarious. The threat of being accused of "homosexuality" is constant. It can be pulled out of the hat at any moment for any reason. If a person wants to harm another person, he or she can spread a rumor or make an accusation of homosexuality. Start a rumor, and it can have extreme consequences for the victim.

Once an allegation is made or a service member initiates discharge, she or he may be subjected to the most extreme forms of harassment and abuse. Negative statements are often posted on bulletin boards; rumors are started. The fact that the military is a separate world and a restricted environment permits many things to occur that never meet the public eye. One of the most egregious violations of human rights occurs in the context of official military investigations of "homosexuality." Investigators, especially in the Naval Investigative Service, often approach this work with a zeal that borders on voyeurism.

The military services have many ways of disciplining people accused of homosexuality. A person can be subjected to intrusive and degrading investigations or other administrative actions for which there is little or no recourse (removal of security clearance, job reassignment, etc.). In addition, a person can be administratively separated from the services for "homosexuality," or for "fraudulent enlistment" (where the person is accused of concealing his or her homosexuality or bisexuality at the point of enlistment or reenlistment). Separation may be initiated by a service member or by the government, most often the latter. Although administrative discharges are ordinarily good ones ("Honorable" or "General"), in recent years the services have found ways of issuing an increasing number of "Other Than Honorable" (OTH) discharges. Normally OTH discharges result in the loss of veterans benefits.

The conditions under which a person may receive Other Than Honorable discharges are known as "aggravating circumstances." These include the use of force, coercion, or intimidation; sex with someone under sixteen; sex in public view (which is interpreted to include physical activity, such as touching, that is observed by a third party even if it does not occur in a public place); sex in a military ship, aircraft or installation; sex for money; and sex with a subordinate. Military investigators often pressure service members to make statements, true or not. All of a sudden what was a relatively minor matter becomes a major ordeal. Most gay

---

[1] Although the same dynamic is at work for heterosexual youth, there is a major difference. Because of the presumption of heterosexuality, most people are forced to act heterosexual even if they are unsure of their orientation. Coming to terms with an alternative sexual orientation is an extra leap.

discharges are not Other Than Honorable, but OTH discharges have been increasing in the last decade. It's a trend worth watching.

Finally, a person may be tried by court-martial for sodomy, the aforementioned "aggravating circumstances," misconduct, or other behaviors considered to be discrediting to the service.

The good news is that a service member who carefully prepares a request for separation is likely to be let go—in peacetime, at least. It is strongly advised that service members avoid admitting to specific acts, partners or incidents. If one can avoid these admissions, get good legal help, and withstand the pressures that may come as a result of an investigation (note: not all cases are investigated), chances of getting out with an Honorable or General discharge are pretty good.

The military's discriminatory policies have had a disproportionate impact on women. Women are two to three times more likely (depending on service branch) to receive discharges for homosexuality than men. Allegations of lesbianism often occur in two contexts: where women hold non-traditional jobs (welding, for example) and in cases where women reject the sexual advances of men.

There is a deeper issue. Homophobia is used as a weapon to enforce sexism, specifically the notion that the military should be a male preserve. Many of the marching chants and motivational activities that are a part of the training regimen demean women.[1] The charge of "lesbianism" is often made by men in order to "put women in their place." There have been reports of increased lesbian baiting in the aftermath of the Tailhook scandal (the sexual harassment and molestation of Navy women by a hoard of male Naval and Marine officers at an aviators convention). Representative Pat Schroeder (D-CO) has alleged that some women who have complained of sexual harassment have had these complaints met by countercharges of lesbianism by the men accused of perpetrating the harassment.

Military investigations of "homosexuality" provide another example of the unique impact of officially-endorsed homophobia on women. Group investigations of service members to identify "homosexuals" (known as "witch hunts") are largely confined to service women. Women are brought in for questioning and are pressured to identify alleged lesbians. Women of all sexual orientations are affected by these witch hunts.

---

[1] Some gay men are affected in a secondary way because they are considered to be effeminate, not "real men." For instance, a male who has difficulty during basic training may be called a "faggot."

The HIV/AIDS issue has complicated matters for lesbian and gay service members. The military, like much of civilian society, tends to view AIDS as a gay disease. If anything, military personnel are less enlightened about the fact that heterosexuals, hemophiliacs and intravenous drug users can get AIDS. Testing for HIV infection is widespread and mandatory in the military, including for reservists. According to the policies, people who are HIV+ are allowed to stay in the military unless they show signs of progressive clinical illness. The standards vary from one service branch to another. Even if a person is allowed to remain in the service, she or he is restricted in what kinds of jobs she or he can hold or where she or he can be stationed. Assignment abroad is normally not a possibility.

Another issue is doctor-patient confidentiality. This has become such a problem that Congress addressed it by passing a law, in 1986, restricting the use of statements made to medical personnel as part of an "epidemiological assessment." In other words, statements made in certain contexts are not supposed to be used against a person in disciplinary or negative administrative actions. In practice, the military often gets around this restriction.

One of the most alarming developments is the prosecution of HIV+ service members for allegedly having unsafe sex. These have been occurring in the military with considerable success for about four years. HIV+ service members who are alleged to have engaged in unprotected sexual intercourse may be prosecuted for assault or for disobeying a direct order (to refrain from certain activities). Many people argue that it is all right to punish people who engage in irresponsible sexual behavior. On the other hand, many public health experts argue that unsafe sex prosecutions will discourage people from coming forth and seeking treatment. I agree with the latter group. AIDS should be treated as a public health issue.

The extent to which the military's AIDS/HIV practices have contributed to an increase in the number of homosexuality discharges is unclear. What appears to be occuring is that HIV+ service members are being discharged at higher rates than other service members. We are not able to tell with certainty whether the grounds are disproportionately for homosexuality or other equally inappropriate reasons (such as personality disorder, misconduct, poor performance, or for medical reasons that do not carry with them disability benefits). To add insult to injury, the military has successfully argued in one case (*Steffan v. Cheney*) that the anti-gay policy can be justified as a reasonable government response to the AIDS crisis.

CIVILIAN ADVOCACY

Much work has been done in the last decade to counter the military's discriminatory practices. The primary focus has been to attack the policy through litigation in civilian courts, Congressional action, and by pressuring institutions that cooperate with the military (such as schools, professional associations, etc.) to restrict the military's presence. In addition, a network of skilled attorneys and volunteer paralegal counselors have assisted individual service members facing personnel actions. As a result of this work, lesbian and gay military issues have achieved an unprecedented level of public visibility.

Litigation has focused on a variety of issues: whether a person may be separated for merely making a public statement that he or she is gay—a First Amendment issue; litigation attacking the basic tenets of the exclusionary policy based on due-process and equal-protection arguments; and whether a person who has been separated for homosexuality must repay the government for the cost of military-funded education. It has been clearly established that the military has the "right" to continue with its policies based on the traditional doctrine of the deference of civilian courts to the military.

There have been some minor victories in isolated instances. A federal court has ruled that the services must show that the discrimination against an individual has a "rational basis that furthers a legitimate government purpose" (*Pruitt v. Cheney*). Another federal court has ruled that the military may not deny reenlistment to a gay service member who had been repeatedly allowed to reenlist in the past despite the fact that he had not concealed his orientation (*Watkins v. United States Army*). However, the basic policy is expected to remain intact until Congressional or executive action is taken.

Much of this advocacy work has been untaken by organizations in a coalition known as the Gay and Lesbian Military Freedom Project.[1] The coalition's members have focused their activity on public education, litigation and lobbying on Capitol Hill. In 1988, the Project organized testimony before the Defense Advisory Committee on Women in the Service (DACOWITS) showing the link between accusations of homosexuality and sexual harassment.

Another major arena is the work to eliminate ROTC on college and university campuses because it violates campus non-discrimination rules or local or state non-discrimination ordinances. Since 1989 major struggles have been waged mostly by lesbian and gay student groups on about 200 campuses nationwide. This movement has been somewhat effective. One

---

[1] Member groups include the National Lawyers Guild (Military Law Task Force), the National Gay and Lesbian Task Force, the National Organization for Women, the American Civil Liberties Union (Lesbian and Gay Rights Project), Lambda Legal Defense and Education Fund, the Midwest Committee for Military Counseling, and several gay veterans organizations.

of the things it has done is develop a whole new body of information about the relationship between the institutions of higher learning and the military. More significantly, there is a real possibility that some military activities will be eliminated.

Most of the efforts to pressure the military by eliminating ROTC and recruiting programs have been met by opposition from school administrators and boards of trustees. Besides being instinctively pro-government, administrators have feared the loss of government funding. In a number of instances the Defense Department has threatened to cut off funding if military programs are eliminated. This has been an empty threat so far.

Faculty members have been more sympathetic, with faculty leadership bodies at many major universities voting in favor of expelling ROTC if the military doesn't change its policy by a certain date. The fallback position of many administrations has been that they're not going to eliminate programs now, but will lobby the Pentagon to change its policies. The lobbying hasn't worked so far. Some university governance bodies and various institutions may now be forced to set a date for the elimination of ROTC if the military does not change its policy. A few schools have already taken such action.

The third arena of struggle is the White House. During the presidential campaign, Bill Clinton pledged to rescind the military gay ban. Initially he promised to issue an executive order to that effect early in his tenure. Hostile reactions by people in government and military circles have been so strong as to force him to hold back. It is likely that a decision about the order will be postponed pending the work of a study commission. One of the dangers in the more recent public statements made by Clinton is that he makes a distinction between homosexual status (which may be acceptable under a future executive order) and homosexual conduct. This distinction may have dangerous ramifications for many allegedly gay or lesbian service members. It would impose a standard that is not normally applied to heterosexual service members. If such a policy is put into place, any activity that is construed as being a gay sexual overture may be treated as sexual misconduct, and punished accordingly. Significant struggles lie ahead for lesbian and gay service members, no matter what action the president takes.

THE GULF WAR EXPERIENCE

Some lesbian and gay service members saw Operation Desert Shield and Desert Storm as an opportunity to prove the ridiculousness of the policy and to open up doors completely. Others opposed the war and the repression and oppression of lesbians and gays in the military.

In my view the war upset the apple cart for many people. For the Pentagon, it upset the way it has dealt with the issue of "homosexuality." At the same time it forced lesbian and gay service members to deal with a range of issues including where they stood on the war. In addition, the war made it tough for lesbian and gay organizations to avoid taking a position on the military, although many tried to avoid doing so by defining issues in narrow civil-rights terms.

For the military, the dilemma is this: do you kick out lesbian and gay service members who come out or are discovered, or do you keep them in for the sake of expediency? Generally the practice has been the latter: people are kept in for expediency during the war and then kicked out after that. To some extent that's what happened during the Gulf war. Donna Lynn Jackson, an Army reservist in California, publicly identified herself as a lesbian, stating that she expected the military to send her to the Gulf notwithstanding. Within about ten days the military released her from the service because of publicity.

In general, people weren't discharged except when they were very public and very visible—the embarrassment factor. For the most part, discharges were delayed. Randy Shilts, the prominent gay journalist who is a reporter for the San Francisco Chronicle, reported Pentagon officials as saying that discharges for "homosexuality" would be deferred until the Gulf crisis was over. That was the typical experience, consistent with what happened in previous wars.

Some lesbian and gay service members were conscientious objectors. There is the case of two women in the Bay Area who submitted their conscientious objector packets simultaneously with a statement that they were lesbians and let the military deal with it. The CO application for at least one of them was turned down, and she was eventually discharged for being a lesbian.

Another event that pointed out the contradictions in the military's policy was the "outing" of Pentagon spokesperson Pete Williams in *The Advocate*. (He was the mild-mannered spokesperson seen on TV every day during the Gulf crisis.) The Secretary of Defense was forced to address the contradiction. He didn't say one way or another whether Pete Williams was gay. He did say that he made a distinction between civilian employees of the Department of Defense and military employees: the policy applies only to military employees.

This series of events created a climate in which two things happened. More lesbian and gay service members publicly challenged the military's policy in the period after the war. This in turn made the policy into an issue in the 1992 presidential campaign.

The question before us is, How do you build a broad movement that both advances human rights and opposes militarism?

I'd like to address this dilemma in the context of two concrete examples: the student anti-ROTC movement, and the the response of civilian lesbian and gay organizations to the Gulf war. What's there is not always what meets the eye.

The movement against ROTC has often been mischaracterized. My observation is that campus-based lesbian and gay activist groups for the most part do not seek to open up access because individual activists want to join the military, or would urge other lesbian and gay young people to do so. Instead I think two things are going on.

First, the military is seen as a symbol of institutionalized oppression against lesbian and gay people. It is considered vulnerable to public criticism because its policy can be shown up as ridiculous. Not only have lesbians and gay men fought in wars, but the military's own internal studies indicate that the specific justifications offered for the policy have no merit. Many lesbian and gay activists believe that a change in military policy will have an impact in the civilian world. The analogy is often made to the 1948 executive order banning segregation in the military. In my view the analogy is overly simplistic and naïve, but there is no question that a change in military policy would have an impact on other institutions.

Second, many lesbian and gay student groups have used this struggle as a way of building a national lesbian and gay student movement that addresses a range of issues of concern to lesbian and gay people.

There was a lively political debate about the war in lesbian and gay organizations. This new development was due to a number of factors.

One of these was that the mainstream lesbian and gay civil rights organizations have felt pushed, visibly and invisibly, from political tendencies such as ACT UP and Queer Nation, which tend to take a more oppositional view of government on a range of social issues, including funding for AIDS and the reactionary social policy of the Bush administration. Those organizations which define issues in narrow civil rights terms felt the greatest push. The National Gay and Lesbian Task Force issued a statement against the war. Then-director Urvashi Vaid said in presenting the Task Force statement: "We remain convinced that war is a tragedy for everyone involved—including those on the battle lines and at home—and that a peaceful, diplomatic settlement best serves the aspirations of all human beings....It is hypocritical and insulting to expect us to support the military when it so blatantly exploits us."

This was significant, but it wasn't reported outside of the gay press. Only 5 of the 19 board members of the Task Force were known to oppose taking that position. Such actions create openings.

Another factor is that the people who staff lesbian and gay organizations, at least a substantial number of them, have a history of involvement in other political and social movements. These people served as advocates for the idea that lesbian and gay organizations could not stand on the sidelines.

Equally significantly, a number of lesbian and gay organizations took the position that they have the right to speak out on issues that are not usually considered lesbian and gay issues. In their view, speaking out on national issues affecting broad public interests is a mark of political maturity. That's a step forward as well.

All this is not to say that the lesbian and gay civil rights movement has become an anti-militarist movement, because for the most part it has not.

This is partly because in addition to the student movement and the traditional civil rights organizations, there is a third constituency in the coalition working to change the military's anti-gay policy. This is made up of lesbian and gay veterans. In general, this element of the coalition is the most conservative of the three. As a result, their presence has led to some unholy alliances.

An extreme example of this conservatism is the case of Miriam Ben-Shalom, a lesbian reservist and former drill sergeant, who has been fighting the military for many years, in a legal ordeal that deserves recognition and support. Ben-Shalom is seen by some as a heroine because she has struggled for a long time. But she says some reactionary things, ultra-patriotic things. For instance, she openly urged lesbian and gay youth to volunteer for military service in the Gulf. I think she is atypical of the people who speak out against the military's policies, but the fact that she has been allowed to play the heroine, and that people invite her to speak, give her awards and then don't explicitly criticize the militaristic parts of her statement is a shortcoming. By and large people like Ben-Shalom are not the spokespersons for the movement, but they do get a lot of press because they've been in the courts for some time.

I must add that although these three constituencies have come together for the purposes of making change on one issue, the military's anti-gay policy, they cannot be said to have a unified commitment to strengthening the military. They work together as a coalition in spite of having different political interests and long-term goals.

Nevertheless, the coalition movement has been effective, and we in the peace movement have to be engaged with it. Ironically, the Gulf war may have opened up more opportunities for dialogue and joint work between lesbian and gay movements and the peace movement.

BUILDING BRIDGES

I believe those of us with commitments to both camps have work to do on both sides. We have an obligation to challenge the peace movement on one hand, and a parallel obligation to challenge lesbian and gay civil rights organizations on the other.

Homophobia within the peace movement prevents people from seeing the active and lively dynamic—the diversity of opinion and debate—going on within lesbian and gay political circles, as I noted earlier. This diversity was not widely reported in peace movement publications during the war.

On the other side, military policies must be challenged. But they should be challenged within a political and moral framework where the purpose and function of the military is called into question. There is no neat separation between those policies and the purpose and function of the military—and we need to say so clearly, both to lesbian and gay civil rights organizations and to peace organizations.

Finally, we need to ask ourselves what we mean by liberation. Liberation does not equal the right to fight. At the same time, repressive and exclusionary policies and institutions must be challenged in our struggle for liberation. Such a challenge can be made, at least to a limited extent, by working against the military's anti-gay policy, and such a challenge will have an impact on how lesbian, gay male and bisexual people are treated in the wider society.

This means finding ways to sponsor and organize dialogue, because there is real work being done, real diversity and debate within lesbian and gay political circles about militarism. We can't score points if we sit on the sidelines. There are things that the heterosexual part of the peace movement can learn from lesbian and gay movements. We can't simply take our perspective and infuse it into other people's work; we have to reconsider some of our absolutist and dogmatic formulations.

Such a dialogue may not be comfortable for many of us. But it will be well worth the energy it takes. There are things all of us, in all our movements for a just and peaceable society, have yet to learn about the nature of oppression. We will be able to learn them only from each other.

AUTHOR'S NOTE

A note about terminology is in order. Throughout this essay I use the term "lesbians and gay men" to refer to all sexual minorities. Also, the military definition of "homosexuality" includes bisexuality.

The author would like to thank Luz Guerra, Kathleen Gilberd, and Richard Cleaver for their insightful comments and their fine work.

DISCUSSION QUESTIONS

1. What campus organizations in your area are working to remove ROTC from their campus? How might coalitions with these folks be organized to address the range of issues that concern lesbians and gay men?

2. The military clearly discriminates against lesbians and gay men. How might a "right-to-fight" campaign be organized which acknowledges the limitations of militarism?

3. In what ways is discrimination in the military seen as a "symbol of oppression against lesbian and gay people?"

SUGGESTIONS FOR FURTHER READING

Katherine Bourdonay. 1985. *Fighting back: Lesbian and gay draft, military, and veterans issues.* Chicago: Midwest Committee for Military Counseling.

Mary Ann Humphrey. 1990. *My country, my right to serve: Experiences of gay men and women in the military, World War II to the present.* New York: HarperCollins.

Mike Hippler. 1989. *Matlovich: The good soldier.* Boston: Alyson.

Kim Westheimer. 1986. Support mixed for lesbian facing discharge. *Gay Community News* (August 3); see also reply by Richard Cleaver, What and whom does the 'service' serve? (November 16–22).

LESBIAN FEMINISM
AND THE GAY RIGHTS MOVEMENT:
ANOTHER VIEW OF MALE SUPREMACY,
ANOTHER SEPARATISM
Marilyn Frye

Most of the articles in this collection have assumed that lesbians and gay men have common aims and interests in the process of social change. This point of view is by no means universal among lesbians, for some of whom gay men's privilege as men overshadows their identity as queer.

Marilyn Frye examines why this may be so, and suggests that the majority of gay men have built their politics in such a way as to prevent women from making common cause with them. She acknowledges that this is not true for all gay men, and in her description of what gay male allies for lesbians might take as the basis for their politics, there is an implied critique of the assimilationist line of strategy in the gay men's movement.

Some gay men may feel that Frye's description does not fit their experience. Before rejecting her insights on that basis, male readers may wish to savor the reversal from the norm such a description presents in a world where men continually describe women's experience without challenge.

Less explicitly, Frye also questions the idea that lesbian or gay male sexual identity is inevitable and unalterable, rather than a choice. (Readers may recall that John D'Emilio's article raised this same question.)

The article is a revision of a talk given in the spring of 1981, under the auspices of the Grand Rapids, Michigan, chapter of Dignity, *the Catholic lesbian and gay men's organization.*

Many gay men and some lesbians and feminists assume that it is reasonable to expect lesbian and feminist support for, or participation in, gay political and cultural organizations and projects, and many people think it is reasonable to expect that gay men will understand and support feminist and lesbian causes. But both of these expectations are, in general, conspicuously not satisfied.

With a few exceptions, lesbians and in particular, feminist lesbians have not seen gay rights as a compelling cause nor found association with gay organizations rewarding enough to hold more than temporary interest. With perhaps even fewer exceptions, gay men do not find feminist or lesbian concerns to be close enough to their own to compel either supportive political action or serious and attentive thought. Gay political and cultural organizations which ostensibly welcome and act in behalf of both gay men and gay women generally have few if any lesbian members, and lesbian and feminist political and cultural organizations, whether or not they seek or accept male membership, have little if any gay male support.

All of us deviants suffer from the fact that the dominant culture is, at least publicly, intolerant of deviations from what might be called "missionary sexuality": sexuality organized around male-dominant, female-subordinate genital intercourse. Lesbians and gay men both are subject to derision and ostracism, abuse and terror, in both cases for reasons that flow somehow out of social and political structures of sex and gender. Popular images of the lesbian and the gay man are images of people who do not fit the patterns of gender imposed on the sexes. She is seen as a female who is not feminine and he as a male who is not masculine. In many states and locales lesbians and gay men find themselves joined under a common political necessity when they must battle a Proposition This-or-That which would legally sanction their civil injury, or are under assault by such groups as the Moral Majority or the Ku Klux Klan. Gay men seem to many women to be less sexist than straight men, presumably because gay men are not interested in women sexually. And the feminist commitment to individual sexual self-determination includes, for most feminists, a commitment to gay rights.

Such things might lead one to suppose that there is, in fact, a cultural and political affinity between gay men on the one hand and women lesbians and/or feminists on the other, and then to assume that the absence of any firm and general alliance here must be explained by there being some sort of hitch or barrier, some accidental factor of style, language or misinformation, which obscures the common interests or makes cooperation difficult. I do not share this supposition and assumption.

A culture hostile to any but missionary sexuality is also hostile to women—the culture is a sexist, a misogynist, a male-supremacist culture. Because of this cultural reality, the worlds of what the clinicians would call "homosexual" women and men are very different: we deviate from very different norms; our deviations are situated very differently in the male-supremacist world view and political structure; we are not objects of the same phobias and loathings. If some of us feel some threads of sympathy connecting us and therefore would want to be friends to each other's causes, the first thing we should do is seek a just understanding of the differences which separate us. But these differences turn out to be so profound as to cast doubt on the assumption that there is any basic cultural or political affinity here at all upon which alliances could be built.

A look at some of the principles and values of male-supremacist society and culture suggests immediately that the male gay rights movement and gay male culture, as they can be known in their public manifestations, are in many central points considerably more congruent than discrepant with this phallocracy, which in turn is so hostile to women and to the woman-loving to which lesbians are committed. Among the most fundamental of those principles and values are the following.

1. The presumption of male citizenship.

2. Worship of the penis.

3. Male homoeroticism, or man-loving.

4. Contempt for women, or woman-hating.

5. Compulsory male heterosexuality.

6. The presumption of general phallic access.

As one explores the meaning of these principles and values, gay and straight male cultures begin to look so alike that it becomes something of a puzzle why straight men do not recognize their gay brothers, as they certainly do not, much to the physical and psychological expense of the latter.

1. The presumption of male citizenship is the principle that if, and only if, someone is male, he has a *prima facie* claim to a certain array of rights, such as the rights to ownership and disposition of property, to physical integrity and freedom of movement, to having a wife and to paternity, to access to resources for making a living, and so forth. Though dominant men accept among themselves certain sorts of justifications for abridging or denying such rights of men (e.g., the necessity of raising an army), the presumption is on the side of their having these rights, if others deny a man these rights arbitrarily, that is, apparently without recognizing that such denial required certain sorts of justification, then the implication arises that he is not really of fully a man or male. If he accepts the burden of proof, this too would suggest that he is not really or fully a man or male. Thus, what is called "discrimination"—the arbitrary abridgment of men's rights, abridgment not accompanied by certain sorts of justification—is felt as "emasculating," and those whose rights are abridged are inclined to respond by asserting their manhood.

Civil rights movements of various sorts in this country, under male leadership, have tended to take this approach, which obviously does not question, but relies on, the underlying presumption of male citizenship. A civil-rights feminism, even one which means to be moderate, is pushed toward challenging this presumption, hence toward a more radical challenge to the prevailing order, by the fact that its constituency is women. Women's only alternative to the more radical challenge is that of claiming the manhood of women, which has been tried and is not in my estimation as absurd at as it may sound; but that claim is not easy to explain or to incorporate in persuasive political rhetoric.

Since the constituency of the male gay rights movement is very overtly and definitively classified and degraded as "womanish" or "effeminate," it might seem that a logical and proud gay political strategy would be to demand citizenship as "women"—the strategy of challenging the presumption of male citizenship. Some individual gay men lean toward this, and thus to political kinship with women, but the gay rights movement generally has taken the course of claiming the manhood of its constituents, supposing that the presumption of gay men's rights will follow upon acknowledgment of this. In so doing, they acquiesce in and support the reservation of full citizenship to males and thus align themselves with the political adversaries of feminism.

It is indeed true that gay men, generally speaking, are really men and thus by the logic of phallocratic thinking really ought to be included under the presumption of male citizenship. In fact, as some gay men have understood (even if the popular mind has not), gay men generally are in significant ways, perhaps in all important ways, only more loyal to masculinity and male-supremacy than other men.

2. In phallocratic culture, the penis is deified, fetishized, mystified and worshipped. Male literature proves with convincing redundancy that straight men identify with their penises and are simultaneously strangely alienated from them. The culture is one in which men are not commonly found laughable when they characterize the female as a castrated male. It is a culture in which an identification of the penis with power, presence and creativity is found plausible—not the brain, the eyes, the mouth or the hand, but the penis. In that culture, any object or image which at all resembles or suggests the proportions of an erect penis will be imbued with or assumed to have special mythic, semantic, psychological or supernatural powers. There is nothing in gay male culture or politics as they appear on the street, in bars, in gay media, which challenges this belief in the magic of the penis. In the straight culture, worship of the penis in symbolic representations is overt and common, but men's love of penises in the flesh tends to be something of a closet affair, expressed privately or covertly, or disguised by humor or rough housing. Gay men

generally are only much more straightforward about it: less ambivalent, less restrained, more overt.

If worship of the phallus is central to phallocratic culture, then gay men, by and large, are more like ardent priests than infidels, and the gay rights movement may be the fundamentalism of the global religion which is Patriarchy. In this matter, the congruence of gay male culture with straight male culture and the chasm between these and women's cultures are great indeed.

Women generally have good experiential reason to associate negative values and feelings with penises, since penises are connected to a great extent with their degradation, terror and pain. The fear or dread this can generate might be a close relative of worship, but there is also the not-so-uncommon experience of boredom, frustration and alienation in the sorts of encounters with penises which are advertised as offering excitement, fulfillment and transcendence. So far as living with the threat of rape permits, many women's attitudes toward penises tend to vacillate between indifference and contempt, attitudes which are contraries of worship. Lesbians and feminists, who may know more securely the dispensability of penises to women's physical gratification and to their identity and authority, may be even more prone than most women to these unworshipful attitudes. It is among women, especially feminists and lesbians, that the unbelievers are to be found. We and gay men are on opposite sides of this part of phallophilic orthodoxy.

Let me interject that though I derogate and mock the worship of the penis, I do not despise its enjoyment. I suspect that if penises were enjoyed a good deal more and worshipped a great deal less, everyone's understanding of both male and female sexuality, of power and of love, would change beyond recognition and much for the better. But I do not read gay male culture of enjoyment, in spite of its hedonistic rhetoric and the number of good cooks it produces. There are suggestions of this heresy at its outer margins only, and I will return to that matter later.

3. The third principle of male-supremacy I listed above is the principle of male homoeroticism. I am not speaking of some sort of "repressed" homosexuality to which the intense heterosexuality of so many men is said to be a reaction. I speak here not of homosexuality but of homoeroticism, and I think it is not in the least repressed.

In the dominant straight male language and world view, "sex" equals what I have called "missionary sex." In spite of the variety of things people actually do with and to each other in private under the rubrics of "having sex" or "being sexual," cultural images of sex and "sexual acts" refer and pertain overwhelmingly to male-dominant, female-subordinate genital intercourse, that is, to fucking. As has often been documented, most men claim, indeed insist, that there is no essential connection between sex (that is, fucking) and love, affection, emotional connection, admiration, honor or any of the other passions of desire and attachment. To say that straight men are heterosexual is only to say that they engage in sex (fucking) exclusively with (or upon or to) the other sex, i.e., women. All or almost all of that which pertains to love, most straight men reserve exclusively for other men. The people whom they admire, respect, adore, revere, honor, whom they imitate, idolize, and form profound attachments to, whom they are willing to teach and from whom they are willing to learn, and whose respect, admiration, recognition, honor, reverence and love they desire...those are, overwhelmingly, other men. In their relations with women, what passes for respect is kindness, generosity or paternalism; what passes for honor is removal to the pedestal. From women they want devotion, service and sex.

Heterosexual male culture is homoerotic; it is man-loving. This is perfectly consistent with its being hetero-sex-ual, since in this scheme sex and love have nothing essential, and very little that is accidental, to do with each other.

Gay male culture is also homoerotic. There is almost nothing of it which suggests any extension of love to women, and all of the elements of passion and attachment, including all kinds of sensual pleasure and desire, are overtly involved in its male-male relations. Man-loving is, if anything, simply more transparent to the lovers and more complete for gay men than for straight men.

Lesbian and lesbian-feminist culture is also, of course, generally homoerotic. Lesbians/feminists tend to reserve passion, attachment and desire for women, and to want them from women. We tend to be relatively indifferent, erotically, to men, so far as socialization and survival in male-supremacist culture permit. Not to love men is, in male-supremacist culture, possibly the single most execrable sin. It is indicative of this, I think, that lesbians' or feminists' indifference to men is identified directly as man-hating. Not to love men is so vile in this scheme of values that it cannot be conceived as the merely negative thing it is, as a simple absence of interest, but must be seen as positive enmity.

If man-loving is the rule of phallocratic culture, as I think it is, and if, therefore, male homoeroticism is compulsory, then gay men should be numbered among the faithful, or the loyal and law-abiding citizens, and lesbians feminists are sinners and criminals, or, if perceived politically, insurgents and traitors.

4. Given the sharpness of the male/female and masculine/feminine dualism of phallocratic thought, woman-hating is an obvious corollary of man-loving.

Contempt for women is such a common thing in this culture that it is sometimes hard to see. It is expressed in a great deal of what passes for humor, and in most popular entertainment. Its presence also in high culture and scholarship has been documented exhaustively by feminist scholars in every field. It is promoted by the advertising and fashion industries. All heterosexual pornography, including man-made so-called "lesbian" pornography for male audiences, exhibits absolutely uncompromising woman-hating. Athletics coaches and military drill sergeants express their disgust when their charges perform inadequately by calling them "women," "ladies," "girls" and other more derogatory names for females.

Woman-hating is a major part of what supports male-supremacy; its functions in phallocratic society are many. Among other things, it supports male solidarity by setting women both apart from and below men. It helps to maintain a clear and definitive boundary between the male "us" and its corresponding "them," and it helps to sustain the illusion of superiority which motivates loyalty. Men not uncommonly act out contempt for women ritually to express and thereby reconfirm for themselves and each other their manhood, that is, their loyal partisanship of the male "us" and their rights to the privileges of membership. This is one of the functions of the exchanges of "conquest" stories, of casual derogation, gang rape, and other such small and large atrocities.

In a woman-hating culture, one of the very nasty things that can happen to a man is his being treated or seen as a woman, or womanlike. This degradation makes him a proper object of rape and derision, and reverses for him the presumption of civil rights. This dreadful fate befalls gay men. In the society at large, if it is known that a man is gay, he is subject to being pegged at the level of sexual status, personal authority and civil rights which are presumptive for women. This is of course, really quite unfair, for most gay men are quite as fully *men* as any men: being gay is not at all inconsistent with being loyal to masculinity and committed to contempt for women. Some of the very things which lead straight people to doubt gay men's manhood are, in fact, proofs of it.

One of the things which persuades the straight world that gay men are not really men is the effeminacy of style of some gay men and the gay institution of the impersonation of women, both of which are associated in the popular mind with male homosexuality. But as I read it, gay men's effeminacy and donning of feminine apparel displays no love of or identification with women or the womanly.

For the most part, this femininity is affected and is characterized by theatrical exaggeration. It is a casual and cynical mockery of women, for whom femininity is the trappings of oppression, but it is also a kind of play, a toying with that which is taboo. It is a naughtiness indulged in, I suspect, more by those who believe in their immunity to contamination than by those with any doubts or fears. Cocky lads who are sure of their immortality are the ones who do acrobatics on the ledge five stories above the pavement. What gay male affectation of femininity seems to me to be is a kind of serious sport in which men may exercise their power and control over the feminine, much as in other sports one exercises physical power and control over elements of the physical universe. Some gay men achieve, indeed, prodigious mastery of the feminine, and they are often treated by those in the know with the respect due to heroes. But the mastery of the feminine is not feminine. It is masculine. It is not a manifestation of woman-loving but of woman-hating. Someone with such mastery may have the very first claim to manhood.

All this suggests that there is more than a little truth in the common claim that homophobia belongs most to those least secure in their masculinity. Blatant and flagrant gay male effeminacy ridicules straight men's anxious and superstitious avoidance of the feminine. And there are gay men who are inclined to cheer this account, to feel smug and delighted at an analysis like this which suggests that they are superior to other men, that is, superior in their masculinity. They clearly reveal thereby that they do indeed pass the Contempt-for-Women test of manhood.

(There is a gentler politic which lies behind some gay men's affectation of the feminine. It can be a kind of fun which involves mockery not of women or of straight men but of the whole institution of gender—a deliberately irreverent fooling around with one of the most sacred foolishnesses of phallocratic culture. This may be the necessarily lighthearted political action of a gender rebel rather than an exercise of masculinity. Certain kinds of lightheartedness in connection with what is, after all, the paraphernalia of women's oppression can become a rather bad joke. But when the silliness stays put as a good joke on patriarchy it betrays a potentially revolutionary levity about the serious matter of manhood and thus may express a politics more congenial to feminism that most gay politics.)

One might have hoped that since gay men themselves can be, in a way, victims of woman-hating, they might have come to an unusual identification with women and hence to political alliance with them. This is a political possibility which is in some degree actualized by some gay men, but for most, such identification is really impossible. They know, even if not articulately, that their classification with women is based on a profound misunderstanding. Like most other men who for one reason or another get a taste of what it's like to be a woman in a woman-hating culture, they are inclined to protest, not the injustice of anyone ever being treated so shabbily, but the injustice of *their* being treated so when *they* are not women. The straight culture's identification of gay men with women usually only serves to intensify gay men's investment in their difference and distinction from the female other. What results is not alliance with women but strategies designed to demonstrate publicly gay men's identification with men, as over and against women. Such strategies must involve one form or another of public acting out of male-dominance and female-subordination.

It is not easy to find ways to stage public actions and appearances which present simultaneously the gayness of gay men and their correct male-supremacist contempt for women. Affected effeminacy does display this, but it is popularly misunderstood. It would be perfect if some of the many gay men who are married would appear with their wives on talk shows where the men would talk animatedly about the joys of loving men and their wives would smile and be suitably supportive, saying they only want their husbands to be happy. But there will not be many volunteers for this work. Who then are the women who will appear slightly to the side of and slightly behind gay men, representing the female other in the proper relation and contrast to their manhood? Lesbians, of course. Gay men can credibly present themselves as men, that is, as beings defined by superiority to women, if there are lesbians in the gay rights movement—given only that males are always or almost always in the visible position of leadership. By having females around, visible but in subordinate positions, gay men can publicly demonstrate their separation and distinction from women and their "appropriate" attitude toward women, which is, at bottom, woman-hating.

Gay male culture and the male gay rights movement, in their publicly visible manifestations, seem to conform quite nicely to the fundamental male-supremacist principle of woman-hating. Anyone who has hung around a gay bar would expect as much: gay men, like other men, commonly, casually and cheerfully makes jokes which denigrate and vilify women, women's bodies, women's genitals. Indeed, in some circles, contempt for women and physical disgust with female bodies are overtly accepted as just the other side of the coin of gay men's attraction to men.

5. The fifth of the principles of male-supremacy which I listed was the principle of compulsory heterosexuality. It is a rule about having sex, that is, about "missionary" fucking. This activity is generally compulsory for males in this culture. Fucking is a large part of how females are kept subordinated to males. It is a ritual enactment of that subordination which constantly reaffirms the fact of subordination and habituates both men and women to it, both in body and in imagination. It is also one of the components of the system of behavior and values which constitutes compulsory motherhood for women. A great deal of fucking is also presumed to preserve and maintain women's belief in their own essential heterosexuality, which in turn (for women as not for men) connects with and reinforces female hetero-eroticism, that is, man-loving in women. It is very important to the maintenance of male-supremacy that men fuck

women, a lot. So it is required; it is compulsory. Doing it is both doing one's duty and an expression of solidarity. A man who does not or will not fuck women is not pulling his share of the load. He is not a loyal and dependable member of the team.

Some gay men certainly are deviants in this respect, and would lobby for tolerance of their deviance without the penalties now attached to it. They would break a rule of phallocracy, but in many cases they are loathe to do their duty only because they have learned all too well their lessons in woman-hating. Their reluctance to play out this part of manhood is due only to an imbalance, where the requisite woman-hating has taken a form and reached an intensity which puts it in tension with this other requirement of manhood. Such divergence of gay life from male-supremacist culture clearly is not a turning from fundamental male-supremacist values, so much as it is a manifestation of the tensions internal to those values.

The unwillingness of some gay men to engage in fucking women seems not to be central to male homosexuality, to "gayness," as it is presented and defended by the male gay rights movement. The latter seems for the most part tolerant of the requirement of heterosexuality; its spokesmen seem to demand merely that men not be limited to heterosexuality, that is, that genital contact and intercourse be permitted as part of their homoerotic relations with other men. They point out that a great many gay men are married, and that many men who engage in what is called homosexuality also do fuck women—that is, they are "normal" and dutiful men. They point out how many gay men are fathers. I do not pretend to know the demographics here: how many gay men do fuck women or have impregnated women, nor even how many are committed to this line of persuasion in their roles as gay rights activists. But this *is* one of the themes in gay rights rhetoric. Men who take such a line are, again, no particular political allies of women. They maintain their solidarity with other men in respect of this aspect of keeping the system going, and only want credit for it in spite of some of their other activities and proclivities.

6. We now come to the only one of the fundamental principles of male-supremacist culture and society where there really is an interesting divergence between it and the values and principles of what it labels male homosexuality. Even here, the situation is ambiguous, for the male gay rights movement only wants too much of something that is really already very dear to straight men.

Men in general in this culture consider themselves, in virtue of their genital maleness, to have a right to access to whatever they want. The kinds of limitations they recognize to this general accessibility of the universe to them are limitations imposed by other men through such things as systems of private property, the existence of the state, and the rules and rituals of limitations of violence among men. In their identification with Mankind, they recognize no limitations whatsoever on their access to anything else in the universe, with the possible exception of those imposed by the physical requirements of Mankind's own survival, and they may even ignore or scoff at those out of some strange belief in Mankind as immortal and eternal. The translation of this cosmic male arrogance to the level of the individual male body is the individual's presumptions of the almost universal right to fuck—to assert his individual male dominance over all that is not himself by using it for his phallic gratification or self-assertion at either a physical or a symbolic level. Any physical object can be urinated on or in, or ejaculated on or in, or penetrated by his penis, as can any nonhuman animal or any woman, subject only to limitations imposed by property rights and local social mores—and even those are far from inviolable by the erect penis which, they say, has no conscience. The one general and nearly inviolable limitation on male phallic access is that males are not supposed to fuck other males, especially adult human males of their own class, tribe, race, etc. This is the one important rule of phallocratic culture that most gay men do violate, and this violation is central to what is defended and promoted by the male gay rights movement.

But note the form of this deviation from the rules of the male-supremacist game. It is refusing a limitation on phallic access; it is a refusal to restrain the male self. It is an excess of phallic arrogance. The fundamental principle is that of universal phallic access. What is in dispute in only a qualification of it. Gay male culture does not deny or shun the principle; it embraces it.

A large part of what maintains male-supremacy is the constant cultivation of masculinity in genital males. Masculinity involves the belief that, as a man, one is the center of a universe which is designed to feed and sustain one and to be ruled by one, as well as the belief that anything which does not conform to one's will may be, perhaps *should* be, brought into line by violence. Thus far, there really would not be room in the universe for more than one masculine being. There must be a balancing factor, something to protect the masculine beings from each other. Sure enough, there is a sort of "incest taboo" built into standard masculinity: a properly masculine being does not prey upon or consume other masculine beings in his kin group. It is a moderating theme like the rule of honor among thieves.

Within the kin group, masculine beings may compete in various well-defined and ritualistic ways, but they identify with each other in such a way that they cannot see each other as the "Other," that is, as raw material for the gratification of the appetites. This blending into a herd with certain other masculine beings, which they sometimes call "male bonding," is what would guarantee masculine beings some crucial bit of security among masculine beings who in infantile solipsistic arrogance would otherwise blindly annihilate each other. The proscription against male-male fucking is the lid on masculinity, the limiting principle which keeps masculinity from being simply an endless firestorm of undifferentiated self. As such, that proscription is necessarily always in tension with the rest of masculinity. This tension gives masculinity its structure, but is also forever problematic. As long as males are socialized constantly to masculinity, the spectre of their running amok is always present. The straight male's phobic reaction to male homosexuality can then be seen as a fear of an unrestricted, unlimited, *ungoverned* masculinity. It is, of course, more than this and more complicated; but is this, among other things.

To assuage this fear, what the rhetoric and ideology of the male gay rights movement has tried to do is to convince straight men that male-male ass-fucking and fellatio are not after all a violation of the rule against men preying upon or consuming other men, but are, on the contrary, expressions of male bonding. I do not pretend to know whether, or how often, male-male ass-fucking or fellatio is basically rape or basically bonding, or how basically it is either, so I will not offer to settle that question. What I want to note is just this: if it is the claim of gay men and their movement that male-male fucking is really a form of male bonding, an intensification and completion of the male homoeroticism which is basic to male-supremacy, then they themselves are arguing that their culture and practices are, after all, perfectly congruent with the culture, practices and principles of male supremacy.

According to the general picture that has emerged here, male homosexuality is congruent with and a logical extension of straight male-supremacist culture. It seems that straight men just don't understand the congruency and are frightened by the "logical extension." In response, the male gay rights movement attempts to educate and encourage straight men to an appreciation of the normalcy and harmlessness of gay men. It does not challenge the principles of male-supremacist culture.

In contrast, any politics which concerns itself with the dignity and welfare of women cannot fail to challenge these principles, and lesbian feminism in particular is totally at odds with them. The feminist lesbian's style, activities, desire and values are obviously and profoundly noncongruent with the principles of male-supremacist culture. She does not love men; she does not preserve all passion and significant exchange for men. She does not hate women. She presupposes the equality of the female and male bodies, or even the superiority or normativeness of the female body. She has no interest in penises beyond some reasonable concern about how men use them against women. She claims civil rights for women without arguing that women are really men with different plumbing. She does not live as the complement to the rule of heterosexuality for men. She is not accessible to the penis; she does not view herself as a natural object of fucking and denies that men have either the right or the duty to fuck her.

Our existence as females not owned by males and not penis-accessible, our values and our attention, our experience of the erotic and the direction of our passion, places us directly in opposition to male-supremacist culture in all respects, so much so that our existence is almost unthinkable within the world view of that culture.

Far from there being a natural affinity between feminist lesbians and the gay civil rights movement, I see their politics as being, in most respects, directly antithetical to each other. The general direction of gay male politics is to claim maleness and male privilege for gay men and to promote the enlargement of the range of presumption of phallic access to the point where it is, in fact, absolutely unlimited. The general direction of lesbian feminist politics is the dismantling of male privilege, the erasure of masculinity, and the reversal of the rule of phallic access, replacing the rule that access is permitted unless specifically forbidden with the rule that it is forbidden unless specifically permitted.

There are other possibilities. Gay men, at least those who are not of the upper economic classes and/or are not white, do experience the hatred and fear and contempt of straight men, do experience ostracism and abridgment of rights, or live with the threat thereof. Gay men are terrorized and victimized significantly more than other men of their class and race by the bullies, muggers and religious zealots of the world. They do tolerate, as do women, legal and nonlegal harassment and insult no self-respecting person should ever tolerate. Out of this marginalization and victimization there could and should come something more constructive, progressive—indeed revolutionary—than a politics of assimilation which consists mainly of claims to manhood and pleas for understanding.

However a man comes to perceive himself as "different" with respect to his relation to the gender categories, in his sensual desires, in his passions, he comes so to perceive himself in a cultural context which offers him the duality masculine/feminine to box himself into. On the one hand, he is "offered" the dominant sexist and heterosexist culture which will label him feminine and castigate him, and on the other hand, he is "offered" a very misogynist and hypermasculine gay male subculture; he is invited to join a basically masculist gay rights movement mediating the two, trying to build bridges of understanding between them. If he has the aesthetic and political good taste to find all of the above repugnant, he can only do what lesbian feminists have been doing: *invent.* He has to move off, as we have, in previously indescribable directions. He has to invent what maleness is when it is not shaped and hardened into straight masculinity, gay hypermasculinity or effeminacy. For a man even to begin to think such invention is worthwhile or necessary is to be disloyal to phallocracy. For a gay man, it is to *be* the traitor to masculinity that the straight man always thought he was.

Any man who would be a friend to women must come to understand the values and principles of phallocratic culture and how his own life is interwoven with them, and must reject them and become disloyal to masculinity. Any man who would do this has to reinvent what being a man is. The initial intuition which many of us have had that gay men may be more prone than straight men to being friends to women has, perhaps, this much truth in it: for gay men, more than for straight men, the seeds both of some motive and of some resources for taking this radical turn are built into their cultural and political situation in the world. The gay man's difference can be the source of the friction which might mother invention and may provide resources for that invention.

One of the privileges of being normal and ordinary is a certain unconsciousness. When one is that which is taken as the norm in one's social environment, one does not have to think about it. Often, in discussions about prejudice and discrimination I hear statements like these: "I don't think of myself as heterosexual;" "I don't think of myself as white;" "I don't think of myself as a man;" "I'm just a person, I just think of myself as a person." If one is the norm, one does not have to know what one is. If one is marginal, one does not have the privilege of not noticing what one is.

This absence of privilege is a presence of knowledge. As such, it can be a great resource, given only that the marginal person does not scorn the knowledge and lust for inclusion in the mainstream, for the unconsciousness of normalcy. I do not say this casually or callously; I know that longing for normalcy and the burden of knowledge. But the knowledge, and the marginality, can be embraced. The alternative to embracing them is erasing the meaning of one's own experience in order to blend in as normal—pretending that one's difference is nothing, really, nothing more significant than a preference for foreign cars, bourbon or western-cut clothes. Gay men and lesbians, all, are sexual deviants: our bodies move in this world on very different paths and encounter other bodies in very different ways and different places than do the bodies of the heterosexual majority. Nothing could be more fundamental. The difference is not "mere," not unimportant. Whatever there is in us that longs for integrity has to go with the knowledge, not with the desire to lose consciousness in normalcy.

I cannot tell another person how the knowledge of her or his marginality will ramify through lifelong experience to more knowledge, but I think it is safe to say that since our marginality has so centrally to do with our bodies and our bodies' nonconformance with the bodily and behavioral categories of the dominant cultures, we have access to knowledge of bodies which is lost and/or hidden in the dominant cultures. In particular, both gay men and lesbians may have access to knowledge of bodily, sensory, sensuous pleasure that is almost totally blocked out in heterosexual male-supremacist cultures, especially in the streams most dominated by white, christian, commercial and militaristic styles and values. To the extent that gay male culture cultivates and explores and expands its tendencies to the pursuit of simple bodily pleasure, as opposed to its tendencies to fetishism, fantasy and alienation, it seems that it could nurture very radical, hitherto unthinkable new conceptions of what it can be to live as a male body.

The phallocratic orthodoxy about the male body's pleasure seems to be that strenuous muscular exertion and the orgasm associated with fucking are its highest and greatest forms. This doctrine suits the purposes of a society which requires both intensive fucking and a population of males who imagine themselves as warriors. But what bodily pleasures there are in the acts which express male supremacy and physical dominance are surely not the paradigms, nor the span nor the height nor depth, of the pleasure available to one living as a male body. There is some intuition of this in gay male culture, and the guardians of male-supremacism do not want it known. A direct and enthusiastic pursuit of the pleasures of the male body will not, I suspect, lead men to masculinity, will not direct men to a life of preying on others and conquering nature, any more than pursuit of bodily pleasure leads women to monogamous heterosexuality and femininity. I can only recommend that men set themselves to discovering and inventing what it *would* lead to.

Another general thing that can safely be said about the resources provided by marginality is that marginality opens the possibility of seeing structures of the dominant culture which are invisible from within it. It is a peculiar blessing both of gay men and of lesbians that in many ways we are both Citizen and Exile, member of the family and stranger. Most of us were raised straight; many have been straight much of the time. Most of us know that straight world from the inside *and*, if we only will, from its outer edge. We can look at it with the accuracy and depth provided by binocular vision. With the knowledge available to us from our different perches at the margins of things, we can base our inventions of ourselves, inventions of what a woman is and of what a man is, on a really remarkable understanding of humans and human society as they have been constructed and misconstructed before. If only we will. The will is a most necessary element.

It has been the political policy of lesbian feminists to present ourselves publicly as persons who have chosen lesbian patterns of desire and sensuality. Whether as individuals we feel ourselves to have been born lesbians or to be lesbians by decision, we claim as morally and politically conscious agents a positive choice to go with it: to claim our lesbianism, to take full advantage of its advantages. This is central to our feminism: that women can know their own bodies and desires, interpret their own erotic currents, create and choose environments which encourage chosen changes in all these; and that a female eroticism that is independent of males and of masculinity *is* possible and *can* be chosen. We claim these things and fight in the world for all women's liberty to live them without punishment and terror, believing also that if the world permits self-determined female eroticism, it will be a wholly different world. It has generally been the political policy of the male-dominated gay rights movement to *deny* that homosexuality is chosen, or worthy of choice. In the public arena that movement's primary stance has been: "We would be straight if we had a choice, but we don't have a choice" supplemented by "We're really just human, just like you." The implication is that it is only human to want to be straight, and only too human to have flaws and hang-ups. While apologizing for difference by excusing it as something over which one has no control, this combination of themes seeks to drown that same difference in a sentimental wash of common humanity.

For the benefits of marginality to be reaped, marginality must in some sense be chosen. Even if, in one's own individual history, one experiences one's patterns of desire as given and not chosen, one may deny, resist, tolerate or embrace them. One can choose a way of life which is devoted to changing them, disguising oneself or escaping the consequences of difference, or a way of life which takes on one's difference as integral to one's stance and location in the world. If one takes the route of denial and avoidance, one cannot take difference as a resource. One cannot see what is to be seen from one's particular vantage point or know what can be known to a body so located if one is preoccupied with wishing one were not there, denying the peculiarity of one's position, disowning oneself.

The power available to those who choose, who decide in favor of deviance from heterosexual norms, can be very great. The choosing, the deciding, challenges doctrines of genetic determinism which obscure the fact that heterosexuality is part of a politics. The choosing challenges the value placed on heterosexual normalcy. And the choosing places the choosing agent in a position to create and explore a different vision.

Many gay men, including many of those in positions of leadership in the gay rights movement, have not wanted this kind of power. They have not wanted any fundamental change of politics and society or any radical new knowledge, but rather have only wanted their proper (usually, white male) share of the booty. But others have begun to understand the potentially healing and revelatory power of difference and are beginning to commit themselves to the project of reinventing maleness from a positive and chosen position at the outer edge of the structures of masculinity and male supremacism.

If there is hope for a coordination of the efforts and insights of lesbian feminists and gay men, it is here at the edges that we may find it, when we are working from chosen foundations in our different differences.

DISCUSSION QUESTIONS
1. How do the attitudes Frye attributes to gay men correspond with the experiences of male readers? With the experiences of female readers?

2. To what extent have the events of the past decade, particularly the power of the religious right and the AIDS crisis, changed the dynamics described in this article? In particular, how have gay men's politics changed? How have they remained the same?

3. Is all sexual activity involving penetration an expression of dominance? How do we reconcile Frye's discussion of the right of phallic access with her suspicion that "if penises were enjoyed a good deal more and worshipped a great deal less, everyone's understanding of both male and female sexuality, of power and love, would change beyond recognition and much for the better?"

4. How does a person choose marginality? What does it mean, in practice, to relinquish privilege? Is it possible to relinquish it fully?

SUGGESTIONS FOR FURTHER READING
Marilyn Frye. 1991. Lesbian "Sex". *An intimate wilderness: Lesbian writers on sexuality.* Judith Barrington, Ed. Portland: Eighth Mountain Press.

Marilyn Frye. 1983. To be and be seen: The politics of reality. *The politics of reality.* Freedom CA: Crossing Press.

Sarah Lucia Hoagland & Julia Penelope, Eds. 1988. *For lesbians only: A separatist anthology.* London: Onlywomen Press.

Ann Japenga. 1990. The separatist revival. *OUT/LOOK* 8, 2(4): 78-83.

Darrell Yates Rist. 1989. AIDS as apocalypse: The deadly costs of an obsession. *The Nation* (February 13) 1+. See also: Exchange: Gay politics and AIDS. *The Nation* (March 20, 1989) 362, which contains responses to this initial essay.

STRATEGIES FOR
ELIMINATING HOMOPHOBIA
Suzanne Pharr

Suzanne Pharr has been active in the women's shelter and domestic violence movements. Her work on homophobia is rooted in the struggles of lesbian and heterosexual women to find ways of working together in that movement. These struggles, as she describes them in Homophobia: A Weapon of Sexism, *from which these suggestions are taken, were both internal and external. The internal struggles arose from homophobia in interpersonal relations. The external ones, which added to the pressure of the internal ones, centered on fears that the work of lesbians would be used to discourage women from seeking shelter and to discredit the movement as a whole.*

Similar dynamics are not unknown in the peace and other social change movements. For example, one of the editors has had the experience of seeing peace march organizers try to prevent publicly-identified lesbian and gay male contingents from appearing. "You can march with us, you just can't carry the sign, it will alienate people and the press will use it against us."

Pharr makes several concrete suggestions for dealing with these problems and clarifies the need for some of the work to be done by allies, not by lesbians and gay men themselves.

As Freud supposedly asked in frustration about women, "What *do* women want?" some feminists might ask about lesbians, "What do they want, anyway? Haven't we given them enough?" It can be argued that many feminist organizations have lesbians in places of leadership, but we have to remember that most of us have had to pay a damaging price in the trade-offs we have made in order to be an accepted part of the organization. And we have to remember how many "unacceptable" lesbians—those who don't reflect heterosexuality—have not been included in the front and visible lines of the women's liberation movement.

So what do lesbians want? We want the elimination of homophobia. We are seeking equality. Equality is more than tolerance, compassion, understanding, acceptance, benevolence, for these still come from a place of implied superiority: favors granted to those less fortunate. These attitudes suggest that there is still something wrong, something not quite right that must be overlooked or seen beyond. The elimination of homophobia requires that homosexual identity be viewed as viable and legitimate and as normal as heterosexual identity. It does not require tolerance; it requires an equal footing. Given the elimination of homophobia, sexual identity—whether homosexual, bisexual, or heterosexual—will not be seen as good or bad but simply as what is.

With homophobia eliminated, we will be able to remove our concern about the gender of the person one loves and apply it instead to those areas where people abuse one another with their sexual practices: incest, rape, objectification of sexual partners, pornography, and all forms of coercive sex, including marital rape. Our concern in relationships can then center on crucial power, dominance, and control issues, not the gender of the relationship partners. There is precious little enough love, affection, and tenderness in the world; it would be a great step forward for humankind if we granted people their right to love.

How then do we begin to eliminate homophobia in our personal lives and in our women's organizations? We must begin the way we begin all the things we do successfully: by setting achievable goals and taking small steps that eventually lead to larger steps. The overall goal is to strip homophobia of its power and thereby eliminate it. To stop that power, we must stop contributing to it.

A very small but powerful and effective first step we can take is to say the word *lesbian*. We must say it in positive ways in our everyday conversations as we affirm different sexual identities, and we must say the word *lesbian* when we talk about our work with women. It is not enough to say that our women's organization is for all women because women from groups that have never been considered the norm are still rendered invisible under the term *all women*. For years people, including feminists, have talked about women and meant *white women* in their assumptions and in their descriptions: women of color were rendered both invisible and left out. The same has been true of old women, differently abled women, women who aren't Christian, poor women, and certainly lesbians. We must bring truth and integrity to our words: when we say all women, we must mean *all* women.

If we are to succeed in the liberation of women, it will have to be through all of us working together for goals that include us all. Therefore, a primary strategy has to be inclusiveness, not only in the ranks but in the decision-making and sharing of power. Because women are affected by other oppressions in addition to sexism, we must understand the connections among those oppressions, work to eliminate them, and acknowledge those groups of women who have been systematically excluded from the privileges shared by those considered the "norm." Until those oppressions are eliminated, we cannot use the expression "all women" and expect women and the world at large to know that every kind of woman is included. Until true inclusion happens, we must name all the women we mean until everyone everywhere understands we are engaged in a movement to free all women.

Moreover, we must demonstrate that we are engaged in work that directly affects different groups of women. What many organizations have done in the past is an ineffective form of "outreach." Women's organizations that are primarily white in their top staff positions and boards of directors begin reaching out to communities of color, asking women to join them in ways that don't include participation in vital decision-making or ownership—and then they are disappointed and angry that women of color do not join. We see battered women's shelters reaching out to women of color or battered lesbians before they have done crucial work on racism and homophobia, thus subjecting women of color and lesbians to the additional violence of racism and homophobia in their organizations. Hence, when we say "all women," we must specify all those we wish to include, and our programs and services must reflect a full commitment to diversity. When we are truly diverse in the ownership of our programs, women will know they are included and will join in the work that touches all of us. Our reputation and our track record will be our "outreach."

At present the word *lesbian* holds tremendous power, is highly charged, and instills fear in heterosexual women and in lesbians who have chosen invisibility. Just as visible lesbians are not so vulnerable to being named lesbian, so are women's organizations less vulnerable to lesbian baiting when they are open and strong about the inclusion of lesbians in their work with all women. The word's power begins to be diminished in the face of those who refuse to concede its negative power.

As long as women's organizations are afraid to use the word *lesbian* in public speeches, in written materials, in grants, then those organizations are not safe places for lesbians to work or to seek services. If the word still holds such power that it cannot be used, then that is clear evidence that the organization is not willing or able to support and defend lesbians in its ranks. If it will not take the initial risk of saying the word, then what would make us believe there would be any risk-taking in the face of threats or controversy? This fear makes fertile ground for lesbian baiting.

Battered women's programs that want to work with battered lesbians must understand that it is not safe for a battered lesbian or lesbian staff to participate if the program does not talk about lesbians in its brochures, public speeches, grant proposals. Needless to say, battered lesbians can't learn about the program unless battered lesbians are talked about in the program's general public information—lesbians are everywhere the general population is. Until programs have worked on homophobia and are prepared to face lesbian baiting, they should not offer services to lesbians within the shelter.

We must find ways to confront lesbian-baiting. One of the most effective is to keep the problem clearly focused on the homophobic person, not on the woman or organization. The problem is with the person who hates, who is prejudiced, not with the victim. If someone says, "I understand your organization has turned into just a bunch of lesbians," then we begin asking questions such as, "What is the problem you have with different sexual identities?" "What is it about you that is threatened by lesbians?" "Why do you think what lesbians are doing is harmful?" "What experiences led you to develop this prejudice?" If we are clear about the right people have to their sexual identity, then it is not necessary for us to be defensive. Nor do we have to be antagonistic or violent. Instead, we can assist people in understanding and accepting people's right to sexual identity or at least understanding that their homophobia, with its restrictions on human relationships, is the problem.

Another small step is to drop assumptions of heterosexual identity on the part of others. Upon first conversation with an adult woman, most people ask, are you married, do you have children? This immediate assumption leaves those who are not married or who have no children to feel there is something wrong with them and their lives and choices or circumstances. The questions also reinforce the belief that woman's most important role is as a married mother. When gatherings and parties are held in women's organizations, many women still assume heterosexuality and ask women to invite husbands or dates instead of simply asking that women invite those we care for, whether they are friends, sexual partners, or relatives.

Along with dropping these assumptions, we need to look at what it is about ourselves that we put forward in order to prove we are acceptable, at the ways we assert that we are heterosexually identified. Is the first thing asserted that one is married or attached to men in some way? How weary I am of feminists who feel they have to be excessively reassuring that they like men. What has always amused and amazed me is that the very worst things I have ever heard said about men have been by married (frequently non-feminist) women, not lesbians, especially longtime lesbians. Still, women feel the necessity to distance themselves from lesbians by asserting how much they *like* men. Liking men is not the issue. Freedom from dominance and control is the issue, and that's why married women talk so angrily and disparagingly about the men who dominate them in traditional marriages that don't have societal support for women's equality.

Instead of distancing oneself from lesbians, one must confront homophobia by being openly supportive of lesbian identity, both in personal and public life and in feminist work. Support means not requiring invisibility or disappearances. Support means being as engaged in the lives of lesbians as in the lives of heterosexual women, sharing sorrow and happiness, participating in the rites of couple bonding, in the rites of passage, and by honoring those things as being important, as being valid events in an individual's life. A lesbian's separation from her partner is no less serious than a heterosexual's divorce. A lesbian falling in love is an occasion for as much joy as a heterosexual falling in love. And we must honor and affirm the choice of both lesbians and heterosexuals to live alone.

Another way to support lesbian identity is to appreciate lesbian culture and to participate in it. On the personal level, this means reading some of the many books and periodicals written by lesbians, listening to lesbian music and attending concerts and music festivals, seeing and discussing lesbian films and videos. It is this participation that will begin the work to eliminate stereotyping, for it is within the lesbian culture that we see the incredible diversity of lesbian lives. To do more than just raise personal consciousness and ensure personal growth, one has to talk about this appreciation and participation in a public way, for it is the sharing of one's growth and consciousness that brings about the social change necessary to eliminate homophobia.

In our women's organizations, we must make lesbian culture visible— in the books and periodicals and records and paintings we purchase and share with our constituencies in an open and proud way. While presenting current lesbian culture, we must also do work to reclaim the past. Because homophobia has been so fierce, lesbian history and work in the movement has been destroyed, has been rendered invisible. Writings about women's history and women's feminist work often read as though contributions were made primarily by white heterosexual women. As we have begun reclaiming women's history from its disappearance among men's history, we now must work harder to reclaim the history of lesbians and women of color.

Along with working on support for lesbian visibility, we must integrate an analysis of homophobia, heterosexism and compulsory heterosexuality in our work against sexism and develop strategies to eliminate these related oppressions. We must make a public commitment to work for a world where sexual identity and sexual roles are not coerced and restricted, a world where no one is granted the socially condoned power to dominate and control others because of sexual gender and identity.

To do this work of eliminating homophobia is no easy task, for there are great risks involved. It is currently acceptable to be overtly homophobic: to make jokes about gays and lesbians, to say in state legislatures that AIDS is only important when it hits the heterosexual population, to pass and uphold sodomy laws, to forbid lesbians and gays from providing foster care to children, to overlook school children calling each other "faggot," to issue court decisions that withhold custody from lesbian mothers, to hold police raids on gay bars and physically and emotionally harass customers, to hear about the beating and killing of gay men and to dismiss it as deserved.

However, overt oppressions exist only when there is covert expression of these oppressions and support for them. As Elie Wiesel said in a television interview after receiving the Nobel Peace Prize, in Nazi Germany when the concentration camps were being developed, the public silence was deafening. Our own silence is a major contributor to overt homophobia—when we laugh at homophobic jokes or don't speak out, when we yield to lesbian baiting, when we require heterosexual behavior from lesbians and gay men, when we stereotype and call the exceptions the good lesbians or gay men, as in "You would never guess she/he was gay."

We must take a very hard look at our complicity with oppressions, all of them. We must see that to give no voice, to take no action to end them is to support their existence. Our options are two: to be racist, or anti-Semitic, or homophobic (or whatever the oppression may be), or to work actively against these attitudes. There is no middle ground. With an oppression such as homophobia where there is so much permission to sustain overt hatred and injustice, one must have the courage to take the risks that may end in loss of privilege. We must keep clearly in mind, however, that privilege earned from oppression is always conditional and is gained at the cost of freedom.

Discussion Questions

1. What experiences of heterosexist exclusion have readers had? What worked in dealing with them? What didn't?

2. What approaches have group members taken to interrupt homophobic behavior in day-to-day life situations? What has worked well? What hasn't?

3. What concrete steps are lesbian, gay male and bisexual activists prepared to take, for themselves, toward ending heterosexism in our groups?

4. What concrete steps are non-gay allies prepared to take, for themselves, toward ending heterosexism in our groups?

5. What are some of the possible connections between anti-gay violence and violence against women?

6. How is homophobia related to sexism?

SUGGESTIONS FOR FURTHER READING

Frédérique Delacoste & Felice Newman. 1981. *Fight back! Feminist resistance to male violence.* Minneapolis: Cleis Press.

Gerre Goodman, George Lakey, Judy Lashof & Erika Thorne. 1983. *No turning back: Lesbian and gay liberation for the 1980s.* Philadelphia: New Society Publishers. See especially sections on "Next Steps."

K. Lobel. 1986. *Naming the violence: Speaking out about lesbian battering.* Seattle: The Seal Press.

JoAnn Loulan. 1987. *Lesbian passion: Loving ourselves and each other.* San Francisco: Spinster's Ink/Aunt Lute.

Liz Margolis, et. al. 1987. Internalized homophobia: Identifying and treating the oppressor within. *Lesbian psychologies: Explorations and challenges.* Boston Lesbian Psychologies Collective, Eds. Urbana: University of Illinois Press.

Kirk Marshall & Hunter Madsen. 1989. *After the ball.* New York: Doubleday.

Suzanne Pharr. 1988. Women in exile: The lesbian experience. *Homophobia: A weapon of sexism.* Inverness, CA: Chardon Press.

STRATEGIES AND VISIONS

Visions

ALLIANCES
Judit

There is a new word in my vocabulary
last night we talked about alliances
I came away with a very clear sense
that we use the word too loosely
and a very real fear
of the pain caused by this confusion
so now there is a new idea in my mind

Alliances arise from differences
there is no one who is automatically my ally
because we are the same
Alliances don't grow wild and unattended
they need constant thought and care
the seed is a common language
not of words and accents
but of worries, concerns and celebrations

Alliances are not accessories to our wardrobe
that we can take off
and hang up with our coats in the closet
when we come home tired
or leave at home because they won't look right
at a certain party
or hide because they will make some people uncomfortable

Alliances are not medals to wear on our chest
to show how many different cultural events
we have been to
or how many friends of the right kind we have
they are not trophies we receive for being "special,"
although unfortunately we are,
just because we care about someone's reality
besides our own

Alliances are really very simple
they arise out of the fact that we are different
and yet may have common goals
they grow on two conditions
that you and I
both of us
understand that we need each other to survive
and that we have the courage
to ask each other what that means.

BRIDGE, DRAWBRIDGE, SANDBAR OR ISLAND:
LESBIANS-OF-COLOR HACIENDA ALIANZAS
Gloria Anzaldúa

*This essay, based on a speech entitled "Lesbian Alliances:
Combatting Heterosexism in the 1980s," given to the National
Women's Studies Association in June of 1988, outlines four positions
that lesbians-of-color might want to consider in their alliances-
coalition work with others. In spite of similarities in experiences
between white lesbians (and gay men) and people-of-color,
Anzaldúa reminds us of at least one critical difference, the ability to
"pass" and hide our queer sexuality. Because of this, white gays
tend to push cultural difference to the side in our insistence on
sameness as a basis for coalitions and alliances. Therefore,
lesbians-of-color might choose to separate (become islands),
mediate (bridge), fluctuate between withdrawal and mediation
(drawbridge), or move naturally between the three as symbolized in
the sandbar.*

La gente hablando se entiende
(People understand each other by talking)
> —Mexican proverb

Buenos días, marimachas, lesberadas, tortilleras, patlaches,[1] dykes,
bulldaggers, butches, femmes, and good morning to you, too, straight
women. This morning when I got up I looked in the mirror to see who I was
(my identity keeps changing), and you know how hair looks when you've
washed it the night before and then slept on it? Yes, that's how mine
looked. Not that I slept that much. I was nervous about making this talk
and I usually never get nervous until just before I'm on. I kept thinking,
What am I going to tell all those women? How am I going to present and
represent myself to them and who, besides myself, am I going to speak to
and for? Last night lying in bed in the dorm room I got disgusted with my
semi-prepared talk, so I wrote another one. I threw that out too. Then I

---

[1] The words *marimachas* and *tortilleras* are derogatory terms that *mujeres* who are
lesbians are called. *Patlache* is the Nahuatl term for women who bond and have sex
with other women. *Lesberadas* is a term I coined, prompted by the word *desperado.*

---

skimmed several papers I was working on, looking for ideas. I realized that I couldn't use any of this material and ordered my unconscious to come up with something by morning or else. This morning I walked over here, picking lint off my shirt, feeling wrinkled, and thinking, Here I am, I'm still the poor little Chicanita from the sticks. What makes me think I have anything useful to say about alliances?

Women-of-color such as myself do have some important things to say about alliance and coalition work. The overlapping communities of struggle that a mestiza lesbian finds herself in allows her to play a pivotal role in alliance work. To be part of an alliance or coalition is to be active, an activist. Why do we make alliances and participate in them? We are searching for powerful, meaning-making experiences. To make our lives relevant, to gain political knowledge, to give our lives a sense of involvement, to respond to social oppression and its debilitating effects. Activists are engaged in a political quest. Activists are alienated from the dominant culture but instead of withdrawing we confront, challenge. Being active meets some basic needs: emotional catharsis, gratification, political epiphanies. But those in an alliance group also feel like a family and squabble and fight like one, complete with a favorite (good child) and a scapegoat (bad child).

THE FRACTURE: AT HOMENESS/ESTRANGEMENT

I look around me and I see my *carnalas*, my *hermanas*, the other half and halves, *mita' y mita'*, (as queer women are called in South Texas), and I feel a great affinity with everyone. But at the same time I feel (as I've felt at other conferences) like I am doing this alone, I feel a great isolation and separateness and differentness from everyone, even though I have many allies. Yet as soon as I have these thoughts—that I'm in this alone, that I have to stand on the ground of my own being, that I have to create my own separate space—the exact opposite thoughts come to me: that we're all in this together, *juntas*, that the ground of our being is a common ground, *la Tierra*, and that at all times we must stand together despite, or because, of the huge splits that lie between our legs, the faults among feminists are like the fractures in the earth. Earthquake country, these feminisms. Like a fracture in the Earth's crust splitting rock, like a splitting rock itself, the quakes shift different categories of women past each other so that we cease to match, and are forever disaligned—colored from white, Jewish from colored, lesbian from straight. If we indeed do not have one common ground but only shifting plots, how can we work and live and love together? Then, too, let us not forget *la mierda* between us, a mountain of *caca* that keeps us from "seeing" each other, being with each other.

Being a mestiza queer person, *una de las otras* ("of the others") is having and living in a lot of worlds, some of which overlap. One is immersed in all the worlds at the same time while also traversing from one to the other. The mestiza queer is mobile, constantly on the move, a traveler, *callejera*, a *cortacalles*. Moving at the blink of an eye, from one space, one world to another, each world with its own peculiar and distinct inhabitants, not comfortable in any one of them, none of them "home," yet none of them "not home" either. I'm flying home to South Texas after this conference, and while I'm there, I'm going to be feeling a lot of the same things that I'm feeling here—a warm sense of being loved and of being at home, accompanied by a simultaneous and uncomfortable feeling of no longer fitting, of having lost my home, of being an outsider. My mother, and my sister and my brothers, are going to continue to challenge me and to argue against the part of me that has community with white lesbians, that has community with feminism, that has community with other *mujeres-de-color*, that has a political community. Because I no longer share their world view, I have become a stranger and an exile in my own home. "When are you coming home again, *Prieta*," my mother asks at the end of my visit, of every visit. "Never, Momma" (Anzaldúa 1983). After I first left home and became acquainted with other worlds, the Prieta that returned was different, thus "home" was different too. It could not completely accommodate the new Prieta, and I could barely tolerate it. Though I continue to go home, I no longer fool myself into believing that I am truly "home."

A few days ago in Montreal at the Third International Feminist Book Fair (June 1988), I felt a great kinship with women writers and publishers from all over the world. I felt both at home and homeless in that foreign yet familiar terrain because of its strangeness (strange because I have never been there). At the conference, and most especially at the lesbian reading, I felt very close to some white lesbian separatist friends. Then they would make exclusionary or racist remarks and I would feel my body heating up, I would feel the space between us widening. Though white lesbians say their oppression in a heterosexist, homophobic society is similar to the suffering of racism that people-of-color experience, they *can* escape from the more overt oppressions by hiding from being gay (just as I can). But what I can't hide from is being Chicana—my color and features give me away. Yes, when I go home I have to put up with a lot of heterosexist bullshit from my family and community, from the whole Chicano nation who want to exclude my feminism, my lesbianism. This I have in common with women-of-all-colors. But what really hurts, however, is to be with people that I love, with you *mujeres-de-todos-colores*, and to *still* feel, after all our dialogues and struggles, that my cultural identity is *still* being pushed off to the side, being minimized by some of my so-called allies who unconciously rank racism a lesser oppression than sexism. Women-of-color feel especially frustrated and depressed when these "allies" participate in alliances dealing with issues of racism or when the theme of the conference we are attending is racism. It is then that white feminists feel they have "dealt" with the issue and can go on to other "more important" matters.

At the Montreal Conference I also felt an empathy with heterosexual women-of-color and with the few men who were there, only to be saddened that they needed to be educated about women-only space. It also made me sad, too, that white lesbians have not accepted the fact that women-of-color have affinities with men in their cultures. White lesbians were unconciously asking women-of-color to choose between women and men, failing to see that there is more than one way to be oppressed. Not all women experience sexism in the same way, and for women-of-color sexism is not the only oppression. White lesbians forget that they too have felt excluded, that they too have interrupted women-of-color-only space, bringing in their agenda and, in their hunger to belong, pushed ours to the side.

Alliance work is the attempt to shift positions, change positions, reposition ourselves regarding our individual and collective identities. In alliance we are confronted with the problem of how we share or don't share space, how we can position ourselves with individuals or groups who are different from and at odds with each other, how we can reconcile one's love for diverse groups when members of these groups do not love each other, cannot relate to each other, and don't know how to work together.

THE ACTIVIST Y LA TAREA DE ALIANZAS

Alliance-coalition work is marked or signaled by framing metacommunication, "This is alliance work" (Bateson 1972). It occurs in bounded specific contexts defined by the ruled and boundaries of that time and space and group. While it professes to do its "work" in the community, its basis is both experiential and theoretical. It has a discourse, a theory that guides it. It stands both inside (the community one is doing the work for) and outside ordinary life (the meeting place, the conference). Ideally one takes alliance work home.

In alliance-coalition work there is an element of role playing, as if one were someone else. Activists possess an unspoken, un-talked-about ability to recognize the unreality and game-playing quality of their work. We very seriously act/perform as well as play at being an ally. We adopt a role model or self-image and behave as if one *were* that model, the person one is trying to be. Activists picture themselves in a scenario: a female hero venturing out and engaging in nonviolent battles against the corrupt dominant world with the help of their trusted *comadronas*. There are various narratives about working at coalition, about making commitments, setting goals and achieving those goals. An activist possesses, in lesser or greater degree, a self-conscious awareness of her "role" and the nature of alliance work. She is aware that not only is the alliance-coalition group struggling to make specific changes in certain institutions (health care, immigration laws, etc.) but in doing so the group often engages in fighting cultural paradigms—the entire baggage of beliefs, values and techniques shared by the community. But in spite of all cultural inscriptions to contrary, the activist with her preconceived self-image, her narrative, and self-reflectivity resists society's "inscribing" cultural norms, practices, and paradigms on her. She elects to be the one "inscribing" herself and her culture. Activists are agents.

IN COLLUSION, IN COALITION, IN COLLISION

For now we women-of-color are doing more solidarity work with each other. Because we occupy the same or similarly oppressed cultural, economic space(s) or share similar oppressions, we can create a solidarity based on a "minority" coalition. We can build alliances around differences, even in groups which are homogenous. Because people-of-color are treated generically by the dominant culture—their seeing and treating us as parts of a whole, rather than just individuals—this forces us to experience ourselves collectively. I have been held accountable by some white people for Richard Rodriguez's views and have been asked to justify Cesar Chavez's political strategies. In classes and conferences I am often called to speak on issues of race and am thereafter responsible for the whole Chicano/Mexicano race. Yet, were I to hold a white woman responsible for Ronald Reagan's acts, she would be shocked because to herself she is an individual (nor is her being white named because it is taken for granted as the norm).

I think we people-of-color can turn this fusion or confusion of individual/collectivity around and use it as a tool for collective strength and not as an oppressive representation. We can subvert it and use it. It could serve as one base for intimate connection between personal and collective in solidarity work and in alliances across differences. For us the issue of alliances affects every aspect of our lives—personal growth, not just social. We are always working with whitewomen or other groups unlike ourselves toward common and specific goals for the time the work of coalition is in process. Lesbians-of-color have always done this. Judit Moschkovitz wrote: "Alliances are made between people who are different." I would add between people who are different but who have a similar conscience that impels them toward certain actions. Alliances are made between persons whose vague unconscious angers, hopes, guilts, and fears grow out of direct experiences of being either perpetrators or victims of racism and sexism.

Feelings of anger, guilt, and fear rose up nine years ago at Storrs, Connecticut, at the 1981 National Women's Studies Association (NWSA) "Women Respond to Racism" Conference, when issues of alliances and racism exploded into the open. Along with many women-of-color I had aspirations, hopes, and visions for multiracial *comunidades*, for communities (in the plural) among all women, of *mundos surdos* (left-handed worlds). Cherríe Moraga and I came bringing an offering, *This Bridge Called My Back: Radical Writings By Radical Women Of Color;* it made its debut at that conference. Some of my aspirations were naïve, but without them, I would not have been there nor would I be here now. This vision of *communidad* is still the carrot that I, the donkey, hunger for and seek at conferences such as this one.

At the 1981 conference we laid bare the splits between whitewomen and women-of-color, white lesbians and lesbians-of-color, separatists and nonseparatists. We risked exposing our true feelings. Anger was the strongest in/visible current at that conference, as it is at this one, though many of us repressed it then and are still repressing it now. Race was the big issue then, as it is now for us. Race, the big difference. When asked what I am, I never say I'm a woman. I say I am a Chicana, a mestiza, a *mexicana*, or I am a woman-of-color—which is different from "woman" (woman always means whitewoman). Monique Wittig (1981) claims that a lesbian is not a woman because woman exists only in relation to men; woman is part of the category of sex (man and woman) which is a heterosexual construct. Similarly, for me a woman-of-color is not just a "woman;" she carries the markings of her race, she is a gendered racial being—not just a gendered being. However, nonintellectual, working-class women-of-color do not have the luxury of thinking of such semantic and theoretical nuances, much less exempting themselves from the category "woman." So though I myself see the distinction, I do not push it.

A large part of my identity is cultural. Despite changes in awareness since the early eighties, racism in the form of, "Your commitment has to be to feminism, forget about your race and its struggles, struggle with us not them" is still the biggest deterrent to coalition work between whitewomen and women-of-color. Some white feminists, displacing race and class and highlighting gender, are still trying to force us to choose between being colored or female, only now they've gone underground and use unconscious covert pressures. It's all very subtle. Our white allies or collegues get a hurt look in their eyes when we bring up their racism in their interactions with us and quickly change the subject. Tired of our own "theme song" (Why aren't you dealing with race and class in your conference, classroom, organization?) and not wanting to hurt them and in retaliation have them turn against us, we drop the subject and, in effect, turn the other cheek. Women-of-color need these and other manipulations named so that we can make our own articulations. Colored and whitewomen doing coalition work together will continue to reflect the dominated/dominator dichotomy UNLESS whitewomen have or are dealing with issues of racial domination in a "real" way. It is up to them *how* they will do this.

Estranged Strangers: A Forced Bonding

Alliance stirs up intimacy issues, issues of trust, relapse of trust, intensely emotional issues "We seem to be more together organizationally and estranged individually" (Uttal 1990). There is always some, no matter how minimal, unease or discomfort between most women-of-color and most whitewomen. Because they can't ignore our ethnicity, getting our approval and acceptance is their way to try to make themselves more comfortable and lessen their unease. It is a great temptation for us to make whitewomen comfortable. (In the past our lives may have depended on not offending a white person.) Some of us get seduced into making a whitewoman an honorary woman-of-color—she wants it so badly. But it makes us fidget, it positions us in a relationship founded on false assumptions. A reversed dependency of them upon us emerges, one that is as unhealthy as our previous reliance on them. There is something parasitic about both of these kinds of dependencies. We need to examine bondings of this sort and to "see through" them to the unconscious motivations. Both white and colored need to look at the history of betrayal, the lies, the secrets and misinformation both have internalized and continue to propagate. We need to ask, Do women-of-color want only partronage from whitewomen? Do white feminists only need and expect acceptance and acknowledgement from women-of-color? Yet there is an inherent potential for achieving results in both personal and political cross-racial alliances. We could stick to each other like velcro, whose two different sides together form a great bond—the teeth of one fasten onto the fabric of the other half and hold with a strength greater than either half alone.

Though the deepest connections colored dykes have is to their native culture, we also have strong links with other races, including whites. Though right now there is a strong return to nationalist feeling, colored lesbian feminists in our everyday interactions are truly more citizens of the planet. "To be a lesbian is to have a world vision" (Dykewomon 1988). In a certain sense I share this vision. If we are to create a lesbian culture, it must be a mestiza lesbian culture, one that partakes of all cultures, one that is not just white in style, theory, or direction, that is not just Chicana, not just Black. We each have a choice as to what people, what cultures, and what issues we want to live with and live in and the roles we want to play. The danger is that white lesbians will "claim" us and our culture as their own in the creation of "our" new space.

"Chusando" Movidas/A Choice of Moves

There are many roles, or ways of being, of acting, and of interacting in the world. For me they boil down to four basic ones: bridge, drawbridge, sandbar, and island. Being a bridge means being a mediator between yourself and your community and white people—lesbians, feminists, white men. You select, consciously or unconsciously, which group to bridge with—or they choose you. Often, the you that's the mediator gets lost in the dichotomies, dualities, or contradictions you're mediating. You have to be flexible yet maintain your ground, or the pull in different directions will dismember you. It's a tough job; not many people can keep the bridge up.

Being a drawbridge means having the option to take two courses of action. The first is being "up," i.e. withdrawing, pulling back from physically connecting with white people (there can never be a complete disconnection because white culture and its perspectives are inscribed on us/into us). You can choose to pull up the drawbridge or retreat to an island in order to be with your colored *hermanas* in a sort of temporary cultural separatism. Many of us choose to "draw up our own bridges" for short periods of time in order to regroup, recharge our energies, and nourish ourselves before wading back into the frontlines. This is also true for whitewomen. The other option is being "down"—that is, being a bridge. Being "down" may mean a partial loss of self. Being "there" for people all the time, mediating all the time means risking being "walked" on, being "used." I and my publishing credentials are often "used" to "colorize" white women's grant proposals, projects, lecture series, and conferences. If I don't cooperate I am letting the whole feminist movement down.

Being an island means there are no causeways, no bridges, maybe no ferries, either, between you and whites. I think that some women-of-color are, in these reactionary times, in these very racist times, choosing to be islands for a little while. These race separatists, small in numbers, are disgusted not only with patriarchal culture, but also with white feminism and the white lesbian community. To be an island, you have to reject certain people. Yet being an island cannot be a way of life—there are no life-long islands because no one is totally self-sufficient. Each person depends on others for the food she eats, the clothes on her back, the books she reads, and though these "goods" may be gotten from within the island, sequestering oneself to some private paradise is not an option for poor people, for most people-of-color.

At this point in time, the infrastructures of bridge and drawbridge feel too man-made and steel-like for me. Still liking the drawbridge concept, I sought and found the sandbar, a submerged or partly exposed ridge of sand built by waves offshore from a beach. To me the sandbar feels like a more "natural" bridge (though nature too, some argue, is a cultural construction). There is a particular type of sandbar that connects an island to a mainland—I forget what it is called. For me the important thing is how we shift from bridge to drawbridge to sandbar to island. Being a sandbar means getting a breather from being a perpetual bridge without having to withdraw completely. The high tides and low tides of your life are factors which help decide whether or where you're a sandbar today, tomorrow. It means that your functioning as a "bridge" may be partially underwater, invisible to others, and that you can somehow choose who to allow to "see" your bridge, who you'll allow to walk on your "bridge," that is, who you'll make connections with. A sandbar is more fluid and shifts locations, allowing for more mobility and more freedom. Of course there are sandbars called shoals, where boats run amuck. Each option comes with its own dangers.

So what do we, lesbians-of-color, choose to be? Do we continue to function as bridges? Do we opt to be drawbridges or sandbars? Do we isolate ourselves as islands? We may choose different options for different stages of our process. While I have been a persistent bridge, I have often been forced to "draw the bridge," or have been driven to be an island. Now I find myself slowly turning into a sandbar—the thing is that I have a fear of drowning.

Mujeres-de-color, mujeres blancas, ask yourselves what are you now, and is this something that you want to be for the next year or five years or ten? Ask yourself if you want to do alliance-coalition work and if so what kind and with whom. The fact that we are so estranged from whitewomen and other women-of-color makes alliance work that much more imperative. It is sad that though conferences allow for short-term alliances, the potential for achieving some feminists' goals is short-circuited by politically correct "performances" by participants instead of more "real" and honest engagement. Choosing to be a bridge, a drawbridge, and a sandbar allows us to connect, heart to heart, *con corazones abiertos*. Even islands come to NWSA conferences—perhaps they come to find other islands.

TERMS OF ENGAGEMENT

Mujeres-of-color, there are some points to keep in mind when doing coalition work with whitewomen. One is not be lulled into forgetting that *coalition work attempts to balance power relations and undermine and subvert the system of domination-subordination* that affects even our most unconscious thoughts. We live in a world where whites dominate colored and we participate in such a system every minute of our lives—the subordination/domination dynamic is that insidious. We, too, operate in a racist system whether we are rebelling against it or are colluding with it. The strategies of defense we use against the dominant culture we also knowingly and unknowingly use on each other. Whites of whatever class always have certain privileges over colored people of whatever class, and class oppression operates among us women-of-color as pervasively as among whites.

Keep in mind that if members of coalitions play at the deadly serious and difficult game of making alliances work we have to set up some ground rules and define the terms we use to name the issues. We need to "see through" some common assumptions. One is that there is no such thing as a common ground. As groups and individuals, we all stand on different plots. Sisterhood in the singular was a utopian fantasy invented by whitewomen, one in which we women-of color were represented by whitewomen, one in which they continued to marginalize us, strip us of our individuality. (One must possess a sense of personhood before one can develop a sense of sisterhood.) It seems to me that through extensive coalitions, various *"hermanidades"* may be created—not one sisterhood but many. We don't all need to come together, *juntas* (total unity may be another utopian myth). Some of us can gather in affinity groups, small grassroots circles and others. All parties involved in coalitions need to recognize the necessity that women-of-color and lesbians define the terms of engagement: that we be listened to, that we articulate who we are, where we have come from (racial past), how we understand oppression to work, how we think we can get out from under, and what strategies we can use in accomplishing the particular tasks we have chosen to perform. When we don't collectively define ourselves and locations, the group will automatically operate under white assumptions, white definitions, white strategies. Formulating a working definition, preferably one subject to change, of alliance/coalition, racism and internalized racism will clear the floor of patriarchal, white, and other kinds of debris and make a clean (well, sort of clean) space for us to work in. I've given you my definitions for alliance and coalition. Racism is the subjugation of a cultural group by another for the purpose of gaining economic advantage, of mastering and having power over the group—the result being harm done, consciously or unconsciously, to its members. We need to defy ethnocentrism, the attitude that the whole culture is superior to all others. Ethnocentrism condones racism. Racism is a theory, it is an ideology, it is a violence perpetuated against colored ethnic cultures.

> The intensity of the violence may range from hidden, indirect forms of discrimination (housing) through overt forms of ethnocidal practices (enforced schooling, religious harassment) to forms of physical and direct violence culminating in genocide (holocaust)....It becomes structurally institutionalized as the basis of hegemony, it turns into systematic racism (Karrer & Lutz).

Internalized racism means the introjecting, from the dominant culture, of negative images and prejudice against outsider groups such as people-of-color and the projection of prejudice by an oppressed person upon another oppressed person or upon her/himself. It is a type of "dumping." On the phone the other day I was telling my mother that I'd confronted my neighbor—a Black man who "parties" every day, from morning till night, with a dozen beer-drinking buddies—and demanded that he not intrude on my space with his noise. She said, "No, don't tell them anything, Black men kill. They'll rape you." This is an example of internalized racism, it is not racism. Chicanos as a group do not have the power to subjugate Black people or any other people. Where did my mother learn about Blacks? There are very few Black people in the Rio Grande Valley of South Texas. My mother has internalized racism from the white dominant culture, from watching television and from our own culture which defers to and prefers light-skinned *gueros* and denies the Black blood in our *mestisaje*—which may be both a race and class prejudice, as darker means being more *indio* or *india*, means poorer. Whites are conditioned to be racist, colored are prone to internalize racism and, for both groups, racism and internalized racism appear to be the given, "the way things are." Prejudice is a "stabilized deception of perception" (Karrer & Lutz, 257). I call this "deception" "selective reality"—the narrow spectrum of reality that human beings choose to perceive and/or what their culture "selects" for them to "see." That which is outside of the range of consensus (white) perception is "blanked-out." Color, race, sexual preferences, and other threatening differences are "unseen" by some whites, certain voices not heard. Such "editing" of reality maintains race, class, and gender oppressions.

Another point to keep in mind is that feminists-of-color threaten the order, coherence, authority, and the concept of white superiority and this makes some white feminists uncomfortable and assimilated colored women uneasy. Feminists of color, in turn, are made uncomfortable by the knowledge that, by virtue of their color, white feminists have privilege and white feminists often focus on gender issues to the exclusion of racial ones. After centuries of colonization, some whitewomen and women-of-color, when interacting with each other, fall into old and familiar patterns: the former will be inclined to patronize and to "instruct;" the latter to fall into subservience and, consciously or unconciously, model herself after the whitewoman. The woman-of-color might see white approval or take on gradations of stances, from meek to hostile, which get her locked into passive-aggressive to violently reactive states.

But how are you to recognize your *aliada*, your ally in a roomful of people? Coalition work is not a sport where members of a particular team go bare-chested or wear T-shirts that say AMIGA (which stands for an actual organization in Texas). It can get confusing unless you can distinguish each other. And once you identify each other, how will you work together?

When calling a foul, do you harangue the other person in a loud voice? Do you take on a *matador* defense—neglect to guard opposing players in favor of taking the limelight to inflate your ego? Will your organization be a collective or a hierachy? Should your *modus operandi* be hands on or hands off? Will your offensive strategies consist of nudges, bumps, shoves or bombs? You may have to accept that there may be no solutions, resolutions or even agreement *ever.* The terms *solution, resolution,* and *progressing* and *moving forward* are Western dominant cultural concepts. Irresolution and disagreement may be more common in life than resolutions and agreements. Coalition work does not thrive on "figurehead" leaders, on grandstanding, "leadership always makes you master and the others slaves" (Lucia 1986, 107). Instead, coalition work succeeds through collective efforts and individual voices being heard. Once we focus on coalition/alliance we come to the questions, How long should we stay together? Should we form temporary *carnalaship* of extended family which leads to strong familial and tribal affiliations but which works against larger coalitions?

IF YOU WOULD BE MY ALLY

Ideally as allies (all lies), we can have no major lies among us, and we would lay our secrets on the conference table—the ones we've internalized and the ones we propagate. In looking at the motivations of those we are in solidarity with (women-of-color) and those who want to make alliances with us (whitewomen), we not only need to look at who they are, the space(s) they occupy, and how they enter our space and maneuver in it, *but* we have to look at our own motivations. Some issues to ponder and questions to ask ourselves: If all political action is founded on subconscious irresolutions and personal conflicts, then we must first look at that baggage we carry with us before sorting through other folks' dirty laundry. Having examined our own motives we can then inquire into the motivations of those who want to be our allies: Do they want us to be like them? Do they want us to hide the parts of ourselves that make them uneasy, i.e., our color, class, and racial identities? If we were to ask white lesbians to leave their whiteness at home, they would be shocked, having assumed that they have deconditioned the negative aspects of being white out of themselves by virtue of being feminist or lesbians. But I see that whiteness bleeds through all the baggage they port around with them and that it even seeps into their bones. Do they want to "take over" and impose their values in order to have power over us? I've had white and colored friends tell me I shouldn't give my energy to male friends, that I shouldn't go to horror movies because of the violence against women in them, that I should only write from the perspective of female characters, that I shouldn't eat meat. I respect women whose values and politics are different from mine, but they do not respect me or give me credit for self-determining my life when they impose trendy politically correct attitudes on me. The assumption they are making in imposing their "political correctness" on me is that I, a woman, a chicana, a lesbian should go to an "outside" authority rather than my own for how to run my life.

When I am asked to leave parts of myself out of the room, out of the kitchen, out of the bed, these people are not getting a whole person. They are only getting a little piece of me. As feminists and lesbians, we need all of us together, *tlan* (from the Nahuatl meaning close together), and each one of us needs all the different aspects and pieces of ourselves to be present and totally engaged in order to survive life in the late twentieth century.

Do they only want those parts of us that they can live with, that are similar to theirs, not different from them? The issue of differences continues to come up over and over again. Are we asked to sit at the table, or be invited to bed, because we bring some color to and look good behind the sheets? Are we there because those who would be our allies happen to have ancestors that were our oppressors and are operating out of a sense of guilt? Does this person want to be "seen" and recognized by us? According to Lacan, every human action, even the most altruistic, comes from a desire for recognition by the Other and from a desire for self-recognition in some form (Lacan 1977). For some, love is the highest and most intense recognition.

Maria Lugones, a Latina philospher, a woman who is at this conference, wrote a paper (1983) with a whitewoman, Vicky Spelman, "Have We Got a Theory For You! Feminist Theory, Cultural Imperialism, and the Demand for 'The Woman's Voice'," in which they posit that the only motivation for alliance work is love and friendship. Nothing else. I have friends that I totally disagree with politically, friends that are not even from the same class, the same race, the same anything, but something keeps us together, keeps us working things out. Perhaps Lugones and Spelman are right. Love and friendship can provide a good basis for alliance work, but there are too many

> tensions in alliance groups to dismiss with a light comment that bonds are based on love and friendship. This reminds me of Dill's critique of sisterhood being based on common (white) interests and alikeness (Uttal 1990).

What may be "saving" the colored and white feminist movements may be a combination of all these factors. Certainly the tensions between opposing theories and political stances vitalize the feminist dialogue. But it may only be combined with respect, partial understanding, love, and friendship that keeps us together in the long run. So, *mujeres,* think about the *carnalas* you want to be in your space, those whose spaces you want to have overlapping yours.

RITUALIZING COALITION AND ALLIANCE BUILDING

Speaking and communicating lay the ground work, but there is a point beyond too much talk that abstracts the experience. What is needed is a symbolic behavior performance made concrete by involving body and emotions with political theories and strategies, rituals that will connect the conscious with the unconscious. Through ritual we can make some deep level changes.

Ritual consecrates the alliance. Breaking bread together, and other group activities that physically and psychically represent the ideals, goals, and attitudes promote a quickening, thickening between us.

Allies, remember that the foreign woman, "the alien," is *nonacayocapo* which in Nahuatl means one who possesses body (flesh) and blood like me. *Aliadas, recuerda que la mujer ajena también es nonacayocapo, la que tiene cuerpo y sangre como yo.* Remember that our hearts are full of compassion, not empty. And the spirit dwells strong within. Remember also that the great emptiness, hollowness within the psyches of whitewomen propels them to coalition with colored. Oh, white sister, where is your soul, your spirit? It has run off in shock, *susto*, and you lack shamans and *curanderas* to call it back. *Sin alma no te puedes animarte pa'nada.* Remember that an equally empty and hollow place within us allows that connection, even needs that linkage.

It is important that whitewomen go out on limbs and fight for women-of-color in workplaces, schools, and universities. It is important that women-of-color in positions of power support their disempowered sisters. The liberation of women is the private, individual, and collective responsibility of colored and white men and women. *Aliada por pactos de alianzas,* united by pacts of alliances we may make some changes—in ourselves and in our societies.

After reading this paper consider making some decisions and setting goals to work on yourself, with another, with others of your race, or with a multiracial group as a bridge, drawbridge, sandbar, island, or in a way that works for you. *En fin quiero tocarlas de cerca*, I want to be allied to some of you. I want to touch you, kinswomen, *parientas*, *compañeras*, *paisanas*, *carnalas*, comrades, and I want you to touch me so that together, each in our separate ways, we can nourish our struggle and keep alive our visions to recuperate, validate, and transform our histories.

AUTHOR'S NOTE

Rather than discussing anti-Semitism, a dialogue I choose not to take on in this paper for reasons of length, boundaries of topic, and ignorance on my part of all its subtleties (though I am aware that there is a connection between racism and anti-Semitism I am not sure what it is), I've decided not to take it on nor even make a token mention of it. I realize that this is a form of "If you don't deal with my racism I won't deal with yours," and that pleading ignorance is no excuse.

DISCUSSION QUESTIONS

1. What might be some of the coalition goals readers could begin to work toward, as informed by the ideas in Anzaldúa's essay?

2. How does Anzaldúa use the word "colored"? What does this suggest about the dangers and potentialities of language as a tool for radical social change?

3. What might a "mestiza lesbian culture" look like? How important is culture-building in our political analyses and actions?

4. How might the adoption of the ground rules Anzaldúa outlines transform our organizations? In what ways have these ideas already informed our actions?

SUGGESTIONS FOR FURTHER READING

Tomás Almaguer. 1991. The cartography of homosexual desire and identity among Chicano men. *Differences: A Journal of Feminist Cultural Studies* 3(2).

Gloria Anzaldúa. 1987. *Borderlands=La frontera: The new mestiza.* San Francisco: Spinsters/Aunt Lute.

Virginia Harris & Trinity Ordoña. 1990. Developing unity among women of color: Crossing the barriers of internalized racism and cross-racial hostility. *Making face, making soul, hacienda caras: Creative and critical perspectives by women of color.* Gloria Anzaldúa, Ed. San Francisco: Aunt Lute Foundation.

Peggy McIntosh. 1992. White privilege and male privilege: A personal account of coming to see the correspondences through work in women's studies. *Race, class, and gender.* Margaret Andersen & Patricia Hill Collins, Eds. Belmont, CA: Wadsworth Publishing.

Bernice Johnson Reagon. 1983. Coalition politics: Turning the century. *Home girls: A black feminist anthology.* Barbara Smith, Ed. New York: Kitchen Table Women of Color Press.

Adrienne Rich. 1979. Disloyal to civilization: feminism, racism, Gynephobia. *On lies, secrets and silence.* New York: W.W. Norton.

Terry Wolverton. 1983. Unlearning complicity, remembering resistance: White women's anti-racism education. *Learning our way: Essays in feminist education.* Charlotte Bunch & Sandra Pollack, Eds. Trumansburg, NY: Crossing Press.

THE WELDER
Cherríe Moraga

I am a welder.
Not an alchemist.
I am interested in the blend
of common elements to make
a common thing.

No magic here.
Only the heat of my desire to fuse
what I already know
exists. Is possible.

We plead to each other,
we all come from the same rock
we all come from the same rock
ignoring the fact that we bend
at different temperatures
that each of us is malleable
up to a point.

Yes, fusion *is* possible
but only if things get hot enough—
all else is temporary adhesion,
patching up.

It is the intimacy of steel melting
into steel, the fire of our individual
passion to take hold of ourselves
that makes sculpture of our lives,
builds buildings.

And I am not talking about skyscrapers,
merely structures that can support us
without fear
of trembling.

For too long a time
the heat of my heavy hands
has been smoldering
in the pockets of other
people's business—
they need oxygen to make fire.

I am now
coming up for air.
Yes, I *am*
picking up the torch.

I am the welder.
I understand the capacity of heat
to change the shape of things.
I am suited to work
within the realm of sparks
out of control.

I am the welder.
I am taking the power
into my own hands.

THE TRANSFORMATION OF SILENCE
INTO LANGUAGE AND ACTION
Audre Lorde

This paper was originally delivered at the Modern Language Association's "Lesbian and Literature Panel" on December 28, 1977. In this moving essay, Lorde describes the pain of oppression and silence and gives us courage to transform that pain and fear. Audre Lorde died of liver cancer on Tuesday, November 17, 1992, at her home in St. Croix. She will be deeply missed.

I have come to believe over and over again that what is most important to me must be spoken, made verbal and shared, even at the risk of having it bruised or misunderstood. That the speaking profits me, beyond any other effect. I am standing here as a Black lesbian poet, and the meaning of all that waits upon the fact that I am still alive, and might not have been. Less that two months ago I was told by two doctors, one female and one male, that I would have to have breast surgery, and that there was a sixty to eighty percent chance that the tumor was malignant. Between that telling and the actual surgery, there was a three week period of the agony of an involuntary reorganization of my entire life. The surgery was completed, and the growth was benign.

But within those three weeks, I was forced to look upon myself and my living with a harsh and urgent clarity that has left me still shaken but much stronger. This is a situation faced by many women, by some of you here today. Some of what I experienced during that time has helped elucidate for me much of what I feel concerning the transformation of silence into language and action.

In becoming forcibly and essentially aware of my mortality, and of what I wished and wanted for my life, however short it might be, priorities and omissions became strongly etched in a merciless light, and what I most regretted were my silences. Of what had I *ever* been afraid? To question or to speak as I believed could have meant pain, or death. But we are all hurt in so many different ways, all the time, and pain will either change or end. Death, on the other hand, is the final silence. And that might be coming quickly, now, without regard for whether I had ever spoken what needed to be said, or had only betrayed myself into small silences, while I planned someday to speak, or waited for someone else's words. And I began to recognize a source of power within myself that comes from the knowledge that while it is most desirable not to be afraid, learning to put fear into perspective gave me great strength.

I was going to die, if not sooner then later, whether or not I had ever spoken myself. My silences had not protected me. Your silence will not protect you. But for every real word spoken, for every attempt I had ever made to speak those truths for which I am still seeking, I had made contact with other women while we examined the words to fit a world in which we all believed, bridging our differences. And it was the concern and caring of all those women which gave me strength and enabled me to scrutinize the essentials of my living.

The women who sustained me through that period were Black and white, old and young, lesbian, bisexual, and heterosexual, and we all shared a war against the tyrannies of silence. They all gave me a strength and concern without which I could not have survived intact. Within those weeks of acute fear came the knowledge—within the war we are all waging with the forces of death, subtle and otherwise, conscious or not—I am not only a casualty, I am also a warrior.

What are the words you do not yet have? What do you need to say? What are the tyrannies you swallow day by day and attempt to make your own, until you sicken and die of them, still in silence? Perhaps for some of you here today, I am the face of one of your fears. Because I am a woman, because I am Black, because I am a lesbian, because I am myself—a Black woman warrior poet doing my work—come to ask you, are you doing yours?

And of course I am afraid, because the transformation of silence into language and action is an act of self-revelation, and that always seems fraught with danger. But my daughter, when I told her of our topic and my difficulty with it, said, "Tell them about how you're never really a whole person if you remain silent, because there's always that one little piece inside you that wants to be spoken out, and if you keep ignoring it, it gets madder and madder and hotter and hotter, and if you don't speak it out one day it will just up and punch you in the mouth from the inside."

In the cause of silence, each of us draws the face of her own fear—fear of contempt, of censure, or some judgment, or recognition, of challenge, of annihilation. But most of all, I think, we fear the visibility without which we cannot truly live. Within this country where racial difference creates a constant, if unspoken, distortion of vision, Black women have on one hand always been highly visible, and so, on the other hand, have been rendered invisible through the depersonalization of racism. Even within the women's movement, we have had to fight, and still do, for that very visibility which also renders us most vulnerable, our Blackness. For to survive in the mouth of this dragon we call America, we have had to learn this first and most vital lesson—that we were never meant to survive. Not as human beings. And neither were most of you here today, Black or not.

And that visibility which makes us most vulnerable is that which also is the source of our greatest strength. Because the machine will try to grind you into dust anyway, whether or not we speak. We can sit in our corners mute forever while our sisters and our selves are wasted, while our children are distorted and destroyed, while our earth is poisoned; we can sit in our safe corners mute as bottles, and we will still be no less afraid.

In my house this year we are celebrating the feast of Kwanza, the African-American festival of harvest which begins the day after Christmas and lasts for seven days. There are seven principles of Kwanza, one for each day. The first principle is Umoja, which means unity, the decision to strive for and maintain unity in self and community. The principle for yesterday, the second day, was Kujichagulia—self-determination—the decision to define ourselves, name ourselves, and speak for ourselves, instead of being defined and spoken for by others. Today is the third day of Kwanza, and the principle for today is Ujima—collective work and responsibility—the decision to build and maintain ourselves and our communities together and to recognize and solve our problems together.

Each of us is here now because in one way or another we share a commitment to language and to the power of language, and to the reclaiming of that language which has been made to work against us. In the transformation of silence into language and action, it is vitally necessary for each one of us to establish or examine her function in that transformation and to recognize her role as vital within that transformation.

For those of us who write, it is necessary to scrutinize not only the truth of what we speak, but the truth of that language by which we speak it. For others, it is to share and spread also those words that are meaningful to us. But primarily for us all, it is necessary to teach by living and speaking those truths which we believe and know beyond understanding. Because in this way alone we can survive, by taking part in a process of life that is creative and continuing, that is growth.

And it is never without fear—of visibility, of the harsh light of scrutiny and perhaps judgment, of pain, of death. But we have lived through all of those already, in silence, except death. And I remind myself all the time now that if I were to have been born mute, or had maintained an oath of silence my whole life long for safety, I would still have suffered, and I would still die. It is very good for establishing perspective.

And where the words of women are crying to be heard, we must each of us recognize our responsibility to seek those words out, to read them and share them and examine them in their pertinence to our lives. That we not hide behind the mockeries of separations that have been imposed upon us and which so often we accept as our own. For instance, "I can't possibly teach Black women's writing—their experience is so different from mine." Yet how many years have you spent teaching Plato and

Shakespeare and Proust? Or another, "She's a white woman and what could she possibly have to say to me?" Or, "She's a lesbian, what would my husband say, or my chairman?" Or again, "This woman writes of her sons and I have no children." And all the other endless ways in which we rob ourselves of ourselves and each other.

We can learn to work and speak when we are afraid in the same way we have learned to work and speak when we are tired. For we have been socialized to respect fear more than our own needs for language and definition, and while we wait in silence for that final luxury of fearlessness, the weight of that silence will choke us.

The fact that we are here and that I speak these words is an attempt to break that silence and bridge some of those differences between us, for it is not difference which immobilizes us, but silence. And there are so many silences to be broken.

DISCUSSION QUESTIONS

1. How does the ACT UP phrase "silence equals death" relate to Lorde's warning that "your silence will not protect you?" What fundamental challenge do these ideas make to lesbian and gay men's "closets"?

2. What specific steps can each of us take to cross the "mockeries of separations that have been imposed on us?" How can we teach about others' lives without presuming to speak *for* others?

3. How are acts of self-revelation fraught with danger?

SUGGESTIONS FOR FURTHER READING

Dennis Altman. 1990. My America and yours: A letter to U.S. lesbian and gay activists. *OUT/LOOK* 8, 2(4):62-65.

James Baldwin. [1949] 1989. Preservation of innocence. *OUT/LOOK* 6, 2(2):40-45.

Robert Bernstein, Jewelle Gomez, Mickey Wheatley, John D'Emilio, Urvashi Vaid & Virginia Apuzzo. 1989. Messages to the movement: Six leaders speak out. *OUT/LOOK* 5, 2(1):53-61.

Audre Lorde. 1988. A burst of light: Living with cancer. *A burst of light*. Ithaca: Firebrand Books.

INVESTMENT OF WORTH
Terri L. Jewell

You value the earthen vase —
    each crack applauded
    for authenticity,
a slave's Freedom Quilt —
    hand-pulled stitchery
    a rare tale relinquished,
Victorian silver hair pins
    with filigreed flowers
    delicate as unconscious.
A collector of ancients
    quite proud of your tastes
    but scornful of
        curled brown leaves
        slight gray webs
        parched desert soil
   of a woman
   turned and tuned to her ripening,
    whose life is dear
    as a signed first edition,
    whose death as costly
    as a polished oak bed.

"Investment of worth," by Terri L. Jewell from WHEN I AM AN OLD WOMAN I SHALL WEAR PURPLE, edited by Sandra Martz, published by Papiermaché Press, Watsonville CA, 1987. Copyright © 1987 by Terri L. Jewell. Reprinted with permission.

REFERENCES

REFERENCES

Adam, Barry D. 1987. *The rise of a gay and lesbian movement.* Boston: Twayne Publishers.

Addams, Jane. [1915] 1984. Interview. *My country is the whole world.* Cambridge Women's Peace Collective, Eds. London: Pandora Press.

Jeffner Allen. 1986. Motherhood: The annihilation of women. *Lesbian Philosophies: Explorations.* Palo Alto, CA: Institute for Lesbian Studies.

Altman, Dennis. 1971. *Homosexual: Oppression and liberation.* New York: Outerbridge & Dienstfrey.

Anzaldúa, Gloria. 1983. Never, Momma. *Third Woman* (Fall).

Arno Press. 1987. Employment of homosexuals and sex perverts in government [reprint]. *Government against homosexuals.* New York: New York Times.

Barnes, Hollister. 1958. I am glad I am homosexual. *ONE Magazine* (August): 6–9.

Barnet, Richard. 1977. *The roots of war.* New York: Penguin Books.

Barnet, Richard. 1990. *The rockets' red glare.* New York: Simon & Schuster.

Bateson, Gregory. 1972. *Steps to an ecology of mind.* New York: Ballantine Books.

Beam, Joseph. 1986. Brother to brother: Words from the heart. *In the life: A black gay anthology.* Joseph Beam, Ed. Boston: Alyson Publications.

Bérubé, Allan. 1990. *Coming out under fire.* New York: Penguin Books.

Bérubé, Allan & John D'Emilio. 1984. The military and lesbians during the McCarthy years. *Signs* 9(4):759-775.

Borosage, Robert. 1970. The making of the national security state. *The Pentagon watchers.* Leonard Rodberg & Derek Shearer, Eds. New York: Doubleday.

El Caudillo. 1975. Excerpted in *Peace News* (July 11).

Carol Cohn. 1990. Clean bombs and clean language. *Women, militarism, and war: Essays in history, politics and social theory.* Jean Bethke Elshtain & Sheila Tobias, Eds. Savage, MD: Rowman & Littlefield Publishers, Inc.

Conrad, Florence. 1965. Research is here to stay. *The Ladder* 9(10/11).

Congregation for the Doctrine of the Faith. 1986. Letter to the bishops of the Catholic church on the pastoral care of homosexual persons. Vatican City: Author.

Cutler, Marvin. 1956. *Homosexuals today.* Los Angeles: ONE, Inc.

Decter, Midge. 1980. The boys on the beach. *Commentary* (September): 35–48.

De Mattei, Victor. 1978. Letter to Helen Michalowski.

D'Emilio, John. 1982. McCarthyism. *The Advocate* 358 (December 23): 26–28.

D'Emilio, John. 1983. *Sexual politics, sexual communities: The making of a homosexual minority in the United States, 1940–1970.* Chicago: University of Chicago Press.

Dykewomon, Elana. 1988. Talk given at Lesbian Separatism panel, Third International Feminist Book Fair, Montreal.

Dyson, Freeman. 1984. *Weapons and hope.* New York: Harper & Row.

Eisenhart, Wayne. 1975. You can't hack it, little girl: A discussion of the covert psychological agenda of modern combat training. *Journal of Social Issues*, 31(4).

Eisenhart, Wayne. 1977. Flower of the dragon: An example of applied humanistic psychology. *Journal of Humanistic Psychology*, 17(1).

Elshtain, Jean Bethke. 1985. Reflections on war and political discourse: Realism, just war and feminism in a nuclear age. *Political Theory* (February): 39-55.

Faderman, Lillian. 1991. *Odd girls and twilight lovers.* New York: Columbia University Press.

Fasteau, Marc Feigen. 1975. Vietnam and the cult of toughness in foreign policy. *The male machine.* New York: Dell.

Foucault, Michael. 1980. *Power/knowledge.* New York: Pantheon.

Goodman, Paul. 1962. Underground writing, 1960. *Utopian essays and practical proposals.* New York: Random House.

Gray, J. Glenn. 1970. *The warriors.* New York: Harper & Row.

Gregory-Lewis, Sasha. 1977. Revelations of a gay informant. *The Advocate* 210 & 211 (February 23 & March 9).

Hantover, Jeffrey. 1980. The Boy Scouts and the validation of masculinity. *The American man.* Elizabeth H. Pleck & Joseph H. Pleck, Eds. Englewood Cliffs, NJ: Prentice-Hall Spectrum.

Harris, Jean. 1986. *Stranger in two worlds.* New York: Macmillan.

Herek, Gregory. 1987. Can functions be measured? A new perspective on the functional approach to attitudes. *Social Psychology Quarterly*, 50: 285-303.

Hernton, Calvin C. 1966. *Sex and racism in America.* New York: Grove Weidenfeld.

Hyde, L., Ed. 1978. *Rat and the Devil: Journal letters of F.O. Matthiessen and Russell Cheney.* Hamden, CT: Shoe String.

Jones, Ann. 1985. *Everyday death: The case of Bernadette Powell.* New York: Holt, Rinehart & Winston.

Julien, Isaac & Kobena Mercer. 1986. True confessions: A discourse on images of black male sexuality. *Ten-8*, 22:6.

Julien, Isaac. 1988. *Looking for Langston.* London: Sankofa Film & Video.

Kameny, Franklin. 1965a. Does research into homosexuality matter? *The Ladder*, 9(8).

Kameny, Franklin. 1965b. Emphasis on research has had its day. *The Ladder*, 10(1).

Steve Karpf. 1991. Getting defensive: Queer patrols hit the streets. *Gay Community News*, 19(5).

Karrer, Wolfgang, & Hartmut Lutz, Eds. [n.d.] *Minority literature in North America: Contemporary perspectives.* Unpublished.

Katz, Jonathan Ned. 1978. *Gay American history.* New York: Avon Discus.

Katz, Jonathan Ned. 1983. *Gay/Lesbian almanac.* New York: Harper Colophon.

Klare, Michael & Peter Kornbluh. 1988. *Low-intensity warfare: Counterinsurgency, proinsurgency and antiterrorism in the eighties.* New York: Pantheon.

Lacan, Jacques. 1977. *Écrits, a selection*. Trans. Alan Sheridan. New York: W. W. Norton.

Licata, Salvatore. 1981. The homosexual rights movement in the United States. *Journal of Homosexuality* 6(1/2): 161–189.

Lifton, Robert J. 1973. *Home from the war: Vietnam veterans, neither victims nor executioners*. New York: Simon & Schuster.

Lloyd, Genevieve. 1984. *The man of reason: "Male" and "female" in Western philosophy*. Minneapolis: University of Minnesota Press.

Lloyd, Genevieve. 1986. Selfhood, war and masculinity. *Feminist challenges: social and political theory*. Carole Pateman & Elizabeth Gross, Eds. Boston: Northeastern University Press.

Lucia, Maria. 1986. Santaella, On passion as (?)Phanevanou (maybe or almost a phenomenology of passion). *Third Woman: Texts & More*, 3 (1/2).

Lugones, Maria, & Elizabeth V. Spelman. 1983. Have we got a theory for you! Feminist theory, cultural imperialism and the demand for "The Woman's Voice." *Women's Studies International Forum*, 6(6): 573-581.

McClusker, Michael. 1972. Statement. *The Winter Soldier Investigation: An Inquiry into American War Crimes*. Vietnam Veterans Against the War, Eds. Boston: Beacon Press.

Macleod, David I. 1983. *Building character in the American boy*. Madison: University of Wisconsin Press.

Marlowe, David H. 1983. The manning of the force and the structure of battle. *Conscripts and volunteers*. R. Fullwinder, Ed. Totowa, NJ: Rowman & Allanheld.

Marotta, Toby. 1981. *The politics of homosexuality*. Boston: Houghton Mifflin.

Melman, Seymour. 1970. *Pentagon capitalism*. New York: McGraw Hill.

Melman, Seymour. 1991. Military state capitalism. *The Nation* (May 20).

Miles, Sara. 1992. The fabulous fight back. *OUT/LOOK 17*, 5(1):54-59.

Mills, C. Wright. 1959. *The power elite*. New York: Oxford University Press.

Myrdal, Gunnar. 1944. *An American dilemma*. New York: Harper & Bros.

Newton, Huey. [1970] 1972. A Letter from Huey to the revolutionary brothers and sisters about the Women's Liberation and Gay Liberation movements. *The homosexual dialectic.* Joseph McCaffrey, Ed. Englewood Cliffs, NJ: Prentice-Hall.

Page, Stewart & Mary Yee. 1985. Conception of male and female homosexual stereotypes among university graduates. *Journal of Homosexuality* 12(1): 109–118.

Prescott, James. 1975. *Bulletin of Atomic Scientists* (November):17.

Podhoretz, Norman. 1977. The culture of appeasement. *Harper's* (October).

Rampersad, Arnold. 1986. *The life of Langston Hughes: Volume I: 1902–1941.* New York: Oxford University Press.

Raskin, Marcus. 1970. The Kennedy hawks assume power from the Eisenhower vultures. *The Pentagon watchers.* Leonard Rodberg & Derek Shearer, Eds. New York: Doubleday.

Raskin, Marcus. 1992. Let's terminate the CIA. *The Nation* (June 8).

Rose, Hilary. 1983. Head, brain and heart. *Signs 9.*

Rose, Hilary. 1986. Women's work, women's knowledge. *What is feminism?* Juliet Mitchell & Ann Oakley, Eds. Oxford: Blackwell.

Rubin, Gayle. 1984. Thinking sex: Notes for a radical theory of the politics of sexuality. *Pleasure and danger: Exploring female sexuality.* Carole Vance, Ed. Boston: Routledge & Kegan Paul.

Russo, Vito. 1981. *The celluloid closet: Homosexuality in the movies.* New York: Harper & Row.

Scarry, Elaine. 1985. *The body in pain.* New York: Oxford University Press.

Schreiner, Olive. [1911] 1978. *Women and labour.* London: Virgo Press.

Smith, Charles Michael. 1986. Bruce Nugent: Bohemian of the Harlem Renaissance. *In the life: A black gay anthology.* Joseph Beam, Ed. Boston: Alyson.

Smith, Clark, Ed. [n.d.] *The short-timers: Soldiering in Vietnam.* Unpublished.

Smith, Michael J. 1983. *Black men/white men.* San Francisco: Gay Sunshine Press.

Stanford, Adrian. 1977. *Black and queer.* Boston: Good Gay Poets Press.

Teal, Donn. 1971. *The gay militants.* New York: Stein & Day.

Timmons, Stuart. 1991. *The trouble with Harry Hay.* Boston: Alyson.

Tobin, Kay & Randy Wicker. 1975. *The gay crusaders.* New York: New York Times Arno Press Reprint Series.

Troupe, Quincy. 1989. *James Baldwin: The legacy.* New York: Simon & Schuster.

Uttal, Lynet. 1990. Personal communication to Gloria Anzaldúa.

Waldeck, R.G. 1960. Homosexual international. *Human Events* (September 29): 453–456.

Welch, Sharon. 1985. *Communities of resistance and solidarity: A feminist theology of liberation.* Maryknoll, NY: Orbis Books.

Wittig, Monique. 1981. One is not born a woman. *Feminist Issues*, 1(2).